SIGN LANGUAGE
AMONG
NORTH AMERICAN INDIANS

Garrick Mallery

DOVER PUBLICATIONS, INC.
Mineola, New York

Bibliographical Note

This Dover edition, first published in 2001, is an unabridged republica-
tion of pages 263–552 of the First Annual Report of the Bureau of
Ethnology of the Smithsonian Institution, 1879–80, published by the
Smithsonian Institution, Washington, in 1881. A table of contents and
introductory Note have been prepared especially for this edition.

Library of Congress Cataloging-in-Publication Data

Mallery, Garrick, 1831–1894.
    Sign language among North American Indians / Garrick Mallery.
      p. cm.
    Originally published: Washington, D. C. : Smithsonian Institution,
1881.
    ISBN-13: 978-0-486-41948-0 (pbk.)
    ISBN-10: 0-486-41948-7 (pbk.)
    1. Indians of North America—Sign language. I. Title.

E98.S5 M258 2001
419.1'089'97—dc21
                                      2001032360

Manufactured in the United States by LSC Communications
41948709   2020
www.doverpublications.com

NOTE

Sign Language among North American Indians is a significant document in the history of American anthropology. It was originally published in 1881 as pages 263–552 of the First Annual Report of the Bureau of Ethnology of the Smithsonian Institution for 1879–80, edited by the Bureau's director, John Wesley Powell. Its author, Garrick Mallery, was a retired U.S. Army officer employed by the Bureau and probably the foremost expert at that time on American Indian sign languages.

In this and in numerous other publications, Mallery collected and published a huge amount of basic research material on American Indian cultures. Though contemporary scholars look critically at some of his assumptions and conclusions, the "errors and naïve assertions"[1] that made their way into his work, Mallery's data is still being cited by anthropologists today. He "had a genuine fascination and respect for sign languages. He defended aboriginal users of sign language against charges that they employed gestures only because their spoken languages were deficient. . . . He argued that the use of sign language was largely a function of the number of disparate languages spoken within a region . . . since, he believed, the primary use of sign language was intertribal communication."[2]

---

1. William D. Hyder, "Some Problems in the Use of Sign Language to Interpret Rock Art," 1988.
2. Douglas C. Baynton, *Forbidden Signs: American Culture and the Campaign Against Sign Language,* 1996.

CONTENTS

LIST OF ILLUSTRATIONS 265

INTRODUCTORY 269

Divisions of Gesture Speech 270

The Origin of Sign Language 273

Some Theories upon Primitive Language 282

History of Gesture Language 285

Modern Use of Gesture Speech 293

Our Indian Conditions Favorable to Sign Language 311

Theories Entertained Respecting Indian Signs 313

Results Sought in the Study of Sign Language 346

Notable Points for Further Researches 387

Mode in Which Researches Have Been Made 395

LIST OF AUTHORITIES AND COLLABORATORS 401

EXTRACTS FROM DICTIONARY 409

Tribal Signs 458

Proper Names 476

Phrases 479

Dialogues 486

Narratives 500

Discourses 521

SIGNALS 529

Signals Executed by Bodily Action 529

Signals in Which Objects Are Used in Connection with Personal Action 532

Signals Made When the Person of the Signalist is Not Visible 536

SCHEME OF ILLUSTRATION 544

Outlines for Arm Positions in Sign Language 545

Types of Hand Positions in Sign Language 547

Examples 550

SMITHSONIAN INSTITUTION——BUREAU OF ETHNOLOGY.

J. W. POWELL, DIRECTOR.

SIGN LANGUAGE

AMONG

NORTH AMERICAN INDIANS

COMPARED WITH THAT AMONG OTHER PEOPLES AND DEAF-MUTES.

BY

GARRICK MALLERY.

LIST OF ILLUSTRATIONS.

	Page.
Fig. 61. Affirmation, approving. Old Roman	286
62. Approbation. Neapolitan.	286
63. Affirmation, approbation. N. A. Indian	286
64. Group. Old Greek. Facing	289
65. Negation. Dakota	290
66. Love. Modern Neapolitan.	290
67. Group. Old Greek. Facing	290
68. Hesitation. Neapolitan..	291
69. Wait. N. A. Indian	291
70. Question, asking. Neapolitan	291
71. Tell me. N. A. Indian	291
72. Interrogation. Australian.	291
73. Pulcinella	292
74. Thief. Neapolitan	292
75. Steal. N. A. Indian	293
76. Public writer. Neapolitan group. Facing	296
77. Money. Neapolitan	297
78. "Hot Corn." Neapolitan Group. Facing	297
79. "Horn" sign. Neapolitan.	298
80. Reproach. Old Roman	298
81. Marriage contract. Neapolitan group. Facing	298
82. Negation. Pai-Ute sign..	299
83. Coming home of bride. Neapolitan group. Facing	299
84. Pretty. Neapolitan.	300
85. "Mano in fica." Neapolitan	300
86. Snapping the fingers. Neapolitan	300
87. Joy, acclamation	300
88. Invitation to drink wine..	300
89. Woman's quarrel. Neapolitan Group. Facing	301
90. Chestnut vender. Facing	301
91. Warning. Neapolitan	302
92. Justice. Neapolitan	302
93. Little. Neapolitan.	302

	Page.
Fig. 94. Little. N. A. Indian	302
95. Little. N. A. Indian	302
96. Demonstration. Neapolitan	302
97. "Fool." Neapolitan	303
98. "Fool." Ib	303
99. "Fool." Ib	303
100. Inquiry. Neapolitan	303
101. Crafty, deceitful. Neapolitan	303
102. Insult. Neapolitan	304
103. Insult. Neapolitan	304
104. Silence. Neapolitan	304
105. Child. Egyptian hieroglyph	304
106. Negation. Neapolitan	304
107. Hunger. Neapolitan	305
108. Mockery. Neapolitan	305
109. Fatigue. Neapolitan	305
110. Deceit. Neapolitan	305
111. Astuteness, readiness. Neapolitan	305
112. Tree. Dakota, Hidatsa.	343
113. To grow. N. A. Indian..	343
114. Rain. Shoshoni, Apache.	344
115. Sun. N. A. Indian	344
116. Sun. Cheyenne	344
117. Soldier. Arikara	345
118. No, negation. Egyptian.	355
119. Negation. Maya	356
120. Nothing. Chinese	356
121. Child. Egyptian figurative	356
122. Child. Egyptian linear.	356
123. Child. Egyptian hieratic	356
124. Son. Ancient Chinese ..	356
125. Son. Modern Chinese...	356
126. Birth. Chinese character	356
127. Birth. Dakota	356
128. Birth, generic. N. A. Indians	357

NOTE: In the Dover edition, Fig. 89 faces page 300.

	Page.
Fig. 129. Man. Mexican	357
130. Man. Chinese character.	357
131. Woman. Chinese character	357
132. Woman. Ute	357
133. Female, generic. Cheyenne	357
134. To give water. Chinese character	357
135. Water, to drink. N. A. Indian	357
136. Drink. Mexican	357
137. Water. Mexican	357
138. Water, giving. Egypt	358
139. Water. Egyptian	358
140. Water, abbreviated	358
141. Water. Chinese character	358
142. To weep. Ojibwa pictograph	358
143. Force, vigor. Egyptian.	358
144. Night. Egyptian	358
145. Calling upon. Egyptian figurative	359
146. Calling upon. Egyptian linear	359
147. To collect, to unite. Egyptian	359
148. Locomotion. Egyptian figurative	359
149. Locomotion. Egyptian linear	359
150. Shun'-ka Lu'-ta. Dakota.	365
151. "I am going to the east." Abnaki	369
152. "Am not gone far." Abnaki	369
153. "Gone far." Abnaki	370
154. "Gone five days' journey." Abnaki	370
155. Sun. N. A. Indian	370
156. Sun. Egyptian	370
157. Sun. Egyptian	370
158. Sun with rays. Ib	371
159. Sun with rays. Ib	371
160. Sun with rays. Moqui pictograph	371
161. Sun with rays. Ib	371
162. Sun with rays. Ib	371
163. Sun with rays. Ib	371
164. Star. Moqui pictograph.	371
165. Star. Moqui pictograph.	371
166. Star. Moqui pictograph.	371
167. Star. Moqui pictograph.	371

	Page.
Fig. 168. Star. Peruvian pictograph	371
169. Star. Ojibwa pictograph.	371
170. Sunrise. Moqui do	371
171. Sunrise. Ib	371
172. Sunrise. Ib	371
173. Moon, month. Californian pictograph	371
174. Pictograph, including sun. Coyotero Apache.	372
175. Moon. N. A. Indian	372
176. Moon. Moqui pictograph	372
177. Moon. Ojibwa pictograph	372
178. Sky. Ib	372
179. Sky. Egyptian character	372
180. Clouds. Moqui pictograph	372
181. Clouds. Ib	372
182. Clouds. Ib	372
183. Cloud. Ojibwa pictograph	372
184. Rain. New Mexican pictograph	373
185. Rain. Moqui pictograph	373
186. Lightning. Moqui pictograph	373
187. Lightning. Ib	373
188. Lightning, harmless. Pictograph at Jemez, N. M.	373
189. Lightning, fatal. Do	373
190. Voice. "The-Elk-that-hollows-walking"	373
191. Voice. Antelope. Cheyenne drawing	373
192. Voice, talking. Cheyenne drawing	374
193. Killing the buffalo. Cheyenne drawing	375
194. Talking. Mexican pictograph	376
195. Talking, singing. Maya character	376
196. Hearing ears. Ojibwa pictograph	376
197. "I hear, but your words are from a bad heart." Ojibwa	376
198. Hearing serpent. Ojibwa pictograph	376
199. Royal edict. Maya	377

Page.

Fig. 200. To kill. Dakota 377
201. "Killed Arm." Dakota.. 377
202 Pictograph, including
"kill." Wyoming Ter. 378
203. Pictograph, including
"kill." Wyoming Ter. 378
204. Pictograph, including
"kill." Wyoming Ter. 379
205. Veneration. Egyptian
character............... 379
206. Mercy. Supplication, favor. Egyptian........ 379
207. Supplication. Mexican
pictograph 380
208. Smoke. Ib 380
209. Fire. Ib 381
210. "Making medicine." Conjuration. Dakota 381
211. Meda. Ojibwa pictograph. 381
212. The God Knuphis. Egyptian................... 381
213. The God Knuphis. Ib... 381
214. Power. Ojibwa pictograph 381
215. Meda's Power. Ib 381
216. Trade pictograph........ 382
217. Offering. Mexican pictograph 382
218. Stampede of horses. Dakota 382
219. Chapultepec. Mexican
pictograph 383
220. Soil. Ib............... 383
221. Cultivated soil. Ib..... 383
222. Road, path. Ib 383
223. Cross-roads and gesture
sign. Mexican pictograph 383
224. Small-pox or measles. Dakota 383
225. "No thoroughfare." Pictograph 383
226. Raising of war party. Dakota 384
227. "Led four war parties."
Dakota drawing....... 384
228. Sociality. Friendship.
Ojibwa pictograph..... 384
229. Peace. Friendship. Dakota 384
230. Peace. Friendship with
whites. Dakota....... 385
231. Friendship. Australian.. 385
232. Friend. Brulé Dakota .. 386

Page.

Fig. 233. Lie, falsehood. Arikara. 393
234. Antelope. Dakota 410
235. Running Antelope. Personal totem............ 410
236. Bad. Dakota 411
237. Bear. Cheyenne 412
238. Bear. Kaiowa, etc...... 413
239. Bear. Ute 413
240. Bear. Moqui pictograph. 413
241. Brave. N. A. Indian 414
242. Brave. Kaiowa, etc..... 415
243. Brave. Kaiowa, etc..... 415
244. Chief. Head of tribe.
Absaroka............... 418
245. Chief. Head of tribe.
Pai-Ute................ 418
246. Chief of a band. Absaroka and Arikara 419
247. Chief of a band. Pai-Ute. 419
248. Warrior. Absaroka, etc. 420
249. Ojibwa gravestone, including "dead"........ 422
250. Dead. Shoshoni and Banak 422
251. Dying. Kaiowa, etc 424
252. Nearly dying. Kaiowa.. 424
253. Log house. Hidatsa 428
254. Lodge. Dakota 430
255. Lodge. Kaiowa, etc 431
256. Lodge. Sahaptin 431
257. Lodge. Pai-Ute......... 431
258. Lodge. Pai-Ute......... 431
259. Lodge. Kutchin 431
260. Horse. N. A. Indian.... 434
261. Horse. Dakota 434
262. Horse. Kaiowa, etc..... 435
263. Horse. Caddo 435
264. Horse. Pima and Papago. 435
265. Horse. Ute 435
266. Horse. Ute 435
267. Saddling a horse. Ute .. 437
268. Kill. N. A. Indian...... 438
269. Kill. Mandan and Hidatsa.................. 439
270. Negation. No. Dakota. 441
271. Negation. No. Pai-Ute. 442
272. None. Dakota.......... 443
273. None. Australian....... 444
274. Much, quantity. Apache. 447
275. Question. Australian ... 449
276. Soldier. Dakota and Arikara 450
277. Trade. Dakota 452
278. Trade. Dakota 452

	Page.
Fig. 279. Buy. Ute	453
280. Yes, affirmation. Dakota.	456
281. Absaroka tribal sign. Shoshoni	458
282. Apache tribal sign. Kaiowa, etc	459
283. Apache tribal sign. Pima and Papago	459
284. Arikara tribal sign. Arapaho and Dakota	461
285. Arikara tribal sign. Absaroka	461
286. Blackfoot tribal sign. Dakota	463
287. Blackfoot tribal sign. Shoshoni	464
288. Caddo tribal sign. Arapaho and Kaiowa	464
289. Cheyenne tribal sign. Arapaho and Cheyenne	464
290. Dakota tribal sign. Dakota	467
291. Flathead tribal sign. Shoshoni	468
292. Kaiowa tribal sign. Comanche	470
293. Kutine tribal sign. Shoshoni	471
294. Lipan tribal sign. Apache.	471
295. Pend d'Oreille tribal sign. Shoshoni	473
296. Sahaptin or Nez Percé tribal sign. Comanche.	473
297. Shoshoni tribal sign. Shoshoni	474
298. Buffalo. Dakota	477
299. Eagle Tail. Arikara	477
300. Eagle Tail. Moqui pictograph	477
301. Give me. Absaroka	480
302. Counting. How many? Shoshoni and Banak	482
303. I am going home. Dakota	485
304. Question. Apache.	486
305. Shoshoni tribal sign. Shoshoni	486
306. Chief. Shoshoni	487
307. Cold, winter, year. Apache	487
308. "Six." Shoshoni	487
309. Good, very well. Apache.	487
310. Many. Shoshoni	488

	Page.
Fig. 311. Hear, heard. Apache	488
312. Night. Shoshoni	489
313. Rain. Shoshoni	489
314. See each other. Shoshoni	490
315. White man, American. Dakota	491
316. Hear, heard. Dakota	492
317. Brother. Pai-Ute	502
318. No, negation. Pai-Ute	503
319. Scene of Na-wa-gi-jig's story. Facing	508
320. We are friends. Wichita.	521
321. Talk, talking. Wichita	521
322. I stay, or I stay right here. Wichita	521
323. A long time. Wichita	522
324. Done, finished. Do	522
325. Sit down. Australian	523
326. Cut down. Wichita	524
327. Wagon. Wichita	525
328. Load upon. Wichita	525
329. White man; American. Hidatsa	526
330. With us. Hidatsa	526
331. Friend. Hidatsa	527
332. Four. Hidatsa	527
333. Lie, falsehood. Hidatsa.	528
334. Done, finished. Hidatsa.	528
335. Peace, friendship. Hualpais. Facing	530
336. Question, ans'd by tribal sign for Pani. Facing	531
337. Buffalo discovered. Dakota. Facing	532
338. Discovery. Dakota. Facing	533
339. Success of war party. Pima. Facing	538
340. Outline for arm positions, full face	545
341. Outline for arm positions, profile	545
342a. Types of hand positions, A to L	547
342b. Types of hand positions, M to Y	548
343. Example. To cut with an ax	550
344. Example. A lie	550
345. Example. To ride	551
346. Example. I am going home	551

SIGN LANGUAGE

AMONG

NORTH AMERICAN INDIANS

COMPARED WITH THAT AMONG OTHER PEOPLES AND DEAF-MUTES.

BY GARRICK MALLERY.

INTRODUCTORY.

During the past two years the present writer has devoted the intervals between official duties to collecting and collating materials for the study of sign language. As the few publications on the general subject, possessing more than historic interest, are meager in details and vague in expression, original investigation has been necessary. The high development of communication by gesture among the tribes of North America, and its continued extensive use by many of them, naturally directed the first researches to that continent, with the result that a large body of facts procured from collaborators and by personal examination has now been gathered and classified. A correspondence has also been established with many persons in other parts of the world whose character and situation rendered it probable that they would contribute valuable information. The success of that correspondence has been as great as could have been expected, considering that most of the persons addressed were at distant points sometimes not easily accessible by mail. As the collection of facts is still successfully proceeding, not only with reference to foreign peoples and to deaf-mutes everywhere, but also among some American tribes not yet thoroughly examined in this respect, no exposition of the subject pretending to be complete can yet be made. In complying, therefore, with the request to prepare the present paper, it is necessary to explain to correspondents and collaborators whom it may reach, that this is not the comprehensive publication by the Bureau of Ethnology for which their assistance has been solicited. With this explanation some of those who have already forwarded contributions will not be surprised at their omission, and others will not desist from the work in which they are still kindly engaged, under the impression that its results will not be received in time to meet with welcome and credit. On the contrary, the urgent appeal for aid before addressed to officers of the Army and Navy of this and other nations, to missionaries, travelers, teachers of deaf-mutes, and philologists generally, is now with equal urgency repeated. It is, indeed, hoped that the continued presentation of the subject to persons either having opportunity for observation or the power to favor with suggestions may, by awakening some additional interest in it, secure new collaboration from localities still unrepresented.

It will be readily understood by other readers that, as the limits assigned to this paper permit the insertion of but a small part of the material already collected and of the notes of study made upon that accumulation, it can only show the general scope of the work undertaken, and not its accomplishment. Such extracts from the collection have been selected as were regarded as most illustrative, and they are preceded by a discussion perhaps sufficient to be suggestive, though by no means exhaustive, and designed to be for popular, rather than for scientific use. In short, the direction to submit a progress-report and not a monograph has been complied with.

DIVISIONS OF GESTURE SPEECH.

These are corporeal motion and facial expression. An attempt has been made by some writers to discuss these general divisions separately, and its success would be practically convenient if it were always understood that their connection is so intimate that they can never be altogether severed. A play of feature, whether instinctive or voluntary, accentuates and qualifies all motions intended to serve as signs, and strong instinctive facial expression is generally accompanied by action of the body or some of its members. But, so far as a distinction can be made, expressions of the features are the result of emotional, and corporeal gestures, of intellectual action. The former in general and the small number of the latter that are distinctively emotional are nearly identical among men from physiological causes which do not affect with the same similarity the processes of thought. The large number of corporeal gestures expressing intellectual operations require and admit of more variety and conventionality. Thus the features and the body among all mankind act almost uniformly in exhibiting fear, grief, surprise, and shame, but all objective conceptions are varied and variously portrayed. Even such simple indications as those for " no" and " yes" appear in several differing motions. While, therefore, the terms sign language and gesture speech necessarily include and suppose facial expression when emotions are in question, they refer more particularly to corporeal motions and attitudes. For this reason much of the valuable contribution of DARWIN in his *Expression of the Emotions in Man and Animals* is not directly applicable to sign language. His analysis of emotional gestures into those explained on the principles of serviceable associated habits, of antithesis, and of the constitution of the nervous system, should, nevertheless, always be remembered. Even if it does not strictly embrace the class of gestures which form the subject of this paper, and which often have an immediate pantomimic origin, the earliest gestures were doubtless instinctive and generally emotional, preceding pictorial, metaphoric, and, still subsequent, conventional gestures even, as, according to DARWIN'S cogent reasoning, they preceded articulate speech.

While the distinction above made between the realm of facial play and that of motions of the body, especially those of the arms and hands, is sufficiently correct for use in discussion, it must be admitted that the features do express intellect as well as emotion. The well-known saying of Charles Lamb that "jokes came in with the candles" is in point, but the most remarkable example of conveying detailed information without the use of sounds, hands, or arms, is given by the late President T. H. Gallaudet, the distinguished instructor of deaf-mutes, which, to be intelligible, requires to be quoted at length:

"One day, our distinguished and lamented historical painter, Col. John Trumbull, was in my school-room during the hours of instruction, and, on my alluding to the tact which the pupil referred to had of reading my face, he expressed a wish to see it tried. I requested him to select any event in Greek, Roman, English, or American history of a scenic character, which would make a striking picture on canvas, and said I would endeavor to communicate it to the lad. 'Tell him,' said he, 'that Brutus (Lucius Junius) condemned his two sons to death for resisting his authority and violating his orders.'

"I folded my arms in front of me, and kept them in that position, to preclude the possibility of making any signs or gestures, or of spelling any words on my fingers, and proceeded, as best I could, by the expression of my countenance, and a few motions of my head and attitudes of the body, to convey the picture in my own mind to the mind of my pupil.

"It ought to be stated that he was already acquainted with the fact, being familiar with the leading events in Roman history. But when I began, he knew not from what portion of history, sacred or profane, ancient or modern, the fact was selected. From this wide range, my delineation on the one hand and his ingenuity on the other had to bring it within the division of Roman history, and, still more minutely, to the particular individual and transaction designated by Colonel Trumbull. In carrying on the process, I made no use whatever of any arbitrary, conventional look, motion, or attitude, before settled between us, by which to let him understand what I wished to communicate, with the exception of a single one, if, indeed, it ought to be considered such.

"The usual sign, at that time, among the teachers and pupils, for a Roman, was portraying an aquiline nose by placing the fore-finger, crooked, in front of the nose. As I was prevented from using my finger in this way, and having considerable command over the muscles of my face, I endeavored to give my nose as much of the aquiline form as possible, and succeeded well enough for my purpose. * * *

"The outlines of the process were the following :

"A stretching and stretching gaze eastward, with an undulating motion of the head, as if looking across and beyond the Atlantic Ocean, to denote that the event happened, not on the western, but eastern continent. This was making a little progress, as it took the subject out of the range of American history.

"A turning of the eyes upward and backward, with frequently-repeated motions of the head backward, as if looking a great way back in past time, to denote that the event was one of ancient date.

"The aquiline shape of the nose, already referred to, indicating that a Roman was the person concerned. It was, of course, an old Roman.

"Portraying, as well as I could, by my countenance, attitude, and manner an individual high in authority, and commanding others, as if he expected to be obeyed.

"Looking and acting as if I were giving out a specific order to many persons, and threatening punishment on those who should resist my authority, even the punishment of death.

"Here was a pause in the progress of events, which I denoted by sleeping as it were during the night and awakening in the morning, and doing this several times, to signify that several days had elapsed.

"Looking with deep interest and surprise, as if at a single person brought and standing before me, with an expression of countenance indicating that he had violated the order which I had given, and that I knew it. Then looking in the same way at another person near him as also guilty. Two offending persons were thus denoted.

"Exhibiting serious deliberation, then hesitation, accompanied with strong conflicting emotions, producing perturbation, as if I knew not how to feel or what to do.

"Looking first at one of the persons before me, and then at the other, and then at both together, *as a father would look*, indicating his distressful parental feelings under such afflicting circumstances.

"Composing my feelings, showing that a change was coming over me, and exhibiting towards the imaginary persons before me the decided look of the inflexible commander, who was determined and ready to order them away to execution. Looking and acting as if the tender and forgiving feelings of *the father* had again got the ascendency, and as if I was about to relent and pardon them.

"These alternating states of mind I portrayed several times, to make my representations the more graphic and impressive.

"At length the father yields, and the stern principle of justice, as expressed in my countenance and manners, prevails. My look and action denote the passing of the sentence of death on the offenders, and the ordering them away to execution.

* * * * * * *

"He quickly turned round to his slate and wrote a correct and complete account of this story of Brutus and his two sons."

While it appears that the expressions of the features are not confined to the emotions or to distinguishing synonyms, it must be remembered that the meaning of the same motion of hands, arms, and fingers is often modified, individualized, or accentuated by associated facial changes and postures of the body not essential to the sign, which emotional changes and postures are at once the most difficult to describe and the most interesting when intelligently reported, not only because they infuse life into the skeleton sign, but because they may belong to the class of innate expressions.

THE ORIGIN OF SIGN LANGUAGE.

In observing the maxim that nothing can be thoroughly understood unless its beginning is known, it becomes necessary to examine into the origin of sign language through its connection with that of oral speech. In this examination it is essential to be free from the vague popular impression that some oral language, of the general character of that now used among mankind, is "natural" to mankind. It will be admitted on reflection that all oral languages were at some past time far less serviceable to those using them than they are now, and as each particular language has been thoroughly studied it has become evident that it grew out of some other and less advanced form. In the investigation of these old forms it has been so difficult to ascertain how any of them first became a useful instrument of inter-communication that many conflicting theories on this subject have been advocated.

Oral language consists of variations and mutations of vocal sounds produced as signs of thought and emotion. But it is not enough that those signs should be available as the vehicle of the producer's own thoughts. They must be also efficient for the communication of such thoughts to others. It has been, until of late years, generally held that thought was not possible without oral language, and that, as man was supposed to have possessed from the first the power of thought, he also from the first possessed and used oral language substantially as at present. That the latter, as a special faculty, formed the main distinction between man and the brutes has been and still is the prevailing doctrine. In a lecture delivered before the British Association in 1878 it was declared that "animal intelligence is unable to elaborate that class of abstract ideas, the formation of which depends upon the faculty of speech." If instead of "speech" the word "utterance" had been used, as including all possible modes of intelligent communication, the statement might pass without criticism. But it may be doubted if there is any more necessary connection between abstract ideas and sounds, the mere signs of thought, that strike the ear, than there is between the same ideas and signs addressed only to the eye.

The point most debated for centuries has been, not whether there was any primitive oral language, but what that language was. Some literalists have indeed argued from the Mosaic narrative that because the Creator, by one supernatural act, with the express purpose to form separate peoples, had divided all tongues into their present varieties, and could, by another similar exercise of power, obliterate all but one which should be universal, the fact that he had not exercised that power showed it not to be his will that any man to whom a particular speech had been given should hold intercourse with another miraculously set apart from him by a different speech. By this reasoning, if the study of a foreign tongue was not impious, it was at least clear that the primitive language had been taken away as a disciplinary punishment, as the Paradisiac Eden had been earlier lost, and that, therefore, the search for it was as fruitless as to attempt the passage of the flaming sword. More liberal Christians have been disposed to regard the Babel story as allegorical, if not mythical, and have considered it to represent the disintegration of tongues out of one which was primitive. In accordance with the advance of linguistic science they have successively shifted back the postulated primitive tongue from Hebrew to Sanscrit, then to Aryan, and now seek to evoke from the vasty deeps of antiquity the ghosts of other rival claimants for precedence in dissolution. As, however, the languages of man are now recognized as extremely numerous, and as the very sounds of which these several languages are composed are so different that the speakers of some are unable to distinguish with the ear certain sounds in others, still less able to reproduce them, the search for one common parent language is more difficult than was supposed by mediæval ignorance.

The discussion is now, however, varied by the suggested possibility that man at some time may have existed without any oral language. It is conceded by some writers that mental images or representations can be formed without any connection with sound, and may at least serve for thought, though not for expression. It is certain that concepts, however formed, can be expressed by other means than sound. One mode of this expression is by gesture, and there is less reason to believe that gestures commenced as the interpretation of, or substitute for words than that the latter originated in, and served to translate gestures. Many arguments have been advanced to prove that gesture language preceded articulate speech and formed the earliest attempt at communication, resulting from the interacting subjective and objective conditions to which primitive man was exposed. Some of the facts on which deductions have been based, made in accordance with well-established modes of scientific research from study of the lower animals, children, idiots, the lower types of mankind, and deaf-mutes, will be briefly mentioned.

GESTURES OF THE LOWER ANIMALS.

Emotional expression in the features of man is to be considered in reference to the fact that the special senses either have their seat in, or are in close relation to the face, and that so large a number of nerves pass to it from the brain. The same is true of the lower animals, so that it would be inferred, as is the case, that the faces of those animals are also expressive of emotion. There is also noticed among them an exhibition of emotion by corporeal action. This is the class of gestures common to them with the earliest made by man, as above mentioned, and it is reasonable to suppose that those were made by man at the time when, if ever, he was, like the animals, destitute of articulate speech. The articulate cries uttered by some animals, especially some birds, are interesting as connected with the principle of imitation to which languages in part owe their origin, but in the cases of forced imitation, the mere acquisition of a vocal trick, they only serve to illustrate that power of imitation, and are without significance. Sterne's starling, after his cage had been opened, would have continued to complain that he could not get out. If the bird had uttered an instinctive cry of distress when in confinement and a note of joy on release, there would have been a nearer approach to language than if it had clearly pronounced many sentences. Such notes and cries of animals, many of which are connected with reproduction and nutrition, are well worth more consideration than can now be given, but regarding them generally it is to be questioned if they are so expressive as the gestures of the same animals. It is contended that the bark of a dog is distinguishable into fear, defiance, invitation, and a note of warning, but it also appears that those notes have been known only since the animal has been domesticated. The gestures of the dog are far more readily distinguished than his bark, as in his preparing for attack, or caressing his master, resenting an injury, begging for food, or simply soliciting attention. The chief modern use of his tail appears to be to express his ideas and sensations. But some recent experiments of Prof. A. GRAHAM BELL, no less eminent from his work in artificial speech than in telephones, shows that animals are more physically capable of pronouncing articulate sounds than has been supposed. He informed the writer that he recently succeeded by manipulation in causing an English terrier to form a number of the sounds of our letters, and particularly brought out from it the words "How are you, Grandmamma?" with distinctness. This tends to prove that only absence of brain power has kept animals from acquiring true speech. The remarkable vocal instrument of the parrot could be used in significance as well as in imitation, if its brain had been developed beyond the point of expression by gesture, in which latter the bird is expert.

The gestures of monkeys, whose hands and arms can be used, are nearly akin to ours. Insects communicate with each other almost entirely by means of the antennæ. Animals in general which, though not deaf, can not be taught by sound, frequently have been by signs, and probably all of them understand man's gestures better than his speech. They exhibit signs to one another with obvious intention, and they also have often invented them as a means of obtaining their wants from man.

GESTURES OF YOUNG CHILDREN.

The wishes and emotions of very young children are conveyed in a small number of sounds, but in a great variety of gestures and facial expressions. A child's gestures are intelligent long in advance of speech; although very early and persistent attempts are made to give it instruction in the latter but none in the former, from the time when it begins *risu cognoscere matrem*. It learns words only as they are taught, and learns them through the medium of signs which are not expressly taught. Long after familiarity with speech, it consults the gestures and facial expressions of its parents and nurses as if seeking thus to translate or explain their words. These facts are important in reference to the biologic law that the order of development of the individual is the same as that of the species.

Among the instances of gestures common to children throughout the world is that of protruding the lips, or pouting, when somewhat angry or sulky. The same gesture is now made by the anthropoid apes and is found strongly marked in the savage tribes of man. It is noticed by evolutionists that animals retain during early youth, and subsequently lose, characters once possessed by their progenitors when adult, and still retained by distinct species nearly related to them.

The fact is not, however, to be ignored that children invent words as well as signs with as natural an origin for the one as for the other. An interesting case was furnished to the writer by Prof. BELL of an infant boy who used a combination of sounds given as "nyum-nyum," an evident onomatope of gustation, to mean "good," and not only in reference to articles of food relished but as applied to persons of whom the child was fond, rather in the abstract idea of "niceness" in general. It is a singular coincidence that a bright young girl, a friend of the writer, in a letter describing a juvenile feast, invented the same expression, with nearly the same spelling, as characteristic of her sensations regarding the delicacies provided. The Papuans met by Dr. Comrie also called "eating" *nam-nam*. But the evidence of all such cases of the voluntary use of articulate speech by young children is qualified by the fact that it has been inherited from very many generations, if not quite so long as the faculty of gesture.

GESTURES IN MENTAL DISORDER.

The insane understand and obey gestures when they have no knowledge whatever of words. It is also found that semi-idiotic children who cannot be taught more than the merest rudiments of speech can receive a considerable amount of information through signs, and can express themselves by them. Sufferers from aphasia continue to use appro-

priate gestures after their words have become uncontrollable. It is further noticeable in them that mere ejaculations, or sounds which are only
the result of a state of feeling, instead of a desire to express thought,
are generally articulated with accuracy. Patients who have been in
the habit of swearing preserve their fluency in that division of their
vocabulary.

UNINSTRUCTED DEAF-MUTES.

The signs made by congenital and uninstructed deaf-mutes to be now
considered are either strictly natural signs, invented by themselves, or
those of a colloquial character used by such mutes where associated.
The accidental or merely suggestive signs peculiar to families, one member of which happens to be a mute, are too much affected by the other
members of the family to be of certain value. Those, again, which are
taught in institutions have become conventional and designedly adapted
to translation into oral speech, although founded by the abbé de l'Épée,
followed by the abbé Sicard, in the natural signs first above mentioned.

A great change has doubtless occurred in the estimation of congenital deaf-mutes since the Justinian Code, which consigned them forever
to legal infancy, as incapable of intelligence, and classed them with the
insane. Yet most modern writers, for instance Archbishop Whately and
Max Müller, have declared that deaf-mutes could not think until after
having been instructed. It cannot be denied that the deaf-mute thinks
after his instruction either in the ordinary gesture signs or in the finger
alphabet, or more lately in artificial speech. By this instruction he has
become master of a highly-developed language, such as English or
French, which he can read, write, and actually talk, but that foreign
language he has obtained through the medium of signs. This is a conclusive proof that signs constitute a real language and one which ad-
mits of thought, for no one can learn a foreign language unless he had
some language of his own, whether by descent or acquisition, by which
it could be translated, and such translation into the new language could
not even be commenced unless the mind had been already in action and
intelligently using the original language for that purpose. In fact the
use by deaf-mutes of signs originating in themselves exhibits a creative
action of mind and innate faculty of expression beyond that of ordinary
speakers who acquired language without conscious effort. The thanks
of students, both of philology and psychology, are due to Prof. SAMUEL
PORTER, of the National Deaf Mute College, for his response to the
question, "Is thought possible without language?" published in the
Princeton Review for January, 1880.

With regard to the sounds uttered by deaf-mutes, the same explanation of heredity may be made as above, regarding the words invented
by young children. Congenital deaf-mutes at first make the same
sounds as hearing children of the same age, and, often being susceptible
to vibrations of the air, are not suspected of being deaf. When that
affliction is ascertained to exist, all oral utterances from the deaf-mute
are habitually repressed by the parents.

GESTURES OF THE BLIND.

The facial expressions and gestures of the congenitally blind are worthy of attention. The most interesting and conclusive examples come from the case of Laura Bridgman, who, being also deaf, could not possibly have derived them by imitation. When a letter from a beloved friend was communicated to her by gesture-language, she laughed and clapped her hands. A roguish expression was given to her face, concomitant with the emotion, by her holding the lower lip by the teeth. She blushed, shrugged her shoulders, turned in her elbows, and raised her eye-brows under the same circumstances as other people. In amazement, she rounded and protruded the lips, opened them, and breathed strongly. It is remarkable that she constantly accompanied her "yes" with the common affirmative nod, and her "no" with our negative shake of the head, as these gestures are by no means universal and do not seem clearly connected with emotion. This, possibly, may be explained by the fact that her ancestors for many generations had used these gestures. A similar curious instance is mentioned by Cardinal Wiseman (*Essays*, III, 547, *London*, 1853) of an Italian blind man, the appearance of whose eyes indicated that he had never enjoyed sight, and who yet made the same elaborate gestures made by the people with whom he lived, but which had been used by them immemorially, as correctly as if he had learned them by observation.

LOSS OF SPEECH BY ISOLATION.

When human beings have been long in solitary confinement, been abandoned, or otherwise have become isolated from their fellows, they have lost speech either partially or entirely, and required to have it renewed through gestures. There are also several recorded cases of children, born with all their faculties, who, after having been lost or abandoned, have been afterwards found to have grown up possessed of acute hearing, but without anything like human speech. One of these was Peter, "the Wild Boy," who was found in the woods of Hanover in 1726, and taken to England, where vain attempts were made to teach him language, though he lived to the age of seventy. Another was a boy of twelve, found in the forest of Aveyron, in France, about the beginning of this century, who was destitute of speech, and all efforts to teach him failed. Some of these cases are to be considered in connection with the general law of evolution, that in degeneration the last and highest acquirements are lost first. When in these the effort at acquiring or re-acquiring speech has been successful, it has been through gestures, in the same manner as missionaries, explorers, and shipwrecked mariners have become acquainted with tongues before unknown to themselves and sometimes to civilization. All persons in such circumstances are obliged to proceed by pointing to objects and making gesticulations, at the same time observing what articulate sounds were associated with those motions by the persons addressed, and thus vocabularies and lists of phrases were formed.

LOW TRIBES OF MAN.

Apart from the establishment of a systematic language of signs under special circumstances which have occasioned its development, the gestures of the lower tribes of men may be generally classed under the emotional or instinctive division, which can be correlated with those of the lower animals. This may be illustrated by the modes adopted to show friendship in salutation, taking the place of our shaking hands. Some Pacific Islanders used to show their joy at meeting friends by sniffing at them, after the style of well-disposed dogs. The Fuegians pat and slap each other, and some Polynesians stroke their own faces with the hand or foot of the friend. The practice of rubbing or pressing noses is very common. It has been noticed in the Lapland Alps, often in Africa, and in Australia the tips of the noses are pressed a long time, accompanied with grunts of satisfaction. Patting and stroking different parts of the body are still more frequent, and prevailed among the North American Indians, though with the latter the most common expression was hugging. In general, the civilities exchanged are similar to those of many animals.

GESTURES AS AN OCCASIONAL RESOURCE.

Persons of limited vocabulary, whether foreigners to the tongue employed or native, but not accomplished in its use, even in the midst of a civilization where gestures are deprecated, when at fault for words resort instinctively to physical motions that are not wild nor meaningless, but picturesque and significant, though perhaps made by the gesturer for the first time. An uneducated laborer, if good-natured enough to be really desirous of responding to a request for information, when he has exhausted his scanty stock of words will eke them out by original gestures. While fully admitting the advice to Coriolanus—

> Action is eloquence, and the eyes of the ignorant
> More learned than the ears —

it may be paraphrased to read that the hands of the ignorant are more learned than their tongues. A stammerer, too, works his arms and features as if determined to get his thoughts out, in a manner not only suggestive of the physical struggle, but of the use of gestures as a hereditary expedient.

GESTURES OF FLUENT TALKERS.

The same is true of the most fluent talkers on occasions when the exact vocal formula desired does not at once suggest itself, or is unsatisfactory without assistance from the physical machinery not embraced in the oral apparatus. The command of a copious vocabulary common to both speaker and hearer undoubtedly tends to a phlegmatic delivery and disdain of subsidiary aid. An excited speaker will, however, generally make a free use of his hands without regard to any effect of that use upon auditors. Even among the gesture-hating English, when they are aroused from torpidity of manner, the hands are involuntarily clapped in approbation, rubbed with delight, wrung in distress, raised in astonishment, and waved in triumph. The fingers are snapped for contempt, the forefinger is vibrated to reprove or threaten, and the fist shaken in defiance. The brow is contracted with displeasure, and the eyes winked to show connivance. The shoulders are shrugged to express disbelief or repugnance, the eyebrows elevated with surprise, the lips bitten in vexation and thrust out in sullenness or displeasure, while a higher degree of anger is shown by a stamp of the foot. Quintilian, regarding the subject, however, not as involuntary exhibition of feeling and intellect, but for illustration and enforcement, becomes eloquent on the variety of motions of which the hands alone are capable, as follows:

"The action of the other parts of the body assists the speaker, but the hands (I could almost say) speak themselves. By them do we not demand, promise, call, dismiss, threaten, supplicate, express abhorrence and terror, question and deny? Do we not by them express joy and sorrow, doubt, confession, repentance, measure, quantity, number, and time? Do they not also encourage, supplicate, restrain, convict, admire, respect? and in pointing out places and persons do they not discharge the office of adverbs and of pronouns?"

Voss adopts almost the words of Quintilian, "*Manus non modo loquéntem adjuvant, sed ipsæ pene loqui videntur,*" while Cresollius calls the hand "the minister of reason and wisdom * * * without it there is no eloquence."

INVOLUNTARY RESPONSE TO GESTURES.

Further evidence of the unconscious survival of gesture language is afforded by the ready and involuntary response made in signs to signs when a man with the speech and habits of civilization is brought into close contact with Indians or deaf-mutes. Without having ever before seen or made one of their signs, he will soon not only catch the meaning of theirs, but produce his own, which they will likewise comprehend, the power seemingly remaining latent in him until called forth by necessity.

NATURAL PANTOMIME.

In the earliest part of man's history the subjects of his discourse must have been almost wholly sensuous, and therefore readily expressed in pantomime. Not only was pantomime sufficient for all the actual needs of his existence, but it is not easy to imagine how he could have used language such as is now known to us. If the best English dictionary and grammar had been miraculously furnished to him, together with the art of reading with proper pronunciation, the gift would have been valueless, because the ideas expressed by the words had not yet been formed.

That the early concepts were of a direct and material character is shown by what has been ascertained of the roots of language, and there does not appear to be much difficulty in expressing by other than vocal instrumentality all that could have been expressed by those roots. Even now, with our vastly increased belongings of external life, avocations, and habits, nearly all that is absolutely necessary for our physical needs can be expressed in pantomime. Far beyond the mere signs for eating, drinking, sleeping, and the like, any one will understand a skillful representation in signs of a tailor, shoemaker, blacksmith, weaver, sailor, farmer, or doctor. So of washing, dressing, shaving, walking, driving, writing, reading, churning, milking, boiling, roasting or frying, making bread or preparing coffee, shooting, fishing, rowing, sailing, sawing, planing, boring, and, in short, an endless list.

Max Müller properly calls touch, scent, and taste the palaioteric, and sight and hearing the neoteric senses, the latter of which often require to be verified by the former. Touch is the lowest in specialization and development, and is considered to be the oldest of the senses, the others indeed being held by some writers to be only its modifications. Scent, of essential importance to many animals, has with man almost ceased to be of any, except in connection with taste, which he has developed to a high degree. Whether or not sight preceded hearing in order of development, it is difficult, in conjecturing the first attempts of man or his hypothetical ancestor at the expression either of percepts or concepts, to connect vocal sounds with any large number of objects, but it is readily conceivable that the characteristics of their forms and movements should have been suggested to the eye—fully exercised before the tongue—so soon as the arms and fingers became free for the requisite simulation or portrayal. There is little distinction between pantomime and a developed sign language, in which thought is transmitted rapidly and certainly from hand to eye as it is in oral speech from lips to ear; the former is, however, the parent of the latter, which is more abbreviated and less obvious. Pantomime acts movements, reproduces forms and positions, presents pictures, and manifests emotions with greater realization than any other mode of utterance. It may readily be supposed that a troglodyte man would desire to communicate the finding of a cave in the vicinity of a pure pool, circled with soft grass, and shaded by trees bearing edible fruit. No sound of nature is connected with any of those objects, but the position and size of the cave, its distance and direction, the water, its quality, and amount, the verdant circling carpet, and the kind and height of the trees could have been made known by pantomime in the days of the mammoth, if articulate speech had not then been established, as Indians or deaf-mutes now communicate similar information by the same agency.

The proof of this fact, as regards deaf-mutes, will hardly be demanded, as their expressive pantomime has been so often witnessed. That of the North American Indians, as distinct from the signs which are generally its abbreviations, has been frequently described in general terms, but it may be interesting to present two instances from remote localities.

A Maricopa Indian, in the present limits of Arizona, was offered an advantageous trade for his horse, whereupon he stretched himself on his horse's neck, caressed it tenderly, at the same time shutting his eyes, meaning thereby that no offer could tempt him to part with his charger.

An A-tco-mâ-wi or Pit River Indian, in Northeastern California, to explain the cause of his cheeks and forehead being covered with tar, represented a man falling, and, despite his efforts to save him, trembling, growing pale (pointing from his face to that of a white man), and sinking to sleep, his spirit winging its way to the skies, which he indicated by imitating with his hands the flight of a bird upwards, his body sleeping still upon the river bank, to which he pointed. The tar upon his face was thus shown to be his dress of mourning for a friend who had fallen and died.

Several descriptions of pure pantomime, intermixed with the more conventionalized signs, will be found in the present paper. In especial, reference is made to the Address of Kin Chē-ĕss, Nátci's Narrative, the Dialogue between Alaskan Indians, and Na-wa-gi-jig's Story.

SOME THEORIES UPON PRIMITIVE LANGUAGE.

Cresollius, writing in 1620, was strongly in favor of giving precedence to gesture. He says, "Man, full of wisdom and divinity, could have appeared nothing superior to a naked trunk or block had he not been adorned with the hand as the interpreter and messenger of his thoughts." He quotes with approval the brother of St. Basil in declaring that had men been formed without hands they would never have been endowed with an articulate voice, and concludes: "Since, then, nature has furnished us with two instruments for the purpose of bringing into light and expressing the silent affections of the mind, language and the hand, it has been the opinion of learned and intelligent men that the former would be maimed and nearly useless without the latter; whereas the hand, without the aid of language, has produced many and wonderful effects."

Rabelais, who incorporated into his satirical work much true learning and philosophy, makes his hero announce the following opinion:

"Nothing less, quoth Pantagruel [Book iii, ch. xix], do I believe than that it is a mere abusing of our understandings to give credit to the words of those who say that there is any such thing as a natural language. All speeches have had their primary origin from the arbitrary institutions, accords, and agreements of nations in their respective condescendments to what should be noted and betokened by them. An articulate voice, according to the dialecticians, hath naturally no signification at all; for that the sense and meaning thereof did totally depend upon the good will and pleasure of the first deviser and imposer of it."

Max Müller, following Professor Heyse, of Berlin, published an ingenious theory of primitive speech, to the effect that man had a creative faculty giving to each conception, as it thrilled through his brain for the first time, a special phonetic expression, which faculty became extinct when its necessity ceased. This theory, which makes each radical of language to be a phonetic type rung out from the organism of the first man or men when struck by an idea, has been happily named the "ding-dong" theory. It has been abandoned mainly through the destructive criticisms of Prof. W. D. WHITNEY, of Yale College. One lucid explanation by the latter should be specially noted: "A word is a combination of sounds which by a series of historical reasons has come to be accepted and understood in a certain community as the sign of a certain idea. As long as they so accept and understand it, it has existence; when every one ceases to use and understand it, it ceases to exist."

Several authors, among them Kaltschmidt, contend that there was but one primitive language, which was purely onomatopœic, that is, imitative of natural sounds. This has been stigmatized as the "bow-wow" theory, but its advocates might derive an argument from the epithet itself, as not only our children, but the natives of Papua, call the dog a "bow-wow." They have, however, gone too far in attempting to trace back words in their shape as now existing to any natural sounds instead of confining that work to the roots from which the words have sprung.

Another attempt has been made, represented by Professor Noiré, to account for language by means of interjectional cries. This Max Müller revengefully styled the "pooh-pooh" theory. In it is included the rhythmical sounds which a body of men make seemingly by a common impulse when engaged in a common work, such as the cries of sailors when hauling on a rope or pulling an oar, or the yell of savages in an attack. It also derives an argument from the impulse of life by which the child shouts and the bird sings. There are, however, very few either words or roots of words which can be proved to have that derivation.

Professor SAYCE, in his late work, *Introduction to the Science of Language, London*, 1880, gives the origin of language in gestures, in onomatopœia, and to a limited extent in interjectional cries. He concludes it to be the ordinary theory of modern comparative philologists that all languages are traced back to a certain number of abstract roots, each of which was a sort of sentence in embryo, and while he does not admit this as usually presented, he believes that there was a time in the history of speech when the articulate or semi-articulate sounds uttered by primitive men were made the significant representations of thought by the gestures with which they were accompanied. This statement is specially gratifying to the present writer as he had advanced much the same views in his first publication on the subject in the following paragraph, now reproduced with greater confidence :

"From their own failures and discordancies, linguistic scholars have recently decided that both the 'bow-wow' and the 'ding-dong' theories are unsatisfactory; that the search for imitative, onomatopœic, and directly expressive sounds to explain the origin of human speech has been too exclusive, and that many primordial roots of language have been founded in the involuntary sounds accompanying certain actions. As, however, the action was the essential, and the consequent or concomitant sound the accident, it would be expected that a representation or feigned reproduction of the action would have been used to express the the idea before the sound associated with that action could have been separated from it. The visual onomatopœia of gestures, which even yet have been subjected to but slight artificial corruption, would therefore serve as a key to the audible. It is also contended that in the pristine days, when the sounds of the only words yet formed had close connection with objects and the ideas directly derived from them, signs were as much more copious for communication than speech, as the sight embraces more and more distinct characteristics of objects than does the sense of hearing."

CONCLUSIONS.

The preponderance of authority is in favor of the view that man, when in the possession of all his faculties, did not choose between voice and gesture, both being originally instinctive, as they both are now, and never, with those faculties, was in a state where the one was used to the absolute exclusion of the other. The long neglected work of Dalgarno, published in 1661, is now admitted to show wisdom when he says: "*non minus naturale fit homini communicare in* Figuris *quam* Sonis: *quorum utrumque dico homini* naturale." With the voice man at first imitated the few sounds of nature, while with gesture he exhibited actions, motions, positions, forms, dimensions, directions, and distances, and their derivatives. It would appear from this unequal division of capacity that oral speech remained rudimentary long after gesture had become an art. With the concession of all purely imitative sounds and of the spontaneous action of the vocal organs under excitement, it is still true that the connection between ideas and words generally depended upon a compact between the speaker and hearer which presupposes the existence of a prior mode of communication. That was probably by gesture, which, in the apposite phrase of Professor SAYCE, "like the rope-bridges of the Himalayas or the Andes, formed the first rude means of communication between man and man." At the very least it may be gladly accepted provisionally as a clue leading out of the labyrinth of philologic confusion.

For the purpose of the present paper there is, however, no need of an absolute decision upon the priority between communication of ideas by bodily motion and by vocal articulation. It is enough to admit that the connection between them was so early and intimate that gestures, in the wide sense indicated of presenting ideas under physical forms, had a direct formative effect upon many words; that they exhibit the earliest condition of the human mind; are traced from the remotest antiquity among all peoples possessing records; are generally prevalent in the savage stage of social evolution; survive agreeably in the scenic pantomime, and still adhere to the ordinary speech of civilized man by motions of the face, hands, head, and body, often involuntary, often purposely in illustration or for emphasis.

It may be unnecessary to explain that none of the signs to be described, even those of present world-wide prevalence, are presented as precisely those of primitive man. Signs as well as words, animals, and plants have had their growth, development, and change, their births and deaths, and their struggle for existence with survival of the fittest. It is, however, thought probable from reasons hereinafter mentioned that their radicals can be ascertained with more precision than those of words.

HISTORY OF GESTURE LANGUAGE.

There is ample evidence of record, besides that derived from other sources, that the systematic use of gesture speech was of great antiquity. Livy so declares, and Quintilian specifies that the " *lex gestus * * * ab illis temporibus heroicis orta est.*" Plato classed its practice among civil virtues, and Chrysippus gave it place among the proper education of freemen. Athenæus tells that gestures were even reduced to distinct classification with appropriate terminology. The class suited to comedy was called Cordax, that to tragedy Eumelia, and that for satire Sicinnis, from the inventor Sicinnus. Bathyllus from these formed a fourth class, adapted to pantomime. This system appears to have been particularly applicable to theatrical performances. Quintilian, later, gave most elaborate rules for gestures in oratory, which are specially noticeable from the importance attached to the manner of disposing the fingers. He attributed to each particular disposition a significance or suitableness which are not now obvious. Some of them are retained by modern orators, but without the same, or indeed any, intentional meaning, and others are wholly disused.

The value of these digital arrangements is, however, shown by their use among the modern Italians, to whom they have directly descended.

From many illustrations of this fact the following is selected. Fig. 61 is copied from Austin's *Chironomia* as his graphic execution of the ges-

ture described by Quintilian : " The fore finger of the right hand joining the middle of its nail to the extremity of its own thumb, and moderately extending the rest of the fingers, is graceful in *approving*." Fig. 62 is taken from De Jorio's plates and descriptions of the gestures

FIG. 61.

among modern Neapolitans, with the same idea of approbation—" good." Both of these may be compared with Fig. 63, a common sign among the North American Indians to express affirmation and approbation. With

the knowledge of these details it is possible to believe the story of Macrobius that Cicero used to vie with Roscius, the celebrated actor, as to which of them could express a sentiment in the greater variety of ways, the one by gesture and the other by speech, with the apparent result of victory to the actor who was so satisfied with the superiority of his art that he wrote a book on the subject.

FIG. 62.

Gestures were treated of with still more distinction as connected with pantomimic dances and representations. Æschylus appears to have brought theatrical gesture to a high degree of perfection, but Telestes, a

dancer employed by him, introduced the dumb show, a dance without marked dancing steps, and subordinated to motions of the hands, arms, and body, which is dramatic pantomime. He was so great an artist, says Athenæus, that when he represented the *Seven before Thebes* he rendered every circumstance manifest by his gestures alone. From Greece, or rather from Egypt, the art was brought to Rome, and in the reign of Augustus was the great delight of that Emperor and his friend Mæcenas.

FIG. 63.

Bathyllus, of Alexandria, was the first to introduce it to the Roman public, but he had a dangerous rival in Pylades. The latter was magnificent, pathetic, and affecting, while Bathyllus was gay and sportive. All Rome was split into factions about their respective merits. Athenæus speaks of a distinguished performer of his own time (he died A. D. 194) named Memphis, whom he calls the " dancing philosopher," because he showed what the Pythagorean philosophy could do by exhibiting in silence everything with stronger evidence than they could who professed to teach the arts of language. In the reign of Nero, a celebrated pantomimist who had heard that the cynic philosopher Demetrius spoke of the art with contempt, prevailed upon him to witness his performance, with the result that the cynic, more and more astonished, at last cried out aloud, "Man, I not only see, but I hear what you do, for to me you appear to speak with your hands!"

Lucian, who narrates this in his work *De Saltatione*, gives another tribute to the talent of, perhaps, the same performer. A barbarian prince of Pontus (the story is told elsewhere of Tyridates, King of Armenia), having come to Rome to do homage to the Emperor Nero, and been taken to see the pantomimes, was asked on his departure by the Emperor what present he would have as a mark of his favor. The barbarian begged that he might have the principal pantomimist, and upon being asked why he made such an odd request, replied that he had many neighbors who spoke such various and discordant languages that he found it difficult to obtain any interpreter who could understand them or explain his commands; but if he had the dancer he could by his assistance easily make himself intelligible to all.

While the general effect of these pantomimes is often mentioned, there remain but few detailed descriptions of them. Apuleius, however, in the tenth book of his *Metamorphosis* or "Golden Ass," gives sufficient details of the performance of the Judgment of Paris to show that it strongly resembled the best form of ballet opera known in modern times. These exhibitions were so greatly in favor that, according to Ammianus Marcellinus, there were in Rome in the year 190 six thousand persons devoted to the art, and that when a famine raged they were all kept in the city, though besides all the strangers all the philosophers were forced to leave. Their popularity continued until the sixth century, and it is evident from a decree of Charlemagne that they were not lost, or at least, had been revived in his time. Those of us who have enjoyed the performance of the original Ravel troupe will admit that the art still survives, though not with the magnificence or perfection, especially with reference to serious subjects, which it exhibited in the age of imperial Rome.

Early and prominent among the post-classic works upon gesture is that of the venerable Bede (who flourished A. D. 672–735) *De Loquelâ per Gestum Digitorum, sive de Indigitatione.* So much discussion had indeed been carried on in reference to the use of signs for the desideratum of a universal mode of communication, which also was designed to be occult and mystic, that Rabelais, in the beginning of the sixteenth century, who, however satirical, never spent his force upon matters of little importance, devotes much attention to it. He makes his English philosopher, Thaumast "The Wonderful" declare, "I will dispute by signs only, without speaking, for the matters are so abstruse, hard, and arduous, that words proceeding from the mouth of man will never be sufficient for unfolding of them to my liking."

The earliest contributions of practical value connected with the subject were made by George Dalgarno, of Aberdeen, in two works, one published in London, 1661, entitled *Ars Signorum, vulgo character universalis et lingua philosophica,* and the other printed at Oxford,

1680, entitled, *Didascalocophus, or the Deaf and Dumb Man's Tutor.* He spent his life in obscurity, and his works, though he was incidentally mentioned by Leibnitz under the name of "M. Dalgarus," passed into oblivion. Yet he undoubtedly was the precursor of Bishop Wilkins in his *Essay toward a Real Character and a Philosophical Language,* published in London, 1668, though indeed the first idea was far older, it having been, as reported by Piso, the wish of Galen that some way might be found out to represent things by such peculiar signs and names as should express their natures. Dalgarno's ideas respecting the education of the dumb were also of the highest value, and though they were too refined and enlightened to be appreciated at the period when he wrote, they probably were used by Dr. Wallis if not by Sicard. Some of his thoughts should be quoted: "As I think the eye to be as docile as the ear; so neither see I any reason but the hand might be made as tractable an organ as the tongue; and as soon brought to form, if not fair, at least legible characters, as the tongue to imitate and echo back articulate sounds." A paragraph prophetic of the late success in educating blind deaf-mutes is as follows: "The soul can exert her powers by the ministry of any of the senses: and, therefore, when she is deprived of her principal secretaries, the eye and the ear, then she must be contented with the service of her lackeys and scullions, the other senses; which are no less true and faithful to their mistress than the eye and the ear; but not so quick for dispatch."

In his division of the modes of "expressing the inward emotions by outward and sensible signs," he relegates to physiology cases "when the internal passions are expressed by such external signs as have a natural connection, by way of cause and effect, with the passion they discover, as laughing, weeping, frowning, &c., and this way of interpretation being common to the brute with man belongs to natural philosophy. And because this goes not far enough to serve the rational soul, therefore, man has invented Sematology." This he divides into Pneumatology, interpretation by sounds conveyed through the ear; Schematology, by figures to the eye, and Haptology, by mutual contact, skin to skin. Schematology is itself divided into Typology or Grammatology, and Cheirology or Dactylology. The latter embraces "the transient motions of the fingers, which of all other ways of interpretation comes nearest to that of the tongue."

As a phase in the practice of gestures in lieu of speech must be mentioned the code of the Cistercian monks, who were vowed to silence except in religious exercises. That they might literally observe their vows they were obliged to invent a system of communication by signs, a list of which is given by Leibnitz, but does not show much ingenuity.

A curious description of the speech of the early inhabitants of the world, given by Swedenborg in his *Arcana Coelestia,* published 1749–1756, may be compared with the present exhibitions of deaf-mutes in institutions for their instruction. He says it was not articulate like the

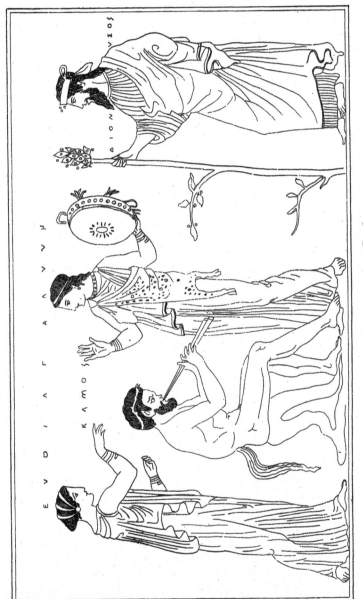

Fig. 64.—Group from an ancient Greek vase.

vocal speech of our time, but was tacit, being produced not by external respiration, but by internal. They were able to express their meaning by slight motions of the lips and corresponding changes of the face.

Austin's comprehensive work, *Chironomia, or a Treatise on Rhetorical Delivery, London*, 1806, is a repertory of information for all writers on gesture, who have not always given credit to it, as well as on all branches of oratory. This has been freely used by the present writer, as has also the volume by the canon Andrea de Jorio, *La Mimica degli Antichi investigata nel Gestire Napoletano, Napoli*, 1832. The canon's chief object was to interpret the gestures of the ancients as shown in their works of art and described in their writings, by the modern gesticulations of the Neapolitans, and he has proved that the general system of gesture once prevailing in ancient Italy is substantially the same as now observed. With an understanding of the existing language of gesture the scenes on the most ancient Greek vases and reliefs obtain a new and interesting significance and form a connecting link between the present and prehistoric times. Two of De Jorio's plates are here reproduced, Figs. 64 and 67, with such explanation and further illustration as is required for the present subject.

The spirited figures upon the ancient vase, Fig. 64, are red upon a black ground and are described in the published account in French of the collection of Sir John Coghill, Bart., of which the following is a free translation:

Dionysos or Bacchus is represented with a strong beard, his head girt with the credemnon, clothed in a long folded tunic, above which is an ample cloak, and holding a thyrsus. Under the form of a satyr, Comus, or the genius of the table, plays on the double flute and tries to excite to the dance two nymphs, the companions of Bacchus—Galené, Tranquility, and Eudia, Serenity. The first of them is dressed in a tunic, above which is a fawn skin, holding a tympanum or classic drum on which she is about to strike, while her companion marks the time by a snapping of the fingers, which custom the author of the catalogue wisely states is still kept up in Italy in the dance of the tarantella. The composition is said to express allegorically that pure and serene pleasures are benefits derived from the god of wine.

This is a fair example of the critical acumen of art-commentators. The gestures of the two nymphs are interesting, but on very slight examination it appears that those of Galené have nothing to do with beat of drum, nor have those of Eudia any connection with music, though it is not so clear what is the true subject under discussion. Aided, however, by the light of the modern sign language of Naples, there seems to be by no means serenity prevailing, but a quarrel between the ladies, on a special subject which is not necessarily pure. The nymph at the reader's left fixes her eyes upon her companion with her index in the same direction, clearly indicating, *thou*. That the address is reproachful is shown from her countenance, but with greater certainty from her attitude and the corresponding one of her companion, who raises both her hands in suprise accompanied with negation. The latter is ex-pressed by the right hand raised toward the shoulder, with the palm op-posed to the person to whom response is made. This is the rejection of the idea presented, and is expressed by some of our Indians, as shown in Fig. 65. A sign of the Dakota tribe of Indians with the same signification is given

FIG. 65.

in Fig. 270, page 441, *infra*. At the same time the upper part of the nymph's body is drawn backward as far as the preservation of equilibrium permits. So a reproach or accu-sation is made on the one part, and denied, whether truthfully or not, on the other. Its subject also may be ascertained. The left hand of Eudia is not mute; it is held towards her rival with the balls of the index and thumb united, the modern Neapolitan sign for *love*, which is drawn more clearly in Fig. 66. It is called the kissing of the thumb and finger, and there is ample authority to show that among the ancient classics it was a sign of marriage. St. Jerome, quoted by Vincenzo Requena, says: "*Nam et ipsa digitorum conjunctio, et quasi molli osculo se complectans et fœderans, maritum pin-git et conjugem;*" and Apuleius clearly alludes to the same gesture as used in the adoration of Venus, by the words "*primore digito in erectum polli-cem residente.*" The gesture is one of the few out of the large number described in various parts of Rabelais' great work, the significance of which is explained. It is made by Naz-de-cabre or Goat's Nose (*Pantagruel*, Book III, Ch. XX), who lifted up into the air his left hand, the whole fingers

FIG. 66.

whereof he retained fistways closed together, except the thumb and the forefinger, whose nails he softly joined and coupled to one another. "I understand, quoth Pantagruel, what he meaneth by that sign. It denotes marriage." The quarrel is thus established to be about love; and the fluting satyr seated between the two nymphs, behind whose back the accusation is furtively made by the jealous one, may well be the object concerning whom jealousy is manifested. Eudia therefore, instead of "serenely" marking time for a "tranquil" tympanist, appears to be cry-ing, "Galené! you bad thing! you are having, or trying to have, an affair with my Comus!"—an accusation which this writer verily believes to have been just. The lady's attitude in affectation of surprised denial is not that of injured innocence.

Fig. 67, taken from a vase in the Homeric Gallery, is rich in natural gestures. Without them, from the costumes and attitudes it is easy to recognize the protagonist or principal actor in the group, and its general subject. The warrior goddess Athené stands forth in the midst of what appears to be a council of war. After the study of modern gesture

Fig. 67.—Group from a vase in the Homeric Gallery.

speech, the votes of each member of the council, with the degree of positiveness or interest felt by each, can be ascertained. Athené in animated motion turns her eyes to the right, and extends her left arm and hand to the left, with her right hand brandishing a lance in the same direction, in which her feet show her to be ready to spring. She is urging the figures on her right to follow her at once to attempt some dangerous enterprise. Of these the elderly

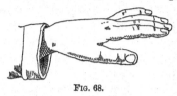 

man, who is calmly seated, holds his right hand flat and reversed, and suspended slightly above his knee. This probably is the ending of the modern Nea-

FIG. 68.   FIG. 69.

politan gesture, Fig. 68, which signifies hesitation, advice to pause before hasty action, "go slowly," and commences higher with a gentle wavering movement downward. This can be compared with the sign of some of our Indians, Fig. 69, for *wait! slowly!* The female figure at the left of the group, standing firmly and decidedly, raises her left hand directed to the goddess with the palm vertical. If

this is supposed to be a stationary gesture it means, "*wait! stop!*" It may, however, be the commencement of the last mentioned gesture, "*go slow.*"

FIG. 70.

Both of these members of the council advise delay and express doubt of the propriety of immediate action.

The sitting warrior on the left of Athené presents his left hand flat and carried well up. This position, supposed to be stationary, now means to *ask, inquire,* and it may be that he inquires of the other veteran what reasons he can produce for his temporizing policy. This may be collated with the modern Neapolitan sign for *ask,*

FIG. 71.

Fig. 70, and the common Indian sign for "*tell me!*" Fig. 71. In connection with this it is also interesting to compare the Australian sign for interrogation, Fig. 72, and also the Comanche Indian sign for *give me,*

FIG. 72.

Fig. 301, page 480, *infra.* If, however, the artist had the intention to represent the flat hand as in motion from below upward, as is probable from the connection, the meaning is *much, greatly.* He strongly disapproves the counsel of the opposite side. Our Indians often express the idea of quantity, *much,* with the same conception of comparative height, by an upward motion of the extended palm, but with them the palm is held downward. The last figure to the right, by the action of his whole body, shows his rejection of the proposed delay, and his right hand gives the modern sign of combined surprise and reproof.

It is interesting to note the similarity of the merely emotional gestures and attitudes of modern Italy with those of the classics. The Pulcinella, Fig. 73, for instance, drawn from life in the streets of Naples, has the same pliancy and *abandon* of the limbs as appears in the supposed foolish slaves of the Vatican Terence.

In close connection with this branch of the study reference must be made

to the gestures exhibited in the works of Italian art only modern in comparison with the high antiquity of their predecessors. A good instance is in the Last Supper of Leonardo da Vinci, painted toward the close of the fifteenth century, and to the figure of Judas as there portrayed. The gospel denounces him as a thief, which is expressed in the painting by the hand extended and slightly curved, imitative of the pilferer's act in clutching and drawing toward him furtively the stolen object, and is the same gesture that now indicates *theft* in Naples, Fig. 74, and among some of the North American Indians, Fig. 75. The pictorial propriety of the sign is preserved by the apparent desire of the traitor to obtain the one white loaf of bread on the table

FIG. 73.

(the remainder being of coarser quality) which lies near where his hand is tending. Raffaelle was equally particular in his exhibition of gesture language, even unto the minutest detail of the arrangement of the fingers. It is traditional that he sketched the Madonna's hands for the Spasimo di Sicilia in eleven different positions before he was satisfied.

FIG. 74.

No allusion to the bibliography of gesture speech, however slight, should close without including the works of Mgr. D. De Haerne, who has, as a member of the Belgian Chamber of Representatives, in addition to his rank in the Roman Catholic Church, been active in promoting the cause of education in general, and especially that of the deaf and dumb. His admirable treatise *The Natural Language of Signs* has been translated and is accessible to American readers in the *American Annals of the Deaf and Dumb*, 1875. In that valuable serial, conducted by Prof. E. A. FAY, of the National Deaf

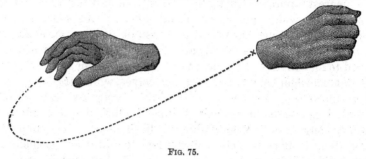

FIG. 75.

Mute College at Washington, and now in its twenty-sixth volume, a large amount of the current literature on the subject indicated by its title can be found.

MODERN USE OF GESTURE SPEECH.

Dr. TYLOR says (*Early History of Mankind*, 44): "We cannot lay down as a rule that gesticulation decreases as civilization advances, and say, for instance, that a Southern Frenchman, because his talk is illustrated with gestures as a book with pictures, is less civilized than a German or Englishman." This is true, and yet it is almost impossible for persons not accustomed to gestures to observe them without associating the idea of low culture. Thus in Mr. Darwin's summing up of those characteristics of the natives of Tierra del Fuego, which rendered it difficult to believe them to be fellow-creatures, he classes their "violent gestures" with their filthy and greasy skins, discordant voices, and hideous faces bedaubed with paint. This description is quoted by the Duke of Argyle in his *Unity of Nature* in approval of those characteristics as evidence of the lowest condition of humanity.

Whether or not the power of the visible gesture relative to, and its influence upon the words of modern oral speech are in inverse proportion to the general culture, it seems established that they do not bear that or any constant proportion to the development of the several languages with which gesture is still more or less associated. The statement has frequently been made that gesture is yet to some highly-advanced languages a necessary modifying factor, and that only when a language has become so artificial as to be completely expressible in written signs—indeed, has been remodeled through their long familiar use—can the bodily signs be wholly dispensed with. The evidence for this statement is now doubted, and it is safer to affirm that a common use of gesture depends more upon the sociologic conditions of the speakers than upon the degree of copiousness of their oral speech.

USE BY OTHER PEOPLES THAN NORTH AMERICAN INDIANS.

The nearest approach to a general rule which it is now proposed to hazard is that where people speaking precisely the same dialect are not numerous, and are thrown into constant contact on equal terms with others of differing dialects and languages, gesture is necessarily resorted to for converse with the latter, and remains for an indefinite time as a habit or accomplishment among themselves, while large bodies enjoying common speech, and either isolated from foreigners, or, when in contact with them, so dominant as to compel the learning and adoption of their own tongue, become impassive in its delivery. The ungesturing English, long insular, and now rulers when spread over continents, may be compared with the profusely gesticulating Italians dwelling in a maze of dialects and subject for centuries either to foreign rule or to the influx of strangers on whom they depended. So common is the use of gestures in Italy, especially among the lower and uneducated classes, that utterance without them seems to be nearly impossible. The driver or boatman will often, on being addressed, involuntarily drop the reins or oars, at the risk of a serious accident, to respond with his arms and fingers in accompaniment of his tongue. Nor is the habit confined to the uneducated. King Ferdinand returning to Naples after the revolt of 1821, and finding that the boisterous multitude would not allow his voice to be heard, resorted successfully to a royal address in signs, giving reproaches, threats, admonitions, pardon, and dismissal, to the entire satisfaction of the assembled lazzaroni. The medium, though probably not the precise manner of its employment, recalls Lucan's account of the quieting of an older tumult—

tumultum
Composuit vultu, dextraque silentia fecit.

This rivalry of Punch would, in London, have occasioned measureless ridicule and disgust. The difference in what is vaguely styled temperament does not wholly explain the contrast between the two peoples, for the performance was creditable both to the readiness of the King in an emergency and to the aptness of his people, the main distinction being that in Italy there was in 1821, and still is, a recognized and cultivated language of signs long disused in Great Britain. In seeking to account for this it will be remembered that the Italians have a more direct descent from the people who, as has been above shown, in classic times so long and lovingly cultivated gesture as a system. They have also had more generally before their eyes the artistic relics in which gestures have been preserved.

It is a curious fact that some English writers, notably Addison (*Spectator*, 407), have contended that it does not suit the genius of that nation to use gestures even in public speaking, against which doctrine Austin vigorously remonstrates. He says: "There may possibly be nations whose livelier feelings incline them more to gesticulation than is common among us, as there are also countries in which plants of excellent use to man grow spontaneously; these, by care and culture, are found to thrive also in colder countries."

It is in general to be remarked that as the number of dialects in any district decreases so will the gestures, though doubtless there is also weight in the fact not merely that a language has been reduced to and modified by writing, but that people who are accustomed generally to read and write, as are the English and Germans, will after a time think and talk as they write, and without the accompaniments still persistent among Hindus, Arabs, and the less literate of European nations.

The fact that in the comparatively small island of Sicily gesture language has been maintained until the present time in a perfection not observed elsewhere in Europe must be considered in connection with the above remark on England's insularity, and it must also be admitted that several languages have prevailed in the latter, still leaving dialects. This apparent similarity of conditions renders the contrast as regards use of gestures more remarkable, yet there are some reasons for their persistence in Sicily which apply with greater force than to Great Britain. The explanation, through mere tradition, is that the common usage of signs dates from the time of Dionysius, the tyrant of Syracuse, who prohibited meetings and conversation among his subjects, under the direst penalties, so that they adopted that expedient to hold communication. It would be more useful to consider the peculiar history of the island. The Sicanians being its aborigines it was colonized by Greeks, who, as the Romans asserted, were still more apt at gesture than themselves. This colonization was also by separate bands of adventurers from several different states of Greece, so that they started with dialects and did not unite in a common or national organization, the separate cities and their territories being governed by oligarchies or tyrants frequently at war with each other, until, in the fifth century B. C., the Carthaginians began to contribute a new admixture of language and blood, followed by Roman, Vandal, Gothic, Herulian, Arab, and Norman subjugation. Thus some of the conditions above suggested have existed in this case, but, whatever the explanation, the accounts given by travelers of the extent to which the language of signs has been used even during the present generation are so marvelous as to deserve quotation. The one selected is from the pen of Alexandre Dumas, who, it is to be hoped, did not carry his genius for romance into a professedly sober account of travel:

"In the intervals of the acts of the opera I saw lively conversations carried on between the orchestra and the boxes. Arami, in particular, recognized a friend whom he had not seen for three years, and who related to him, by means of his eyes and his hands, what, to judge by the eager gestures of my companion, must have been matters of great interest. The conversation ended, I asked him if I might know without impropriety what was the intelligence which had seemed to interest him so deeply. 'O, yes,' he replied, 'that person is one of my good friends, who has been away from Palermo for three years, and he has been telling me that he was married at Naples; then traveled with his wife in

Austria and in France; there his wife gave birth to a daughter, whom he had the misfortune to lose; he arrived by steamboat yesterday, but his wife had suffered so much from sea-sickness that she kept her bed, and he came alone to the play.' 'My dear friend,' said I to Arami, 'if you would have me believe you, you must grant me a favor.' 'What is it?' said he. 'It is, that you do not leave me during the evening, so that I may be sure you give no instructions to your friend, and when we join him, that you ask him to repeat aloud what he said to you by signs.' 'That I will,' said Arami. The curtain then rose; the second act of Norma was played; the curtain falling, and the actors being re-called, as usual, we went to the side-room, where we met the traveler. 'My dear friend,' said Arami, 'I did not perfectly comprehend what you wanted to tell me; be so good as to repeat it.' The traveler repeated the story word for word, and without varying a syllable from the trans-lation which Arami had made of his signs; it was marvelous indeed.

"Six weeks after this, I saw a second example of this faculty of mute communication. This was at Naples. I was walking with a young man of Syracuse. We passed by a sentinel. The soldier and my com-panion exchanged two or three grimaces, which at another time I should not even have noticed, but the instances I had before seen led me to give attention. 'Poor fellow,' sighed my companion. 'What did he say to you?' I asked. 'Well,' said he, 'I thought that I recognized him as a Sicilian, and I learned from him, as we passed, from what place he came; he said he was from Syracuse, and that he knew me well. Then I asked him how he liked the Neapolitan service; he said he did not like it at all, and if his officers did not treat him better he should certainly finish by deserting. I then signified to him that if he ever should be reduced to that extremity, he might rely upon me, and that I would aid him all in my power. The poor fellow thanked me with all his heart, and I have no doubt that one day or other I shall see him come.' Three days after, I was at the quarters of my Syracusan friend, when he was told that a man asked to see him who would not give his name; he went out and left me nearly ten minutes. 'Well,' said he, on returning, 'just as I said.' 'What?' said I. 'That the poor fellow would desert.'"

After this there is an excuse for believing the tradition that the revolt called "the Sicilian Vespers," in 1282, was arranged throughout the island without the use of a syllable, and even the day and hour for the massacre of the obnoxious foreigners fixed upon by signs only. In-deed, the popular story goes so far as to assert that all this was done by facial expression, without even manual signs.

NEAPOLITAN SIGNS.

It is fortunately possible to produce some illustrations of the modern Neapolitan sign language traced from the plates of De Jorio, with trans-lations, somewhat condensed, of his descriptions and remarks.

In Fig. 76 an ambulant secretary or public writer is seated at his

FIG. 76.—Neapolitan public letter-writer and clients.

Fig. 78.—Neapolitan hot-corn vender.

little table, on which are the meager tools of his trade. He wears spectacles in token that he has read and written much, and has one seat at his side to accommodate his customers. On this is seated a married woman who asks him to write a letter to her absent husband. The secretary, not being told what to write about, without surprise, but somewhat amused, raises his left hand with the ends of the thumb and finger joined, the other fingers naturally open, a common sign for *inquiry.* "What shall the letter be about?" The wife, not being ready of speech, to rid herself of the embarrassment, resorts to the mimic art, and, without opening her mouth, tells with simple gestures all that is in her mind. Bringing her right hand to her heart, with a corresponding glance of the eyes she shows that the theme is to be *love.* For emphasis also she curves the whole upper part of her body towards him, to exhibit the intensity of her passion. To complete the mimic story, she makes with her left hand the sign of *asking* for something, which has been above described (see page 291). The letter, then, is to assure her husband of her love and to beg him to return it with corresponding affection. The other woman, perhaps her sister, who has understood the whole direction, regards the request as silly and fruitless and is much disgusted. Being on her feet, she takes a step toward the wife, who she thinks is unadvised, and raises her left hand with a sign of disapprobation. This position of the hand is described in full as open, raised high, and oscillated from right to left. Several of the Indian signs have the same idea of oscillation of the hand raised, often near the head, to express *folly, fool.* She clearly says, "What a thing to ask! what a fool you are!" and at the same time makes with the right hand the sign of *money.* This is made by the extremities of the thumb and index rapidly rubbed against each other,

FIG. 77.

and is shown more clearly in Fig. 77. It is taken from the handling and counting of coin. This may be compared with an Indian sign, see Fig. 115, page 344.

So the sister is clearly disapproving with her left hand and with her right giving good counsel, as if to say, in the combination, "What a fool you are to ask for his love; you had better ask him to send you some money."

In Naples, as in American cities, boiled ears of green corn are vended with much outcry. Fig. 78 shows a boy who is attracted by the local cry " *Pollanchelle tenerelle!* " and seeing the sweet golden ears still boiling in the kettle from which steams forth fragrance, has an ardent desire to taste the same, but is without a *soldo.* He tries begging. His right open hand is advanced toward the desired object with the sign of *asking* or *begging,* and he also raises his left forefinger to indicate the number *one*—" Pretty girl, please only give me one!" The pretty girl is by no means cajoled, and while her left hand holds the ladle ready to use if he dares to touch her merchandise, she replies by gesture " *Te voglio dà no cuorno !*" freely translated, " I'll give you one *in a horn !*" This gesture is drawn with clearer outline in Fig. 79, and has many significations,

FIG. 79.

according to the subject-matter and context, and also as applied to different parts of the body. Applied to the head it has allusion, descending from high antiquity, to a marital misfortune which was probably common in prehistoric times as well as the present. It is also often used as an amulet against the *jettatura* or evil eye, and misfortune in general, and directed toward another person is a prayerful wish for his or her preservation from evil. This use is ancient, as is shown on medals and statues, and is supposed by some to refer to the horns of animals slaughtered in sacrifice. The position

of the fingers, Fig. 80, is also given as one of Quintilian's oratorical gestures by the words "*Duo quoque medii sub pollicem veniunt,*" and is said by him to be vehement and connected with reproach or argument. In the present case, as a response to an impertinent

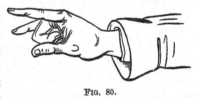

FIG. 80.

or disagreeable petition, it simply means, "instead of giving what you ask, I will give you nothing but what is vile and useless, as horns are."

Fig. 81 tells a story which is substantially the foundation of the slender plot of most modern scenic pantomimes preliminary to the bursting forth from their chrysalides of Harlequin, Columbine, Pantaloon, and company. A young girl, with the consent of her parents, has for some time promised her hand to an honest youth. The old mother, in despite of her word, has taken a caprice to give her daughter to another suitor. The father, though much under the sway of his spouse, is in his heart desirous to keep his engagement, and has called in the notary to draw the contract. At this moment the scene begins, the actors of which, for greater perspicuity and brevity, may be provided with stage names as follows:

Cecca, diminutive for Francisca, the mother of—
Nanella, diminutive of Antoniella, the betrothed of—
Peppino, diminutive of Peppe, which is diminutive of Guiseppe.
Pasquale, husband of Cecca and father of Nanella.
Tonno, diminutive of Antonio, favored by Cecca.
D. Alfonso, notary.

Cecca tries to pick a quarrel with Peppino, and declares that the contract shall not be signed. He reminds her of her promise, and accuses her of breach of faith. In her passion she calls on her daughter to repudiate her lover, and casting her arms around her, commands her to make the sign of breaking off friendship—"*scocchiare*"—which she has herself made to Peppino, and which consists in extending the hand

FIG. 81.—Disturbance at signing of Neapolitan marriage contract.

FIG. 83.—Coming home of Neapolitan bride.

with the joined ends of finger and thumb before described, see Fig. 66, and then separating them, thus breaking the union. This the latter reluctantly pretends to do with one hand, yet with the other, which is concealed from her irate mother's sight, shows her constancy by continuing with emphatic pressure the sign of *love*. According to the gesture vocabulary, on the sign *scocchiare* being made to a person who is willing to accept the breach of former affection, he replies in the same manner, or still more forcibly by inserting the index of the other hand between the index and thumb of the first, thus showing the separation by the presence of a material obstacle. Simply refraining from holding out the hand in any responsive gesture is sufficient to indicate that the breach is not accepted, but that the party addressed desires to continue in friendship instead of resolving into enmity. This weak and inactive negative, however, does not suit Peppino's vivacity, who, placing his left hand on his bosom, makes, with his right, one of the signs for emphatic negation. This consists of the palm turned to the person addressed with the index somewhat extended and separated from the other fingers, the whole hand being oscillated from right to left.  This gesture appears on ancient Greek vases, and is compound, the index being demonstrative and the negation shown by the horizontal oscillation, the whole being translatable as, " That thing I want not, won't have, reject." The sign is virtually the same as that made by Arapaho and Cheyenne Indians (see EXTRACTS FROM DICTIONARY, page 440, *infra.*). The conception of oscillation to show negation also appears with different execution in the sign of the Jicarilla Apaches and the Pai-Utes, Fig. 82. The same sign is reported from Japan, in the same sense.

FIG. 82.

Tonno, in hopes that the quarrel is definitive, to do his part in stopping the ceremony, proceeds to blow out the three lighted candles, which are an important traditional feature of the rite. The good old man Pasquale, with his hands extended, raised in surprised displeasure and directed toward the insolent youth, stops his attempt. The veteran notary, familiar with such quarrels in his experience, smiles at this one, and, continuing in his quiet attitude, extends his right hand placidly to Peppino with the sign of *adagio*, before described, see Fig. 68, advising him not to get excited, but to persist quietly, and all would be well.

Fig. 83 portrays the first entrance of a bride to her husband's house. She comes in with a tender and languid mien, her pendent arms indicating soft yielding, and the right hand loosely holds a handkerchief, ready to apply in case of overpowering emotion. She is, or feigns to be, so timid and embarrassed as to require support by the arm of a friend who introduces her. She is followed by a male friend of the family, whose joyful face is turned toward supposed by-standers, right hand pointing to the new acquisition, while with his left he makes the sign of horns before described, see Fig. 79, which in this connection is to wish prosperity and avert misfortune, and is equivalent to the words in the Neopolitan dialect, "*Mal'uocchie non nce pozzano*"—may evil eyes never have power over her.

The female confidant, who supports and guides her embarrassed friend with her right arm, brings her left hand into the sign of *beautiful*—"See what a beauty she is!" This sign is made by the thumb and index open and severally lightly touching each side of the lower cheek, the other fingers open. It is given on a larger scale and slightly varied in Fig. 84,

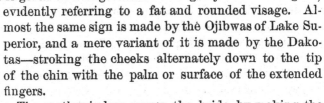

evidently referring to a fat and rounded visage. Almost the same sign is made by the Ojibwas of Lake Superior, and a mere variant of it is made by the Dakotas—stroking the cheeks alternately down to the tip of the chin with the palm or surface of the extended fingers.

The mother-in-law greets the bride by making the sign *mano in fica* with her right hand. This sign, made with the hand clenched and the point of the thumb between and projecting beyond the fore and middle fingers, is more distinctly shown in Fig. 85. It has a very

FIG. 84.

ancient origin, being found on Greek antiques that have escaped the destruction of time, more particularly in bronzes, and undoubtedly refers to the *pudendum muliebre*. It is used offensively and ironically, but

also—which is doubtless the case in this instance— as an invocation or prayer against evil, being more forcible than the horn-shaped gesture before described. With this sign the Indian sign for *female*, see Fig. 132, page 357, *infra*, may be compared.

FIG. 85.

The mother-in-law also places her left hand hollowed in front of her abdomen, drawing with it her gown slightly forward, thereby making a pantomimic representation of the state in which "women wish to be who love their lords"; the idea being plainly an expressed hope that the household will be blessed with a new generation.

Next to her is a hunchback, who is present as a familiar clown or

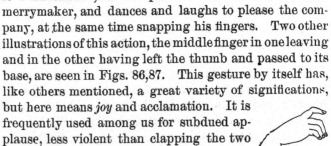

merrymaker, and dances and laughs to please the company, at the same time snapping his fingers. Two other illustrations of this action, the middle finger in one leaving and in the other having left the thumb and passed to its base, are seen in Figs. 86, 87. This gesture by itself has, like others mentioned, a great variety of significations, but here means *joy* and acclamation. It is frequently used among us for subdued applause, less violent than clapping the two hands, but still oftener to express negation with disdain, and also carelessness. Both

FIG. 86.   FIG. 87.

these uses of it are common in Naples, and appear in Etruscan vases and

FIG. 89.—Quarrel between Neapolitan women.

FIG. 90.—The cheating Neapolitan chestnut huckster.

Pompeian paintings, as well as in the classic authors. The significance of the action in the hand of the contemporary statue of Sardanapalus at Anchiale is clearly *worthlessness*, as shown by the inscription in Assyrian, "Sardanapalus, the son of Anacyndaraxes, built in one day Anchiale and Tarsus. Eat, drink, play; the rest is not worth *that!*"

The bridegroom has left his mother to do the honors to the bride, and himself attends to the rest of the company, inviting one of them to drink some wine by a sign, enlarged in Fig. 88, which is not merely pointing to the mouth with the thumb, but the hand with the incurved fingers represents the body of the common glass flask which the Neapolitans use, the extended thumb being its neck; the invitation is therefore specially to drink wine. The guest, however, responds by a very obvious gesture that he don't wish anything to drink, but he would like to eat some macaroni, the fingers being disposed as if handling that comestible in the fashion of vulgar Italians. If the idea were only to eat generally, it would have been expressed by the fingers and thumb united in a point and moved several times near and toward the mouth, not raised above it, as is necessary for suspending the strings of macaroni.

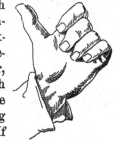

FIG. 88.

In Fig. 89 the female in the left of the group is much disgusted at seeing one of her former acquaintances, who has met with good fortune, promenade in a fine costume with her husband. Overcome with jealousy, she spreads out her dress derisively on both sides, in imitation of the hoop skirts once worn by women of rank, as if to say "So you are playing the great lady!" The insulted woman, in resentment, makes with both hands, for double effect, the sign of horns, before described, which in this case is done obviously in menace and imprecation. The husband is a pacific fellow who is not willing to get into a woman's quarrel, and is very easily held back by a woman and small boy who happen to join the group. He contents himself with pretending to be in a great passion and biting his finger, which gesture may be collated with the emotional clinching of the teeth and biting the lips in anger, common to all mankind.

In Fig. 90 a contadina, or woman from the country, who has come to the city to sell eggs (shown to be such by her head-dress and the form of the basket which she has deposited on the ground), accosts a vender of roast chestnuts and asks for a measure of them. The chestnut huckster says they are very fine and asks a price beyond that of the market; but a boy sees that the rustic woman is not sharp in worldly matters and desires to warn her against the cheat. He therefore, at the moment when he can catch her eye, pretending to lean upon his basket, and moving thus a little behind the huckster, so as not to be seen, points him out with his index finger, and lays his left forefinger under his eye, pulling down the skin slightly, so as to deform the regularity of the lower eyelid. This is a *warning against a cheat*, shown more clearly in Fig. 91. This sign primarily indicates a squinting person, and metaphorically one

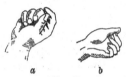

whose looks cannot be trusted, even as in a squinting person you cannot be certain in which direction he is looking.

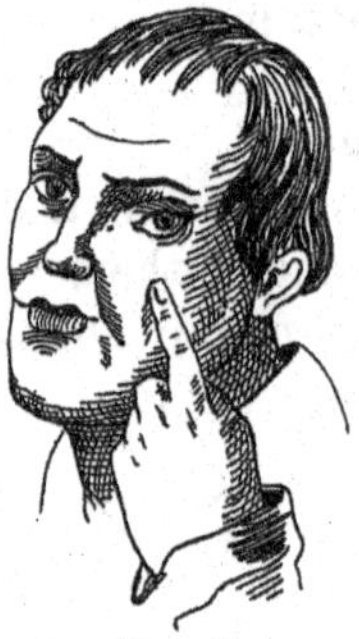

Fig. 92 shows the extremities of the index and thumb closely joined in form of a cone, and turned down, the other fingers held at pleasure, and the hand and arm advanced to the point and held steady. This signifies *justice*, a just person, that

which is just and right. The

FIG. 91.

FIG 92.

same sign may denote friendship, a menace, which specifically is that of being brought to justice, and snuff, *i. e.* powdered tobacco; but the expression of the countenance and the circumstance of

a   *b*

FIG. 93.

the use of the sign determine these distinctions. Its origin is clearly the balance or emblem of justice, the office of which consists in ascertaining physical weight, and thence comes the moral idea of distinguishing clearly what is just and accurate and what is not. The hand is presented in the usual manner of holding the balance to weigh articles.

Fig. 93 signifies *little, small*, both as regards the size of physical objects or figuratively, as of a small degree of talent, affection, or the like.

It is made either by the point of the thumb placed under the end of the index (*a*), or *vice versâ* (*b*), and the other fingers held at will,

FIG. 94.

FIG. 95.

but separated from those mentioned. The intention is to exhibit a small portion either of the thumb or index separated from the rest of the hand. The gesture is found in Herculanean bronzes, with obviously the same signification. The signs made by some tribes of Indians for the same conception are very similar, as is seen by Figs. 94 and 95.

Fig. 96 is simply the index extended by itself. The other fingers are generally bent inwards and pressed down by the thumb, as mentioned by Quintilian, but that is not necessary to the gesture if the forefinger is distinctly separated from the rest. It is most commonly used for indication, pointing out, as it is over all the world, from which comes the name index, applied by the Romans as also by us, to the forefinger. In different relations to the several parts of the body and arm positions it has many significations, *e. g.*,

FIG. 96.

attention, meditation, derision, silence, number, and demonstration in general.

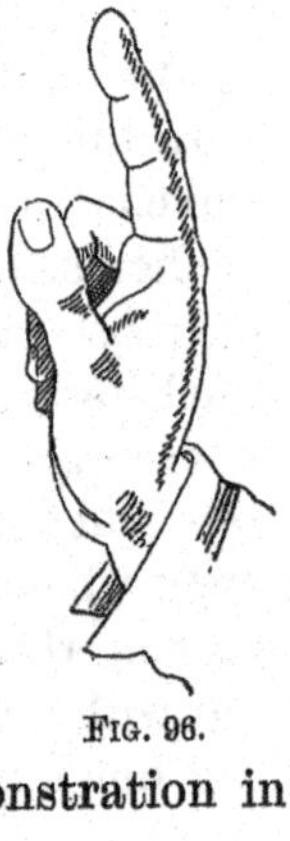

Fig. 97 represents the head of a jackass, the thumbs being the ears, and the separation of the little from the third fingers showing the jaws. Fig. 98 is intended to portray the head of the same animal in a front

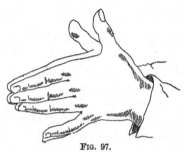

view, the hands being laid upon each other, with thumbs extending on each side to represent the ears. In each case the thumbs are generally moved forward and back, in

FIG. 97.

FIG. 98.

the manner of the quadruped, which, without much apparent reason, has been selected as the emblem of stupidity. The sign, therefore, means *stupid, fool*. Another mode of executing the same conception—the ears of an ass—is shown in Fig. 99, where the end of the thumb is applied to the ear or temple

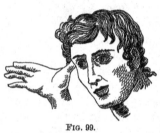

and the hand is wagged up and down. Whether the ancient Greeks had the same low opinion of the ass as is now entertained is not clear, but they regarded long ears with derision, and Apollo, as a punishment to Midas for his foolish decision, be-

FIG. 99.

FIG. 100.

stowed on him the lengthy ornaments of the patient beast.

Fig. 100 is the fingers elongated and united in a point, turned upwards. The hand is raised slightly toward the face of the gesturer and shaken a few times in the direction of the person conversed with. This is *inquiry*, not a mere interrogative, but to express that the person addressed has not been clearly understood, perhaps from the vagueness or diffusiveness of his expressions. The idea appears to suggest the gathering of his thoughts together into one distinct expression, or to be *pointed* in what he wishes to say.

Crafty, deceitful, Fig. 101. The little fingers of both reversed hands are hooked together, the others open but slightly curved,

FIG. 101.

and, with the hands, moved several times to the right and left. The gesture is intended to represent a crab and the tortuous movements of the crustacean, which are likened to those of a man who cannot be depended on in his walk through life. He is not straight.

Figs. 102 and 103 are different positions of the hand in which the approximating thumb and forefinger form a circle. This is the direst insult that can be given. The amiable canon De Jorio only hints at its special significance, but it may be evident to persons aware of a practice disgraceful to Italy. It is very ancient.

Fig. 104 is easily recognized as a request or command to be *silent*, either on the occasion or on the subject. The mouth, supposed to be forcibly closed, prevents speaking, and the natural gesture, as might be supposed, is historically ancient, but the instance, frequently adduced from the attitude of the god Harpokrates, whose finger is on his lips, is an error. The Egyptian hieroglyphists, notably in the designation of Horus, their dawn-god, used the finger in or on the lips for "child." It

FIG. 102.

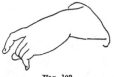

FIG. 103.

FIG. 104.

has been conjectured in the last instance that the gesture implied, not the mode of taking nourishment, but inability to speak—*in-fans*. This conjecture, however, was only made to explain the blunder of the Greeks, who saw in the hand placed connected with the mouth in the hieroglyph of Horus (the) son, "Hor–(p)–chrot," the gesture familiar to themselves of a finger on the lips to express "silence," and so, mistaking both the name and the characterization, invented the God of Silence, Harpokrates. A careful examination of all the linear hieroglyphs given by Champollion (*Dictionnaire Egyptien*) shows that the finger or the hand to the mouth of an adult (whose posture is always distinct from that of a child) is always in connection with the positive ideas of voice, mouth, speech, writing, eating, drinking, &c., and never with the negative idea of silence. The special character for *child*, Fig. 105, always has the above-mentioned part of the sign with reference to nourishment from the breast.

FIG. 106.

Fig. 106 is a forcible *negation*. The outer ends of the fingers united in a point under the chin are violently thrust forward. This is the rejection of an idea or proposition, the same conception being executed in several different modes by the North American Indians.

FIG. 105.

Fig. 107 signifies *hunger*, and is made by extending the thumb and index under the open mouth and turning them horizontally and vertically several times. The idea is emptiness and desire to be filled. It is also expressed by beating the ribs with the flat hands, to show that the sides meet or are weak for the want of something between them.

Fig. 108 is made in mocking and ridicule. The open and oscillating hand touches the point of the nose with that of the thumb. It has the particular sense of stigmatizing the person addressed or in question as a dupe. A credulous person is generally imagined with a gaping mouth

and staring eyes, and as thrusting forward his face, with pendant chin, so that the nose is well advanced and therefore most prominent in the profile. A dupe is therefore called *naso lungo* or long-nose, and with Italian writers *"restare con un palmo di naso"*—to be left with a palm's length of nose—means

FIG. 107.

FIG. 108.

to have met with loss, injury, or disappointment.

The thumb stroking the forehead from one side to the other, Fig. 109, is a natural sign of *fatigue*, and of the physical toil that produces fatigue. The wiping off of perspiration is obviously indicated. This gesture is often used ironically.

As a *dupe* was shown above, now the *duper* is signified, by Fig. 110. The gesture is to place the fingers between the cravat and the neck and rub the latter with the back of the hand. The idea is that the de-

FIG. 109.

FIG. 110.

ceit is put within the cravat, taken in and down, similar to our phrase to "swallow" a false and deceitful story, and a "cram" is also an English slang word for an incredible lie. The conception of the slang term is nearly related to that of the Neapolitan sign, viz., the artificial enlargement of the œsophagus of the person victimized or on whom imposition is attempted to be practiced, which is necessary to take it down.

Fig. 111 shows the ends of the index and thumb stroking the two sides of the nose from base to point. This means *astute, attentive, ready*. Sharpness of the nasal organ is popularly associated with subtlety and finesse. The old Romans by *homo emunctœ naris* meant an acute man attentive to his interests. The sign is often used in a bad sense, then signifying *too* sharp to be trusted.

This somewhat lengthy but yet only partial list of Neapolitan gesture-signs must conclude

FIG. 111.

with one common throughout Italy, and also among us with a somewhat different signification, yet perhaps also derived from classic times. To express suspicion of a person the forefinger of the right hand is placed upon the side of the nose. It means *tainted*, not sound. It is used to give an unfavorable report of a person inquired of and to warn against such.

The Chinese, though ready in gesticulation and divided by dialects, do not appear to make general use of a systematic sign language, but they adopt an expedient rendered possible by the peculiarity of their written characters, with which a large proportion of their adults are acquainted, and which are common in form to the whole empire. The inhabitants of different provinces when meeting, and being unable to converse orally, do not try to do so, but write the characters of the words upon the ground or trace them on the palm of the hand or in the air. Those written characters each represent words in the same manner as do the Arabic or Roman numerals, which are the same to Italians, Germans, French, and English, and therefore intelligible, but if expressed in sound or written in full by the alphabet, would not be mutually understood. This device of the Chinese was with less apparent necessity resorted to in the writer's personal knowledge between a Hungarian who could talk Latin, and a then recent graduate from college who could also do so to some extent, but their pronunciation was so different as to occasion constant difficulty, so they both wrote the words on paper, instead of attempting to speak them.

The efforts at intercommunication of all savage and barbarian tribes, when brought into contact with other bodies of men not speaking an oral language common to both, and especially when uncivilized inhabitants of the same territory are separated by many linguistic divisions, should in theory resemble the devices of the North American Indians. They are not shown by published works to prevail in the Eastern hemisphere to the same extent and in the same manner as in North America. It is, however, probable that they exist in many localities, though not reported, and also that some of them survive after partial or even high civilization has been attained, and after changed environment has rendered their systematic employment unnecessary. Such signs may be, first, unconnected with existing oral language, and used in place of it; second, used to explain or accentuate the words of ordinary speech, or third, they may consist of gestures, emotional or not, which are only noticed in oratory or impassioned conversation, being, possibly, survivals of a former gesture language.

From correspondence instituted it may be expected that a considerable collection of signs will be obtained from West and South Africa, India, Arabia, Turkey, the Fiji Islands, Sumatra, Madagascar, Ceylon, and especially from Australia, where the conditions are similar in many respects to those prevailing in North America prior to the Columbian discovery. In the *Aborigines of Victoria, Melbourne*, 1878, by R. Brough Smythe, the author makes the following curious remarks: "It is believed that they have several signs, known only to themselves, or to those among the whites who have had intercourse with them for lengthened periods, which convey information readily and accurately. Indeed, because of their use of signs, it is the firm belief of many (some uneducated and some educated) that the natives of Australia are acquainted with the secrets of Freemasonry."

In the *Report of the cruise of the United States Revenue steamer Corwin in the Arctic Ocean, Washington,* 1881, it appears that the Innuits of the northwestern extremity of America use signs continually. Captain Hooper, commanding that steamer, is reported by Mr. Petroff to have found that the natives of Nunivak Island, on the American side, below Behring Strait, trade by signs with those of the Asiatic coast, whose language is different. Humboldt in his journeyings among the Indians of the Orinoco, where many small isolated tribes spoke languages not understood by any other, found the language of signs in full operation. Spix and Martius give a similar account of the Puris and Coroados of Brazil.

It is not necessary to enlarge under the present heading upon the signs of deaf-mutes, except to show the intimate relation between sign language as practiced by them and the gesture signs, which, even if not "natural," are intelligible to the most widely separated of mankind. A Sandwich Islander, a Chinese, and the Africans from the slaver Amistad have, in published instances, visited our deaf-mute institutions with the same result of free and pleasurable intercourse; and an English deaf-mute had no difficulty in conversing with Laplanders. It appears, also, on the authority of Sibscota, whose treatise was published in 1670, that Cornelius Haga, ambassador of the United Provinces to the Sublime Porte, found the Sultan's mutes to have established a language among themselves in which they could discourse with a speaking interpreter, a degree of ingenuity interfering with the object of their selection as slaves unable to repeat conversation. A curious instance has also been reported to the writer of operatives in a large mill where the constant rattling of the machinery rendered them practically deaf during the hours of work and where an original system of gestures was adopted.

In connection with the late international convention, at Milan, of persons interested in the instruction of deaf-mutes which, in the enthusiasm of the members for the new system of artificial articulate speech, made war upon all gesture-signs, it is curious that such prohibition of gesture should be urged regarding mutes when it was prevalent to so great an extent among the speaking people of the country where the convention was held, and when the advocates of it were themselves so dependent on gestures to assist their own oratory if not their ordinary conversation. Artificial articulation surely needs the aid of significant gestures more, when in the highest perfection to which it can attain, than does oral speech in its own high development. The use of artificial speech is also necessarily confined to the oral language acquired by the interlocutors and throws away the advantage of universality possessed by signs.

USE BY MODERN ACTORS AND ORATORS.

Less of practical value can be learned of sign language, considered as a system, from the study of gestures of actors and orators than would appear without reflection. The pantomimist who uses no words whatever is obliged to avail himself of every natural or imagined connection between thought and gesture, and, depending wholly on the latter, makes himself intelligible. On the stage and the rostrum words are the main reliance, and gestures generally serve for rythmic movement and to display personal grace. At the most they give the appropriate representation of the general idea expressed by the words, but do not attempt to indicate the idea itself. An instance is recorded of the addition of significance to gesture when it is employed by the gesturer, himself silent, to accompany words used by another. Livius Andronicus, being hoarse, obtained permission to have his part sung by another actor while he continued to make the gestures, and he did so with much greater effect than before, as Livy, the historian, explains, because he was not impeded by the exertion of the voice; but the correct explanation probably is, because his attention was directed to ideas, not mere words.

GESTURES OF ACTORS.

To look at the performance of a play through thick glass or with closed ears has much the same absurd effect that is produced by also stopping the ears while at a ball and watching the apparently objectless capering of the dancers, without the aid of musical accompaniment. Diderot, in his *Lettre sur les sourds muets*, gives his experience as follows:

"I used frequently to attend the theater and I knew by heart most of our good plays. Whenever I wished to criticise the movements and gestures of the actors I went to the third tier of boxes, for the further I was from them the better I was situated for this purpose. As soon as the curtain rose, and the moment came when the other spectators disposed themselves to listen, I put my fingers into my ears, not without causing some surprise among those who surrounded me, who, not understanding, almost regarded me as a crazy man who had come to the play only not to hear it. I was very little embarrassed by their comments, however, and obstinately kept my ears closed as long as the action and gestures of the players seemed to me to accord with the discourse which I recollected. I listened only when I failed to see the appropriateness of the gestures. * * * There are few actors capable of sustaining such a test, and the details into which I could enter would be mortifying to most of them."

It will be noticed that Diderot made this test with regard to the appropriate gestural representation of plays that he knew by heart, but if he had been entirely without any knowledge of the plot, the difficulty in his comprehending it from gestures alone would have been enormously increased. When many admirers of Ristori, who were wholly unac-

quainted with the language in which her words were delivered, declared
that her gesture and expression were so perfect that they understood
every sentence, it is to be doubted if they would have been so delighted
if they had not been thoroughly familiar with the plots of Queen Eliz-
abeth and Mary Stuart. This view is confirmed by the case of a deaf-
mute, told to the writer by Professor FAY, who had prepared to enjoy
Ristori's acting by reading in advance the advertised play, but on his
reaching the theater another play was substituted and he could derive no
idea from its presentation. The experience of the present writer is that
he could gain very little meaning in detail out of the performance at a
Chinese theater, where there is much more true pantomime than in the
European, without a general notion of the subject as conveyed from
time to time by an interpreter. A crucial test on this subject was made
at the representation at Washington, in April, 1881, of *Frou-Frou* by
Sarah Bernhardt and the excellent French company supporting her.
Several persons of special intelligence and familiar with theatrical performances, but who did not understand spoken French, and had not heard
or read the play before or even seen an abstract of it, paid close attention to ascertain what they could learn of the plot and incidents from
the gestures alone. This could be determined in the special play the
more certainly as it is not founded on historic events or any known
facts. The result was that from the entrance of the heroine during the
first scene in a peacock-blue riding habit to her death in a black walking-
suit, three hours or five acts later, none of the students formed any distinct conception of the plot. This want of apprehension extended even
to uncertainty whether *Gilberte* was married or not; that is, whether her
adventures were those of a disobedient daughter or a faithless wife,
and, if married, which of the half dozen male personages was her husband. There were gestures enough, indeed rather a profusion of them,
and they were thoroughly appropriate to the words (when those were
understood) in which fun, distress, rage, and other emotions were
expressed, but in no cases did they interpret the motive for those emotions. They were the dressing for the words of the actors as the superb
millinery was that of their persons, and perhaps acted as varnish to
bring out dialogues and soliloquies in heightened effect. But though
varnish can bring into plainer view dull or faded characters, it cannot
introduce into them significance where none before existed. The simple
fact was that the gestures of the most famed histrionic school, the
Comédie Française, were not significant, far less self-interpreting, and
though praised as the perfection of art, have diverged widely from
nature. It thus appears that the absence of absolute self-interpretation
by gesture is by no means confined to the lower grade of actors, such as
are criticised in the old lines:

> When to enforce some very tender part
> His left hand sleeps by instinct on the heart;
> His soul, of every other thought bereft,
> Seems anxious only—where to place the left!

Without relying wholly upon the facts above mentioned, it will be admitted upon reflection that however numerous and correct may be the actually significant gestures made by a great actor in the representation of his part, they must be in small proportion to the number of gestures not at all significant, and which are no less necessary to give to his declamation precision, grace, and force. Significant gestures on the stage may be regarded in the nature of high seasoning and ornamentation, which by undue use defeat their object and create disgust. Histrionic perfection is, indeed, more shown in the slight shades of movement of the head, glances of the eye, and poises of the body than in violent attitudes; but these slight movements are wholly unintelligible without the words uttered with them. Even in the expression of strong emotion the same gesture will apply to many and utterly diverse conditions of fact. The greatest actor in telling that his father was dead can convey his grief with a shade of difference from that which he would use if saying that his wife had run away, his son been arrested for murder, or his house burned down; but that shade would not without words inform any person, ignorant of the supposed event, which of the four misfortunes had occurred. A true sign language, however, would fully express the exact circumstances, either with or without any exhibition of the general emotion appropriate to them.

Even among the best sign-talkers, whether Indian or deaf-mute, it is necessary to establish some *rapport* relating to theme or subject-matter, since many gestures, as indeed is the case in a less degree with spoken words, have widely different significations, according to the object of their exhibition, as well as the context. Panurge (*Pantagruel*, Book III, ch. xix) hits the truth upon this point, however ungallant in his application of it to the fair sex. He is desirous to consult a dumb man, but says it would be useless to apply to a woman, for " whatever it be that they see they do always represent unto their fancies, and imagine that it hath some relation to love. Whatever signs, shows, or gestures we shall make, or whatever our behavior, carriage, or demeanor shall happen to be in their view and presence, they will interpret the whole in reference to androgynation." A story is told to the same point by Guevara, in his fabulous life of the Emperor Marcus Aurelius. A young Roman gentleman encountering at the foot of Mount Celion a beautiful Latin lady, who from her very cradle had been deaf and dumb, asked her in gesture what senators in her descent from the top of the hill she had met with, going up thither. She straightway imagined that he had fallen in love with her and was eloquently proposing marriage, whereupon she at once threw herself into his arms in acceptance. The experience of travelers on the Plains is to the same general effect, that signs commonly used to men are understood by women in a sense so different as to occasion embarrassment. So necessary was it to strike the mental key-note of the spectators by adapting their minds to time, place, and circumstance, that even in the palmiest days of pantomime it was customary for the crier to give some short preliminary explanation of what was to be acted, which advantage is now retained by our play-bills, always more specific when the performance is in a foreign language, unless, indeed, the management is interested in the sale of librettos.

GESTURES OF OUR PUBLIC SPEAKERS.

If the scenic gestures are so seldom significant, those appropriate to oratory are of course still less so. They require energy, variety, and precision, but also a degree of simplicity which is incompatible with the needs of sign language. As regards imitation, they are restrained within narrow bounds and are equally suited to a great variety of sentiments. Among the admirable illustrations in Austin's *Chironomia* of gestures applicable to the several passages in Gay's "Miser and Plutus" one is given for "But virtue's sold" which is perfectly appropriate, but is not in the slightest degree suggestive either of virtue or of the transaction of sale. It could be used for an indefinite number of thoughts or objects which properly excited abhorrence, and therefore without the words gives no special interpretation. Oratorical delivery demands general grace—cannot rely upon the emotions of the moment for spontaneous appropriateness, and therefore requires preliminary study and practice, such as are applied to dancing and fencing with a similar object; indeed, accomplishment in both dancing and fencing has been recommended as of use to all orators. In reference to this subject a quotation from Lord Chesterfield's letters is in place: "I knew a young man, who, being just elected a member of Parliament, was laughed at for being discovered, through the key-hole of his chamber door, speaking to himself in the glass and forming his looks and gestures. I could not join in that laugh, but, on the contrary, thought him much wiser than those that laughed at him, for he knew the importance of those little graces in a public assembly and they did not."

OUR INDIAN CONDITIONS FAVORABLE TO SIGN LANGUAGE.

In no other thoroughly explored part of the world has there been found spread over so large a space so small a number of individuals divided by so many linguistic and dialectic boundaries as in North America. Many wholly distinct tongues have for an indefinitely long time been confined to a few scores of speakers, verbally incomprehensible to all others on the face of the earth who did not, from some rarely operating motive, laboriously acquire their language. Even when the American race, so styled, flourished in the greatest population of which we have any evidence (at least according to the published views of the present writer, which seem to have been generally accepted), the immense number of languages and dialects still preserved, or known by early recorded fragments to have once existed, so subdivided it that only the dwellers in a very few villages could talk together with ease. They were all interdistributed among unresponsive vernaculars, each to the other being *bar-bar-ous* in every meaning of the term. The number of known stocks or families of Indian languages within the territory of the United States amounts now to sixty-five, and these differ among themselves as radically as each differs from the Hebrew, Chinese, or English. In each of these linguistic families there are several, sometimes as many as twenty, separate languages, which also differ from each other as much as do the English, French, German, and Persian divisions of the Aryan linguistic stock.

The use of gesture-signs, continued, if not originating, in necessity for communication with the outer world, became entribally convenient from the habits of hunters, the main occupation of all savages, depending largely upon stealthy approach to game, and from the sole form of their military tactics—to surprise an enemy. In the still expanse of virgin forests, and especially in the boundless solitudes of the great plains, a slight sound can be heard over a large area, that of the human voice being from its rarity the most startling, so that it is now, as it probably has been for centuries, a common precaution for members of a hunting or war party not to speak together when on such expeditions, communicating exclusively by signs. The acquired habit also exhibits itself not only in formal oratory and in impassioned or emphatic conversation, but also as a picturesque accompaniment to ordinary social talk. Hon. LEWIS H. MORGAN mentions in a letter to this writer that he found a silent but happy family composed of an Atsina (commonly called Gros Ventre of the Prairie) woman, who had been married two years to a Frenchman, during which time they had neither of them attempted to learn each other's language; but the husband having taken kindly to the language of signs, they conversed together by that means with great contentment. It is also often resorted to in mere laziness, one gesture saving many words. The gracefulness, ingenuity, and apparent spontaneity of the greater part of the signs can never be realized until actually witnessed, and their beauty is much heightened by the free play to which the arms of these people are accustomed, and the small and well-shaped hands for which they are remarkable. Among them can seldom be noticed in literal fact—

> The graceless action of a heavy hand—

which the Bastard metaphorically condemns in King John.

The conditions upon which the survival of sign language among the Indians has depended is well shown by those attending its discontinuance among certain tribes.

Many instances are known of the discontinuance of gesture speech with no development in the native language of the gesturers, but from the invention for intercommunication of one used in common. The

Kalapuyas of Southern Oregon until recently used a sign language, but have gradually adopted for foreign intercourse the composite tongue, commonly called the Tsinuk or Chinook jargon, which probably arose for trade purposes on the Columbia River before the advent of Europeans, founded on the Tsinuk, Tsihali, Nutka, &c., but now enriched by English and French terms, and have nearly forgotten their old signs. The prevalence of this mongrel-speech, originating in the same causes that produced the pigeon-English or *lingua-franca* of the Orient, explains the marked scantiness of sign language among the tribes of the Northwest coast.

Where the Chinook jargon has not extended on the coast to the North, the Russian language commences, used in the same manner, but it has not reached so deeply into the interior of the continent as the Chinook, which has been largely adopted within the region bounded by the eastern line of Oregon and Washington, and has become known even to the Pai-Utes of Nevada. The latter, however, while using it with the Oregonian tribes to their west and north, still keep up sign language for communication with the Banaks, who have not become so familiar with the Chinook. The Alaskan tribes on the coast also used signs not more than a generation ago, as is proved by the fact that some of the older men can yet converse by this means with the natives of the interior, whom they occasionally meet. Before the advent of the Russians the coast tribes traded their dried fish and oil for the skins and paints of the eastern tribes by visiting the latter, whom they did not allow to come to the coast, and this trade was conducted mainly in sign language. The Russians brought a better market, so the travel to the interior ceased, and with it the necessity for the signs, which therefore gradually died out, and are little known to the present generation on the coast, though still continuing in the interior, where the inhabitants are divided by dialects.

No explanation is needed for the disuse of a language of signs for the special purpose now in question when the speech of surrounding civilization is recognized as necessary or important to be acquired, and gradually becomes known as the best common medium, even before it is actually spoken by many individuals of the several tribes. When it has become general, signs, as systematically employed before, gradually fade away.

THEORIES ENTERTAINED RESPECTING INDIAN SIGNS.

In this paper it is not designed to pronounce upon theories, and certainly none will be advocated in a spirit of dogmatism. The writer recognizes that the subject in its novelty specially requires an objective and not a subjective consideration. His duty is to collect the facts as they are, and this as soon as possible, since every year will add to the confusion and difficulty. After the facts are established the theories will take care of themselves, and their final enunciation will be in the hands of men more competent than the writer will ever pretend to be, although his knowledge, after careful study of all data attainable, may be considerably increased. The mere collection of facts, however, cannot be prosecuted to advantage without predetermined rules of judgment, nor can they be classified at all without the adoption of some principle which involves a tentative theory. More than a generation ago Baader noticed that scientific observers only accumulated great masses of separate facts without establishing more connection between them than an arbitrary and imperfect classification; and before him Goethe complained of the indisposition of students of nature to look upon the universe as a whole. But since the great theory of evolution has been brought to general notice no one will be satisfied at knowing a fact without also trying to establish its relation to other facts. Therefore a working hypothesis, which shall not be held to with tenacity, is not only allowable but necessary. It is also important to examine with proper respect the theories advanced by others. Some of these, suggested in the few publications on the subject and also by correspondents, will be mentioned.

NOT CORRELATED WITH MEAGERNESS OF LANGUAGE.

The story has been told by travelers in many parts of the world that various languages cannot be clearly understood in the dark by their possessors, using their mother tongue between themselves. The evidence for this anywhere is suspicious; and when it is asserted, as it often has been, in reference to some of the tribes of North American Indians, it is absolutely false, and must be attributed to the error of travelers who, ignorant of the dialect, never see the natives except when trying to make themselves intelligible to their visitors by a practice which they have found by experience to have been successful with strangers to their tongue, or perhaps when they are guarding against being overheard by others. Captain Burton, in his *City of the Saints*, specially states that the Arapahos possess a very scanty vocabulary, pronounced in a quasi-unintelligible way, and can hardly converse with one another in the dark. The truth is that their vocabulary is by no means scanty, and they do converse with each other with perfect freedom without any gestures when they so please. The difficulty in speaking or understanding their language is in the large number of guttural and interrupted sounds which are not helped by external motions of the mouth and lips in articulation, and the light gives little advantage to its comprehension so far as concerns the vocal apparatus, which, in many languages, can be seen as well as heard, as is proved by the modern deaf-mute practice of artificial speech. The corresponding story that no white man ever learned Arapaho is also false. A member of Frémont's party so long ago as 1842 spoke the language. Burton in the same connection gives a story "of a man who, being sent among the Cheyennes to qualify himself for interpreting, returned in a week and proved his competency; all he did, however, was to go through the usual pantomime with a running accompaniment of grunts." And he might as well have omitted the grunts, for he obviously only used sign language. Lieutenant Abert, in 1846–'47, made much more sensible remarks from his actual observation than Captain Burton repeated at second-hand from a Mormon met by him at Salt Lake. He said: "Some persons think that it [the Cheyenne language] would be incomplete without gesture, because the Indians use gestures constantly. But I have been assured that the language is in itself capable of bodying forth any idea to which one may wish to give utterance."

In fact, individuals of those American tribes specially instanced in these reports as unable to converse without gesture, often, in their domestic *abandon*, wrap themselves up in robes or blankets with only breathing holes before the nose, so that no part of the body is seen, and chatter away for hours, telling long stories. If in daylight they thus voluntarily deprive themselves of the possibility of making signs, it is clear that their preference for talks around the fire at night is explicable by very natural reasons wholly distinct from the one attributed. The inference, once carelessly made from the free use of gesture by some of the Shoshonian stock, that their tongue was too meager for use without signs, is refuted by the now ascertained fact that their vocabulary is remarkably copious and their parts of speech better differentiated than those of many people on whom no such stigma has been affixed. The proof of this was seen in the writer's experience, when Ouray, the head chief of the Utes, was at Washington, in the early part of 1880, and after an interview with the Secretary of the Interior made report of it to the rest of the delegation who had not been present. He spoke without pause in his own language for nearly an hour, in a monotone and without a single gesture. The reason for this depressed manner was undoubtedly because he was very sad at the result, involving loss of land and change of home; but the fact remains that full information was communicated on a complicated subject without the aid of a manual sign, and also without even such change of inflection of voice as is common among Europeans. All theories based upon the supposed poverty of American languages must be abandoned.

The grievous accusation against foreign people that they have no intelligible language is venerable and general. With the Greeks the term ἄγλωσσος, "tongueless," was used synonymous with βάρβαρος, "barbarian" of all who were not Greek. The name "Slav," assumed by a grand division of the Aryan family, means "the speaker," and is contradistinguished from the other peoples of the world, such as the Germans, who are called in Russian "Njemez," that is, "speechless." In Isaiah (xxxiii, 19) the Assyrians are called a people "of a stammering tongue, that one cannot understand." The common use of the expression "tongueless" and "speechless," so applied, has probably given rise, as TYLOR suggests, to the mythical stories of actually speechless tribes of savages, and the considerations and instances above presented tend to discredit the many other accounts of languages which are incomplete without the help of gesture.   The theory that sign language was in whole or in chief the original utterance of mankind would be strongly supported by conclusive evidence to the truth of such travelers' tales, but does not depend upon them.   Nor, considering the immeasurable period during which, in accordance with modern geologic views, man has been on the earth, is it probable that any existing races can be found in which speech has not obviated the absolute necessity for gesture in communication among themselves.   The signs survive for convenience, used together with oral language, and for special employment when language is unavailable.

A comparison sometimes drawn between sign language and that of our Indians, founded on the statement of their common poverty in abstract expressions, is not just to either.   This paper will be written in vain if it shall not suggest the capacities of gesture speech in that regard, and a deeper study into Indian tongues has shown that they are by no means so confined to the concrete as was once believed.

ITS ORIGIN FROM ONE TRIBE OR REGION.

Col. Richard I. Dodge, United States Army, whose long experience among the Indians entitles his opinion to great respect, says in a letter:

"The embodiment of signs into a systematic language is, I believe, confined to the Indians of the Plains.   Contiguous tribes gain, here and there, a greater or less knowledge of this language; these again extend the knowledge, diminished and probably perverted, to their neighbors, until almost all the Indian tribes of the United States east of the Sierras have some little smattering of it.   The Plains Indians believe the Kiowas to have invented the sign language, and that by them its use was communicated to other Plains tribes.   If this is correct, analogy would lead us to believe that those tribes most nearly in contact with the Kiowas would use it most fluently and correctly, the knowledge becoming less as the contact diminishes.   Thus the Utes, though nearly contiguous (in territory) to the Plains Indians, have only the merest 'picked up' knowledge of this language, and never use it among themselves, simply because, they and the Plains tribes having been, since the memory of their oldest men, in a chronic state of war, there has been no social contact."

In another communication Colonel Dodge is still more definite:

"The Plains Indians themselves believe the sign language was invented by the Kiowas, who holding an intermediate position between the Comanches, Tonkaways, Lipans, and other inhabitants of the vast plains of Texas, and the Pawnees, Sioux, Blackfeet, and other northern tribes, were the general go-betweens, trading with all, making peace or war with or for any or all. It is certain that the Kiowas are at present more universally proficient in this language than any other Plains tribe. It is also certain that the tribes furthest away from them and with whom they have least intercourse use it with least facility."

Dr. William H. Corbusier, assistant surgeon United States Army, a valued contributor, gives information as follows:

"The traditions of the Indians point toward the south as the direction from which the sign language came. They refer to the time when they did not use it; and each tribe say they learned it from those south of them. The Comanches, who acquired it in Mexico, taught it to the Arapahoes and Kiowas, and from these the Cheyennes learned it. The Sioux say that they had no knowledge of it before they crossed the Missouri River and came in contact with the Cheyennes, but have quite recently learned it from them. It would thus appear that the Plains Indians did not invent it, but finding it adapted to their wants adopted it as a convenient means of communicating with those whose language they did not understand, and it rapidly spread from tribe to tribe over the Plains. As the sign language came from Mexico, the Spaniards suggest themselves as the introducers of it on this continent. They are adepts in the use of signs. Cortez as he marched through Mexico would naturally have resorted to signs in communicating with the numerous tribes with which he came in contract. Finding them very necessary, one sign after another would suggest itself and be adopted by Spaniards and Indians, and, as the former advanced, one tribe after another would learn to use them. The Indians on the Plains, finding them so useful, preserved them and each tribe modified them to suit their convenience, but the signs remained essentially the same. The Shoshones took the sign language with them as they moved northwest, and a few of the Piutes may have learned it from them, but the Piutes as a tribe do not use it."

Mr. Ben. Clarke, the respected and skillful interpreter at Fort Reno writes to the same general effect:

"The Cheyennes think that the sign language used by the Cheyennes, Arapahoes, Ogallala and Brulé Sioux, Kiowas, and Comanches originated with the Kiowas. It is a tradition that, many years ago, when the Northern Indians were still without horses, the Kiowas often raided among the Mexican Indians and captured droves of horses on these trips. The Northern Plains Indians used to journey to them and trade for horses. The Kiowas were already proficient in signs, and the others learned from them. It was the journeying to the South that finally divided the Cheyennes, making the Northern and Southern Cheyennes. The same may be said of the Arapahoes. That the Kiowas were the first sign talkers is only a tradition, but as a tribe they are now considered to be the best or most thorough of the Plains Indians."

Without engaging in any controversy on this subject it may be noticed that the theory advanced supposes a comparatively recent origin of sign language from one tribe and one region, whereas, so far as can be traced, the conditions favorable to a sign language existed very long ago and were co-extensive with the territory of North America occupied by any of the tribes. To avoid repetition reference is made to the discussion below under the heads of universality, antiquity, identity, and permanence. At this point it is only desired to call attention to the ancient prevalence of signs among tribes such as the Iroquois, Wyandot, Ojibwa, and at least three generations back among the Crees beyond our northern boundary and the Mandans and other far-northern Dakotas, not likely at that time to have had communication, even through intertribal channels, with the Kaiowas. It is also difficult to understand how their signs would have in that manner reached the Kutchin of Eastern Alaska and the Kutine and Selish of British Columbia, who use signs now. At the same time due consideration must be given to the great change in the intercommunication of tribes, produced by the importation of the horse, by which the habits of those Indians now, but not very anciently, inhabiting the Plains were entirely changed. It is probable that a sign language before existing became, contemporaneously with nomadic life, cultivated and enriched.

As regards the Spanish origin suggested, there is ample evidence that the Spaniards met signs in their early explorations north of and in the northern parts of Mexico, and availed themselves of them but did not introduce them. It is believed also that the elaborate picture writing of Mexico was founded on gesture signs.

With reference to the statement that the Kaiowas are the most expert sign talkers of the Plains, a number of authorities and correspondents give the precedence to the Cheyennes, and an equal number to the Arapahos. Probably the accident of meeting specially skillful talkers in the several tribes visited influences such opinions.

The writer's experience, both of the Utes and Pai-Utes, is different from the above statement respecting the absence of signs among them. They not only use their own signs but fully understand the difference between the signs regarded as their own and those of the Kaiowas. On special examination they understood some of the latter only as words of a foreign language interpolated in an oral conversation would be comprehended from the context, and others they would recognize as having seen before among other tribes without adoption. The same is true regarding the Brulé Sioux, as was clearly expressed by Medicine Bull, their chief. The Pimas, Papagos, and Maricopas examined had a copious sign language, yet were not familiar with many Kaiowa signs presented to them.

Instead of referring to a time past when they did not use signs, the Indians examined by the writer and by most of his correspondents speak of a time when they and their fathers used it more freely and copiously than at present, its disuse being from causes before mentioned. It, however, may be true in some cases that a tribe, having been for a long time in contact only with others the dialect of which was so nearly akin as to be comprehensible, or from any reason being separated from those of a strange speech, discontinued sign language for a time, and then upon migration or forced removal came into circumstances where it was useful, and revived it. It is asserted that some of the Muskoki and the Ponkas now in the Indian Territory never saw sign language until they arrived there. Yet there is some evidence that the Muskoki did use signs a century ago, and some of the Ponkas still remaining on their old homes on the Missouri remember it and have given their knowledge to an accurate correspondent, Rev. J. O. Dorsey, though for many years they have not been in circumstances to require its employment.

Perhaps the most salutary criticism to be offered regarding the theory would be in the form of a query whether sign language has ever been invented by any one body of people at any one time, and whether it is not simply a phase in evolution, surviving and reviving when needed. Criticism on this subject is made reluctantly, as it would be highly interesting to determine that sign language on this continent came from a particular stock, and to ascertain that stock. Such research would be similar to that into the Aryan and Semitic sources to which many modern languages have been traced backwards from existing varieties, and if there appear to be existing varieties in signs their roots may still be found to be *sui generis*. The possibility that the discrepancy between signs was formerly greater than at present will receive attention in discussing the distinction between the identity of signs and their common use as an art. It is sufficient to add now that not only does the burden of proof rest unfavorably upon the attempt to establish one parent stock for sign language in North America, but it also comes under the stigma now fastened upon the immemorial effort to name and locate the original oral speech of man. It is only next in difficulty to the old persistent determination to decide upon the origin of the whole Indian "race," in which most peoples of antiquity in the eastern hemisphere, including the lost tribes of Israel, the Gipsies, and the Welsh, have figured conspicuously as putative parents.

IS THE INDIAN SYSTEM SPECIAL AND PECULIAR?

This inquiry is closely connected with the last. If the system of signs was invented here in the correct sense of that term, and by a known and existing tribe, it is probable that it would not be found prevailing in any important degree where the influence of the inventors could not readily have penetrated. An affirmative answer to the question also presupposes the same answer to another question, viz, whether there is any one uniform system among the North American Indians which can therefore be compared with any other system. This last inquiry will be considered in its order. In comparing the system as a whole with others, the latter are naturally divided into signs of speaking men foreign to America and those of deaf-mutes.

COMPARISONS WITH FOREIGN SIGNS.

The generalization of TYLOR that "gesture language is substantially the same among savage tribes all over the world," interpreted by his remarks in another connection, is understood as referring to their common use of signs, and of signs formed on the same principles, but not of precisely the same signs to express the same ideas. In this sense of the generalization the result of the writer's study not only sustains it, but shows a surprising number of signs for the same idea which are substantially identical, not only among savage tribes, but among all peoples that use gesture signs with any freedom. Men, in groping for a mode of communication with each other, and using the same general methods, have been under many varying conditions and circumstances which have determined differently many conceptions and their semiotic execution, but there have also been many of both which were similar. Our Indians have no special superstition concerning the evil-eye like the Italians, nor have they been long familiar with the jackass so as to make him emblematical of stupidity; therefore signs for these concepts are not cisatlantic, but even in this paper many are shown which are substantially in common between our Indians and Italians. The large collection already obtained, but not now published, shows many others identical, not only with those of the Italians and the classic Greeks and Romans, but of other peoples of the Old World, both savage and civilized. The generic uniformity is obvious, while the occasion of specific varieties can be readily understood.

COMPARISON WITH DEAF-MUTE SIGNS.

The Indians who have been shown over the civilized East have often succeeded in holding intercourse, by means of their invention and application of principles in what may be called the voiceless mother utterance, with white deaf-mutes, who surely have no semiotic code more nearly connected with that attributed to the plain-roamers than is derived from their common humanity. They showed the greatest pleasure in meeting deaf-mutes, precisely as travelers in a foreign country are rejoiced to meet persons speaking their language, with whom they can hold direct communication without the tiresome and often suspected medium of an interpreter. When they met together they were found to pursue the same course as that noticed at the meeting of deaf-mutes who were either not instructed in any methodical dialect or who had received such instruction by different methods. They often disagreed in the signs at first presented, but soon understood them, and finished by adopting some in mutual compromise, which proved to be those most strikingly appropriate, graceful, and convenient; but there still remained in some cases a plurality of fitting signs for the same idea or object. On one of the most interesting of these occasions, at the Pennsylvania Institution for the Deaf and Dumb, in 1873, it was remarked that the signs of the deaf-mutes were much more readily understood by the Indians, who were Absaroka or Crows, Arapahos, and Cheyennes, than were theirs by the deaf-mutes, and that the latter greatly excelled in pantomimic effect. This need not be surprising when it is considered that what is to the Indian a mere adjunct or accomplishment is to the deaf-mute the natural mode of utterance, and that there is still greater freedom from the trammel of translating words into action—instead of acting the ideas themselves—when, the sound of words being unknown, they remain still as they originated, but another kind of sign, even after the art of reading is acquired, and do not become entities as with us. The " action, action, action," of Demosthenes is their only oratory, not the mere heightening of it, however valuable.

On March 6, 1880, the writer had an interesting experience in taking to the National Deaf-Mute College at Washington seven Utes (which tribe, according to report, is unacquainted with sign language), among whom were Augustin, Alejandro, Jakonik, Severio, and Wash. By the kind attention of President GALLAUDET a thorough test was given, an equal number of deaf-mute pupils being placed in communication with the Indians, alternating with them both in making individual signs and in telling narratives in gesture, which were afterwards interpreted in speech by the Ute interpreter and the officers of the college. Notes of a few of them were taken, as follows:

Among the signs was that for *squirrel*, given by a deaf-mute. The right hand was placed over and facing the left, and about four inches above the latter, to show the height of the animal; then the two hands were held edgewise and horizontally in front, about eight inches apart (showing *length*); then imitating the grasping of a small object and biting it rapidly with the incisors, the extended index was pointed upward and forward (*in a tree*).

This was not understood, as the Utes have no sign for the tree squirrel, the arboreal animal not being now found in their region.

Deaf-mute sign for *jack-rabbit*: The first two fingers of each hand extended (the remaining fingers and thumbs closed) were placed on either side of the head, pointing upward; then arching the hands, palm down, quick, interrupted, jumping movements forward were made.

This was readily understood.

The signs for the following narrative were given by a deaf-mute: When he was a boy he mounted a horse without either bridle or saddle, and as the horse began to go he grasped him by the neck for support; a dog flew at the horse, began to bark, when the rider was thrown off and considerably hurt.

In this the sign for *dog* was as follows: Pass the arched hand forward from the lower part of the face, to illustrate elongated nose and mouth, then with both forefingers extended, remaining fingers and thumbs closed, place them upon either side of the lower jaw, pointing upward, to show lower canines, at the same time accompanying the gesture with an expression of withdrawing the lips so as to show the teeth snarling;

then, with the fingers of the right hand extended and separated throw them quickly forward and slightly upward (*voice* or *talking*).

This sign was understood to mean *bear*, as that for *dog* is different among the Utes, *i. e.*, by merely showing the height of the dog and pushing the flat hand forward, finger-tips first.

Another deaf-mute gestured to tell that when he was a boy he went to a melon-field, tapped several melons, finding them to be green or unripe; finally reaching a good one he took his knife, cut a slice, and ate it. A man made his appearance on horseback, entered the patch on foot, found the cut melon, and detecting the thief, threw the melon towards him, hitting him in the back, whereupon he ran away crying. The man mounted and rode off in an opposite direction.

All of these signs were readily comprehended, although some of the Indians varied very slightly in their translation.

When the Indians were asked whether, if they (the deaf-mutes) were to come to the Ute country they would be scalped, the answer was given, " Nothing would be done to you; but we would be friends," as follows:

The palm of the right hand was brushed toward the right over that of the left (*nothing*), and the right hand made to grasp the palm of the left, thumbs extended over and lying upon the back of the opposing hand.

This was readily understood by the deaf-mutes.

Deaf-mute sign of milking a cow and drinking the milk was fully and quickly understood.

The narrative of a boy going to an apple-tree, hunting for ripe fruit and filling his pockets, being surprised by the owner and hit upon the head with a stone, was much appreciated by the Indians and completely understood.

A deaf-mute asked Alejandro how long it took him to come to Washington from his country. He replied by placing the index and second finger of the right hand astride the extended forefinger (others closed) of the left; then elevating the fingers of the left hand (except thumb and forefinger) back forward (*three*); then extending the fingers of both hands and bringing them to a point, thumbs resting on palmar sides and extended, placing the hands in front of the body, the tips opposite the opposing wrist, and about four inches apart; then, revolving them in imitation of *wheels*, he elevated the extended forefinger of the left hand (*one*); then placing the extended flat hands, thumbs touching, the backs sloping downward towards the respective right and left sides, like the roof of a house; then repeating the sign of wheels as in the preceding, after which the left hand was extended before the body, fingers toward the right, horizontal, palm down and slightly arched, the right wrist held under it, the fingers extending upward beyond it, and quickly and repeatedly snapped upward (*smoke*); the last three signs being *covered—wagon—smoke, i. e. cars*; then elevating four fingers of the left hand (*four*).

Translation.—Traveled three days on horseback, one in a wagon, and four in the cars.

The deaf-mutes understood all but the sign for wheel, which they make as a large circle, with *one* hand.

Another example: A deaf-mute pretended to hunt something; found birds, took his bow and arrows and killed several.

This was fully understood.

A narrative given by Alejandro was also understood by the deaf-mutes, to the effect that he made search for deer, shot one with a gun, killed and skinned it, and packed it up.

It will be observed that many of the above signs admitted of and were expressed by pantomime, yet that was not the case with all that were made. President GALLAUDET made also some remarks in gesture which were understood by the Indians, yet were not strictly pantomimic.

The opinion of all present at the test was that two intelligent mimes would seldom fail of mutual understanding, their attention being exclusively directed to the expression of thoughts by the means of comprehension and reply equally possessed by both, without the mental confusion of conventional sounds only intelligible to one.

A large collection has been made of natural deaf-mute signs, and also of those more conventional, which have been collated with those of the several tribes of Indians. Many of them show marked similarity, not only in principle but often in detail.

The result of the studies so far as prosecuted is that what is called *the* sign language of Indians is not, properly speaking, one language, but that it and the gesture systems of deaf-mutes and of all peoples constitute together one language—the gesture speech of mankind—of which each system is a dialect.

TO WHAT EXTENT PREVALENT AS A SYSTEM.

The assertion has been made by many writers, and is currently repeated by Indian traders and some Army officers, that all the tribes of North America have long had and still use a *common* and *identical* sign language, in which they can communicate freely without oral assistance. Although this remarkable statement is at variance with some of the principles of the formation and use of signs set forth by Dr. E. B. TYLOR, whose admirable chapters on gesture speech in his *Researches into the Early History of Mankind* have in a great degree prompted the present inquiries, that eminent authority did not see fit to discredit it. He repeats the report as he received it, in the words that "the same signs serve as a medium of converse from Hudson Bay to the Gulf of Mexico." Its truth or falsity can only be established by careful comparison of lists or vocabularies of signs taken under test conditions at widely different times and places. For this purpose lists have been collated by the writer, taken in different parts of the country at several dates, from the last century to the last month, comprising together several thousand signs, many of them, however, being mere variants or synonyms for the same object or quality, some being repetitions of others and some of small value from uncertainty in description or authority, or both.

ONCE PROBABLY UNIVERSAL IN NORTH AMERICA.

The conclusion reached from the researches made is to the effect that before the changes wrought by the Columbian discovery the use of gesture illustrated the remark of Quintilian upon the same subject (l. xi, c. 3) that "*In tanta per omnes gentes nationesque linguæ diversitate hic mihi omnium hominum communis sermo videatur.*"

Quotations may be taken from some old authorities referring to widely separated regions. The Indians of Tampa Bay, identified with the Timucua, met by Cabeça de Vaca in 1528, were active in the use of signs, and in his journeying for eight subsequent years, probably through Texas and Mexico, he remarks that he passed through many dissimilar tongues, but that he questioned and received the answers of the Indians by signs "just as if they spoke our language and we theirs." Michaëlius, writing in 1628, says of the Algonkins on or near the Hudson River : "For purposes of trading as much was done by signs with the thumb and fingers as by speaking." In Bossu's *Travels through that part of North America formerly called Louisiana, London,* 1771 (Forster's translation), an account is given of Monsieur de Belle Isle some years previously captured by the Atak-apa, who remained with them two years and "conversed in their pantomimes with them." He was rescued by Governor Bienville and was sufficiently expert in the sign language to interpret between Bienville and the tribe. In Bushmann's *Spuren,* p. 424, there is a reference to the "Accocessaws on the west side of the Colorado, two hundred miles southwest of Nacogdoches," who use thumb signs which they understand : "*Theilen sich aber auch durch Daum-Zeichen mit, die sie alle verstehen.*"

Omitting many authorities, and for brevity allowing a break in the continuity of time, reference may be made to the statement in Major Long's expedition of 1819, concerning the Arapahos, Kaiowas, Ietans, and Cheyennes, to the effect that, being ignorant of each other's languages, many of them when they met would communicate by means of signs, and would thus maintain a conversation without the least difficulty or interruption. A list of the tribes reported upon by Prince Maximilian von Wied-Neuweid, in 1832–'34, appears elsewhere in this paper. In Frémont's expedition of 1844 special and repeated allusion is made to the expertness of the Pai-Utes in signs, which is contradictory to the statement above made by correspondents. The same is mentioned regarding a band of Shoshonis met near the summit of the Sierra Nevada, and one of "Diggers," probably Chemehuevas, encountered on a tributary of the Rio Virgen.

Ruxton, in his *Adventures in Mexico and the Rocky Mountains, New York,* 1848, p. 278, sums up his experience with regard to the Western

tribes so well as to require quotation: "The language of signs is so perfectly understood in the Western country, and the Indians themselves
are such admirable pantomimists, that, after a little use, no difficulty
whatever exists in carrying on a conversation by such a channel; and
there are few mountain men who are at a loss in thoroughly understanding and making themselves intelligible by signs alone, although they
neither speak nor understand a word of the Indian tongue."

Passing to the correspondents of the writer from remote parts of
North America, it is important to notice that Mr. J. W. Powell, Indian
superintendent, reports the use of sign language among the Kutine, and
Mr. James Lenihan, Indian agent, among the Selish, both tribes of
British Columbia. The Very Rev. Edward Jacker, while contributing information upon the present use of gesture language among the Ojibwas of
Lake Superior, mentions that it has fallen into comparative neglect because
for three generations they had not been in contact with tribes of a different speech. Dr. Francis H. Atkins, acting assistant surgeon, United
States Army, in forwarding a contribution of signs of the Mescalero
Apaches remarks: "I think it probable that they have used sign language rather less than many other Indians. They do not seem to use
it to any extent at home, and abroad the only tribes they were likely
to come into contact with were the Navajos, the Lipans of old Mexico,
and the Comanches. Probably the last have been almost alone their
visiting neighbors. They have also seen the Pueblos a little, these appearing to be, like the Phœnicians of old, the traders of this region."
He also alludes to the effect of the Spanish, or rather *lingua Mexicana*,
upon all the Southern tribes and, indeed, upon those as far north as the
Utes, by which recourse to signs is now rendered less necessary.

Before leaving this particular topic it is proper to admit that, while
there is not only recorded testimony to the past use of gesture signs by
several tribes of the Iroquoian and Algonkian families, but evidence
that it still remains, it is, however, noticeable that these families when
met by their first visitors do not appear to have often impressed the
latter with their reliance upon gesture language to the same extent as
has always been reported of the tribes now and formerly found farther
inland. An explanation may be suggested from the fact that among
those families there were more people dwelling near together in commu-
nities speaking the same language, though with dialectic peculiarities,
than became known later in the farther West, and not being nomadic their
intercourse with strange tribes was less individual and conversational.
Some of the tribes, in especial the Iroquois proper, were in a comparatively
advanced social condition. A Mohawk or Seneca would probably have
repeated the arrogance of the old Romans, whom in other respects they
resembled, and compelled persons of inferior tribes to learn his language
if they desired to converse with him, instead of resorting to the compromise of gesture speech, which he had practiced before the prowess and
policy of the confederated Five Nations had gained supremacy and which
was still used for special purposes between the members of his own tribe.

The studies thus far pursued lead to the conclusion that at the time of the discovery of North America all its inhabitants practiced sign language, though with different degrees of expertness, and that while under changed circumstances it was disused by some, others, in especial those who after the acquisition of horses became nomads of the Great Plains, retained and cultivated it to the high development now attained, from which it will surely and speedily decay.

MISTAKEN DENIAL THAT SIGN LANGUAGE EXISTS.

The most useful suggestion to persons interested in the collection of signs is that they shall not too readily abandon the attempt to discover recollections of them even among tribes long exposed to European influence and officially segregated from others. The instances where their existence, at first denied, has been ascertained are important with reference to the theories advanced.

Rev. J. Owen Dorsey has furnished a considerable vocabulary of signs finally procured from the Poncas, although, after residing among them for years, with thorough familiarity with their language, and after special and intelligent exertion to obtain some of their disused gesture language, he had before reported it to be entirely forgotten. A similar report was made by two missionaries among the Ojibwas, though other trustworthy authorities have furnished a copious list of signs obtained from that tribe. This is no imputation against the missionaries, as in October, 1880, five intelligent Ojibwas from Petoskey, Mich., told the writer that they had never heard of gesture language. An interesting letter from Mr. B. O. Williams, sr., of Owasso, Mich., explains the gradual decadence of signs used by the Ojibwas in his recollection, embracing sixty years, as chiefly arising from general acquaintance with the English language. Further discouragement came from an Indian agent giving the decided statement, after four years of intercourse with the Pai-Utes, that no such thing as a communication by signs was known or even remembered by them, which, however, was less difficult to bear because on the day of the receipt of that well-intentioned missive some officers of the Bureau of Ethnology were actually talking in signs with a delegation of that very tribe of Indians then in Washington, from one of whom, Nátci, a narrative printed in this paper (page 500), was received.

The report from missionaries, army officers, and travelers in Alaska was unanimous against the existence of a sign language there until Mr. Ivan Petroff, whose explorations had been more extensive, gave the excellent exposition and dialogue now produced (see page 492). Collections were also obtained from the Apaches and Zuñi, Pimas, Papagos, and Maricopas, after agents and travelers had denied them to be possessed of any knowledge on the subject.

For the reasons mentioned under the last heading, little hope was entertained of procuring a collection from any of the Iroquoian stock, but the intelligent and respectable chief of the Wyandots, Hénto (Gray Eyes), came to the rescue. His tribe was moved from Ohio in July, 1843, to the territory now occupied by the State of Kansas, and then again moved to Indian Territory, in 1870. He asserts that about one-third of the tribe, the older portion, know many signs, a partial list of which he gave with their descriptions. He was sure that those signs were used before the removal from Ohio, and he saw them used also by Shawnees, Delawares, and Senecas there.

Unanimous denial of any existence of sign language came from the British provinces of Ontario and Quebec, and was followed by the collection obtained by the Hon. Horatio Hale. His statement of the time and manner of its being procured by him is not only interesting but highly instructive:

"The aged Mohawk chief, from whom the information on this subject has been obtained, is commonly known by his English name of John Smoke Johnson. 'Smoke' is a rude version of his Indian name, *Sakayenkwaraton*, which may be rendered 'Disappearing Mist.' It is the term applied to the haze which rises in the morning of an autumn day, and gradually passes away. Chief Johnson has been for many years 'speaker' of the great council of the Six Nations. In former times he was noted as a warrior, and later has been esteemed one of the most eloquent orators of his race. At the age of eighty-eight years he retains much of his original energy. He is considered to have a better knowledge of the traditions and ancient customs of his people than any other person now living. This superior knowledge was strikingly apparent in the course of the investigations which were made respecting the sign language. Two other members of his tribe, well-educated and very intelligent men of middle age, the one a chief and government interpreter, the other a clergyman now settled over a white congregation, had both been consulted on the subject and both expressed the opinion that nothing of the sign language, properly speaking, was known among the Six Nations. They were alike surprised and interested when the old chief, in their presence, after much consideration, gradually drew forth from the stores of his memory the proofs of an accomplishment which had probably lain unused for more than half a century."

One of the most conclusive instances of the general knowledge of sign language, even when seldom used, was shown in the visit of five Jicarilla Apaches to Washington in April, 1880, under the charge of Dr. Benjamin Thomas, their agent. The latter said he had never heard of any use of signs among them. But it happened that there was a delegation of Absaroka (Crows) at the same hotel, and the two parties from such widely separated regions, not knowing a word of each other's language, immediately began to converse in signs, resulting in a decided sensation. One of the Crows asked the Apaches whether they ate horses, and it happening that the sign for *eating* was misapprehended for that known by the Apaches for *many*, the question was supposed to be whether the latter had many horses, which was answered in the affirmative. Thence ensued a misunderstanding on the subject of hippophagy, which was curious both as showing the general use of signs as a practice and the diversity in special signs for particular meanings. The surprise of the agent at the unsuspected accomplishment of his charges was not unlike that of a hen who, having hatched a number of duck eggs, is perplexed at the instinct with which the brood takes to the water.

The denial of the use of signs is often faithfully though erroneously reported from the distinct statements of Indians to that effect. In that, as in other matters, they are often provokingly reticent about their old habits and traditions. Chief Ouray asserted to the writer, as he also did to Colonel Dodge, that his people, the Utes, had not the practice of sign talk, and had no use for it. This was much in the proud spirit in which an Englishman would have made the same statement, as the idea involved an accusation against the civilization of his people, which he wished to appear highly advanced. Still more frequently the Indians do not distinctly comprehend what is sought to be obtained. Some-times, also, the art, abandoned in general, only remains in the memories of a few persons influenced by special circumstances or individual fancy.

In this latter regard a comparison may be made with the old science of heraldry, once of practical use and a necessary part of a liberal education, of which hardly a score of persons in the United States have any but the vague knowledge that it once existed; yet the united memories of those persons could, in the absence of records, reproduce all essential points on the subject.

Another cause for the mistaken denial in question must be mentioned. When travelers or sojourners have become acquainted with signs in any one place they may assume that those signs constitute *the* sign language, and if they afterwards meet tribes not at once recognizing those signs, they remove all difficulty about the theory of a "one and indivisible" sign language by simply asserting that the tribes so met do not understand *the* sign language, or perhaps that they do not use signs at all. This precise assertion has, as above mentioned, been made regarding the Utes and Apaches. Of course, also, Indians who have not been brought into sufficient contact with certain tribes using different signs, for the actual trial which would probably result in mutual comprehension, tell the travelers the same story. It is the venerable one of "ἄγλωσσος," "Njemez," "barbarian," and "stammering," above noted, applied to the hands instead of the tongue. Thus an observer possessed by a restrictive theory will find no signs where they are in plenty, while another determined on the universality and identity of sign language can, as elsewhere explained, produce, from perhaps the same individuals, evidence in his favor from the apparently conclusive result of successful communication.

PERMANENCE OF SIGNS.

In connection with any theory it is important to inquire into the permanence of particular gesture signs to express a special idea or object when the system has been long continued. Many examples have been given above showing that the gestures of classic times are still in use by the modern Italians with the same signification; indeed that the former on Greek vases or reliefs or in Herculanean bronzes can only be interpreted by the latter. In regard to the signs of instructed deaf-mutes in this country there appears to be a permanence beyond expectation. Mr. Edmund Booth, a pupil of the Hartford Institute half a century ago, and afterwards a teacher, says in the "*Annals*" for April, 1880, that the signs used by teachers and pupils at Hartford, Philadelphia, Washington, Council Bluffs, and Omaha were nearly the same as he had learned. "We still adhere to the old sign for President from Monroe's three-cornered hat, and for governor we designate the cockade worn by that dignitary on grand occasions three generations ago."

The specific comparisons made, especially by Dr. Washington Matthews and Dr. W. C. Boteler, of the signs reported by the Prince of Wied in 1832 with those now used by the same tribes from whom he obtained them, show a remarkable degree of permanency in many of those that were so clearly described by the Prince as to be proper subjects of any comparison. If they have persisted for half a century their age is probably much greater. In general it is believed that signs, constituting as they do a natural mode of expression, though enlarging in scope as new ideas and new objects require to be included and though abbreviated as hereinafter explained, do not readily change in their essentials.

The writer has before been careful to explain that he does not present any signs as precisely those of primitive man, not being so carried away by enthusiasm as to suppose them possessed of immutability and immortality not found in any other mode of human utterance. Yet such signs as are generally prevalent among Indian tribes, and also in other parts of the world, must be of great antiquity. The use of derivative meanings to a sign only enhances this presumption. At first there might not appear to be any connection between the ideas of *same* and *wife*, expressed by the sign of horizontally extending the two forefingers side by side. The original idea was doubtless that given by the Welsh captain in Shakspere's Henry V: "'Tis so like as my fingers is to my fingers," and from this similarity comes "equal," "companion," and subsequently the close life-companion "wife." The sign is used in each of these senses by different Indian tribes, and sometimes the same tribe applies it in all of the senses as the context determines. It appears also in many lands with all the significations except that of "wife." It is proper here to mention that the suggestion of several correspondents that the Indian sign as applied to "wife" refers to "lying together" is rendered improbable by the fact that when the same tribes desire to express the sexual relation of marriage it is gestured otherwise.

Many signs but little differentiated were unstable, while others that
have proved the best modes of expression have survived as definite and
established.   Their prevalence and permanence being mainly determined
by the experience of their utility, it would be highly interesting to ascertain how long a time was required for a distinctly new conception or
execution to gain currency, become "the fashion," so to speak, over a
large part of the continent, and to be supplanted by a new "mode."   A
note may be made in this connection of the large number of diverse
signs for *horse*, all of which must have been invented within a comparatively recent period, and the small variation in the signs for *dog*,
which are probably ancient.

SURVIVAL IN GESTURE.

Even when the specific practice of sign language has been generally
discontinued for more than one generation, either from the adoption
of a jargon or from the common use of the tongue of the conquering
English, French, or Spanish, some of the gestures formerly employed as
substitutes for words may survive as a customary accompaniment to oratory or impassioned conversation, and, when ascertained, should be carefully noted.   An example, among many, may be found in the fact that
the now civilized Muskoki or Creeks, as mentioned by Rev. H. F. Buckner, when speaking of the height of children or women, illustrate their
words by holding their hands at the proper elevation, palm up; but
when describing the height of "soulless" animals or inanimate objects,
they hold the palm downward.   This, when correlated with the distinctive signs of other Indians, is an interesting case of the survival of a
practice which, so far as yet reported, the oldest men of the tribe now
living only remember to have once existed.   It is probable that a collection of such distinctive gestures among the most civilized Indians
would reproduce enough of their ancient system to be valuable, while
possibly the persistent inquirer might in his search discover some of its
surviving custodians even among Chahta or Cheroki, Innuit or Abnaki,
Klamath or Nutka.

DISTINCTION BETWEEN IDENTITY OF SIGNS AND THEIR USE AS AN ART.

The general report that there is but one sign language in North America, any deviation from which is either blunder, corruption, or a dialect in
the nature of provincialism, may be examined in reference to some of the
misconceived facts which gave it origin and credence.   It may not appear
to be necessary that such examination should be directed to any mode of
collecting and comparing signs which would amount to their distortion.
It is useful, however, to explain that distortion would result from following the views of a recent essayist, who takes the ground that the description of signs should be made according to a "mean" or average.   There
can be no philosophic consideration of signs according to a "mean" of observations.   The proper object is to ascertain the radical or essential part

as distinct from any individual flourish or mannerism on the one hand, and from a conventional or accidental abbreviation on the other; but a mere average will not accomplish that object. If the hand, being in any position whatever, is, according to five observations, moved horizontally one foot to the right, and, according to five other observations, moved one foot horizontally to the left, the "mean" or resultant will be that it is stationary, which sign does not correspond with any of the ten observations. So if six observations give it a rapid motion of one foot to the right and five a rapid motion of the same distance to the left, the mean or resultant would be somewhat difficult to express, but perhaps would be a slow movement to the right for an inch or two, having certainly no resemblance either in essentials or accidents to any of the signs actually observed. In like manner the tail of the written letter " y " (which, regarding its mere formation, might be a graphic sign) may have in the chirography of several persons various degrees of slope, may be a straight line, or looped, and may be curved on either side; but a "mean" taken from the several manuscripts would leave the unfortunate letter without any tail whatever, or travestied as a " u " with an amorphous flourish. A definition of the radical form of the letter or sign by which it can be distinguished from any other letter or sign is a very different proceeding. Therefore, if a "mean" or resultant of any number of radically different signs to express the same object or idea, observed either among several individuals of the same tribe or among different tribes, is made to represent those signs, they are all mutilated and ignored as distinctive signs, though the result may possibly be made intelligible in practice, according to principles mentioned in the present paper. The expedient of a "mean" may be practically useful in the formation of a mere interpreter's jargon, but it elucidates no principle. It is also convenient for any one determined to argue for the uniformity of sign language as against the variety in unity apparent in all the realms of nature. On the "mean" principle, he only needs to take his two-foot rule and arithmetical tables and make all signs his signs and his signs all signs. Of course they are uniform, because he has made them so after the brutal example of Procrustes.

In this connection it is proper to urge a warning that a mere sign talker is often a bad authority upon principles and theories. He may not be liable to the satirical compliment of Dickens's "brave courier," who "understood all languages indifferently ill."; but many men speak some one language fluently, and yet are wholly unable to explain or analyze its words and forms so as to teach it to another person, or even to give an intelligent summary or classification of their own knowledge. What such a sign talker has learned is by memorizing, as a child may learn English, and though both the sign talker and the child may be able to give some separate items useful to a philologist or foreigner, such items are spoiled when colored by the attempt of ignorance to theorize.

A German who has studied English to thorough mastery, except in the mere facility of speech, may in a discussion upon some of its principles be contradicted by any mere English speaker, who insists upon his superior knowledge because he actually speaks the language and his antagonist does not, but the student will probably be correct and the talker wrong. It is an old adage about oral speech that a man who understands but one language understands none. The science of a sign talker possessed by a restrictive theory is like that of Mirabeau, who was greater as an orator than as a philologist, and who on a visit to England gravely argued that there was something seriously wrong in the British mind because the people would persist in saying " give me some bread" instead of " *donnez-moi du pain*," which was so much easier and more natural. A designedly ludicrous instance to the same effect was Hood's arraignment of the French because they called their mothers "mares" and their daughters "fillies." It is necessary to take with caution any statement from a person who, having memorized or hashed up any number of signs, large or small, has decided in his conceit that those he uses are the only genuine Simon Pure, to be exclusively employed according to his direction, all others being counterfeits or blunders. His vocabulary has ceased to give the signs of any Indian or body of Indians whatever, but becomes his own, the proprietorship of which he fights for as if secured by letters-patent. When a sign is contributed by one of the present collaborators, which such a sign talker has not before seen or heard of, he will at once condemn it as bad, just as a United States Minister to Vienna, who had been nursed in the mongrel Dutch of Berks County, Pennsylvania, declared that the people of Germany spoke very bad German.

An argument for the uniformity of the signs of our Indians is derived from the fact that those used by any of them are generally understood by others. But signs may be understood without being identical with any before seen. The entribal as well as intertribal exercise of Indians for generations in gesture language has naturally produced great skill both in expression and reception, so as to render them measurably independent of any prior mutual understanding, or what in a system of signals is called preconcert. Two accomplished army signalists can, after sufficient trial, communicate without having any code in common between them, one being mutually devised, and those specially designed for secrecy are often deciphered. So, if any one of the more conventional signs is not quickly comprehended, an Indian skilled in the principle of signs resorts to another expression of his flexible art, perhaps reproducing the gesture unabbreviated and made more graphic, perhaps presenting either the same or another conception or quality of the same object or idea by an original portraiture.

An impression of the community of signs is the more readily made because explorers and officials are naturally brought into contact more closely with those individuals of the tribes visited who are experts in sign language than with their other members, and those experts, on account of their skill as interpreters, are selected as guides to accompany the visitors. The latter also seek occasion to be present when signs are used, whether with or without words, in intertribal councils, and then the same class of experts comprises the orators, for long exercise in gesture speech has made the Indian politicians, with no special effort, masters of the art acquired by our public speakers only after laborious apprenticeship. The whole theory and practice of sign language being that all who understand its principles can make themselves mutually intelligible, the fact of the ready comprehension and response among all the skilled gesturers gives the impression of a common code. Furthermore, if the explorer learn to employ with ingenuity the signs used by any of the tribes, he will probably be understood in any other by the same class of persons who will surround him in the latter, thereby confirming him in the "common" theory. Those of the tribe who are less skilled, but who are not noticed, might be unable to catch the meaning of signs which have not been actually taught to them, just as ignorant persons among us cannot derive any sense from newly-coined words or those strange to their habitual vocabulary, which, though never before heard, linguistic scholars would instantly understand and might afterward adopt.

It is also common experience that when Indians find that a sign which has become conventional among their tribe is not understood by an interlocutor, a self-expressive sign is substituted for it, from which a visitor may form the impression that there are no conventional signs. It may likewise occur that the self-expressive sign substituted will be met with by a visitor in several localities, different Indians, in their ingenuity, taking the best and the same means of reaching the exotic intelligence.

There is some evidence that where sign language is now found among Indian tribes it has become more uniform than ever before, simply because many tribes have for some time past been forced to dwell near together at peace. A collection was obtained in the spring of 1880, at Washington, from a united delegation of the Kaiowa, Comanche, Apache, and Wichita tribes, which was nearly uniform, but the individuals who gave the signs had actually lived together at or near Anadarko, Indian Territory, for a considerable time, and the resulting uniformity of their signs might either be considered as a jargon or as the natural tendency to a compromise for mutual understanding—the unification so often observed in oral speech, coming under many circumstances out of former heterogeneity. The rule is that dialects precede languages and that out of many dialects comes one language. It may be found that other individuals of those same tribes who have from any cause not lived in the union explained may have signs for the same ideas different from those in the collection above mentioned. This is probable, because some signs of other representatives of one of the component bodies—Apache—have actually been reported differing from those for the same ideas given by the Anadarko group. The uniformity of the signs of those Arapahos, Cheyennes, and Sioux who have been secluded for years at one particular reservation, so far as could be done by governmental power, from the outer world, was used in argument by a correspondent; but some collected signs of other Cheyennes and Sioux differ, not only from those on the reservation, but among each other. Therefore the signs used in common by the tribes at the reservation seem to have been modified and to a certain extent unified.

The result of the collation and analysis of the large number of signs collected is that in numerous instances there is an entire discrepancy between the signs made by different bodies of Indians to express the same idea, and that if any of these are regarded as rigidly determinate, or even conventional with a limited range, and used without further devices, they will fail in conveying the desired impression to any one unskilled in gesture as an art, who had not formed the same precise conception or been instructed in the arbitrary motion. Few of the gestures that are found in current use are, in their origin, conventional. They are only portions, more or less elaborate, of obvious natural pantomime, and those proving efficient to convey most successfully at any time the several ideas became the most widely adopted, liable, however, to be superseded by more appropriate conceptions and delineations. The skill of any tribe and the copiousness of its signs are proportioned first to the necessity for their use, and secondly to the accidental ability of the individuals in it who act as custodians and teachers, so that the several tribes at different times vary in their degree of proficiency, and therefore both the precise mode of semiotic expression and the amount of its general use are always fluctuating. Sign language as a product of evolution has been developed rather than invented, and yet it seems probable that each of the separate signs, like the several steps that lead to any true invention, had a definite origin arising out of some appropriate occasion, and the same sign may in this manner have had many independent origins due to identity in the circumstances, or if lost, may have been reproduced.

The process is precisely the same as that observed among deaf-mutes. One of those unfortunate persons, living with his speaking relatives, may invent signs which the latter are taught to understand, though strangers sometimes will not, because they may be by no means the fittest expressions. Should a dozen or more deaf-mutes, possessed only of such crude signs, come together, they will be able at first to communicate only on a few common subjects, but the number of those and the general scope of expression will be continually enlarged. Each one commences with his own conception and his own presentment of it, but the universality of the medium used makes it sooner or later understood. This independent development, thus creating diversity, often renders the first interchange of thought between strangers slow, for the signs must be self-interpreting. There can be no natural universal language which is absolute and arbitrary. When used without convention, as sign language alone of all modes of utterance can be, it must be tentative, experimental, and flexible. The mutes will also resort to the invention of new signs for new ideas as they arise, which will be made intelligible, if necessary, through the illustration and definition given by signs formerly adopted, so that the fittest signs will be evolved, after rivalry and trial, and will survive. But there may not always be such a preponderance of fitness that all but one of the rival signs shall die out, and some, being equal in value to express the same idea or object, will continue to be used indifferently, or as a matter of individual taste, without confusion. A multiplication of the numbers confined together, either of deaf-mutes or of Indians whose speech is diverse, will not decrease the resulting uniformity, though it will increase both the copiousness and the precision of the vocabulary. The Indian use of signs, though maintained by linguistic diversities, is not coincident with any linguistic boundaries. The tendency is to their uniformity among groups of people who from any cause are brought into contact with each other while still speaking different languages. The longer and closer such contact, while no common tongue is adopted, the greater will be the uniformity of signs.

Colonel Dodge takes a middle ground with regard to the identity of the signs used by our Indians, comparing it with the dialects and provincialisms of the English language, as spoken in England, Ireland, Scotland, and Wales. But those dialects are the remains of actually diverse languages, which to some speakers have not become integrated. In England alone the provincial dialects are traceable as the legacies of Saxons, Angles, Jutes, and Danes, with a varying amount of Norman influence. A thorough scholar in the composite tongue, now called English, will be able to understand all the dialects and provincialisms of English in the British Isles, but the uneducated man of Yorkshire is not able to communicate readily with the equally uneducated man of Somersetshire. This is the true distinction to be made. A thorough sign talker would be able to talk with several Indians who have no signs in common, and who, if their knowledge of signs were only memorized, could not communicate together. So also, as an educated Englishman will understand the attempts of a foreigner to speak in very imperfect and broken English, a good Indian sign expert will apprehend the feeble efforts of a tyro in gestures. But Colonel Dodge's conclusion that there is but one true Indian sign language, just as there is but one true English language, is not proved unless it can be shown that a much larger proportion of the Indians who use signs at all, than present researches show to be the case, use identically the same signs to express the same ideas. It would also seem necessary to the parallel that the signs so used should be absolute, if not arbitrary, as are the words of an oral language, and not independent of preconcert and self-interpreting at the instant of their invention or first exhibition, as all true signs must originally have been and still measurably remain. All Indians, as all gesturing men, have many natural signs in common and many others which are now conventional. The conventions by which the latter were established occurred during long periods, when the tribes forming them were so separated as to have established altogether diverse customs and mythologies, and when the several tribes were with such different environment as to have formed varying conceptions needing appropriate sign expression. The old error that the North American Indians constitute one homogeneous race is now abandoned. Nearly all the characteristics once alleged as segregating them from the rest of mankind have proved not to belong to the whole of the pre-Columbian population, but only to those portions of it first explored. The practice of scalping is not now universal, even among the tribes least influenced by civilization, if it ever was, and therefore the cultivation of the scalp-lock separated from the rest of the hair of the head, or with the removal of all other hair, is not a general feature of their appearance. The arrangement of the hair is so different among tribes as to be one of the most convenient modes for their pictorial distinction. The war paint, red in some tribes, was black in others; the mystic rites of the calumet were in many regions unknown, and the use of wampum was by no means extensive. The wigwam is not the type of native dwellings, which show as many differing forms as those of Europe. In color there is great variety, and even admitting that the term "race" is properly applied, no competent observer would characterize it as red, still less copper-colored. Some tribes differ from each other in all respects nearly as much as either of them do from the lazzaroni of Naples, and more than either do from certain tribes of Australia. It would therefore be expected, as appears to be the case, that the conventional signs of different stocks and regions differ as do the words of English, French, and German, which, nevertheless, have sprung from the same linguistic roots. No one of those languages is a dialect of any of the others; and although the sign systems of the several tribes have greater generic unity with less specific variety than oral languages, no one of them is necessarily the dialect of any other.

Instead, therefore, of admitting, with present knowledge, that the signs of our Indians are "identical" and "universal," it is the more accurate statement that the systematic attempt to convey meaning by signs is universal among the Indians of the Plains, and those still comparatively unchanged by civilization. Its successful execution is by an *art*, which, however it may have commenced as an instinctive mental process, has been cultivated, and consists in actually pointing out objects in sight not only for designation, but for application and predication, and in suggesting others to the mind by action and the airy forms produced by action. To insist that sign language is uniform were to assert that it is perfect—"That faultless monster that the world ne'er saw."

FORCED AND MISTAKEN SIGNS.

Examination into the identity of signs is complicated by the fact that in the collection and description of Indian signs there is danger lest the civilized understanding of them may be mistaken or forced. The liability to those errors is much increased when the collections are not taken directly from the Indians themselves, but are given as obtained at second-hand from white traders, trappers, and interpreters, who, through misconception in the beginning and their own introduction or modification of gestures, have produced a jargon in the sign, as well as in the oral intercourse. An Indian talking in signs, either to a white man or to another Indian using signs which he never saw before, catches the meaning of that which is presented and adapts himself to it, at least for the occasion. Even when he finds that his interlocutor insists upon understanding and presenting a certain sign in a manner and with a significance widely different from those to which he has been accustomed, it is within the very nature, tentative and elastic, of the gesture art—both performers being on an equality—that he should adopt the one that seems to be recognized or that is pressed upon him, as with much greater difficulty he has learned and adopted many foreign terms used with whites before attempting to acquire their language, but never with his own race. Thus there is now, and perhaps always has been, what may be called a *lingua-franca* in the sign vocabulary. It is well known that all the tribes of the Plains having learned by experience that white visitors expect to receive certain signs really originating with the latter, use them in their intercourse just as they sometimes do the words "squaw" and "papoose," corruptions of the Algonkian, and once as meaningless in the present West as the English terms "woman" and "child," but which the first pioneers, having learned them on the Atlantic coast, insisted upon treating as generally intelligible.

The perversity in attaching through preconceived views a wrong significance to signs is illustrated by an anecdote found in several versions and in several languages, but repeated as a veritable Scotch legend by Duncan Anderson, esq., Principal of the Glasgow Institution for the Deaf and Dumb, when he visited Washington in 1853.

King James I. of England, desiring to play a trick upon the Spanish ambassador, a man of great erudition, but who had a crotchet in his head upon sign language, informed him that there was a distinguished professor of that science in the university at Aberdeen. The ambassador set out for that place, preceded by a letter from the King with instructions to make the best of him. There was in the town one Geordy, a butcher, blind of one eye, a fellow of much wit and drollery. Geordy is told to play the part of a professor, with the warning not to speak a word; is gowned, wigged, and placed in a chair of state, when the ambassador is shown in and they are left alone together. Presently the nobleman came out greatly pleased with the experiment, claiming that his theory was demonstrated. He said: "When I entered the room I raised one finger to signify there is one God. He replied by raising two fingers to signify that this Being rules over two worlds, the material and the spiritual. Then I raised three fingers, to say there are three persons in the Godhead. He then closed his fingers, evidently to say these three are one." After this explanation on the part of the nobleman the professors sent for the butcher and asked him what took place in the recitation room. He appeared very angry and said: "When the crazy man entered the room where I was he raised one finger, as much as to say I had but one eye, and I raised two fingers to signify that I could see out of my one eye as well as he could out of both of his. When he raised three fingers, as much as to say there were but three eyes between us, I doubled up my fist, and if he had not gone out of that room in a hurry I would have knocked him down."

The readiness with which a significance may be found in signs when none whatever exists is also shown in the great contest narrated by Rabelais between Panurge and the English philosopher, Thaumast, commencing as follows:

"Everybody then taking heed in great silence, the Englishman lifted his two hands separately, clinching the ends of his fingers in the form that at Chion they call the fowl's tail. Then he struck them together by the nails four times. Then he opened them and struck one flat upon the other with a clash once; after which, joining them as above, he struck twice, and four times afterwards, on opening them. Then he placed them, joined and extended the one above the other, seeming to pray God devoutly.

" Panurge suddenly moved his right hand in the air, placed the right-hand thumb at the right-hand nostril, holding the four fingers stretched out and arrayed in parallel lines with the point of the nose; shutting the left eye entirely, and winking with the right, making a profound depression with eyebrow and eyelid. Next he raised aloft the left with a strong clinching and extension of the four fingers and elevation of the thumb, and held it in line directly corresponding with the position of the right, the distance between the two being a cubit and a half. This done, in the like manner he lowered towards the ground both hands, and finally held them in the midst as if aiming straight at the Englishman's nose."

And so on at great length. The whole performance of Panurge was to save the credit of Pantagruel by making fantastic and mystic motions in pretended disputation with the signs given by Thaumast in good faith. Yet the latter confessed himself conquered, and declared that he had derived inestimable information from the purposely meaningless gestures. The satire upon the diverse interpretations of the gestures of Naz-de-cabre (*Pantagruel*, Book III, chap. xx) is to the same effect, showing it to have been a favorite theme with Rabelais.

ABBREVIATIONS.

A lesson was learned by the writer as to the abbreviation of signs, and the possibility of discovering the original meaning of those most obscure, from the attempts of a Cheyenne to convey the idea of *old man.*

He held his right hand forward, bent at elbow, fingers and thumb closed sidewise. This not conveying any sense, he found a long stick, bent his back, and supported his frame in a tottering step by the stick held, as was before only imagined. Here at once was decrepit age dependent on a staff. The principle of abbreviation or reduction may be illustrated by supposing a person, under circumstances forbidding the use of the voice, seeking to call attention to a particular bird on a tree, and failing to do so by mere indication. Descriptive signs are resorted to, perhaps suggesting the bill and wings of the bird, its manner of clinging to the twig with its feet, its size by seeming to hold it between the hands, its color by pointing to objects of the same hue; perhaps by the action of shooting into a tree, picking up the supposed fallen game, and plucking feathers. These are continued until understood, and if one sign or combination of signs proves to be successful it will be repeated on the next occasion by both persons engaged, and after becoming familiar between them and others will be more and more abbreviated. Conventionality in signs largely consists in the form of abbreviation which is agreed upon. When the signs of the Indians have from ideographic form thus become demotic, they may be called conventional, but still not arbitrary. In them, as in all his actions, man had at the first a definite meaning or purpose, together with method in their subsequent changes or modifications.

Colonel Dodge gives a clear account of the manner in which an established sign is abbreviated in practice, as follows: "There are an almost infinite number and variety of abbreviations. For instance, to tell a man to 'talk,' the most common formal sign is made thus: Hold the right hand in front of, the back near, the mouth, end of thumb and index-finger joined into an 'O,' the outer fingers closed on the palm; throw the hand forward sharply by a quick motion of the wrist, and at the same time flip forward the index-finger. This may be done once or several times.

"The formal sign to 'cease' or 'stop doing' anything is made by bringing the two hands open and held vertically in front of the body, one behind the other, then quickly pass one upward, the other downward, simulating somewhat the motion of the limbs of a pair of scissors, meaning 'cut it off.' The latter sign is made in conversation in a variety of ways, but habitually with one hand only.

"The formal sign to 'stop talking' is first to make the formal sign for 'talk,' then the formal sign for 'cut;' but this is commonly abbreviated by first making the formal sign for 'talk' with the right hand, and then immediately passing the same hand, open, fingers extended, downward across and in front of the mouth, 'talk, cut.'

"But though the Plains Indian, if asked for the sign to 'stop talking,' will properly give the sign either in its extended or abbreviated form as above, he in conversation abbreviates it so much further that the sign loses almost all resemblance to its former self. Whatever the position of the hand, a turn of the wrist, a flip of the forefinger, and a turn of the wrist back to its original position is fully equivalent to the elaborate signs."

It may be added that nearly every sign which to be intelligibly de-scribed and as exhibited in full requires the use of both hands, is out-lined, with one hand only, by skillful Indians gesturing between them-selves, so as to be clearly understood between them. Two Indians, whose blankets are closely held to their bodies by the left hand, which is neces-sarily rendered unavailable for gesture, will severally thrust the right from beneath the protecting folds and converse freely. The same is true when one hand of each holds the bridle of a horse.

The Italian signs are also made in such abbreviated forms as to be little more than hinted at, requiring a perfect knowledge of the full and original form before the slight and often furtive suggestion of it can be understood. Deaf-mutes continually seek by tacit agreement to shorten their signs more and more. While the original of each may be pre-served in root or stem, it is only known to the proficient, as the root or stem of a plant enables botanists, but no others, to distinguish it. Thus the natural character of signs, the universal significance which is their peculiarly distinctive feature, may and often does become lost. From the operation of the principle of independent and individual ab-breviation inherent in all sign language, without any other cause, that of the Indians must in one or two generations have become diverse, even if it had in fact originated from one tribe in which all conceptions and executions were absolute.

ARE SIGNS CONVENTIONAL OR INSTINCTIVE?

There has been much discussion on the question whether gesture signs were originally invented, in the strict sense of that term, or whether they result from a natural connection between them and the ideas repre-sented by them, that is whether they are conventional or instinctive. Cardinal Wiseman (*Essays*, III, 537) thinks that they are of both char-acters; but referring particularly to the Italian signs and the proper mode of discovering their meaning, observes that they are used prima-rily with words and from the usual accompaniment of certain phrases. "For these the gestures become substitutes, and then by association express all their meaning, even when used alone." This would be the process only where systematic gestures had never prevailed or had been so disused as to be forgotten, and were adopted after elaborate oral phrases and traditional oral expressions had become common. In other parts of this paper it is suggested that conventionality chiefly consists in abbreviation, and that signs are originally self-interpreting, independ-ent of words, and therefore in a certain sense instinctive.

Another form of the above query, having the same intent, is whether signs are arbitrary or natural. The answer will depend upon what the observer considers to be natural to himself. A common sign among both deaf-mutes and Indians for *woman* consists in designating the arrangement of the hair, but such a represented arrangement of hair familiar to the gesturer as had never been seen by the person addressed would not seem "natural" to the latter. It would be classed as arbitrary, and could not be understood without context or explanation, indeed without translation such as is required from foreign oral speech. Signs most naturally, that is, appropriately, expressing a conception of the thing signified, are first adopted and afterwards modified by circumstances of environment, so as to appear, without full understanding, conventional and arbitrary, yet they are as truly "natural" as the signs for hearing, seeing, eating, and drinking, which continue all over the world as they were first formed because there is no change in those operations.

CLASSES OF DIVERSITIES IN SIGNS.

While there is not sufficient evidence that any exhibition of sign language in any tribe is a dialect derived or corrupted from an ascertained language in any other tribe, it still is convenient to consider the different forms appearing in different tribes as several dialects (in the usual mode of using that term) of a common language. Every sign talker necessarily has, to some extent, a dialect of his own. No one can use sign language without original invention and without modification of the inventions of others; and all such new inventions and modifications have a tendency to spread and influence the production of other variations. The diversities thus occasioned are more distinct than that mere individuality of style or expression which may be likened to the differing chirography of men who write, although such individual characteristics also constitute an important element of confusion to the inexperienced observer. In differing handwriting there is always an attempt or desire to represent an alphabet which is essentially determinate, but no such fixedness or limited condition of form restricts gesture speech.

Those variations and diversities of form and connected significance specially calling for notice may be: 1st. In the nature of synonyms. 2d. Substantially the same form with such different signification as not to be synonymous. 3d. Difference in significance produced by such slight variation in form as to be, to a careless observer, *symmorphic.*

SYNONYMS.

In this division are placed signs of differing forms which are used in senses so nearly the same as to have only a slight shade of distinction, or sometimes to be practically interchangeable. The comprehensive and metaphorical character of signs renders more of them interchangeable than is the case with words; still, like words, some signs with essential resemblance of meaning have partial and subordinate differences made by etymology or usage. Doubtless signs are purposely selected as delineating the most striking outlines of an object, or the most characteristic features of an action; but different individuals, and likewise different bodies of people, would not always agree in the selection of those outlines and features. Taking the illustration of the attempt to invent a sign for *bird*, before used, any one of a dozen signs might have been agreed upon with equal appropriateness, and, in fact, a number have been so selected by several individuals and tribes, each one, therefore, being a synonym of the other. Another example of this is in the signs for *deer*, designated by various modes of expressing fleetness, by his gait when not in rapid motion, by the shape of his horns, by the color of his tail, and sometimes by combinations of several of those characteristics. Each of these signs may be indefinitely abbreviated, and therefore create indefinite diversity. Another illustration, in which an association of ideas is apparent, is in the upward raising of the index in front of and above the head, which means *above* (sometimes containing the religious conception of *heaven, great spirit*, &c.), and also *now, to-day*. Not unfrequently these several signs to express the same ideas are used interchangeably by the same people, and some one of the duplicates or triplicates may have been noticed by separate observers to the exclusion of the others. On the other hand, they might all have been noticed, but each one among different bodies. Thus confusing reports would be received, which might either be erroneous in deducing the prevalence of particular signs or the opposite. Sometimes the synonym may be recognized as an imported sign, used with another tribe known to affect it. Sometimes the diverse signs to express the same thing are only different trials at reaching the intelligence of the person addressed. An account is given by Lieut. Heber M. Creel, Seventh Cavalry, U. S. A., of an old Cheyenne squaw, who made about twenty successive and original signs to a recruit of the Fourth Cavalry to let him know that she wanted to obtain out of a wagon a piece of cloth belonging to her, to wipe out an oven preparatory to baking bread. Thus by tradition, importation, recent invention, or from all these causes together, several signs entirely distinct are produced for the same object or action.

THE SAME SIGN WITH DIVERSE MEANINGS.

This class is not intended to embrace the cases common both to sign and oral language where the same sign has several meanings, according to the expression, whether facial or vocal, and the general manner accompanying its delivery. The sign given for "stop talking" on page 339 may be used in simple acquiescence, "very well," "all right!" or for comprehension, "I understand;" or in impatience, "you have talked enough!" which may be carried further to express actual anger in the violent "shut up!" But all these grades of thought accompany the idea of a cessation of talk. In like manner an acquaintance of the writer asking the same favor (a permission to go through their camp) of two chiefs, was answered by both with the sign generally used for repletion after eating, viz., the index and thumb turned toward the body, passed up from the abdomen to the throat; but in the one case, being made with a gentle motion and pleasant look, it meant, "I am satisfied," and granted the request; in the other, made violently, with the accompaniment of a truculent frown, it read, "I have had enough of that!" But these two meanings might also have been expressed by different intonations of the English word "enough." The class of signs now in view is better exemplified by the French word *souris*, which is spelled and pronounced precisely the same with the two wholly distinct and independent significations of *smile* and *mouse*. From many examples may be selected the Omaha sign for *think*, *guess*, which is precisely the same as that of the Absaroka, Shoshoni and Banak for *brave*, see page 414. The context alone, both of the sign and the word, determines in what one of its senses it is at the time used, but it is not discriminated merely by a difference in expression.

It would have been very remarkable if precisely the same sign were not used by different or even the same persons or bodies of people with wholly distinct significations. The graphic forms for objects and ideas are much more likely to be coincident than sound is for similar expressions, yet in all oral languages the same precise sound is used for utterly diverse meanings. The first conception of many different objects must have been the same. It has been found, indeed, that the homophony of words and the homomorphy of ideographic pictures is noticeable in opposite significations, the conceptions arising from the opposition itself. The differentiation in portraiture or accent is a subsequent and remedial step not taken until after the confusion has been observed and become inconvenient. Such confusion and contradiction would only be eliminated if sign language were absolutely perfect as well as absolutely universal.

SYMMORPHS.

In this class are included those signs conveying different ideas, and really different in form of execution as well as in conception, yet in which the difference in form is so slight as practically to require attention and discrimination. An example from oral speech may be found in the English word "desert," which, as pronounced "des'-ert" or "desert'," and in a slightly changed form, "dessert," has such widely varying significations. These distinctions relating to signs require graphic illustration.

FIG. 112.

The sign made by the Dakota, Hidatsa, and several other tribes, for *tree* is made by holding the right hand before the body, back forward, fingers and thumb separated, then pushing it slightly upward, Fig. 112. That for *grass* is the same made near the ground; that for *grow* is made

FIG. 113.

like *grass*, though instead of holding the back of the hand near the ground the hand is pushed upward in an interrupted manner, Fig. 113. For *smoke*, the hand (with the back down, fingers pointing upward as in *grow*) is thrown upward several times from the same place instead of continuing the whole motion upward. Frequently the fingers are thrown forward from under the thumb with each successive upward motion. For *fire*, the hand is employed as in the gesture for *smoke*, but the motion is frequently more waving, and in other cases made higher from the ground.

The sign for *rain*, made by the Shoshoni, Apache, and other Indians,

is by holding the hand (or hands) at the height of and before the shoulder, fingers pendent, palm down, then pushing it downward a short distance, Fig. 114. That for *heat* is the same, with the difference that the hand is held above the head and thrust downward toward the forehead; that for *to weep* is made by holding the hand as in *rain*, and the gesture made from the eye downward over the cheek, back of the fingers nearly touching the face.

FIG. 114.

The common sign for *sun* is made by bringing the tips of the thumb and index together so as to form a circle; remaining fingers closed. The hand is then held toward the sky, Fig. 115. The motion with the same circular position of index and thumb is for *want*, by bringing the hand backward toward the mouth, in a curve forming a short arch between the origin and termination of the gesture.

For *drink* the gesture by several tribes is the same as for *want*, with the slight difference in the position of the last three fingers, which are not so tightly clinched, forming somewhat the shape of a cup; and that for *money* is made by holding out the hand with the same arrangement of fingers

FIG. 115.

in front of the hips, at a distance of about twelve or fifteen inches.

Another sign for *sun*, made by the Cheyennes, is by placing the tips of the partly separated thumb and index of one hand against those of

the other, approximating a circle, and holding them toward the sky, Fig. 116, and that for *various things*, observed among the Brulé Sioux with the same position of the hands, is made by placing the circle horizontal, and moving it interruptedly toward the right side, each

FIG. 116.

movement forming a short arch. Compare also the sign for *village*, described on page 386.

The Arikara sign for *soldier* is by placing the clinched hands together before the breast, thumbs touching, then drawing them horizontally outward toward their respective sides, Fig. 117. That for *done*, made by the Hidatsa, is shown below in this paper, see Fig. 334, page 528. That for *much* (*Cheyenne* I, *Comanche* III), see Fig. 274, page 447, is to be correlated with the above.

The sign for *to be told* or *talked to*, and for the reception of speech, by the tribes generally, is made
by placing the   x------------------>------------------x
flat right hand,
palm upward,

FIG. 117.

about fifteen inches in front of the right side of the face or breast, fingers pointing to the left, then drawing the hand toward the bottom of the chin, and is illustrated in Fig. 71, page 291. The Comanche sign for *give* or *asking* is shown in Fig. 301, page 480 (*Comanche* III), and is made by bringing the hand toward the body but a short distance, and the motion repeated, the tips of the fingers indicating the outline of a circle.

The tribal sign for *Kaiowa*, illustrated in its place among the TRIBAL SIGNS, is made by holding the hand with extended and separated fingers and thumb near the side of the head, back outward, and giving it a rotary motion. This gesture is made in front of the face by many tribes. The generic sign for *deer*, made by the Dakota and some others, is by holding the hand motionless at the side of the head, with extended and separated thumb and fingers, representing the branched antlers. That for *fool*, reported from the same Indians, is the same as above described for *Kaiowa*, which it also signifies, though frequently only one or two fingers are used.

The tribal sign both for the *Sahaptin* or *Nez Percés* and for *Caddo* (see TRIBAL SIGNS) is made by passing the extended index, pointing under the nose from right to left. When the second finger is not tightly closed it strongly resembles the sign often made for *lie, falsehood*, by passing the extended index and second fingers separated toward the left, over the mouth.

The tribal sign for Cheyenne (see TRIBAL SIGNS) differs from the sign for *spotted* only in the finger (or hand) in the latter being alternately passed across the upper and lower sides of the left forearm.

The sign for *steal, theft*, see Fig. 75, page 293, is but slightly different from that for *bear*, see Fig. 239, page 413, especially when the latter is made with one hand only. The distinction, however, is that the grasping in the latter sign is not followed by the idea of concealment in the former, which is executed by the right hand, after the motion of grasping, being brought toward and sometimes under the left armpit.

Cold and *winter*, see Tendoy-Huerito Dialogue, page 486, may be compared with *love*, see Kin Chē-ĕss' speech, page 521, and with *prisoner*. In these the difference consists in that *cold* and *winter* are represented by crossing the arms with clinched hands before the breast; *love* by crossing the arms so as to bring the fists more under the chin, and *prisoner* by holding the crossed wrists a foot in front of the breast.

Melon, squash, muskmelon, used by the Utes and Apaches, is made by holding the hand arched, fingers separated and pointing forward, and pushing the hand forward over a slight curve near the ground, and the generic sign for *animals* by the Apaches is made in the same manner at the height intended to represent the object.

The sign for *where?*, and *to search, to seek for*, made by the Dakota (IV), is by holding the back of the hand upward, index pointing forward, and carrying it from left to right about eight inches, raising and lowering it several times while so doing, as if quickly pointing at different objects. That for *some of them*, a part of a number of things or persons, made by the Kaiowa, Comanche, Wichita, and Apache Indians is nearly identical, the gesture being made less rapidly.

RESULTS SOUGHT IN THE STUDY OF SIGN LANGUAGE.

These may be divided into (1) its practical application, (2) its aid to philologic researches in general with (3) particular reference to the grammatic machinery of language, and (4) its archæologic relations.

PRACTICAL APPLICATION.

The most obvious application of Indian sign language will for its practical utility depend, to a large extent, upon the correctness of the view submitted by the present writer that it is not a mere semaphoric repetition of motions to be memorized from a limited traditional list, but is a cultivated art, founded upon principles which can be readily applied by travelers and officials, so as to give them much independence of professional interpreters—as a class dangerously deceitful and tricky. This advantage is not merely theoretical, but has been demonstrated to be practical by a professor in a deaf mute college who, lately visiting several of the wild tribes of the plains, made himself understood among all of them without knowing a word of any of their languages; nor would it only be experienced in connection with American tribes, being applicable to intercourse with savages in Africa and Asia, though it is not pretended to fulfill by this agency the schoolmen's dream of an ecumenical mode of communication between all peoples in spite of their dialectic divisions.

It must be admitted that the practical value of signs for intercourse with the American Indians will not long continue, their general progress in the acquisition of English or of Spanish being so rapid that those languages are becoming, to a surprising extent, the common medium, and signs are proportionally disused. Nor is a systematic use of signs of so great assistance in communicating with foreigners, whose speech is not understood, as might at first be supposed, unless indeed both parties agree to cease all attempt at oral language, relying wholly upon gestures. So long as words are used at all, signs will be made only as their accompaniment, and they will not always be ideographic.

An amusing instance in which savages showed their preference to signs instead of even an onomatope may be quoted from Wilfred Powell's *Observations on New Britain and neighboring Islands during Six Years' Exploration*, in *Proc. Roy. Geog. Soc.*, vol. iii, No. 2 (new monthly series), February, 1881, p. 89, 90: "On one occasion, wishing to purchase a pig, and not knowing very well how to set about it, being ignorant of the dialect, which is totally different from that of the natives in the north, I asked Mr. Brown how I should manage, or what he thought would be the best way of making them understand. He said, 'Why don't you try grunting?' whereupon I began to grunt most vociferously. The effect was magical. Some of them jumped back, holding their spears in readiness to throw; others ran away, covering their eyes with their hands, and all exhibited the utmost astonishment and alarm. In fact, it was so evident that they expected me to turn into a pig, and their alarm was so irresistibly comic, that Mr. Brown and I both burst out laughing, on which they gradually became more reassured, and those that had run away came back, and seeing us so heartily amused, and that I had not undergone any metamorphosis, began to laugh too; but when I drew a pig on the sand with a piece of stick, and made motions of eating, it suddenly seemed to strike them what was the matter, for they all burst out laughing, nodding their heads, and several of them ran off, evidently in quest of the pig that was required."

POWERS OF SIGNS COMPARED WITH SPEECH.

Sign language, being the mother utterance of nature, poetically styled by Lamartine the visible attitudes of the soul, is superior to all others in that it permits every one to find in nature an image to express his thoughts on the most needful matters intelligently to any other person. The direct or substantial natural analogy peculiar to it prevents a confusion of ideas. It is to some extent possible to use words without understanding them which yet may be understood by those addressed, but it is hardly possible to use signs without full comprehension of them. Separate words may also be comprehended by persons hearing them without the whole connected sense of the words taken together being caught, but signs are more intimately connected. Even those most appropriate will not be understood if the subject is beyond the comprehension of their beholders. They would be as unintelligible as the wild clicks of his instrument, in an electric storm, would be to the telegrapher, or as the semaphore, driven by wind, to the signalist. In oral speech even onomatopes are arbitrary, the most strictly natural sounds striking the ear of different individuals and nations in a manner wholly diverse. The instances given by SAYCE are in point. Exactly the same sound was intended to be reproduced in the "*bilbit* amphora" of Nævius, the "*glut glut* murmurat unda sonans" of the Latin Anthology, and the "*puls*" of Varro. The Persian "*bulbul*," the "*jugjug*" of Gascoigne, and the "*whitwhit*" of others are all attempts at imitating the note of the nightingale. Successful signs must have a much closer analogy and establish a *consensus* between the talkers far beyond that produced by the mere sound of words.

Gestures, in the degree of their pantomimic character, excel in graphic and dramatic effect applied to narrative and to rhetorical exhibition, and beyond any other mode of description give the force of reality.   Speech, when highly cultivated, is better adapted to generalization and abstraction ; therefore to logic and metaphysics.   The latter must ever henceforth be the superior in formulating thoughts.   Some of the enthusiasts in signs have contended that this unfavorable distinction is not from any inherent incapability, but because their employment has not been continued unto perfection, and that if they had been elaborated by the secular labor devoted to spoken language they might in resources and distinctiveness have exceeded many forms of the latter. Gallaudet, Peet, and others may be right in asserting that man could by his arms, hands, and fingers, with facial and bodily accentuation, express any idea that could be conveyed by words.

The combinations which can be made with corporeal signs are infinite. It has been before argued that a high degree of culture might have been attained by man without articulate speech and it is but a further step in the reasoning to conclude that if articulate speech had not been possessed or acquired, necessity would have developed gesture language to a degree far beyond any known exhibition of it. The continually advancing civilization and continually increasing intercourse of countless ages has perfected oral speech, and as both civilization and intercourse were possible with signs alone it is to be supposed that they would have advanced in some corresponding manner.   But as sign language has been chiefly used during historic time either as a scaffolding around a more valuable structure to be thrown aside when the latter was completed, or as an occasional substitute, such development was not to be expected.

The process of forming signs to express abstract ideas is only a variant from that of oral speech, in which the words for the most abstract ideas, such as law, virtue, infinitude, and immortality, are shown by Max Müller to have been derived and deduced, that is, abstracted, from sensuous impressions.   In the use of signs the countenance and manner as well as the tenor decide whether objects themselves are intended, or the forms, positions, qualities, and motions of other objects which are suggested, and signs for moral and intellectual ideas, founded on analogies, are common all over the world as well as among deaf-mutes.   Concepts of the intangible and invisible are only learned through percepts of tangible and visible objects, whether finally expressed to the eye or to the ear, in terms of sight or of sound.

Sign language is so faithful to nature, and so essentially living in its expression, that it is not probable that it will ever die.   It may become disused, but will revert.   Its elements are ever natural and universal, by recurring to which the less natural signs adopted dialectically or for expedition can always, with some circumlocution, be explained. This power of interpreting itself is a peculiar advantage, for spoken languages, unless explained by gestures or indications, can only be interpreted by means of some other spoken language. When highly cultivated, its rapidity on familiar subjects exceeds that of speech and approaches to that of thought itself. This statement may be startling to those who only notice that a selected spoken word may convey in an instant a meaning for which the motions of even an expert in signs may require a much longer time, but it must be considered that oral speech is now wholly conventional, and that with the similar development of sign language conventional expressions with hands and body could be made more quickly than with the vocal organs, because more organs could be worked at once. Without such supposed development the habitual communication between deaf-mutes and among Indians using signs is perhaps as rapid as between the ignorant class of speakers upon the same subjects, and in many instances the signs would win at a trial of speed. At the same time it must be admitted that great increase in rapidity is chiefly obtained by the system of preconcerted abbreviations, before explained, and by the adoption of arbitrary forms, in which naturalness is sacrificed and conventionality established, as has been the case with all spoken languages in the degree in which they have become copious and convenient.

There is another characteristic of the gesture speech that, though it cannot be resorted to in the dark, nor where the attention of the person addressed has not been otherwise attracted, it has the countervailing benefit of use when the voice could not be employed. This may be an advantage at a distance which the eye can reach, but not the ear, and still more frequently when silence or secrecy is desired. Dalgarno recommends it for use in the presence of great people, who ought not to be disturbed, and curiously enough "Disappearing Mist," the Iroquois chief, speaks of the former extensive use of signs in his tribe by women and boys as a mark of respect to warriors and elders, their voices, in the good old days, not being uplifted in the presence of the latter. The decay of that wholesome state of discipline, he thinks, accounts partly for the disappearance of the use of signs among the modern impudent youth and the dusky claimants of woman's rights.

An instance of the additional power gained to a speaker of ordinary language by the use of signs, impressed the writer while dictating to two amanuenses at the same moment, to the one by signs and the other by words, on different subjects, a practice which would have enabled Cæsar to surpass his celebrated feat. It would also be easy to talk to a deaf and blind man at once, the latter being addressed by the voice and the former in signs.

RELATIONS TO PHILOLOGY.

The aid to be derived from the study of sign language in prosecuting researches into the science of language was pointed out by LEIBNITZ, in his *Collectanea Etymologica*, without hitherto exciting any thorough or scientific work in that direction, the obstacle to it probably being that scholars competent in other respects had no adequate data of the gesture speech of man to be used in comparison. The latter will, it is hoped, be supplied by the work now undertaken.

In the first part of this paper it was suggested that signs played an important part in giving meaning to spoken words. Philology, comparing the languages of earth in their radicals, must therefore include the graphic or manual presentation of thought, and compare the elements of ideography with those of phonics. Etymology now examines the ultimate roots, not the fanciful resemblances between oral forms, in the different tongues ; the internal, not the mere external parts of language. A marked peculiarity of sign language consists in its limited number of radicals and the infinite combinations into which those radicals enter while still remaining distinctive. It is therefore a proper field for etymologic study.

From these and other considerations it is supposed that an analysis of the original conceptions of gestures, studied together with the holophrastic roots in the speech of the gesturers, may aid in the ascertainment of some relation between concrete ideas and words. Meaning does not adhere to the phonic presentation of thought, while it does to signs. The latter are doubtless more flexible and in that sense more mutable than words, but the ideas attached to them are persistent, and therefore there is not much greater metamorphosis in the signs than in the cognitions. The further a language has been developed from its primordial roots, which have been twisted into forms no longer suggesting any reason for their original selection, and the more the primitive significance of its words has disappeared, the fewer points of contact can it retain with signs. The higher languages are more precise because the consciousness of the derivation of most of their words is lost, so that they have become counters, good for any sense agreed upon and for no other.

It is, however, possible to ascertain the included gesture even in many English words. The class represented by the word *supercilious* will occur to all readers, but one or two examples may be given not so obvious and more immediately connected with the gestures of our Indians. *Imbecile*, generally applied to the weakness of old age, is derived from the Latin *in*, in the sense of on, and *bacillum*, a staff, which at once recalls the Cheyenne sign for *old man*, mentioned above, page 339. So *time* appears more nearly connected with τείνω, to stretch, when information is given of the sign for *long time*, in the Speech of Kin Chĕ-ĕss, in this paper, viz., placing the thumbs and forefingers in such a position as if a small thread was held between the thumb and forefinger of each hand, the hands first touching each other, and then moving slowly from each other, as if *stretching* a piece of gum-elastic.

In the languages of North America, which have not become arbitrary to the degree exhibited by those of civilized man, the connection between the idea and the word is only less obvious than that still unbroken between the idea and the sign, and they remain strongly affected by the concepts of outline, form, place, position, and feature on which gesture is founded, while they are similar in their fertile combination of radicals.

Indian language consists of a series of words that are but slightly differentiated parts of speech following each other in the order suggested in the mind of the speaker without absolute laws of arrangement, as its sentences are not completely integrated. The sentence necessitates parts of speech, and parts of speech are possible only when a language has reached that stage where sentences are logically constructed. The words of an Indian tongue, being synthetic or undifferentiated parts of speech, are in this respect strictly analogous to the gesture elements which enter into a sign language. The study of the latter is therefore valuable for comparison with the words of the former. The one language throws much light upon the other, and neither can be studied to the best advantage without a knowledge of the other.

Some special resemblances between the language of signs and the character of the oral languages found on this continent may be mentioned. Dr. J. HAMMOND TRUMBULL remarks of the composition of their words that they were " so constructed as to be thoroughly self-defining and immediately intelligible to the hearer." In another connection the remark is further enforced: " Indeed, it is a requirement of the Indian languages that every word shall be so framed as to admit of immediate resolution to its significant elements by the hearer. It must be thoroughly *self-defining*, for (as Max Müller has expressed it) 'it requires tradition, society, and literature to maintain words which can no longer be analyzed at once.' * * * In the ever-shifting state of a nomadic society no debased coin can be tolerated in language, no obscure legend accepted on trust. The metal must be pure and the legend distinct."

Indian languages, like those of higher development, sometimes exhibit changes of form by the permutation of vowels, but often an incorporated particle, whether suffix, affix, or infix, shows the etymology which often, also, exhibits the same objective conception that would be executed in gesture. There are, for instance, different forms for standing, sitting, lying, falling, &c., and for standing, sitting, lying on or falling from the same level or a higher or lower level. This resembles the pictorial conception and execution of signs.

Major J. W. POWELL, with particular reference to the disadvantages of the multiplied inflections in Indian languages, alike with the Greek and Latin, when the speaker is compelled, in the choice of a word to express his idea, to think of a great multiplicity of things, gives the following instance:

"A Ponca Indian in saying that a man killed a rabbit, would have to say: the man, he, one, animate, standing, in the nominative case, purposely killed, by shooting an arrow, the rabbit, he, the one, animate, sitting, in the objective case; for the form of a verb to kill would have to be selected, and the verb changes its form by inflection and incorporated particles to denote person, number, and gender as animate or inanimate, and gender as standing, sitting, or lying, and case; and the form of the verb would also express whether the killing was done accidentally or purposely, and whether it was by shooting or by some other process, and, if by shooting, whether by bow and arrow, or with a gun; and the form of the verb would in like manner have to express all of these things relating to the object; that is, the person, number, gender, and case of the object; and from the multiplicity of paradigmatic forms of the verb to kill, this particular one would have to be selected." This is substantially the mode in which an Indian sign talker would find it necessary to tell the story, as is shown by several examples given below in narratives, speeches, and dialogues.

Indian languages exhibit the same fondness for demonstration which is necessary in sign language. The two forms of utterance are alike in their want of power to express certain words, such as the verb " to be," and in the criterion of organization, so far as concerns a high degree of synthesis and imperfect differentiation, they bear substantially the same relation to the English language.

It may finally be added that as not only proper names but nouns generally in Indian languages are connotive, predicating some attribute of the object, they can readily be expressed by gesture signs, and therefore among them, if anywhere, it is to be expected that relations may be established between the words and the signs.

ETYMOLOGY OF WORDS FROM GESTURES.

There can be no attempt in the present limits to trace the etymology of any large number of words in the several Indian languages to a gestural origin, nor, if the space allowed, would it be satisfactory. The signs have scarcely yet been collected, verified, and collated in sufficient numbers for such comparison, even with the few of the Indian languages the radicals of which have been scientifically studied. The signs will, in a future work, be frequently presented in connection with the corresponding words of the gesturers, as is done now in a few instances in another part of this paper. For the present the subject is only indicated by the following examples, introduced to suggest the character of the study in which the students of American linguistics are urgently requested to assist:

The Dakota word *Shaⁿte-suta*—from *shaⁿte*, heart, and *suta*, strong—*brave*, not cowardly, literally strong-hearted, is made by several tribes of that stock, and particularly by the Brulé Sioux, in gestures by collecting the tips of the fingers and thumb of the right hand to a point, and then placing the radial side of the hand over the heart, finger tips pointing downward—*heart;* then place the left fist, palm inward, horizontally before the lower portion of the breast, the right fist back of the left, then raise the right and throw it forcibly over and downward in front of the left—*brave, strong.* See Fig. 242, page 415.

The Arikaras make the sign for *brave* by striking the clinched fist forcibly toward the ground in front of and near the breast.

Brave, or "strong-hearted," is made by the Absaroka, Shoshoni, and Banak Indians by merely placing the clinched fist to the breast, the latter having allusion to the heart, the clinching of the hand to strength, vigor, or force.

An Ojibwa sign for *death, to die,* is as follows:

Place the palm of the hand at a short distance from the side of the head, then withdraw it gently in an oblique downward direction, inclining the head and upper part of the body in the same direction.

The same authority, The Very Rev. E. Jacker, who contributes it, notes that there is an apparent connection between this conception and execution and the etymology of the corresponding terms in Ojibwa. "He dies," is *nibo;* "he sleeps," is *niba.* The common idea expressed by the gesture is a sinking to rest. The original significance of the root *nib* seems to be "leaning;" *anibeia,* "it is leaning"; *anibekweni,* "he inclines the head sidewards." The word *niba* or *nibe* (only in compounds) conveys the idea of "night," perhaps as the falling over, the going to rest, or the death of the day.

Ogima, the Ojibwa term for *chief,* is derived from a root which signifies "above" (*Ogidjaii,* upon; *ogidjina,* above; *ogidaki,* on a hill or mountain, etc.). *Ogitchida,* a brave, a hero (Otawa, *ogida*), is probably from the same root.

Sagima, the Ojibwa form of sachem, is from the root *sag,* which implies a coming forth, or stretching out. These roots are to be considered in connection with several gestures described under the head of *Chief,* in EXTRACTS FROM DICTIONARY, *infra.*

Onijishin, it is *good* (Ojibwa), originally signifies "it lies level." This may be compared with the sign for *good,* in the Tendoy-Huerito Dialogue, Fig. 309, page 487, and also that for *happy, contentment,* in the Speech of Kin Chĕ-ĕss, page 523.

In Klamath the radix *lam* designates a whirling motion, and appears in the word *láma,* "to be crazy, mad," readily correlated with the common gesture for *madman* and *fool,* in which the hand is rotated above and near the head.

Evening, in Klamath, is *litkhi,* from *luta,* to hang down, meaning the time when the sun hangs down, the gesture for which, described elsewhere in this paper (see Nátci's Narrative, page 503), is executive of the same conception, which is allied to the etymology usually given for *eve, even,* "the decline of the day." These Klamath etymologies have been kindly contributed by Mr. A. S. Gatschet.

The Very Rev. E. Jacker also communicates a suggestive *excursus exegeticus* upon the probable gestural origin of the Ojibwa word *tibishko,* "opposite in space; just so; likewise:"

"The adverb *tibishko* (or *dibishko*) is an offshoot of the root *tib* (or *dib*), which in most cases conveys the idea of measuring or weighing, as appears from the following samples: *dibaige*, he measures; *dibowe*, he settles matters by his speech or word, *e. g.*, as a juryman; *dibaamage*, he pays out; *dibakonige*, he judges; *dibabishkodjige*, he weighs; *dibamenimo*, he restricts himself, *e. g.*, to a certain quantity of food; *dibissitchige*, he fulfills a promise; *dibijigan*, a pattern for cutting clothes.

"The original meaning of *tib*, however, must be supposed to have been more comprehensive, if we would explain other (apparent) derivatives, such as: *tibi*, 'I don't know where, where to, where from,' &c; *tibik*, night; *dibendjige*, he is master or owner; *titibisse*, it rolls (as a ball), it turns (as a wheel); *dibaboweigan*, the cover of a kettle. The notion of measuring does not very naturally enter into the ideas expressed by these terms.

"The difficulty disappears if we assume the root *tib* or *dib* to have been originally the phonetic equivalent of a *gesture* expressive of the notion of covering as well as of that of measuring. This gesture would seem to be the holding of one hand above the other, horizontally, at some distance, palms opposite or both downwards. This, or some similar gesture would most naturally accompany the above terms. As for *tibik*, night, compare (*Dunbar*): 'The two hands open and extended, crossing one another horizontally.' The idea of covering evidently enters into this conception. The strange adverb *tibi* ('I don't know where,' &c., or 'in a place unknown to me'), if derived from the same root, would originally signify 'covered.' In *titibisse*, or *didibisse* (it rolls, it turns), the reduplication of the radical syllable indicates the repetition of the gesture, by holding the hands alternately above one another, palms downwards, and thus producing a rotary motion.

"In German, the clasping of the hands in a horizontal position, expressive of a promise or the conclusion of a bargain, is frequently accompanied by the interjection *top!* the same radical consonants as in *tib*. Compare also the English *tap*, the French *tape*, the Greek, τύπτω the Sanscrit *tup* and *tub*, &c."

GESTURES CONNECTED WITH THE ORIGIN OF WRITING.

Though written characters are generally associated with speech, they are shown, by successful employment in hieroglyphs and by educated deaf-mutes to be representative of ideas without the intervention of sounds, and so also are the outlines of signs. This will be more apparent if the motions expressing the most prominent feature, attribute, or function of an object are made, or supposed to be made, so as to leave a luminous track impressible upon the eye separate from the members producing it. The actual result is an immateriate graphic representation of visible objects and qualities which, invested with substance, has become familiar to us as the *rebus*, and also appears in the form of heraldic blazonry styled punning or "canting."

Gesture language is, in fact, not only a picture language, but is actual writing, though dissolving and sympathetic, and neither alphabetic nor phonetic.

Dalgarno aptly says: " *Qui enim caput nutat, oculo connivet, digitum movet in aëre, &c., (ad mentis cogitata exprimendum); is non minus vere scribit, quam qui Literas pingit in Charta, Marmore, vel œre.*"

It is neither necessary nor proper to enter now upon any prolonged account of the origin of alphabetic writing. There is, however, propriety, if not necessity, for the present writer, when making any remarks under this heading and under some others in this paper indicating special lines of research, to disclaim all pretension to being a Sinologue or Egyptologist, or even profoundly versed in Mexican antiquities. His partial and recently commenced studies only enable him to present suggestions for the examination of scholars. These suggestions may safely be introduced by the statement that the common modern alphabetic characters, coming directly from the Romans, were obtained by them from the Greeks, and by the latter from the Phœnicians, whose alphabet was connected with that of the old Hebrew. It has also been of late the general opinion that the whole family of alphabets to which the Greek, Latin, Gothic, Runic, and others belong, appearing earlier in the Phœnician, Moabite, and Hebrew, had its beginning in the ideographic pictures of the Egyptians, afterwards used by them to express sounds. That the Chinese, though in a different manner from the Egyptians, passed from picture writing to phonetic writing, is established by delineations still extant among them, called *ku-wăn*, or " ancient pictures," with which some of the modern written characters can be identified. The ancient Mexicans also, to some extent, developed phonetic expressions out of a very elaborate system of ideographic picture writing. Assuming that ideographic pictures made by ancient peoples would be likely to contain representations of gesture signs, which subject is treated of below, it is proper to examine if traces of such gesture signs may not be found in the Egyptian, Chinese, and Aztec characters. Only a few presumptive examples, selected from a considerable number, are now presented in which the signs of the North American Indians appear to be included, with the hope that further investigation by collaborators will establish many more instances not confined to Indian signs.

A typical sign made by the Indians for *no, negation,* is as follows: The hand extended or slightly curved is held in front of the body, a little to the right of the median line; it is then carried with a rapid sweep a foot or more farther to the right. (*Mandan and Hidatsa* I.)

One for *none, nothing,* sometimes used for simple negation, is also given: Throw both hands outward toward their respective sides from the breast. (*Wyandot* I.)

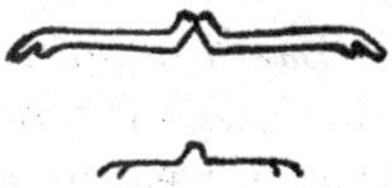

With these compare the two forms of the Egyptian character for *no, negation,* Fig. 118, taken from Champollion, *Grammaire Égyptienne, Paris,* 1836, p. 519.

FIG. 118.

No vivid fancy is needed to see the hands indicated at the extremities of arms extended symmetrically from the body on each side.

Also compare the Maya character for the same idea of negation,

Fig. 119, found in Landa, *Relation des Choses de Yucatan, Paris*, 1864, 316. The Maya word for negation is *"ma,"* and the word *"mak,"* a six-foot measuring rod, given by Brasseur de Bourbourg in his dictionary, apparently having connection with this character, would in use separate the hands as illustrated, giving the same form as the gesture made without the rod.

FIG. 119.

Another sign for *nothing, none*, made by the Comanches, is: Flat hand thrown forward, back to the ground, fingers pointing forward and downward. Frequently the right hand is brushed over the left thus thrown out.

Compare the Chinese character for the same meaning, Fig. 120. This will not be recognized as a hand without study of similar characters, which generally have a cross-line cutting off the wrist. Here the wrist bones follow under the cross cut, then the metacarpal bones, and last the fingers, pointing forward and downward.

FIG. 120.

The Arapaho sign for *child, baby*, is the forefinger in the mouth, *i. e.*, a nursing child, and a natural sign of a deaf-mute is the same. The Egyptian figurative character for the same is seen in Fig. 121. Its linear form is Fig. 122, and its hieratic is Fig. 123 (Champollion, *Dictionnaire Égyptien, Paris*, 1841, p. 31.)

FIG. 121.

FIG. 122.

FIG. 123.

These afford an interpretation to the ancient Chinese form for *son*, Fig. 124, given in *Journ. Royal Asiatic Society*, I, 1834, p. 219, as belonging to the Shang dynasty, 1756, 1112 B. C., and the modern Chinese form, Fig. 125, which, without the comparison, would not be supposed to have any pictured reference to an infant with hand or finger at or approaching the mouth, denoting the taking of nourishment. Having now suggested this, the

FIG. 124.   FIG. 125.   FIG. 126.

Chinese character for *birth*, Fig. 126, is understood as the expression of a common gesture among the Indians, particularly reported from the Dakota, for *born, to be born*, viz: Place the left hand in front of the body, a little to the right, the palm downward and slightly arched, then pass the extended right hand downward, forward, and upward, forming a short curve underneath the left, as in Fig. 127 (*Dakota* V). This is based upon the curve followed by the head of the child during birth, and is used generically. The same curve, when made with one hand, appears in Fig. 128.

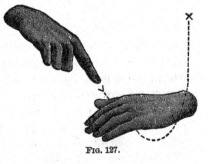

FIG. 127.

It may be of interest to compare with the Chinese *child* the Mexican abbreviated character for *man*, Fig. 129, found in Pipart in *Compte Rendu du Cong. Inter. des Américanistes, 2ᵐᵉ Session, Luxembourg*, 1877, 1878, II, 359. The figure on the right is called the abbreviated form of that by its side, yet its origin may be different.

The Chinese character for *man*, is Fig. 130, and may have the same obvious conception as a Dakota sign for the same signification: "Place the extended index, pointing upward and forward before the lower portion of the abdomen."

FIG. 129.

The Chinese specific character for *woman* is Fig. 131, the cross mark denoting the wrist, and if the remainder be considered the hand, the fingers may be imagined in the position made by many tribes, and especially the Utes, as depicting the *pudendum muliebre*, Fig. 132.

FIG. 130.

FIG. 131.   The Egyptian generic character   FIG. 128.
for *female* is ⌒ (Champollion, *Dict.*,) believed to represent the curve of the mammæ supposed to be cut off or separated from the chest, and the gesture with the same meaning was made by the Cheyenne Titchkematski, and photographed, as in Fig. 133. It forms the same figure as the Egyptian character as well as can be done by a position of the human hand.

The Chinese character for *to give water* is Fig. 134, which may be compared with the common Indian gesture *to drink, to give water*, viz: "Hand held with tips of fingers brought together and passed to the mouth,

FIG. 133.   FIG. 132.

as if scooping up water", Fig. 135, obviously from the primitive custom, as with Mojaves, who still drink with scooped hands.

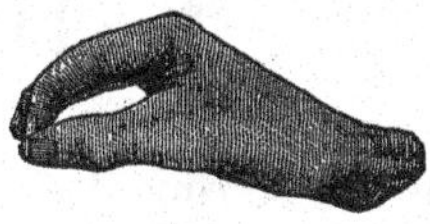

Another common Indian gesture sign for *water to drink, I want to drink*, is: "Hand brought downward past the mouth with loosely extended fingers, palm toward the face." This appears in the Mexican character for *drink*, Fig. 136, taken from Pipart, *loc. cit.*, p. 351. *Water, i. e.*, the pouring out of water with the drops falling or about to fall, is shown in Fig. 137, taken from the same author (p. 349), being the same arrangement of them as in the sign for *rain*, Fig. 114, p. 344, the hand, however, being inverted. *Rain* in the Mexican picture writing is shown by small circles inclosing a dot, as in the last two figures, but not connected together, each having a short line upward marking the line of descent.

FIG. 134.

FIG. 136.    FIG. 137.

FIG. 135.

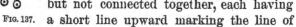

With the gesture for *drink* may be compared Fig. 138, the Egyptian Goddess Nu in the sacred sycamore tree, pouring out the water of life to the Osirian and his soul, represented as a bird, in Amenti (Sharpe, from a funereal stelē in the British Museum, in *Cooper's Serpent Myths*, p. 43).

FIG. 138.

The common Indian gesture for *river* or *stream, water,* is made by passing the horizontal flat hand, palm down, forward and to the left from the right side in a serpentine manner.

The Egyptian character for the same is Fig. 139 (Champollion, *Dict.*, p. 429). The broken line is held to represent the movement of the water on the surface of the stream. When made with one line less angular and more waving it means *water*. It is interesting to compare with this the identical character in the syllabary invented by a West African negro, Mormoru Doalu Bukere, for *water*, ⌇, mentioned by TYLOR in his *Early History of Mankind*, p. 103.

FIG. 139.

The abbreviated Egyptian sign for *water* as a stream is Fig. 140 (Champollion, *loc. cit.*), and the Chinese for the same is as in Fig. 141.

In the picture-writing of the Ojibwa the Eyptian abbreviated character, with two lines instead of three, appears with the same signification.

The Egyptian character for *weep*, Fig. 142, an eye, with tears falling, is also found in the pictographs of the Ojibwa (Schoolcraft, I, pl. 54, Fig. 27), and is also

FIG. 140.

FIG. 141.

made by the Indian gesture of drawing lines by the index repeatedly downward from the eye, though perhaps more frequently made by the full sign for *rain*, described on page 344, made with the back of the hand downward from the eye—"eye rain."

The Egyptian character for *to be strong* is Fig. 143 (Champollion, *Dict.*, p. 91), which is sufficiently obvious, but may be compared with the sign for *strong*, made by some tribes as follows: Hold the clinched fist in front of the right side, a little higher than the elbow, then throw it forcibly about six inches toward the ground.

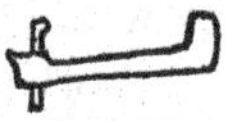

FIG. 142.

FIG. 143.

A typical gesture for *night* is as follows: Place the flat hands, horizontally, about two feet apart, move them quickly in an upward curve toward one another until the right lies across the left. "Darkness covers all." See Fig. 312, page 489.

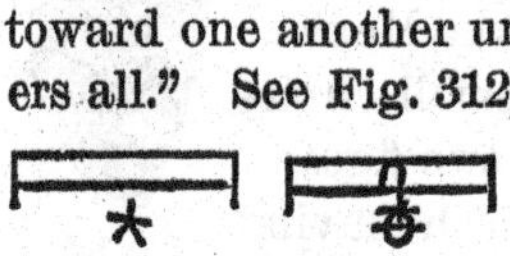

FIG. 144.

The conception of covering executed by delineating the object covered beneath the middle point of an arch or curve, appears also clearly in the Egyptian characters for *night*, Fig. 144 (Champollion, *Dict.*, p. 3).

The upper part of the character is taken separately to form that for *sky* (see page 372, *infra*).

The Egyptian figurative and linear characters, Figs. 145 and 146 (Champollion, *Dict.*, p. 28), for *calling upon* and *invocation*, also used as an interjection, scarcely require the quotation of an Indian sign, being common all over the world.

The gesture sign made by several tribes for *many* is as follows: Both hands, with spread and slightly curved fingers, are held pendent about two feet apart before the thighs; then bring them toward one another,

FIG. 145.

FIG. 146.

horizontally, drawing them upward as they come together. (*Absaroka* I; *Shoshoni and Banak* I; *Kaiowa* I; *Comanche* III; *Apache* II; *Wichita* II.) "An accumulation of objects." This may be the same motion indicated by the Egyptian character, Fig. 147, meaning to *gather together* (Champollion, *Dict.*, p. 459).

FIG. 147.

The Egyptian character, Fig. 148, which in its linear form is represented in Fig. 149, and meaning to *go*, to *come*, *locomotion*, is presented to show readers unfamiliar with hieroglyphics how a corporeal action may be included in a linear character without being obvious or at least certain, unless it should be made clear by comparison with the full figurative form or by other means. This linear form might be noticed many times without certainty or perhaps suspicion that it represented the human legs and feet in the act of walking. The same difficulty, of course, as also the same prospect of success by careful research, attends the tracing of other corporeal motions which more properly come under the head of gesture signs.

FIG. 148.

FIG. 149.

SIGN LANGUAGE WITH REFERENCE TO GRAMMAR.

Apart from the more material and substantive relations between signs and language, it is to be expected that analogies can by proper research be ascertained between their several developments in the manner of their use, that is, in their grammatic mechanism, and in the genesis of the sentence. The science of language, ever henceforward to be studied historically, must take account of the similar early mental processes in which the phrase or sentence originated, both in sign and oral utterance. In this respect, as in many others, the North American Indians may be considered to be living representatives of prehistoric man.

SYNTAX.

The reader will understand without explanation that there is in the gesture speech no organized sentence such as is integrated in the languages of civilization, and that he must not look for articles or particles or passive voice or case or grammatic gender, or even what appears in those languages as a substantive or a verb, as a subject or a predicate, or as qualifiers or inflexions. The sign radicals, without being specifically any of our parts of speech, may be all of them in turn. There is, however, a grouping and sequence of the ideographic pictures, an arrangement of signs in connected succession, which may be classed under the scholastic head of syntax. This subject, with special reference to the order of deaf-mute signs as compared with oral speech, has been the theme of much discussion, some notes of which, condensed from the speculations of M. Rémi Valade and others, follow in the next paragraph without further comment than may invite attention to the profound remark of LEIBNITZ.

In mimic construction there are to be considered both the order in which the signs succeed one another and the relative positions in which they are made, the latter remaining longer in the memory than the former, and spoken language may sometimes in its early infancy have reproduced the ideas of a sign picture without commencing from the same point. So the order, as in Greek and Latin, is very variable. In nations among whom the alphabet was introduced without the intermediary to any impressive degree of picture-writing, the order being (1) language of signs, almost superseded by (2) spoken language, and (3) alphabetic writing, men would write in the order in which they had been accustomed to speak. But if at a time when spoken language was still rudimentary, intercourse being mainly carried on by signs, figurative writing had been invented, the order of the figures would be the order of the signs, and the same order would pass into the spoken language. Hence LEIBNITZ says truly that "the writing of the Chinese might seem to have been invented by a deaf person." The oral language has not known the phases which have given to the Indo-European tongues their formation and grammatical parts. In the latter, signs were conquered by speech, while in the former, speech received the yoke.

Sign language cannot show by inflection the reciprocal dependence of words and sentences. Degrees of motion corresponding with vocal intonation are only used rhetorically or for degrees of comparison. The relations of ideas and objects are therefore expressed by placement, and their connection is established when necessary by the abstraction of ideas. The sign talker is an artist, grouping persons and things so as to show the relations between them, and the effect is that which is seen in a picture. But though the artist has the advantage in presenting in a permanent connected scene the result of several transient signs, he can only present it as it appears at a single moment. The sign talker has the succession of time at his disposal, and his scenes move and act, are localized and animated, and their arrangement is therefore more varied and significant.

It is not satisfactory to give the order of equivalent words as representative of the order of signs, because the pictorial arrangement is wholly lost; but adopting this expedient as a mere illustration of the sequence in the presentation of signs by deaf-mutes, the following is quoted from an essay by Rev. J. R. Keep, in *American Annals of the*

Deaf and Dumb, vol. xvi, p. 223, as the order in which the parable of the Prodigal Son is translated into signs:

"Once, man one, sons two. Son younger say, Father property your divide: part my, me give. Father so.—Son each, part his give. Days few after, son younger money all take, country far go, money spend, wine drink, food nice eat. Money by and by gone all. Country everywhere food little: son hungry very. Go seek man any, me hire. Gentleman meet. Gentleman son send field swine feed. Son swine husks eat, see—self husks eat want—cannot—husks him give nobody. Son thinks, say, father my, servants many, bread enough, part give away can—I none—starve, die. I decide: Father I go to, say I bad, God disobey, you disobey—name my hereafter *son*, no—I unworthy. You me work give servant like. So son begin go. Father far look: son see, pity, run, meet, embrace. Son father say, I bad, you disobey, God disobey—name my hereafter *son*, no—I unworthy. But father servants call, command robe best bring, son put on, ring finger put on, shoes feet put on, calf fat bring, kill. We all eat, merry. Why? Son this my formerly dead, now alive: formerly lost, now found: rejoice."

It may be remarked, not only from this example, but from general study, that the verb "to be" as a copula or predicant does not have any place in sign language. It is shown, however, among deaf-mutes as an assertion of presence or existence by a sign of stretching the arms and hands forward and then adding the sign of affirmation. *Time* as referred to in the conjunctions *when* and *then* is not gestured. Instead of the form, "When I have had a sleep I will go to the river," or "After sleeping I will go to the river," both deaf-mutes and Indians would express the intention by "Sleep done, I river go." Though time present, past, and future is readily expressed in signs (see page 366), it is done once for all in the connection to which it belongs, and once established is not repeated by any subsequent intimation, as is commonly the case in oral speech. Inversion, by which the object is placed before the action, is a striking feature of the language of deaf-mutes, and it appears to follow the natural method by which objects and actions enter into the mental conception. In striking a rock the natural conception is not first of the abstract idea of striking or of sending a stroke into vacancy, seeing nothing and having no intention of striking anything in particular, when suddenly a rock rises up to the mental vision and receives the blow; the order is that the man sees the rock, has the intention to strike it, and does so ; therefore he gestures, "I rock strike." For further illustration of this subject, a deaf-mute boy, giving in signs the compound action of a man shooting a bird from a tree, first represented the tree, then the bird as alighting upon it, then a hunter coming toward and looking at it, taking aim with a gun, then the report of the latter and the falling and the dying gasps of the bird. These are undoubtedly the successive steps that an artist would have taken in drawing the picture, or rather successive pictures, to illustrate the story. It is, however, urged that this pictorial order natural to deaf-mutes is not natural to the congenitally blind who are not deaf-mute, among whom it is found to be rythmical. It is asserted that blind persons not carefully educated usually converse in a metrical cadence, the action usually coming first in the structure of the sentence. The deduction is that all the senses when intact enter into the mode of intellectual conception in proportion to their relative sensitiveness and intensity, and hence no one mode of ideation can be insisted on as normal to the exclusion of others.

Whether or not the above statement concerning the blind is true, the conceptions and presentations of deaf-mutes and of Indians using sign language because they cannot communicate by speech, are confined to optic and, therefore, to pictorial arrangement.

The abbé Sicard, dissatisfied with the want of tenses and conjunctions, indeed of most of the modern parts of speech, in the natural signs, and with their inverted order, attempted to construct a new language of signs, in which the words should be given in the order of the French or other spoken language adopted, which of course required him to supply a sign for every word of spoken language. Signs, whatever their character, could not become associated with words, or suggest them, until words had been learned. The first step, therefore, was to explain by means of natural signs, as distinct from the new signs styled methodical, the meaning of a passage of verbal language. Then each word was taken separately and a sign affixed to it, which was to be learned by the pupil. If the word represented a physical object, the sign would be the same as the natural sign, and would be already understood, provided the object had been seen and was familiar; and in all cases the endeavor was to have the sign convey as strong a suggestion of the meaning of the word as was possible. The final step was to gesticulate these signs, thus associated with words, in the exact order in which the words were to stand in a sentence. Then the pupil would write the very words desired in the exact order desired. If the previous explanation in natural signs had not been sufficiently full and careful, he would not understand the passage. The methodical signs did not profess to give him the ideas, except in a very limited degree, but only to show him how to express ideas according to the order and methods of spoken language. As there were no repetitions of time in narratives in the sign language, it became necessary to unite with the word-sign for verbs others, to indicate the different tenses of the verbs, and so by degrees the methodical signs not only were required to comprise signs for every word, but also, with every such sign, a grammatical sign to indicate what part of speech the word was, and, in the case of verbs, still other signs to show their tenses and corresponding inflections. It was, as Dr. Peet remarks, a cumbrous and unwieldly vehicle, ready at every step to break down under the weight of its own machinery. Nevertheless, it was industriously taught in all our schools from the date of the founding of the American Asylum in 1817 down to about the year 1835, when it was abandoned.

The collection of narratives, speeches, and dialogues of our Indians in sign language, first systematically commenced by the present writer, several examples of which are in this paper, has not yet been sufficiently complete and exact to establish conclusions on the subject of the syntactic arrangement of their signs. So far as studied it seems to be similar to that of deaf-mutes and to retain the characteristic of pantomimes in figuring first the principal idea and adding the accessories successively in the order of importance, the ideographic expressions being in the ideologic order. If the examples given are not enough to establish general rules of construction, they at least show the natural order of ideas in the minds of the gesturers and the several modes of inversion by which they pass from the known to the unknown, beginning with the dominant idea or that supposed to be best known. Some special instances of expedients other than strictly syntactic coming under the machinery broadly designated as grammar may be mentioned.

DEGREES OF COMPARISON.

Degrees of comparison are frequently expressed, both by deaf-mutes and by Indians, by adding to the generic or descriptive sign that for "big" or "little." *Damp* would be "wet—little"; *cool*, "cold—little"; *hot*, "warm—much." The amount or force of motion also often indicates corresponding diminution or augmentation, but sometimes expresses a different shade of meaning, as is reported by Dr. Matthews with reference to the sign for *bad* and *contempt*, see page 411. This change in degree of motion is, however, often used for emphasis only, as is the raising of the voice in speech or italicizing and capitalizing in print. The Prince of Wied gives an instance of a comparison in his sign for *excessively hard*, first giving that for *hard*, viz: Open the left hand, and strike against it several times with the right (with the backs of the fingers). Afterwards he gives *hard, excessively*, as follows: Sign for *hard*, then place the left index-finger upon the right shoulder, at the same time extend and raise the right arm high, extending the index-finger upward, perpendicularly.

Rev. G. L. Deffenbaugh describes what may perhaps be regarded as an intensive sign among the Sahaptins in connection with the sign for *good; i. e., very good*. "Place the left hand in position in front of the body with all fingers closed except first, thumb lying on second, then with forefinger of right hand extended in same way point to end of forefinger of left hand, move it up the arm till near the body and then to a point in front of breast to make the sign *good*." For the latter see EXTRACTS FROM DICTIONARY page 487, *infra*. The same special motion is prefixed to the sign for *bad* as an intensive.

Another intensive is reported by Mr. Benjamin Clark, interpreter at the Kaiowa, Comanche, and Wichita agency, Indian Territory, in which after the sign for *bad* is made, that for *strong* is used by the Comanches as follows: Place the clinched left fist horizontally in front of the breast, back forward, then pass the palmar side of the right fist downward in front of the knuckles of the left.

Dr. W. H. Corbusier, assistant surgeon U. S. A., writes as follows in response to a special inquiry on the subject: "By carrying the right fist from behind forward over the left, instead of beginning the motion six inches above it, the Arapaho sign for *strong* is made. For *brave*, first strike the chest over the heart with the right fist two or three times, and then make the sign for *strong*.

"The sign for *strong* expresses the superlative when used with other signs; with coward it denotes a base coward; with hunger, starvation; and with sorrow, bitter sorrow. I have not seen it used with the sign for pleasure or that of hunger, nor can I learn that it is ever used with them."

OPPOSITION.

The principle of opposition, as between the right and left hands, and between the thumb and forefinger and the little finger, appears among Indians in some expressions for "above," "below," "forward," "back," but is not so common as among the methodical, distinguished from the natural, signs of deaf-mutes. It is also connected with the attempt to express degrees of comparison. *Above* is sometimes expressed by holding the left hand horizontal, and in front of the body, fingers open, but joined together, palm upward. The right hand is then placed horizontal, fingers open but joined, palm downward, an inch or more above the left, and raised and lowered a few inches several times, the left hand being perfectly still. If the thing indicated as "above" is only a *little* above, this concludes the sign, but if it be *considerably* above, the right hand is raised higher and higher as the height to be expressed is greater, until, if *enormously* above, the Indian will raise his right hand as high as possible, and, fixing his eyes on the zenith, emit a duplicate grunt, the more prolonged as he desires to express the greater height. All this time the left hand is held perfectly motionless. *Below* is gestured in a corresponding manner, all movement being made by the left or lower hand, the right being held motionless, palm downward, and the eyes looking down.

The code of the Cistercian monks was based in large part on a system of opposition which seems to have been wrought out by an elaborate process of invention rather than by spontaneous figuration, and is more of mnemonic than suggestive value. They made two fingers at the right side of the nose stand for "friend," and the same at the left side for "enemy," by some fanciful connection with right and wrong, and placed the little finger on the tip of the nose for "fool" merely because it had been decided to put the forefinger there for "wise man."

PROPER NAMES.

It is well known that the names of Indians are almost always connotive, and particularly that they generally refer to some animal, predicating often some attribute or position of that animal. Such names readily admit of being expressed in sign language, but there may be sometimes a confusion between the sign expressing the animal which is taken as a name-totem, and the sign used, not to designate that animal, but as a proper name. A curious device to differentiate proper names was observed as resorted to by a Brulé Dakota. After making the sign of the animal he passed his index forward from the mouth in a direct line, and explained it orally as "that is his name," *i. e.*, the name of the person referred to. This approach to a grammatic division of substantives may be correlated with the mode in which many tribes, especially the Dakotas, designate names in their pictographs, *i. e.*, by a line from the mouth of the figure drawn representing a man to the animal, also drawn with proper color or position. Fig. 150 thus shows the name of Shu^n·ka

Luta, Red Dog, an Ogallalla chief, drawn by himself. The shading of the dog by vertical lines is designed to represent red, or *gules*, according to the heraldic scheme of colors, which is used in other parts of this paper where it seemed useful to designate

FIG. 150.

particular colors. The writer possesses in painted robes many examples in which lines are drawn from the mouth to a name-totem.

It would be interesting to dwell more than is now allowed upon the peculiar objectiveness of Indian proper names with the result, if not the intention, that they can all be signified in gesture, whereas the best sign-talker among deaf-mutes is unable to translate the proper names occurring in his speech or narrative and, necessarily ceasing signs, resorts to the dactylic alphabet. Indians are generally named at first according to a clan or totemic system, but later in life often acquire a new name or perhaps several names in succession from some exploit or adventure. Frequently a sobriquet is given by no means complimentary. All of the subsequently acquired, as well as the original names, are connected with material objects or with substantive actions so as to be expressible in a graphic picture, and, therefore, in a pictorial sign. The determination to use names of this connotive character is shown by the objective translation, whenever possible, of those European names which it became necessary to introduce into their speech. William Penn was called "Onas," that being the word for feather-quill in the Mohawk dialect. The name of the second French governor of Canada was "Montmagny" which was translated by the Iroquois "Onontio"— "Great Mountain," and becoming associated with the title, has been applied to all successive Canadian governors, though the origin being generally forgotten, it has been considered as a metaphorical compliment. It is also said that Governor Fletcher was not named by the Iroquois "Cajenquiragoe," "the great swift arrow," because of his speedy arrival at a critical time, but because they had somehow been informed of the etymology of his name—"arrow maker" (*Fr. fléchier*).

GENDER.

This is sometimes expressed by different signs to distinguish the sex of animals, when the difference in appearance allows of such varied portraiture. An example is in the signs for the male and female buffalo, given by the Prince of Wied. The former is, "Place the tightly closed hands on both sides of the head, with the fingers forward;" the latter is, "Curve the two forefingers, place them on the sides of the head and move them several times." The short stubby horns of the bull appear to be indicated, and the cow's ears are seen moving, not being covered by the bull's shock mane. Tribes in which the hair of the women is differently arranged from that of men often denote their females by corresponding gesture. In many cases the sex of animals is indicated by the addition of a generic sign for male or female.

TENSE.

While it has been mentioned that there is no inflection of signs to express tense, yet the conception of present, past, and future is gestured without difficulty. A common mode of indicating the present time is by the use of signs for *to-day*, one of which is, "(1) both hands extended, palms outward; (2) swept slowly forward and to each side, to convey the idea of openness." (*Cheyenne* II.) This may combine the idea of *now* with *openness*, the first part of it resembling the general deaf-mute sign for *here* or *now*.

Two signs nearly related together are also reported as expressing the meaning *now, at once*, viz.: "Forefinger of the right hand extended, upright, &c. (J), is carried upward in front of the right side of the body and above the head so that the extended finger points toward the center of the heavens, and then carried downward in front of the right breast, forefinger still pointing upright." (*Dakota* I.) "Place the extended index, pointing upward, palm to the left, as high as and before the top of the head; push the hand up and down a slight distance several times, the eyes being directed upward at the time." (*Hidatsa* I; *Kaiowa* I; *Arikara* I; *Comanche* III; *Apache* II; *Wichita* II.)

Time past is not only expressed, but some tribes give a distinct modification to show a short or long time past. The following are examples:

Lately, recently.—Hold the left hand at arm's length, closed, with forefinger only extended and pointing in the direction of the place where the event occurred; then hold the right hand against the right shoulder, closed, but with index extended and pointing in the direction of the left. The hands may be exchanged, the right extended and the left retained, as the case may require for ease in description. (*Absaroka* I; *Shoshoni and Banak* I.)

Long ago.—Both hands closed, forefingers extended and straight; pass one hand slowly at arm's length, pointing horizontally, the other against the shoulder or near it, pointing in the same direction as the opposite one. Frequently the tips of the forefingers are placed together, and the hands drawn apart, until they reach the positions described. (*Absaroka* I; *Shoshoni and Banak* I.)

The Comanche, Wichita, and other Indians designate a *short time ago* by placing the tips of the forefinger and thumb of the left hand together, the remaining fingers closed, and holding the hand before the body with forefinger and thumb pointing toward the right shoulder; the index and thumb of the right hand are then similarly held and placed against those of the left, when the hands are slowly drawn apart a short distance. For a *long time ago* the hands are similarly held, but drawn farther apart. Either of these signs may be and frequently is preceded by those for *day, month,* or *year,* when it is desired to convey a definite idea of the time past.

A sign is reported with the abstract idea of *future,* as follows: "The arms are flexed and hands brought together in front of the body as in type-position (W). The hands are made to move in wave-like motions up and down together and from side to side." (*Oto* I.) The authority gives the poetical conception of "Floating on the tide of time."

The ordinary mode of expressing future time is, however, by some figurative reference, as the following: Count off fingers, then shut all the fingers of both hands several times, and touch the hair and tent or other white object. (*Apache* III.) "Many years; when I am old (white-haired)."

CONJUNCTIONS.

An interesting instance where the rapid connection of signs has the effect of the conjunction *and* is shown in NÁTCI'S NARRATIVE, *infra.*

PREPOSITIONS.

In the TENDOY-HUERITO DIALOGUE (page 489) the combination of gestures supplies the want of the proposition *to.*

PUNCTUATION.

While this is generally accompanied by facial expression, manner of action, or pause, instances have been noticed suggesting the device of interrogation points and periods.

Mark of interrogation.

The Shoshoni, Absaroka, Dakota, Comanche, and other Indians, when desiring to ask a question, precede the gestures constituting the information desired by a sign intended to attract attention and "asking for," viz., by holding the flat right hand, with the palm down, directed to the individual interrogated, with or without lateral oscillating motion; the gestural sentence, when completed, being closed by the same sign and a look of inquiry. This recalls the Spanish use of the interrogation points before and after the question.

Period.

A Hidatsa, after concluding a short statement, indicated its conclusion by placing the inner edges of the clinched hands together before the breast, and passing them outward and downward to their respective sides in an emphatic manner, Fig. 334, page 528. This sign is also used in other connections to express *done*.

The same mode of indicating the close of a narrative or statement is made by the Wichitas, by holding the extended left hand horizontally before the body, fingers pointing to the right, palm either toward the body or downward, and cutting edgewise downward past the tips of the left with the extended right hand. This is the same sign given in the ADDRESS OF KIN CHE-ĖSS as *cut off*, and is illustrated in Fig. 324, page 522. This is more ideographic and convenient than the device of the Abyssinian Galla, reported by M. A. d'Abbadie, who denoted a comma by a slight stroke of a leather whip, a semicolon by a harder one, and a full stop by one still harder.

GESTURES AIDING ARCHÆOLOGIC RESEARCH.

The most interesting light in which the Indians of North America can be regarded is in their present representation of a stage of evolution once passed through by our own ancestors. Their signs, as well as their myths and customs, form a part of the paleontology of humanity to be studied in the history of the latter as the geologist, with similar object, studies all the strata of the physical world. At this time it is only possible to suggest the application of gesture signs to elucidate pictographs, and also their examination to discover religious, sociologic, and historic ideas preserved in them, as has been done with great success in the radicals of oral speech.

SIGNS CONNECTED WITH PICTOGRAPHS.

The picture writing of Indians is the sole form in which they recorded events and ideas that can ever be interpreted without the aid of a traditional key, such as is required for the signification of the wampum belts of the Northeastern tribes and the *quippus* of Peru. Strips of bark, tablets of wood, dressed skins of animals, and the smooth surfaces of rock have been and still are used for such records, those most ancient, and therefore most interesting, being of course the rock etchings; but they can only be deciphered, if at all, by the ascertained principles on which the more modern and the more obvious are made. Many of the numerous and widespread rock carvings are mere idle sketches of natural objects, mainly animals, and others are as exclusively mnemonic as the wampum above mentioned. Even since the Columbian discovery some tribes have employed devices yet ruder than the rudest pictorial attempt as markers for the memory. An account of one of these is given in E. Winslow's Relation (A. D. 1624), *Col. Mass. Hist. Soc.*, 2d series, ix, 1822, p. 99, as follows:

"Instead of records and chronicles they take this course: Where any remarkable act is done, in memory of it, either in the place or by some pathway near adjoining, they make a round hole in the ground about a foot deep, and as much over, which, when others passing by behold, they inquire the cause and occasion of the same, which being once known, they are careful to acquaint all men as occasion serveth therewith. And lest such holes should be filled or grown over by any accident, as men pass by they will often renew the same; by which means many things of great antiquity are fresh in memory. So that as a man traveleth, if he can understand his guide, his journey will be the less tedious, by reason of the many historical discourses which will be related unto him."

Gregg, in *Commerce of the Prairies, New York*, 1844, II, 286, says of the Plains tribes: "When traveling, they will also pile heaps of stones upon mounds or conspicuous points, so arranged as to be understood by their passing comrades; and sometimes they set up the bleached buffalo heads, which are everywhere scattered over those plains, to indicate the direction of their march, and many other facts which may be communicated by those simple signs."

A more ingenious but still arbitrary mode of giving intelligence is

FIG. 151.

practiced at this day by the Abnaki, as reported by H. L. Masta, chief of that tribe, now living at Pierreville, Quebec. When they are in the woods, to say "I am going to the east," a stick is stuck in the ground pointing to that direction, Fig. 151. "Am not gone far," another stick is stuck across the former, close to the ground, Fig. 152. "Gone far" is the reverse, Fig. 153.. The number of days journey of proposed absence is shown by the same number of sticks across the first; thus Fig. 154 signifies five days' journey. Cutting the bark off from a tree on one, two, three or four sides near the butt means "Have had poor, poorer, poorest luck." Cutting it off all around the tree means "I am starving." Smoking a piece of birch bark and hanging it on a tree means "I am sick."

FIG. 152.

Where there has existed any form of artistic representation, however rude, and at the same time a system of ideographic gesture signs prevailed, it would be expected that the form of the latter would appear in

the former. The sign of *river* and *water* mentioned on page 358 being established, when it became necessary or desirable to draw a character or design to convey the same idea, nothing would be more natural than to use the graphic form of delineation which is also above described.

FIG. 153.

It was but one more and an easy step to fasten upon bark, skins, or rocks the evanescent air pictures that still in pigments or carvings preserve their skeleton outline, and in their ideography approach, as has been shown above, the rudiments of the phonetic alphabets that have been constructed by other peoples. A transition stage between gestures and pictographs, in which the left hand is used as a supposed drafting surface upon which the index draws lines,

FIG. 154.

is exhibited in the DIALOGUE BETWEEN ALASKAN INDIANS, *infra*, page 498. This device is common among deaf-mutes, without equal archæologic importance, as it may have been suggested by the art of writing, with which they are generally acquainted, even if not instructed in it.

The reproduction of apparent gesture lines in the pictographs made by our Indians has, for obvious reasons, been most frequent in the attempt to convey those subjective ideas which were beyond the range of an artistic skill limited to the direct representation of objects, so that the part of the pictographs which is still the most difficult of interpretation is precisely the one which the study of sign language is likely to elucidate. The following examples of pictographs of the Indians, in some cases compared with those from foreign sources, have been selected because their interpretation is definitely known and the gestures corresponding with or suggested by them are well determined.

The common Indian gesture sign for *sun* is: "Right hand closed, the index and thumb curved, with tips touching, thus approximating a circle, and held toward the sky," the position of the fingers of the hand forming a circle being shown in Fig. 155. Two

FIG. 155.

FIG. 156.   FIG. 157.

of the Egyptian characters for *sun*, Figs. 156 and 157, are plainly the universal conception of the disk. The latter, together with indications of rays, Fig. 158, and in its linear form, Fig. 159, (Champollion, *Dict.*, 9),

constitutes the Egyptian character for *light*. The rays emanating from
the whole disk appear in Figs. 160 and 161, taken from a MS. contributed by Mr. G. K. GILBERT of the United States Geological Survey, from the rock etchings
of the Moqui pueblos in Arizona. The
same authority gives from the same

FIG. 158.   FIG. 159.

FIG. 160.   FIG. 161.

locality Figs. 162 and 163 for *sun*,
which may be distinguished from several other similar etchings for *star*
also given by him, Figs. 164, 165, 166, 167, by always showing some indication of a face, the latter being absent in the characters denoting *star*.

With the above characters for sun compare Fig. 168, found at Cuzco, Peru, and
taken from Wiener's *Pérou et Bolivie,
Paris*, 1880, p. 706.

The Ojibwa pictograph for sun is seen
in Fig. 169, taken from Schoolcraft, *loc.
cit.*, v. 1, pl. 56, Fig. 67.

FIG. 162.   FIG. 168.

A gesture sign for *sunrise, morning*, is: Forefinger of right hand
crooked to represent half of the sun's disk and pointed or extended to the
left, then slightly elevated.
(*Cheyenne* II.) In this connection it may be noted that when
the gesture is care-
fully made in open
country the pointing
would generally be

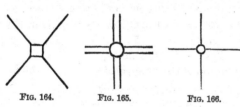

FIG. 164.   FIG. 165.   FIG. 166.   FIG. 167.

to the east, and the body turned so that its left would be in that direction. In a room in a city, or under circumstances where the points of
the compass are not specially attended to, the left side supposes the east, and the gestures relating to sun, day, &c., are
made with such reference. The half only of the disk
represented in the above gesture appears in the following Moqui pueblo etchings for *morning* and
sunrise, Figs. 170, 171, and 172. (Gilbert, *MS.*)

FIG. 169.

FIG. 168.

A common gesture for *day* is when the index and thumb form a circle
(remaining fingers closed) and are passed from east to west.

Fig. 173 shows a pictograph found in Owen's Valley, California, a sim-

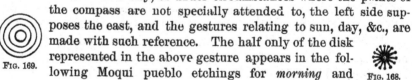

FIG 170.   FIG. 171.   FIG. 172.   FIG. 173.

ilar one being reported in the *Ann. Rep. Geog. Survey west of the* 100th
Meridian for 1876, *Washington*, 1876, pl. opp. p. 326, in which the circle
may indicate either *day* or *month* (both these gestures having the same
execution), the course of the sun or moon being represented perhaps in
mere contradistinction to the vertical line, or perhaps the latter signifies *one*.

Fig. 174 is a pictograph of the Coyotero Apaches, found at Camp Apache, in Arizona, reported in the *Tenth Ann. Rep. U. S. Geolog. and Geograph. Survey of the Territories for* 1876, *Washington,* 1878, pl. lxxvii. The sun and the ten spots of approximately the same shape represent

FIG. 175.

the days, eleven, which the party with five pack mules passed in traveling through the country. The separating lines are the nights, and may include the conception of covering over and consequent obscurity above referred to (page 354).

A common sign for *moon, month,* is the right hand closed, leaving the thumb and index extended, but curved to form a half circle and the hand held toward the sky, in a position which is illustrated in Fig. 175, to which curve the Moqui etching, Fig. 176, and the identical form in the ancient Chinese has an obvious resemblance.

The crescent, as we commonly figure the satellite, appears also in the Ojibwa pictograph, Fig. 177 (Schoolcraft, I, pl. 58), which is the same, with a slight addition, as the Egyptian figurative character.

FIG. 174.

FIG. 176.    FIG. 177.

The sign for *sky,* also *heaven,* is generally made by passing the index from east to west across the zenith. This curve is apparent in the Ojibwa pictograph Fig. 178, reported in Schoolcraft, I, pl. 18, Fig. 21, and is abbreviated in the Egyptian character with the same meaning, Fig. 179 (Champollion, *Dict.,* p. 1).

FIG. 178.   FIG. 179.

A sign for *cloud* is as follows: (1) Both hands partially closed, palms facing and near each other, brought up to level with or slightly above, but in front of the head; (2) suddenly separated sidewise, describing a curve like a scallop; this scallop motion is repeated for "many clouds." (*Cheyenne* II.)

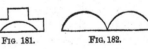

FIG. 180.   FIG. 181.   FIG. 182.

The same conception is in the Moqui etchings, Figs. 180, 181, and 182 (Gilbert *MS.*)

The Ojibwa pictograph for *cloud* is more elaborate, Fig. 183, reported in Schoolcraft, I, pl. 58. It is composed of the sign for *sky,* to which that for *clouds* is added, the latter being reversed as compared with the Moqui etchings, and picturesquely hanging from the sky.

FIG. 183.

The gesture sign for *rain* is described and illustrated on page 344. The pictograph, Fig. 184, reported as found in New Mexico by

Lieutenant Simpson (*Ex. Doc. No.* 64, *Thirty-first Congress, first session,* 1850, pl. 9) is said to represent Montezuma's adjutants sounding a blast

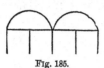

Fig. 185.

to him for rain. The small character inside the curve which represents the sky, corresponds with the gesturing hand. The Moqui etching (Gilbert *MS.*) for *rain, i. e.*, a cloud from which the drops are falling, is given in Fig. 185.

FIG. 184.

The same authority gives two signs for *lightning*, Figs.

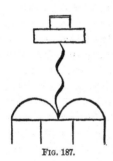

FIG. 186.

186 and 187. In the latter the sky is shown, the changing direction of the streak, and clouds with rain falling. The part relating specially to the streak is portrayed in a sign as follows: Right hand elevated before and above the head, forefinger pointing upward, brought down with great rapidity with a sinuous, undulating motion; finger still ex-

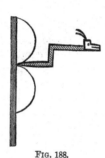

FIG. 187.

FIG. 188.

FIG. 189.

tended diagonally downward toward the right. (*Cheyenne* II.)

Figs. 188 and 189 also represent *lightning*, taken by Mr. W. H. Jack-

FIG. 190.

son, photographer of the late U. S. Geolog. and Geog. Survey, from the decorated walls of an estufa in the Pueblo de Jemez, New Mexico. The former is blunt, for harmless, and the latter terminating in an arrow or spear point, for destructive or fatal, lightning.

A common sign for *speech, speak,* among the Indians is the repeated motion of the index in a straight line forward from the mouth. This line, indicating the voice, is shown in Fig.

FIG. 191.

190, taken from the *Dakota Calendar*, being the expression for the fact that "the-Elk-that-hollows walking," a Minneconjou chief, "made medicine." The ceremony is indicated by the head of an albino buffalo. A more graphic portraiture of the conception of *voice* is in Fig. 191, representing an antelope and the whistling sound produced by the animal on being surprised or alarmed. This is taken from MS. drawing book

Fig. 192.

of an Indian prisoner at Saint Augustine, Fla., now in the Smithsonian Institution, No. 30664.

Fig. 192 is the exhibition of wrestling for a turkey, the point of interest in the present connection being the lines from the mouth to the objects of conversation. It is taken from the above-mentioned MS. drawing book.

The wrestlers, according to the foot prints, had evidently come together, when, meeting the returning hunter, who is wrapped in his blanket with only one foot protruding, they separated and threw off their blankets, leggings, and moccasins, both endeavoring to win the turkey, which lies between them and the donor.

In Fig. 193, taken from the same MS. drawing book, the conversation is about the lassoing, shooting, and final killing of a buffalo which has wandered to a camp. The dotted lines indicate footprints. The Indian drawn under the buffalo having secured the animal by the fore feet, so informs his companions, as indicated by the line drawn from his mouth to the object mentioned; the left-hand figure, having also secured the buffalo by the horns, gives his nearest comrade an opportunity to strike it with an ax, which he no

doubt announces that he will do, as the line from his mouth to the head
of the animal suggests.   The Indian in the upper left-hand corner is told
by a squaw to take an arrow and join his companions, when he turns his
head to inform her that he has one already, which fact he demonstrates
by holding up the weapon.

FIG. 193.

The Mexican pictograph, Fig. 194, taken from Kingsborough, II, pt.
1, p. 100, is illustrative of the sign made by the Arikara and Hidatsa for
tell and *conversation*.   *Tell me* is: Place the flat right hand, palm upward, about fifteen inches in front of the right side of the face, fingers
pointing to the left and front; then draw the hand inward toward and
against the bottom of the chin.   For *conversation*, talking between two
persons, both hands are held before the breast, pointing forward, palms
up, the edges being moved several times toward one another.   Perhaps,
however, the picture in fact only means the common poetical image of
"flying words."

Fig. 195 is one of Landa's characters, found in *Rel. des choses de Yucatan*, p. 316, and suggests one of the gestures for *talk* and more especially

FIG. 194.

that for *sing*, in which the extended and separated fingers are passed forward and slightly downward from the mouth—"many voices." Although the last opinion about the bishop is unfavorable to the authenticity of his work, yet even if it were prepared by a Maya, under his supervision, the latter would probably have given him some genuine native conceptions, and among them gestures would be likely to occur.

The natural sign for *hear*, made both by Indians and deaf-mutes, consisting in the motion of the index, or the index and thumb joined, in a straight line to the ear, is illustrated in the Ojibwa pictograph Fig. 196, "hearing ears," and those of the same people, Figs. 197 and 198, the latter

of which is a hearing serpent, and the former means "I hear, but your words are from a bad heart," the hands being thrown out as in the final part of a gesture for *bad heart*, which is made by the hand being closed and held near the breast, with the back toward the breast, then as the arm is suddenly extended the hand is opened and the fingers separated from each other. (*Mandan and Hidatsa* I.)

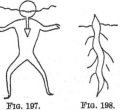

FIG. 195.   FIG. 196.

FIG. 197.   FIG. 198.

The final part of the gesture, representing the idea of *bad*, not connected with heart, is illustrated in Fig. 236 on page 411.

The above Ojibwa pictographs are taken from Schoolcraft, *loc. cit.* I, plates 58, 53, 59.

Fig. 199, a bas-relief taken from Dupaix's Monuments of New Spain, in Kingsborough, *loc. cit.* IV, pt. 3, p. 31, has been considered to be a royal edict or command. The gesture *to hear* is plainly depicted, and the

Fig. 199.

right hand is directed to the persons addressed, so the command appears to be uttered with the preface of *Hear Ye! Oyez!*

The typical sign for *kill* or *killed* is: Right hand clinched, thumb lying along finger tips, elevated to near the shoulder, strike downward and outward vaguely in the direction of the object to be killed. The abbreviated sign is simply to clinch the right hand in the manner described and strike it down and out from the right side. (*Cheyenne* II.) This gesture also appears among the Dakotas and is illustrated in Fig. 200.

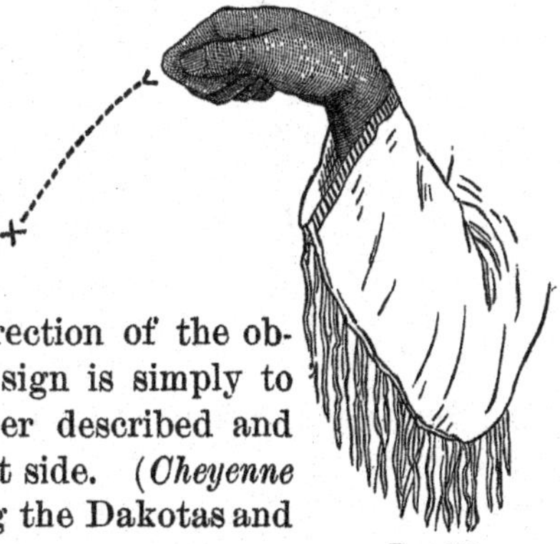

FIG. 201.

FIG. 200.

Fig. 201, taken from the *Dakota Calendar*, illustrates this gesture. It represents the year in which a Minneconjou chief was stabbed in the shoulder by a Gros Ventre, and afterwards named "Dead Arm" or "Killed Arm." At first the figure was supposed to show the perma· nent drawing up of the arm by anchylosis, but that would not be likely to be the result of the wound described, and with knowledge of the gesture the meaning is more clear.

Fig. 202, taken from *Report upon the Reconnaissance of Northwestern*

FIG. 202.

Wyoming, &c., Washington, 1875, p. 207, Fig. 53, found in the Wind River Valley, Wyoming Territory, was interpreted by members of a Shoshoni and Banak delegation to Washington in 1880 as "an Indian killed another." The latter is very roughly delineated in the horizontal figure, but is also represented by the line under the hand of the upright figure, meaning the same individual. At the right is the scalp taken and the two feathers showing the dead warrior's rank. The arm nearest the prostrate foe shows the gesture for *killed.*

The same gesture appears in Fig. 203, from the same authority and

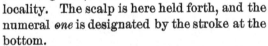

locality. The scalp is here held forth, and the numeral *one* is designated by the stroke at the bottom.

Fig. 204, from the same locality and authority, was also interpreted by the Shoshoni and Banak. It appears from their description that a Blackfoot had attacked the habitation of some of his own people. The right-hand upper figure represents his horse with the lance suspended from the side. The lower figure illustrates the log house built against a stream. The dots are the prints of the horse's hoofs, while the two lines running outward from the upper inclosure show that two thrusts of the

FIG. 203.

lance were made over the wall of the house, thus killing the occupant and securing two bows and five arrows, as represented in the left-hand group. The right-hand figure of that group shows the hand raised in the attitude of making the gesture for *kill.*

As the Blackfeet, according to the interpreters, were the only Indians in the locality mentioned who constructed log houses, the drawing becomes additionally interesting, as an attempt appears to have been made to illustrate the crossing of the logs at the corners, the gesture for which (*log-house*) will be found on page 428.

Fig. 205 is the Egyptian character for *veneration, to glorify* (Champollion, *Dict.*, 29), the author's understanding being that the hands are raised in surprise, astonishment.

The Menomoni Indians now begin their prayers by raising their hands in the same manner. They may have been influenced in this respect by the attitudes of their missionaries in prayer and benediction. The Apaches, who have received less civilized tuition, in a religious gesture corresponding with prayer spread their hands opposite the face, palms up and backward, apparently expressing the desire to *receive*.

Fig. 206 is a copy of an Egyptian tablet reproduced from Cooper's *Serpent Myths*, page 28. A priest kneels before the great goddess Ranno, while supplicating her favor. The conception of the author is that the hands are raised by the supplicant to shield his face from the glory of the divinity. It may be compared with signs for asking for

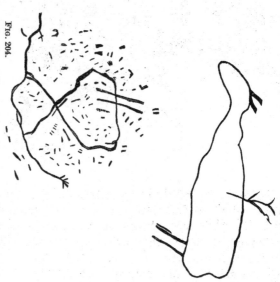

Fig. 204.

mercy and for giving mercy to another, the former being: Extend both forefingers, pointing upward, palms toward the breast, and hold the hands before the chest; then draw them inward toward their respective sides, and pass them upward as high as the sides of the head by either cheek.

(*Kaiowa* I; *Comanche* III; *Apache* II; *Wichita* II.)   The latter, *to have mercy on another*, as made by the same tribes, is: Hold both hands nearly side by side before the chest, palms forward, forefinger only extended and pointing upward; then move them forward and upward, as if passing them by the cheeks of another person from the breast to the sides of the head.

A similar gesture for *supplication* appears in Fig. 207, taken from Kingsborough, *loc. cit.*, III, pt. I, p. 24.

FIG. 205.   An Indian gesture sign for *smoke*, and also one for *fire*, has been de-

FIG. 206.

scribed above, page 344. With the former is connected the Aztec design (Fig. 208) taken from Pipart, *loc. cit.*, II, 352, and the latter appears in Fig. 209, taken from Kingsborough, III, pt. I, p. 21.

A sign for *medicine-man, shaman*, is thus described: "With its index-

finger extended and pointing upward, or all the fingers extended, back of hand outward, move the right hand from just in front of the forehead, spirally upward, nearly to arm's length, from left to right." (*Dakota* IV.)

Fig. 210, from the *Dakota Calendar*, represents the making of medicine or conjuration. In that case the head and horns of a white buffalo cow were used.

FIG. 207.

Fig. 211 is an Ojibwa pictograph taken from Schoolcraft, *loc. cit.*, representing *medicine-man, meda*. With these horns and spiral may be collated Fig. 212 which portrays the ram-headed Egyptian god Knuphis, or Chnum, the spirit, in a shrine on the boat of the sun, canopied by the serpent-goddess Ranno, who is also seen facing him inside the shrine. This is reproduced from Cooper's *Serpent Myths*, p. 24. The same deity is represented in Champollion, *Gram.*, p. 113, as reproduced in Fig. 213.

FIG. 208.

Fig. 214 is an Ojibwa pictograph found in Schoolcraft, I, pl. 58, and given as *power*. It corresponds with the sign for *doctor*, or *medicine-man*, made by the Absarokas by passing the extended and separated index and second finger of the right hand upward from the forehead, spirally, and is considered to indicate "superior knowledge." Among the Otos,

FIG. 209.

as part of the sign with the same meaning, both hands are raised to the side of the head, and the extended in-

FIG. 210.

dices pressing the temples.

Fig. 215 is also an Ojibwa pictograph from Schoolcraft I, pl. 59, and is said to signify *Meda's power*. It corresponds with another sign made for *medicine-man* by the Absarokas and Comanches, viz, The hand passed upward before the forehead, with in-

FIG. 211.

dex loosely extended. Combined with the sign for *sky*, before given, page 372, it means knowledge of superior matters; spiritual power.

The common sign for *trade* is made by extending the forefingers, holding them obliquely upward, and crossing them at right angles to one another, usually in front of the chest. This is often abbreviated by merely crossing the forefingers, see Fig. 278, page 452.

FIG. 212.

It is illustrated in Fig. 216, taken from the Prince of Wied's *Travels in the Interior of North America; London*, 1843, p. 352.

FIG. 213.

To this the following explanation is given: "The cross signifies, 'I will barter or trade.' Three animals are drawn on the right hand of the cross; one is a buffalo; the two others, a weasel (*Mustela Canadensis*) and an otter. The writer offers in exchange for the skins of these animals (probably meaning that of a white buffalo) the articles which he has drawn on the left side of the cross.

FIG. 214.

FIG. 215.

He has, in the first place, depicted a beaver very plainly, behind which there is a gun; to the left of the beaver are thirty strokes, each ten separated by a longer line; this means, I will give thirty beaver skins and a gun for the skins of the three animals on the right hand of the cross."

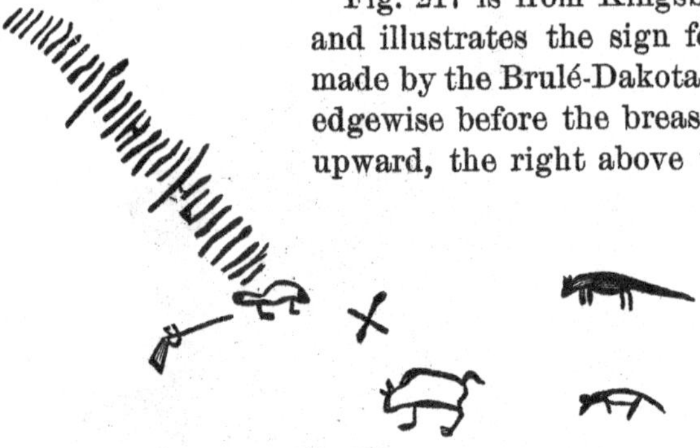

Fig. 217 is from Kingsborough, III, pt. 1, p. 25, and illustrates the sign for *to give* or *to present*, made by the Brulé-Dakotas by holding both hands edgewise before the breast, pointing forward and upward, the right above the left, then throwing them quickly downward until the forearms reach a horizontal position.

Fig. 218 is taken from the *Dakota Calendar*, representing a successful raid of the Absarokas or Crows upon the Brulé-Sioux, in which the village of the latter was surprised and a large number of horses captured. That

FIG. 216.

capture is exhibited by the horse-tracks moving from the *village*, the gesture sign for which is often made by a circle formed either by the opposed thumbs and forefingers of both hands or by a circular motion of both hands, palms inward, toward each other. In some cases there is a motion of

FIG. 217.

the circle, from above downward, as formed.

Fig. 219, from Kingsborough I, pt. 3, p. 10, represents *Chapultepec*, "Mountain of the Locust," by one enormous locust on top of a hill. This shows the mode of augmentation in the same manner as is often done by an exaggerated gesture. The curves at the base of the mountain are intelligible only as being formed in the sign for *many*, described on pages 359 and 488.

FIG. 218.

Fig. 220, taken from Pipart, *loc. cit.*, is the Mexican pictograph for *soil cultivated*, i. e., tilled and planted. Fig. 221, from the same authority, shows the sprouts coming from the cultivated soil, and may be compared with the signs for *grass* and *grow* on page 343.

The gesture sign for *road, path,* is sometimes made by indicating two

lines forward from the body, then imitating walking with the hands upon the imaginary road. The same natural representation of road is seen in Fig. 222, taken from Pipart, *loc. cit.,* page 352. A place where two roads meet— cross-roads—is shown in Fig. 223, from Kingsborough. Two persons are evidently having a chat in sign language at the cross-roads.

FIG. 220.

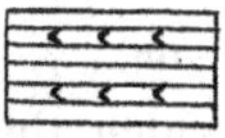

If no gesture is actually included in all of the foregoing pictographs, it is seen that a gesture sign is made with the same conception

FIG. 219.

FIG. 221.

which is obvious in the ideographic pictures. They are selected as specially transparent and clear.

Many others less distinct are now the subject of examination for elucidation. The following examples are added to show the ideographic style of pictographs not connected with gestures, lest it may be suspected that an attempt is made to prove that gestures are always included in or connected with them.

FIG. 222.

Fig. 224, from the *Dakota Calendar,* refers to the small-pox which broke out in the

FIG. 224.

FIG. 223.

year (1802) which it specifies. Fig. 225 shows in the design at the

FIG. 225.

left, a warning or notice, that though a goat can climb up the rocky trail a horse will tumble—"No Thoroughfare." This was contributed by Mr. J. K. Hillers, photographer of the United States Geological Survey, as observed by him in Cañon De Chelly, New Mexico, in 1880.

SIGNS CONNECTED WITH ETHNOLOGIC FACTS.

The present limits permit only a few examples of the manner in which the signs of Indians refer to sociologic, religious, historic, and other ethnologic facts. They may incite research to elicit further information of the same character.

The Prince of Wied gives in his list of signs the heading *Partisan*, a term of the Canadian voyageurs, signifying a leader of an occasional or volunteer war party, the sign being reported as follows: Make first the sign of the pipe, afterwards open the thumb and index-finger of the right hand, back of the hand outward, and move it forward and upward in a curve. This is explained by the author's account in a different connection, that to become recognized as a leader of such a war party as above mentioned, the first act among the tribes using the sign was the consecration, by fasting succeeded by feasting, of a medicine pipe without ornament, which the leader of the expedition afterward bore before him as his

FIG. 226.

FIG. 227.

badge of authority, and it therefore naturally became an emblematic sign. This sign with its interpretation supplies a meaning to Fig. 226 from the *Dakota Calendar* showing "One Feather," a Sioux chief who raised in that year a large war party against the Crows, which fact is simply denoted by his holding out demonstratively an unornamented pipe. In connection with this subject, Fig. 227, drawn and explained by Two Strike, an Ogalala Dakota, relating to his own achievements, displays four plain pipes to exhibit the fact that he had led four war parties.

The sign of the pipe or of smoking is made in a different manner, when used to mean *friend*, as follows: (1) Tips of the two first fingers of the right hand placed against or at right angles to the mouth; (2) suddenly elevated upward and outward to imitate smoke expelled. (*Cheyenne* II). "We two smoke together." This is illustrated in the Ojibwa pictograph, Fig. 228, taken from Schoolcraft I, pl. 59.

FIG. 228.   A ceremonial sign for *peace, friendship*,   FIG. 229.

is the extended fingers, separated (R), interlocked in front of the breast, hands horizontal, backs outward. (*Dakota* I.) Fig. 229 from the *Dakota Calendar* exhibits the beginning of this gesture. When the idea conveyed is peace or friendship with the whites, the hand shaking of the latter is adopted as in Fig. 230, also taken from the *Dakota Calendar*, and referring to the peace made in 1855 by General Harney, at Fort Pierre, with a number of the tribes of the Dakotas.

FIG. 230.

It is noticeable that while the ceremonial gesture of uniting or linking hands is common and ancient in token of peace, the practice of shaking hands on meeting, now the annoying etiquette of the Indians in their intercourse with whites, was not until very recently and is even now seldom used by them between each other, and is clearly a foreign importation. Their fancy for affectionate greeting was in giving a pleasant bodily sensation by rubbing each other on the breast, abdomen, and limbs, or by a hug. The senseless and inconvenient custom of shaking hands is, indeed, by no means general throughout the world, and in the extent to which it prevails in the United States is a subject of ridicule by foreigners. The Chinese, with a higher conception of politeness, shake their own hands. The account of a recent observer of the meeting of two polite Celestials is: "Each placed the fingers of one hand over the fist of the other, so that the thumbs met, and then standing a few feet apart raised his hands gently up and down in front of his breast. For special courtesy, after the foregoing gesture, they place the hand which had been the actor in it on the stomach of its owner, not on that part of the interlocutor, the whole proceeding being subjective, but perhaps a relic of objective performance." In Miss Bird's *Unbeaten Tracks in Japan*, London, 1880, the following is given as the salutatory etiquette of that empire: "As acquaintances come in sight of each other they slacken their pace and approach with downcast eyes and averted faces as if neither were worthy of beholding each other; then they bow low, so low as to bring the face, still kept carefully averted, on a level with the knees, on which the palms of the hands are pressed. Afterwards, during the friendly strife of each to give the *pas* to the other, the palms of the hands are diligently rubbed against each other."

The interlocking of the fingers of both hands above given as an Indian sign (other instances being mentioned under the head of SIGNALS, *infra*) is also reported by R. Brough Smyth, *Aborigines of Victoria, loc. cit.*, Vol. II, p. 308, as made by the natives of Cooper's

FIG. 231.

Creek, Australia, to express the highest degree of friendship, including a special form of hospitality in which the wives of the entertainer performed a part. Fig. 231 is reproduced from a cut in the work referred to.

But besides this interlocked form of signifying the union of friendship the hands are frequently grasped together. Sometimes the sign is abbreviated by simply extending the hand as if about to grasp that of another, and sometimes the two forefingers are laid side by side, which last sign also means, *same, brother* and *companion*. For description and

25 A E

illustration of these three signs, see respectively pages 521, 527, and 317. A different execution of the same conception of union or linking to signify *friend* is often made as follows: Hook the curved index over the curved forefinger of the left hand, the palm of the latter pointing forward, the palm of the right hand being turned toward the face; remaining fingers and thumbs being closed. (*Dakota* VIII.) Fig. 232.

Wied's sign for *medicine* is "Stir with the right hand into the left, and afterward blow into the latter." All persons familiar with the Indians will understand that the term "medicine," foolishly enough adopted by both French and English to express the aboriginal magic arts, has no therapeutic significance. Very few even pretended remedies were administered to the natives and

FIG. 232.

probably never by the professional shaman, who worked by incantation, often pulverizing and mixing the substances mystically used, to prevent their detection. The same mixtures were employed in divination. The author particularly mentions Mandan ceremonies, in which a white "medicine" stone, as hard as pyrites, was produced by rubbing in the hand snow or the white feathers of a bird. The blowing away of the disease, considered to be introduced by a supernatural power foreign to the body, was a common part of the juggling performance.

A sign for *stone* is as follows: With the back of the arched right hand (H) strike repeatedly in the palm of the left, held horizontal, back outward, at the height of the breast and about a foot in front; the ends of the fingers point in opposite directions. (*Dakota* I.) From its use when the stone was the only hammer.

A suggestive sign for *knife* is reported, viz: Cut past the mouth with the raised right hand. (*Wied.*) This probably refers to the general practice of cutting off food, as much being crammed into the mouth as can be managed and then separated from the remaining mass by a stroke of a knife. This is specially the usage with fat and entrails, the Indian delicacies.

An old sign for *tomahawk, ax*, is as follows: Cross the arms and slide the edge of the right hand, held vertically, down over the left arm. (*Wied.*) This is still employed, at least for a small hatchet, or "dress tomahawk," and would be unintelligible without special knowledge. The essential point is laying the extended right hand in the bend of the left elbow. The sliding down over the left arm is an almost unavoidable but quite unnecessary accompaniment to the sign, which indicates the way in which the hatchet is usually carried. Pipes, whips, bows and arrows, fans, and other dress or emblematic articles of the "buck" are seldom or never carried in the bend of the left elbow as is the ax. The pipe is usually held in the left hand.

The following sign for *Indian village* is given by Wied: Place the open thumb and forefinger of each hand opposite to each other, as if to make a circle, but leaving between them a small interval; afterward move them from above downward simultaneously. The villages of the tribes with which the author was longest resident, particularly the Mandans and Arikaras, were surrounded by a strong circular stockade, spaces or breaks in the circle being left for entrance or exit.

Signs for *dog* are made by some of the tribes of the plains essentially the same as the following: Extend and spread the right, fore, and middle fingers, and draw the hand about eighteen inches from left to right across the front of the body at the height of the navel, palm downward, fingers pointing toward the left and a little downward, little and ring fingers to be loosely closed, the thumb against the ring-finger. (*Dakota* IV.) The sign would not be intelligible without knowledge of the fact that before the introduction of the horse, and even yet, the dog has been used to draw the tent- or lodge-poles in moving camp, and the sign represents the trail. Indians less nomadic, who built more substantial lodges, and to whom the material for poles was less precious than on the plains, would not have comprehended this sign without such explanation as is equivalent to a translation from a foreign language, and the more general one is the palm lowered as if to stroke gently in a line conforming to the animal's head and neck. It is abbreviated by simply lowering the hand to the usual height of the wolfish aboriginal breed, and suggests *the* animal *par excellence* domesticated by the Indians and made a companion.

Several examples connected with this heading may be noticed under the preceding head of gestures connected with pictographs, and others of historic interest will be found among the TRIBAL SIGNS, *infra*.

NOTABLE POINTS FOR FURTHER RESEARCHES.

It is considered desirable to indicate some points to which for special reasons the attention of collaborators for the future publication on the general subject of sign language may be invited. These now follow:

INVENTION OF NEW SIGNS.

It is probable that signs will often be invented by individual Indians who may be pressed for them by collectors to express certain ideas, which signs of course form no part of any current language; but while that fact should, if possible, be ascertained and reported, the signs so invented are not valueless merely because they are original and not traditional, if they are made in good faith and in accordance with the principles of sign formation. Less error will arise in this direction than from the misinterpretation of the idea intended to be conveyed by spontaneous signs. The process resembles the coining of new words to which the higher languages owe their copiousness. It is observed in the signs invented by Indians for each new product of civilization brought to their notice.

An interesting instance is in the sign for *steamboat*, made at the request of the writer by White Man (who, however, did not like that sobriquet and announced his intention to change his name to Lean Bear), an Apache, in June, 1880, who had a few days before seen a steamboat for the first time. After thinking a moment he gave an original sign, described as follows:

Make the sign for *water*, by placing the flat right hand before the face, pointing upward and forward, the back forward, with the wrist as high as the nose; then draw it down and inward toward the chin; then with both hands indicate the outlines of a horizontal oval figure from before the body back to near the chest (being the outline of the deck); then place both flat hands, pointing forward, thumbs higher than the outer edges, and push them forward to arms'-length (illustrating the powerful forward motion of the vessel).

An original sign for *telegraph* is given in NATCI'S NARRATIVE, *infra*.

An Indian skilled in signs, as also a deaf-mute, at the sight of a new object, or at the first experience of some new feeling or mental relation, will devise some mode of expressing it in pantomimic gesture or by a combination of previously understood signs, which will be intelligible to others, similarly skilled, provided that they have seen the same objects or have felt the same emotions. But if a number of such Indians or deaf-mutes were to see an object—for instance an elephant—for the first time, each would perhaps hit upon a different sign, in accordance with the characteristic appearance most striking to him. That animal's trunk is generally the most attractive lineament to deaf-mutes, who make a sign by pointing to the nose and moving the arm as the trunk is moved. Others regard the long tusks as the most significant feature, while others are struck by the large head and small eyes. This diversity of conception brings to mind the poem of "The Blind Men and the Elephant," which with true philosophy in an amusing guise explains how the sense of touch led the "six men of Indostan" severally to liken the animal to a wall, spear, snake, tree, fan, and rope. A consideration of invented or original signs, as showing the operation of the mind of an Indian or other uncivilized gesturer, has a psychologic interest, and as connected with the vocal expression, often also invented at the same time, has further value.

DANGER OF SYMBOLIC INTERPRETATION.

In the examination of sign language it is important to form a clear distinction between signs proper and symbols. The terms signs and symbols are often used interchangeably, but with liability to misconstruction, as many persons, whether with right or wrong lexical definition, ascribe to symbols an occult and mystic signification. All characters in Indian picture-writing have been loosely styled symbols, and, as there is no logical distinction between the characters impressed with enduring form and when merely outlined in the ambient air, all Indian gestures, motions, and attitudes might with equal appropriateness be called symbolic. While, however, all symbols come under the generic head of signs, very few signs are in accurate classification symbols. S. T. Coleridge has defined a symbol to be a sign included in the idea it represents. This may be intelligible if it is intended that an ordinary sign is extraneous to the concept and, rather than suggested by it, is invented to express it by some representation or analogy, while a symbol may be evolved by a process of thought from the concept itself; but it is no very exhaustive or practically useful distinction. Symbols are less obvious and more artificial than mere signs, require convention, are not only abstract, but metaphysical, and often need explanation from history, religion, and customs. They do not depict but suggest subjects; do not speak directly through the eye to the intelligence, but presuppose in the mind knowledge of an event or fact which the sign recalls. The symbols of the ark, dove, olive branch, and rainbow would be wholly meaningless to people unfamiliar with the Mosaic or some similar cosmology, as would be the cross and the crescent to those ignorant of history. The last named objects appeared in the class of *emblems* when used in designating the conflicting powers of Christendom and Islamism. Emblems do not necessarily require any analogy between the objects representing, and the objects or qualities represented, but may arise from pure accident. After a scurrilous jest the beggar's wallet became the emblem of the confederated nobles, the Gueux of the Netherlands; and a sling, in the early minority of Louis XIV, was adopted from the refrain of a song by the Frondeur opponents of Mazarin. The portraiture of a fish, used, especially by the early Christians, for the name and title of Jesus Christ was still more accidental, being, in the Greek word ἰχθύς, an acrostic composed of the initials of the several Greek words signifying that name and title. This origin being unknown to persons whose religious enthusiasm was as usual in direct proportion to their ignorance, they expended much rhetoric to prove that there was some true symbolic relation between an actual fish and the Saviour of men. Apart from this misapplication, the fish undoubtedly became an emblem of Christ and of Christianity, appearing frequently on the Roman catacombs and at one time it was used hermeneutically.

The several tribal signs for the Sioux, Arapahos, Cheyennes, &c., are their emblems precisely as the star-spangled flag is that of the United States, but there is nothing symbolic in any of them. So the signs for individual chiefs, when not merely translations of their names, are emblematic of their family totems or personal distinctions, and are no more symbols than are the distinctive shoulder-straps of army officers. The *crux ansata* and the circle formed by a snake biting its tail are symbols, but *consensus* as well as invention was necessary for their establishment, and the Indians have produced nothing so esoteric, nothing which they intended for hermeneutic as distinct from descriptive or mnemonic purposes. Sign language can undoubtedly be and is employed to express highly metaphysical ideas, but to do that in a symbolic system requires a development of the mode of expression consequent upon a similar development of the mental idiocrasy of the gesturers far beyond any yet found among historic tribes north of Mexico. A very few of their signs may at first appear to be symbolic, yet even those on closer examination will probably be relegated to the class of emblems.

The point urged is that while many signs can be used as emblems and both can be converted by convention into symbols or be explained as such by perverted ingenuity, it is futile to seek for that form of psychologic exuberance in the stage of development attained by the tribes now under consideration. All predetermination to interpret either their signs or their pictographs on the principles of symbolism as understood or pretended to be understood by its admirers, and as are sometimes properly applied to Egyptian hieroglyphs, results in mooning mysticism. This was shown by a correspondent who enthusiastically lauded the *Dakota Calendar* (edited by the present writer, and which is a mere figuration of successive occurrences in the history of the people), as a numerical exposition of the great doctrines of the Sun religion in the equations of time, and proved to his own satisfaction that our Indians preserved hermeneutically the lost geometric cultus of pre-Cushite scientists.

Another exhibition of this vicious practice was recently made in the interpretation of an inscribed stone alleged to have been unearthed near Zanesville, Ohio. Two of the characters were supposed, in liberal exercise of the imagination, to represent the *A* and *Ω* of the Greek alphabet. At the comparatively late date when the arbitrary arrangement of the letters of that alphabet had become fixed, the initial and concluding letters might readily have been used to represent respectively the beginning and the end of any series or number of things, and this figure of speech was employed in the book of Revelations. In the attempted interpretation of the inscription mentioned, which was hawked about to many scientific bodies, and published over the whole country, the supposed alpha and omega were assumed to constitute a universal as well as sacred symbol for the everlasting Creator. The usual *menu* of Roman feasts, commencing with eggs and ending with apples, was also commonly known at the time when the book of Revelations was written, and the phrase "*ab ovo usque ad mala*" was as appropriate as "from alpha to omega" to express "from the beginning to the end." In deciphering the stone it would, therefore, be as correct in principle to take one of its oval and one of its round figures, call them egg and apple, and make them the symbols of eternity. In fact, not depending wholly for significance upon the order of courses of a feast or the accident of alphabetical position, but having intrinsic characteristics in reference to the origin and fruition of life, the egg and apple translation would be more acceptable to the general judgment, and it is recommended to enthusiasts who insist on finding symbols where none exist.

SIGNS USED BY WOMEN AND CHILDREN.

For reasons before given it is important to ascertain the varying extent of familiarity with sign language among the members of the several tribes, how large a proportion possesses any skill in it, and the average amount of their vocabulary. It is also of special interest to learn the degree to which women become proficient, and the age at which children commence its practice; also whether they receive systematic instruction in it. The statement was made by Titchkemátski that the Kaiowa and Comanche women know nothing of sign language, while the Cheyenne women are versed in it. As he is a Cheyenne, however, he may not have a large circle of feminine acquaintances beyond his own tribe, and his negative testimony is not valuable. Rev. A. J. Holt, from large experience, asserts that the Kaiowa and Comanche women do know and practice sign language, though the Cheyenne either are more familiar with it than the Kaiowa or have a greater degree of expertness. The Comanche women, he says, are the peers of any sign-talkers. Colonel Dodge makes the broad assertion that even among the Plains tribes only the old, or at least middle-aged, men use signs properly, and that he has not seen any women or even young men who were at all reliable in signs. He gives this statement to show the difficulty in acquiring sign language; but it is questionable if the fact is not simply the result of the rapid disuse of signs, in many tribes, by which cause women, not so frequently called upon to employ them, and the younger generation, who have had no necessity to learn them, do not become expert. Disappearing Mist, as before mentioned, remembers a time when the Iroquois women and children used signs more than the men.

It is also asserted, with some evidence, that the signs used by males and females are different, though mutually understood, and some minor points for observation may be indicated, such as whether the commencement of counting upon the fingers is upon those of the right or the left hand, and whether Indians take pains to look toward the south when suggesting the course of the sun, which would give the motion from left to right.

A suggestion has been made by a correspondent that some secret signs of affiliation are known and used by the members of the several associations, religious and totemic, which have been often noticed among several Indian tribes. No evidence of this has been received, but the point is worth attention.

POSITIVE SIGNS RENDERED NEGATIVE.

In many cases positive signs to convey some particular idea are not reported, and in their place a sign with the opposite signification is given, coupled with the sign of negation. In other words, the only mode of expressing the intended meaning is supposed to be by negation of the reverse of what it is desired to describe. In this manner "fool—no," would be "wise," and "good—no," would be "bad." This mode of expression is very frequent as a matter of option when the positive signs are in fact also used. The reported absence of positive signs for the ideas negatived is therefore often made with as little propriety as if when an ordinary speaker chose to use the negative form "not good," it should be inferred that he was ignorant of the word "bad." It will seldom prove, on proper investigation, that where sign language has reached and retained any high degree of development it will show such poverty as to require the expedient of negation of an affirmative to express an idea which is intrinsically positive.

DETAILS OF POSITIONS OF FINGERS.

The signs of the Indians appear to consist of motions more often than of positions—a fact enhancing the difficulty both of their description and illustration—and the motions when not designedly abbreviated are generally large, free, and striking, seldom minute. It seems also to be the general rule among Indians as among deaf-mutes that the point of the finger is used to trace outlines and the palm of the hand to describe surfaces. From an examination of the identical signs made to each other for the same object by Indians of the same tribe and band, they appear to make many gestures with little regard to the position of the fingers and to vary in such arrangement from individual taste. Some of the elaborate descriptions, giving with great detail the attitude of the fingers of any particular gesturer and the inches traced by his motions, are of as little necessity as would be, when quoting a written word, a careful reproduction of the flourishes of tailed letters and the thickness of down-strokes in individual chirography. The fingers must be in *some* position, but that is frequently accidental, not contributing to the general and essential effect. An example may be given in the sign for *white man* which Medicine Bull, *infra*, page 491, made by drawing the palmar surface of the extended index across the forehead, and in LEAN WOLF'S COMPLAINT, *infra*, page 526, the same motion is made by the back of the thumb pressed upon the middle joint of the index, fist closed. The execution as well as the conception in both cases was the indication of the line of the hat on the forehead, and the position of the fingers in forming the line is altogether immaterial. There is often also a custom or "fashion" in which not only different tribes, but different persons in the same tribe, gesture the same sign with different degrees of beauty, for there is calligraphy in sign language, though no recognized orthography. It is nevertheless better to describe and illustrate with unnecessary minuteness than to fail in reporting a real distinction. There are, also, in fact, many signs formed by mere positions of the fingers, some of which are abbreviations, but in others the arrangement of the fingers in itself forms a picture. An instance of the latter is one of the signs given for the *bear*, viz.: Middle and third finger of right hand clasped down by the thumb, fore and little finger extended crooked downward. See

EXTRACTS FROM DICTIONARY, *infra*. This reproduction of the animal's peculiar claws, with the hand in any position relative to the body, would suffice without the pantomime of scratching in the air, which is added only if the sign without it should not be at once comprehended.

MOTIONS RELATIVE TO PARTS OF THE BODY.

The specified relation of the positions and motions of the hands to different parts of the body is essential to the formation and description of many signs. Those for *speak*, *hear*, and *see*, which must be respectively made relative to the mouth, ear and eye, are manifest examples; and there are others less obviously dependent upon parts of the body, such as the heart or head, which would not be intelligible without apposition. There are also some directly connected with height from the ground and other points of reference. In, however, a large proportion of the signs noted the position of the hands with reference to the body can be varied or disregarded. The hands making the motions can be held high or low, as the gesturer is standing or sitting, or the person addressed is distant or near by. These variations have been partly discussed under the head of abbreviations. While descriptions made with great particularity are cumbrous, it is desirable to give the full detail of that gesture which most clearly carries out the generic conception,

with, if possible, also the description of such deviations and abbreviations as are most confusing. For instance, it is well to explain that signs for *yes* and *no*, described with precise detail as in EXTRACTS FROM DICTIONARY, *infra*, are also often made by an Indian when wrapped in his blanket with only a forefinger protruding, the former by a mere downward and the latter by a simple outward bend of that finger. An example may be also taken from the following sign for *lie, falsehood*, made by an Arikara, Fig. 233. in which

Fig. 233.

the separated index and second fingers are moved sidewise in a downward line near but below the mouth, which may be compared with other executions of the motion with the same position of the fingers directly forward from the mouth, and with that given in LEAN WOLF'S COMPLAINT, illustrated on page 528, in which the motion is made carelessly across the body. The original sign was undoubtedly made directly from the mouth, the conception being " two tongues," two accounts or opposed statements, one of which must be false, but the finger-position coming to be established for two tongues has relation to the original conception whether or not made near or in reference to the mouth, the latter being understood.

It will thus be seen that sometimes the position of the fingers is material as forming or suggesting a figure without reference to motion, while in other cases the relative position of the hands to each other and to parts of the body are significant without any special arrangement of the fingers. Again, in others, the lines drawn in the air by the hand or hands execute the conception without further detail. In each case only the essential details, when they can be ascertained, should be minutely described.

SUGGESTIONS FOR COLLECTING SIGNS.

The object always should be, not to translate from English into signs, but to ascertain the real signs and their meaning. By far the most satisfactory mode of obtaining this result is to induce Indians or other gesturers observed to tell stories, make speeches, or hold talks in gesture, with one of themselves as interpreter in his own oral language if the latter is understood by the observer, and, if not, the words, not the signs, should be translated by an intermediary linguistic interpreter. It will be easy afterward to dissect and separate the particular signs used. This mode will determine the genuine shade of meaning of each sign, and corresponds with the plan now adopted by the Bureau of Ethnology for the study of the tribal vocal languages, instead of that arising out of exclusively missionary purposes, which was to force a translation of the Bible from a tongue not adapted to its terms and ideas, and then to compile a grammar and dictionary from the artificial result. A little ingenuity will direct the more intelligent or complaisant gesturers to the expression of the thoughts, signs for which are specially sought; and full orderly descriptions of such tales and talks with or even without analysis and illustration are more desired than any other form of contribution.

The original authorities, or the best evidence, for Indian signs—*i. e.*, the Indians themselves—being still accessible, the collaborators in this work should not be content with secondary authority. White sign talkers and interpreters may give some genuine signs, but they are very apt to interpolate their own improvements. Experience has led to the apparently paradoxical judgment that the direct contribution of signs purporting to be those of Indians, made by a habitual practitioner of signs who is not an Indian, is less valuable than that of a discriminating observer who is not himself an actor in gesture speech. The former, being to himself the best authority, unwittingly invents and modifies signs, or describes what he thinks they ought to be, often with a very different conception from that of an Indian. Sign language not being fixed and limited, as is the case with oral languages, expertness in it is not necessarily a proof of accuracy in any one of its forms. The proper inquiry is not what a sign might, could, would, or should be, or what is the best sign for a particular meaning, but what is any sign actually used for such meaning. If any one sign is honestly invented or adopted by any one man, whether Indian, African, Asiatic, or deaf-mute, it has its value, but it should be identified to be in accordance with the fact and should not be subject to the suspicion that it has been assimilated or garbled in interpretation. Its prevalence and special range present considerations of different interest and requiring further evidence.

The genuine signs alone should be presented to scholars, to give their studies proper direction, while the true article can always be adulterated into a composite jargon by those whose ambition is only to be sign talkers instead of making an honest contribution to ethnologic and philologic science. The few direct contributions of interpreters to the present work are, it is believed, valuable, because they were made without expression of self-conceit or symptom of possession by a pet theory.

MODE IN WHICH RESEARCHES HAVE BEEN MADE.

It is proper to give to all readers interested in the subject, but particularly to those whose collaboration for the more complete work above mentioned is solicited, an account of the mode in which the researches have thus far been conducted and in which it is proposed to continue them. After study of all that could be obtained in printed form, and a considerable amount of personal correspondence, the results were embraced in a pamphlet issued by the Bureau of Ethnology in the early part of 1880, entitled "*Introduction to the Study of Sign Language among the North American Indians as Illustrating the Gesture Speech of Mankind.*" In this, suggestions were made as to points and manner of observation and report, and forms prepared to secure uniformity and accuracy were explained, many separate sheets of which with the pamphlet were distributed, not only to all applicants, but to all known and accessible persons in this country and abroad who, there was reason to hope, would take sufficient interest in the undertaking to contribute their assistance. Those forms, TYPES OF HAND POSITIONS, OUTLINES OF ARM POSITIONS, AND EXAMPLES, thus distributed, are reproduced at the end of this paper.

The main object of those forms was to eliminate the source of confusion produced by attempts of different persons at the difficult description of positions and motions. The comprehensive plan required that many persons should be at work in many parts of the world. It will readily be understood that if a number of persons should undertake to describe in words the same motions, whether of pantomimists on the stage or of other gesturers, even if the visual perception of all the observers should be the same in the apprehension of the particular gestures, their language in description might be so varied as to give very diverse impressions to a reader who had never seen the gestures described. But with a set form of expressions for the typical positions, and skeleton outlines to be filled up and, when necessary, altered in a uniform style, this source of confusion is greatly reduced. The graphic lines drawn to represent the positions and motions on the same diagrams will vary but little in comparison with the similar attempt of explanation in writing. Both modes of description were, however, requested, each tending to supplement and correct the other, and provision was also made for the notation of such striking facial changes or emotional postures as might individualize or accentuate the gestures. It was also pointed out that the prepared sheets could be used by cutting and pasting them in the proper order, for successive signs forming a speech or story, so as to exhibit the semiotic syntax. Attention was specially directed to the importance of ascertaining the intrinsic idea or conception of all signs, which it was urged should be obtained directly from the persons using them and not by inference.

In the autumn of 1880 the prompt and industrious co-operation of many observers in this country, and of a few from foreign lands, had supplied a large number of descriptions which were collated and collected into a quarto volume of 329 pages, called "*A Collection of Gesture Signs and Signals of the North American Indians, with some comparisons.*"

This was printed on sized paper with wide margins to allow of convenient correction and addition. It was not published, but was regarded as proof, a copy being sent to each correspondent with a request for his annotations, not only in revision of his own contribution, but for its comparison with those made by others. Even when it was supposed that mistakes had been made in either description or reported conception, or both, the contribution was printed as received, in order that a number of skilled and disinterested persons might examine it and thus ascertain the amount and character of error. The attention of each contributor was invited to the fact that, in some instances, a sign as described by one of the other contributors might be recognized as intended for the same idea or object as that furnished by himself, and the former might prove to be the better description. Each was also requested to examine if a peculiar abbreviation or fanciful flourish might not have induced a difference in his own description from that of another contributor with no real distinction either in conception or essential formation. All collaborators were therefore urged to be candid in admitting, when such cases occurred, that their own descriptions were mere unessential variants from others printed, otherwise to adhere to their own and explain the true distinction. When the descriptions showed substantial identity, they were united with the reference to all the authorities giving them.

Many of these copies have been returned with valuable annotations, not only of correction but of addition and suggestion, and are now being collated again into one general revision.

The above statement will, it is hoped, give assurance that the work of the Bureau of Ethnology has been careful and thorough. No scheme has been neglected which could be contrived and no labor has been spared to secure the accuracy and completeness of the publication still in preparation. It may also be mentioned that although the writer has made personal observations of signs, no description of any sign has been printed by him which rests on his authority alone. Personal controversy and individual bias were thus avoided. For every sign there is a special reference either to an author or to some one or more of the collaborators. While the latter have received full credit, full responsibility was also imposed, and that course will be continued.

No contribution has been printed which asserted that any described sign is used by "all Indians," for the reason that such statement is not admissible evidence unless the authority had personally examined all Indians. If any credible person had affirmatively stated that a certain identical, or substantially identical, sign had been found by him, actually used by Abnaki, Absaroka, Arikara, Assiniboins, etc., going through the whole list of tribes, or any definite portion of that list, it would have been so inserted under the several tribal heads. But the expression "all Indians," besides being insusceptible of methodical classification, involves hearsay, which is not the kind of authority desired in a serious study. Such loose talk long delayed the recognition of Anthropology as a science. It is true that some general statements of this character are made by some old authors quoted in the Dictionary, but their descriptions are reprinted, as being all that can be used of the past, for whatever weight they may have, and they are kept separate from the linguistic classification given below.

Regarding the difficulties met with in the task proposed, the same motto might be adopted as was prefixed to Austin's *Chironomia*: "*Non sum nescius, quantum susceperim negotii, qui motus corporis exprimere verbis, imitari scriptura conatus sim voces.*" *Rhet. ad Herenn*, 1. 3. If the descriptive recital of the signs collected had been absolutely restricted to written or printed words the work would have been still more difficult and the result less intelligible. The facilities enjoyed of presenting pictorial illustrations have been of great value and will give still more assistance in the complete work than in the present paper.

In connection with the subject of illustrations it may be noted that a writer in the *Journal of the Military Service Institution of the United States*, Vol. II, No. 5, the same who had before invented the mode of describing signs by "means" mentioned on page 330 *supra*, gives a curious distinction between deaf-mute and Indian signs regarding their respective capability of illustration, as follows: "This French system is taught, I believe, in most of the schools for deaf-mutes in this country, and in Europe; but so great has been the difficulty of fixing the hands in space, either by written description or illustrated cuts, that no text books are used. I must therefore conclude that the Indian sign language is not only the more natural, but the more simple, as the gestures can be described quite accurately in writing, and I think can be illustrated." The readers of this paper will also, probably, "think" that the signs of Indians can be illustrated, and as the signs of deaf-mutes are often identical with the Indian, whether expressing the same or different ideas, and when not precisely identical are always made on the same principle and with the same members, it is not easy to imagine any greater difficulty either in their graphic illustration or in their written description. The assertion is as incorrect as if it were paraphrased to declare that a portrait of an Indian in a certain attitude could be taken by a pencil or with the camera while by some occult influence the same artistic skill would be paralysed in attempting that of a deaf-mute in the same attitude. In fact, text books on the "French system" are used and one in the writer's possession published in Paris twenty-five years ago, contains over four hundred illustrated cuts of deaf-mute gesture signs.

The proper arrangement and classification of signs will always be troublesome and unsatisfactory. There can be no accurate translation either of sentences or of words from signs into written English. So far from the signs representing words as logographs, they do not in their presentation of the ideas of actions, objects, and events, under physical forms, even suggest words, which must be skillfully fitted to them by the glossarist and laboriously derived from them by the philologer. The use of words in formulation, still more in terminology, is so wide a departure from primitive conditions as to be incompatible with the only primordial language yet discovered. No vocabulary of signs will be exhaustive for the simple reason that the signs are exhaustless, nor will it be exact because there cannot be a correspondence between signs and words taken individually. Not only do words and signs both change their meaning from the context, but a single word may express a complex idea, to be fully rendered only by a group of signs, and, *vice versâ*, a single sign may suffice for a number of words. The elementary principles by which the combinations in sign and in the oral languages of civilization are effected are also discrepant. The attempt must therefore be made to collate and compare the signs according to general ideas, conceptions, and, if possible, the ideas and conceptions of the gesturers themselves, instead of in order of words as usually arranged in dictionaries.

The hearty thanks of the writer are rendered to all his collaborators, a list of whom is given below, and will in future be presented in a manner more worthy of them. It remains to give an explanation of the mode in which a large collection of signs has been made directly by the officers of the Bureau of Ethnology. Fortunately for this undertaking, the policy of the government brought to Washington during the year

1880 delegations, sometimes quite large, of most of the important tribes. Thus the most intelligent of the race from many distant and far separated localities were here in considerable numbers for weeks, and indeed, in some cases, months, and, together with their interpreters and agents, were, by the considerate order of the honorable Secretary of the Interior, placed at the disposal of this Bureau for all purposes of gathering ethnologic information. The facilities thus obtained were much greater than could have been enjoyed by a large number of observers traveling for a long time over the continent for the same express purpose. The observations relating to signs were all made here by the same persons, according to a uniform method, in which the gestures were obtained directly from the Indians, and their meaning (often in itself clear from the context of signs before known) was translated sometimes through the medium of English or Spanish, or of a native language known in common by some one or more of the Indians and by some one of the observers. When an interpreter was employed, he translated the words used by an Indian in his oral paraphrase of the signs, and was not relied upon to explain the signs according to his own ideas. Such translations and a description of minute and rapidly-executed signs, dictated at the moment of their exhibition, were sometimes taken down by a phonographer, that there might be no lapse of memory in any particular, and in many cases the signs were made in successive motions before the camera, and prints secured as certain evidence of their accuracy. Not only were more than one hundred Indians thus examined individually, at leisure, but, on occasions, several parties of different tribes, who had never before met each other, and could not communicate by speech, were examined at the same time, both by inquiry of individuals whose answers were consulted upon by all the Indians present, and also by inducing several of the Indians to engage in talk and story-telling in signs between themselves. Thus it was possible to notice the difference in the signs made for the same objects and the degree of mutual comprehension notwithstanding such differences. Similar studies were made by taking Indians to the National Deaf Mute College and bringing them in contact with the pupils.

By far the greater part of the actual work of the observation and record of the signs obtained at Washington has been ably performed by Dr. W. J. HOFFMAN, the assistant of the present writer. When the latter has made personal observations the former has always been present, taking the necessary notes and sketches and superintending the photographing. To him, therefore, belongs the credit for all those references in the following "LIST OF AUTHORITIES AND COLLABORATORS," in which it is stated that the signs were obtained at Washington from Indian delegations. Dr. HOFFMAN acquired in the West, through his service as acting assistant surgeon, United States Army, at a large reservation, the indispensable advantage of becoming acquainted with the Indian character so as to conduct skillfully such researches as that in question, and in addition has the eye and pencil of an artist, so that he seizes readily, describes with physiological accuracy, and reproduces in action and in permanent illustration all shades of gesture exhibited. Nearly all of the pictorial illustrations in this paper are from his pencil. For the remainder, and for general superintendence of the artistic department of the work, thanks are due to Mr. W. H. HOLMES, whose high reputation needs no indorsement here.

LIST OF AUTHORITIES AND COLLABORATORS.

1. A list prepared by WILLIAM DUNBAR, dated Natchez, June 30, 1800, collected from tribes then "west of the Mississippi," but probably not from those very far west of that river, published in the *Transactions of the American Philosophical Society*, vol. vi, pp. 1–8, as read January 16, 1801, and communicated by Thomas Jefferson, president of the society.

2. The one published in *An Account of an Expedition from Pittsburgh to the Rocky Mountains, performed in the years* 1819–1820, *Philadelphia*, 1823, vol. i, pp. 378–394. This expedition was made by order of the Hon. J. C. Calhoun, Secretary of War, under the command of Maj. S. H. LONG, of the United States Topographical Engineers, and is commonly called· James' Long's Expedition. This list appears to have been collected chiefly by Mr. T. Say, from the Pani, and the Kansas, Otos, Missouris, Iowas, Omahas, and other southern branches of the great Dakota family.

3. The one collected by Prince MAXIMILIAN von WIED-NEUWIED in *Reise in das Innere Nord-America in den Jahren* 1832 *bis* 1834. *Coblenz*, 1839 [— 1841], vol. ii, pp. 645–653. His statement is, "the Arikaras, Mandans, Minnitarris [Hidatsa], Crows [Absaroka], Cheyennes, Snakes [Shoshoni], and Blackfeet [Satsika] all understand certain signs, which, on the contrary, as we are told, are unintelligible to the Dakotas, Assiniboins, Ojibwas, Krihs [Crees], and other nations. The list gives examples of the sign language of the former." From the much greater proportion of time spent and information obtained by the author among the Mandans and Hidatsa then and now dwelling near Fort Berthold, on the Upper Missouri, it might be safe to consider that all the signs in his list were in fact procured from those tribes. But as the author does not say so, he is not made to say so in this work. If it shall prove that the signs now used by the Mandans and Hidatsa more closely resemble those on his list than do those of other tribes, the internal evidence will be verified. This list is not published in the English edition, *London*, 1843, but appears in the German, above cited, and in the French, *Paris*, 1840. Bibliographic reference is often made to this distinguished explorer as "Prince Maximilian," as if there were but one possessor of that Christian name among princely families. For brevity the reference in this paper will be *Wied*.

No translation of this list into English appears to have been printed in any shape before that recently published by the present writer in the *American Antiquarian*, vol. ii, No. 3, while the German and French editions are costly and difficult of access, so the collection cannot readily be compared by readers with the signs now made by the same tribes.

The translation now presented is based upon the German original, but in a few cases where the language was so curt as not to give a clear idea, was collated with the French edition of the succeeding year, which, from some internal evidence, appears to have been published with the assistance or supervision of the author.   Many of the descriptions are, however, so brief and indefinite in both their German and French forms that they necessarily remain so in the present translation. The princely explorer, with the keen discrimination shown in all his work, doubtless observed what has escaped many recent reporters of Indian signs, that the latter depend much more upon motion than mere position, and are generally large and free, seldom minute.   His object was to express the general effect of the motion rather than to describe it with such precision as to allow of its accurate reproduction by a reader who had never seen it.   To have presented the signs as now desired for comparison, toilsome elaboration would have been necessary, and even that would not in all cases have sufficed without pictorial illustration.

On account of the manifest importance of determining the prevalence and persistence of the signs as observed half a century ago, an exception is made to the general arrangement hereafter mentioned by introducing after the *Wied* signs remarks of collaborators who have made special comparisons, and adding to the latter the respective names of those collaborators—as, (*Matthews*), (*Boteler*).   It is hoped that the work of those gentlemen will be imitated, not only regarding the *Wied* signs, but many others.

4. The signs given to publication by Capt. R. F. BURTON, which, it would be inferred, were collected in 1860–'61, from the tribes met or learned of on the overland stage route, including Southern Dakotas, Utes, Shoshoni, Arapahos, Crows, Pani, and Apaches.   They are contained in *The City of the Saints, New York*, 1862, pp. 123–130.

Information has been recently received to the effect that this collection was not made by the distinguished English explorer from his personal observation, but was obtained by him from one man in Salt Lake City, a Mormon bishop, who, it is feared, gave his own ideas of the formation and use of signs rather than their faithful description.

5. A list read by Dr. D. G. MACGOWAN, at a meeting of the American Ethnological Society, January 23, 1866, and published in the *Historical Magazine*, vol. x, 1866, pp. 86, 87, purporting to be the signs of the Caddos, Wichitas, and Comanches.

6. Annotations by Lieut. HEBER M. CREEL, Seventh United States Cavalry, received in January, 1881.   This officer is supposed to be specially familiar with the Cheyennes, among whom he lived for eighteen months; but his recollection is that most of the signs described by him were also observed among the Arapaho, Sioux, and several other tribes.

7. A special contribution from Mr. F. F. GERARD, of Fort A. Lincoln, D. T., of signs obtained chiefly from a deaf-mute Dakota, who has trav-

eled among most of the Indian tribes living between the Missouri River and the Rocky Mountains. Mr. Gerard's own observations are based upon the experience of thirty-two years' residence in that country, during which long period he has had almost daily intercourse with Indians. He states that the signs contributed by him are used by the Blackfeet, (Satsika), Absaroka, Dakota, Hidatsa, Mandan, and Arikara Indians, who may in general be considered to be the group of tribes referred to by the Prince of Wied.

In the above noted collections the generality of the statements as to locality of the observation and use of the signs rendered it impossible to arrange them in the manner considered to be the best to study the diversities and agreements of signs. For that purpose it is more convenient that the names of the tribe or tribes among which the described signs have been observed should catch the eye in immediate connection with them than that those of the observers only should follow. Some of the latter indeed have given both similar and different signs for more than one tribe, so that the use of the contributor's name alone would create confusion. To print in every case the name of the contributor, together with the name of the tribe, would seriously burden the paper and be unnecessary to the student, the reference being readily made to each authority through this LIST which also serves as an index. The seven collections above mentioned will therefore be referred to by the names of the authorities responsible for them. Those which now follow are arranged alphabetically by tribes, under headings of Linguistic Families according to Major J. W. POWELL's classification, which are also given below in alphabetic order. Example: The first authority is under the heading ALGONKIAN, and, concerning only the Abnaki tribe, is referred to as (*Abnaki* I), Chief MASTA being the personal authority.

ALGONKIAN.

Abnaki I. A letter dated December 15, 1879, from H. L. MASTA, chief of the Abnaki, residing near Pierreville, Quebec.

Arapaho I. A contribution from Lieut. H. R. LEMLY, Third United States Artillery, compiled from notes and observations taken by him in 1877, among the Northern Arapahos.

Arapaho II. A list of signs obtained from O-QO-HIS′-SA (the Mare, better known as Little Raven) and NA′-WATO (Left Hand), members of a delegation of Arapaho and Cheyenne Indians, from Darlington, Ind. T., who visited Washington during the summer of 1880.

Cheyenne I. Extracts from the *Report of Lieut.* J. W. ABERT, *of his Examination of New Mexico in the years* 1846–'47, in Ex. Doc. No. 41, Thirtieth Congress, first session, Washington, 1848, p. 417, *et seq.*

Cheyenne II. A list prepared in July, 1879, by Mr. FRANK H. CUSHING, of the Smithsonian Institution, from continued interviews with TITO-KE-MA′-TSKI (Cross-Eyes), an intelligent Cheyenne, then employed at that Institution.

Cheyenne III. A special contribution with diagrams from Mr. BEN CLARK, scout and interpreter, of signs collected from the Cheyennes during his long residence among that tribe.

Cheyenne IV. Several communications from Col. RICHARD I. DODGE, A. D. C., United States Army, author of *The Plains of the Great West and their Inhabitants, New York*, 1877, relating to his large experience with the Indians of the prairies.

Cheyenne V. A list of signs obtained from WA-Uⁿ' (Bob-tail) and MO-HI'NUK-MA-HA'-IT (Big Horse), members of a delegation of Arapaho and Cheyenne Indians from Darlington, Ind. T., who visited Washington during the summer of 1880.

Ojibwa I. The small collection of J. G. KOHL, made about the middle of the present century, among the Ojibwas around Lake Superior. Published in his *Kitchigami. Wanderings Around Lake Superior, London*, 1860.

Ojibwa II. Several letters from the Very Rev. EDWARD JACKER, Pointe St. Ignace, Mich., respecting the Ojibwas.

Ojibwa III. A communication from Rev. JAMES A. GILFILLAN, White Earth, Minn., relating to signs observed among the Ojibwas during his long period of missionary duty, still continuing.

Ojibwa IV. A list from Mr. B. O. WILLIAMS, Sr., of Owosso, Mich., from recollection of signs observed among the Ojibwas of Michigan sixty years ago.

Ojibwa V. Contributions received in 1880 and 1881 from Mr. F. JACKER, of Portage River, Houghton County, Michigan, who has resided many years among and near the tribe mentioned.

Sac, Fox, and Kickapoo I. A list from Rev. H. F. BUCKNER, D. D., of Eufaula, Ind. T., consisting chiefly of tribal signs observed by him among the Sac and Fox, Kickapoos, &c., during the early part of the year 1880.

DAKOTAN.

Absaroka I. A list of signs obtained from DE-E'-KI-TCIS (Pretty Eagle), É-TCI-DI-KA-HĂTC'-KI (Long Elk), and PE-RI'-TCI-KA'-DI-A (Old Crow), members of a delegation of Absaroka or Crow Indians from Montana Territory, who visited Washington during the months of April and May, 1880.

Dakota I. A comprehensive list, arranged with great care and skill, from Dr. CHARLES E. MCCHESNEY, acting assistant surgeon, United States Army, of signs collected among the Dakotas (Sioux) near Fort Bennett, Dakota, during the year 1880. Dr. McChesney requests that recognition should be made of the valuable assistance rendered to him by Mr. WILLIAM FIELDEN, the interpreter at Cheyenne Agency, Dakota Territory.

Dakota II. A short list from Dr. BLAIR D. TAYLOR, assistant surgeon, United States Army, from recollection of signs observed among the Sioux during his late service in the region inhabited by that tribe.

Dakota III. A special contribution from Capt. A. W. CORLISS, Eighth United States Infantry, of signs observed by him during his late service among the Sioux.

Dakota IV. A copious contribution with diagrams from Dr. WILLIAM H. CORBUSIER, assistant surgeon, United States Army, of signs obtained from the Ogalala Sioux at Pine Ridge Agency, Dakota Territory, during 1879–'80.

Dakota V. A report of Dr. W. J. HOFFMAN, from observations among the Teton Dakotas while acting assistant surgeon, United States Army, and stationed at Grand River Agency, Dakota, during 1872–'73.

Dakota VI. A list of signs obtained from PE-ZHI' (Grass), chief of the Blackfoot Sioux; NA-ZU'-LA-TA^n-KA (Big Head), chief of the Upper Yanktonais; and CE-TA$^{n'}$-KI^n-YA^n (Thunder Hawk), chief of the Uncpapas, Teton Dakotas, located at Standing Rock, Dakota Territory, while at Washington in June, 1880.

Dakota VII. A list of signs obtained from SHUN'-KA LU-TA (Red Dog), an Ogalala chief from the Red Cloud Agency, who visited Washington in company with a large delegation of Dakotas in June, 1880.

Dakota VIII. A special list obtained from TA-TA$^{n'}$KA WA-KA^n (Medicine Bull), and other members of a delegation of Lower Brulé Dakotas, while at Washington during the winter of 1880–'81.

Hidatsa I. A list of signs obtained from TCE-CAQ'-A-DAQ-A-QIC (Lean Wolf), chief of the Hidatsa, located at Fort Berthold, Dakota Territory, while at Washington with a delegation of Sioux Indians, in June, 1880.

Mandan and Hidatsa I. A valuable and illustrated contribution from Dr. WASHINGTON MATTHEWS, assistant surgeon, United States Army, author of *Ethnography and Philology of the Hidatsa Indians, Washington*, 1877, &c., lately prepared from his notes and recollections of signs observed during his long service among the Mandan and Hidatsa Indians of the Upper Missouri.

Omaha I. A special list from Rev. J. OWEN DORSEY, lately missionary at Omaha Agency, Nebraska, from observations made by him at that agency in 1880.

Oto I. An elaborate list, with diagrams, from Dr. W. C. BOTELER, United States Indian service, collected from the Otos at the Oto Agency, Nebraska, during 1879–'80.

Oto and Missouri I. A similar contribution by the same authority respecting the signs of the Otos and Missouris, of Nebraska, collected during the winter of 1879–'80, in the description of many of which he was joined by Miss KATIE BARNES.

Ponka I. A short list from Rev. J. OWEN DORSEY, obtained by him in 1880 from the Ponkas in Nebraska.

Ponka II. A short list obtained at Washington from KHI-DHA-SKĂ, (White Eagle), and other chiefs, a delegation from Kansas in January, 1881.

IROQUOIAN.

Iroquois I. A list of signs contributed by the Hon. HORATIO HALE, author of "Philology" of the Wilkes Exploring Expedition, &c., now

residing at Clinton, Ontario, Canada, obtained in June, 1880, from
SAKAYENKWARATON (Disappearing Mist), familiarly known as John
Smoke Johnson, chief of the Canadian division of the Six Nations, or
Iroquois proper, now a very aged man, residing at Brantford, Canada.

Wyandot I. A list of signs from HEN'-TO (Gray Eyes), chief of the
Wyandots, who visited Washington during the spring of 1880, in the
interest of that tribe, now dwelling in Indian Territory.

KAIOWAN.

Kaiowa I. A list of signs from SITTIMGEA (Stumbling Bear), a Kaiowa
chief from Indian Territory, who visited Washington in June, 1880.

KUTINEAN.

Kutine I. A letter from J. W. POWELL, Esq., Indian superintendent,
British Columbia, relating to his observations among the Kutine and
others.

PANIAN.

Arikara I. A list of signs obtained from KUA-NUQ'-KNA-UI'-UQ (Son of
the Star), chief of the Arikaras, residing at Fort Berthold, Dakota Territory, while at Washington with a delegation of Indians, in June, 1880.

Pani I. A short list obtained from "ESAU," a Pani Indian, acting as
interpreter to the Ponka delegation at Washington, in January, 1881.

PIMAN.

Pima and Papago I. A special contribution obtained from ANTONITO,
son of the chief of the Pima Indians in Arizona Territory, while on a
visit to Washington in February, 1881.

SAHAPTIAN.

Sahaptin I. A list contributed by Rev. G. L. DEFFENBAUGH, of Lap-
wai, Idaho, giving signs obtained at Kamiah, Idaho, chiefly from FELIX,
chief of the Nez Percés, and used by the Sahaptin or Nez Percés.

SHOSHONIAN.

Comanche I. Notes from Rev. A. J. HOLT, Denison, Texas, respecting
the Comanche signs, obtained at Anadarko, Indian Territory.

Comanche II. Information obtained at Washington, in February, 1880,
from Maj. J. M. HAWORTH, Indian inspector, relating to signs used by
the Comanches of Indian Territory.

Comanche III. A list of signs obtained from KOBI (Wild Horse), a
Comanche chief from Indian Territory, who visited Washington in June,
1880.

Pai-Ute I. Information obtained at Washington from NA'TCI, a Pai-
Ute chief, who was one of a delegation of that tribe to Washington in
January, 1880.

Shoshoni and Banak I. A list of signs obtained from TENDOY (The
Climber), TISIDIMIT, PETE, and WI'AGAT, members of a delegation of

Shoshoni and Banak chiefs from Idaho, who visited Washington during the months of April and May, 1880.

Ute I. A list of signs obtained from ALEJANDRE, GA-LO-TE, AUGUS-TIN, and other chiefs, members of a delegation of Ute Indians of Colorado, who visited Washington during the early months of the year 1880.

TINNEAN.

Apache I. A list of signs obtained from HUERITO (Little Blonde), AGUSTIN VIJEL, and SANTIAGO LARGO (James Long), members of a delegation of Apache chief from Tierra Amarilla, New Mexico, who were brought to Washington in the months of March and April, 1880.

Apache II. A list of signs obtained from NA'-KA'-NA'-NI-TEN (White Man), an Apache chief from Indian Territory, who visited Washington in June, 1880.

Apache III. A large collection made during the summer of 1880, by Dr. FRANCIS H. ATKINS, acting assistant surgeon, United States Army, from the Mescalero Apaches, near South Fork, N. Mex.

Kutchin I. A communication, received in 1881, from Mr. IVAN PE-TROFF, special agent United States census, transmitting a dialogue, taken down by himself in 1866, between the Kenaitze Indians on the lower Kinnik River, in Alaska, and some natives of the interior who called themselves *Tennanah* or *Mountain-River-Men*, belonging to the Tinne Kutchin tribe.

WICHITAN.

Wichita I. A list of signs from Rev. A. J. HOLT, missionary, obtained from KIN CHE-ESS (Spectacles), medicine-man of the Wichitas, at the Wichita Agency, Indian Territory, in 1879.

Wichita II. A list of signs from TSODIÁKO (Shaved Head Boy), a Wichita chief, from Indian Territory, who visited Washington in June, 1880.

ZUÑIAN.

Zuñi I. Some preliminary notes received in 1880 from Rev. TAYLOR F. EALY, missionary among the Zuñi, upon the signs of that body of Indians.

FOREIGN CORRESPONDENCE.

Valuable contributions have been received in 1880–'81 and collated under their proper headings, from the following correspondents in distant countries :

Rev. HERMAN N. BARNUM, D. D., of Harpoot, Turkey, furnishes a list of signs in common use among Turks, Armenians, and Koords in that region.

Miss L. C. LLOYD, Charleton House, Mowbray, near Cape Town, Africa, gives information concerning the gestures and signals of the Bushmen.

Rev. LORIMER FISON, Navuloa, Fiji, notes in letters comparisons between the signs and gestures of the Fijians and those of the North American Indians. As this paper is passing through the press a *Col-*

lection is returned with annotations by him and also by Mr. WALTER CAREW, Commissioner for the Interior of Navitilevu. The last named gentleman describes some signs of a Fijian uninstructed deaf-mute.

Mr. F. A. VON RUPPRECHT, Kepahiang, Sumatra, supplies information and comparisons respecting the signs and signals of the Redjangs and Lelongs, showing agreement with some Dakota, Comanche, and Ojibwa signs.

Letters from Mr. A. W. HOWITT, F. G. S., Sale, Gippsland, Victoria, upon Australian signs, and from Rev. JAMES SIBREE, jr., F. R. G. S., relative to the tribes of Madagascar, are gratefully acknowledged.

Many other correspondents are now, according to their kind promises, engaged in researches, the result of which have not yet been received. The organization of those researches in India and Ceylon has been accomplished through the active interest of Col. H. S. OLCOTT, U. S. Commissioner, Breach Candy, Bombay.

Grateful acknowledgment must be made to Prof. E. A. FAY, of the National Deaf Mute College, through whose special attention a large number of the natural signs of deaf-mutes, remembered by them as having been invented and used before instruction in conventional signs, indeed before attending any school, was obtained. The gentlemen who made the contributions in their own MS., and without prompting, are as follows: Messrs. M. BALLARD, R. M. ZIEGLER, J. CROSS, PHILIP J. HASENSTAB, and LARS LARSON. Their names respectively follow their several descriptions. Mr. BALLARD is an instructor in the college, and the other gentlemen were pupils during the session of 1880.

Similar thanks are due to Mr. J. L. NOYES, superintendent of the Minnesota Institution for the education of the Deaf and Dumb, Faribault, Minn., and to Messrs. GEORGE WING and D. H. CARROLL, teachers in that institution, for annotations and suggestions respecting deaf-mute signs. The notes made by the last named gentlemen are followed by their respective names in reference.

Special thanks are also rendered to Prof. JAMES D. BUTLER, of Madison, Wis., for contribution of Italian gesture-signs, noted by him in 1843, and for many useful suggestions.

Other Italian signs are quoted from the Essay on Italian gesticulations by his eminence Cardinal WISEMAN, in his *Essays on Various Subjects* London, 1855, Vol. III, pp. 533–555. Many Neapolitan signs are extracted from the illustrated work of the canon ANDREA DE JORIO, *La Mimica degli Antichi investigata nel gestire Napoletano, Napoli,* 1832.

A small collection of Australian signs has been extracted from R. BROUGH SMYTH'S *The Aborigines of Victoria, London,* 1878.

EXTRACTS FROM DICTIONARY.

In the printed but unpublished *Collection* before mentioned, page 396, nearly three hundred quarto pages are devoted to descriptions of signs arranged in alphabetic order. A few of these are now presented to show the method adopted. They have been selected either as having connection with the foregoing discussion of the subject or because for some of them pictorial illustrations had already been prepared. There is propriety in giving all the signs under some of the title words when descriptions of only one or two of those signs have been used in the foregoing remarks. This prevents an erroneous inference that the signs so mentioned are the only or the common or the generally prevailing signs for the idea conveyed. This course has involved some slight repetition both of descriptions and of illustrations, as it seemed desirable that they should appear to the eye in the several connections indicated. The extracts are rendered less interesting and instructive by the necessity for omitting cross-references which would show contrasts and similarities for comparison, but would require a much larger part of the collected material to be now printed than is consistent with the present plan. Instead of occupying in this manner the remaining space allotted to this paper, it was decided to present, as of more general interest, the descriptions of TRIBAL SIGNS, PROPER NAMES, PHRASES, DIALOGUES, NARRATIVES, DISCOURSES, and SIGNALS, which follow the EXTRACTS.

It will be observed that in the following extracts there has been an attempt to supply the conceptions or origin of the several signs. When the supposed conception, obtained through collaborators, is printed before the authority given as reference, it is understood to have been gathered from an Indian as being his own conception, and is there fore of special value. When printed after the authority and within quotation marks it is in the words of the collaborator as offered by himself. When printed after the authority and without quotation marks it is suggested by this writer.

The letters of the alphabet within parentheses, used in some of the descriptions, refer to the corresponding figures in TYPES OF HAND POSITIONS at the end of this paper. When such letters are followed by Arabic numerals it is meant that there is some deviation, which is described in the text, from that type of hand position corresponding with the letter which is still used as the basis of description. Example: In the first description from (*Sahaptin* I) for *bad, mean*, page 412, (G) refers to the type of hand position so marked, being identically that position, but in the following reference, to (R 1), the type referred to by the letter

R has the palm to the front instead of backward, being in all other respects the position which it is desired to illustrate; (R), therefore, taken in connection with the description, indicates that change, and that alone. This mode of reference is further explained in the EXAMPLES at the end of this paper.

References to another title word as explaining a part of a description or to supply any other portions of a compound sign will always be understood as being made to the description by the same authority of the sign under the other title-word. Example: In the second description by (*Sahaptin* I) for *bad, mean*, above mentioned, the reference to GOOD is to that sign for *good* which is contributed by Rev. G. L. DEFFEN-BAUGH, and is referred to as (*Sahaptin* I.).

ANTELOPE.

Pass the open right hand outward from the small of the back. (*Wied.*) This, as explained by Indians lately examined, indicates the lighter coloration upon the animal's flanks. A Ute who could speak Spanish accompanied it with the word *blanco*, as if recognizing that it required explanation.

With the index only extended, hold the hand eighteen or twenty inches transversely in front of the head, index pointing to the left, then rub the sides of the body with the flat hands. (*Cheyenne* IV; *Dakota* VI.) "The latter sign refers to the white sides of the animal; the former could not be explained."

Extend and separate the forefingers and thumbs, nearly close all the other fingers, and place the hands with backs outward above and a little in front of the ears, about four inches from the head, and shake them back and

FIG. 234.

FIG. 235.

forth several times. Antelope's horns. This is an Arapaho sign. (*Dakota* I, II, IV.)

Close the right hand, leaving the end of the index in the form of a hook, and the thumb extended as in Fig. 234; then wave the hand quickly back and forth a short distance, opposite the temple. (*Hidatsa* I; *Arikara* I.) "Represents the pronged horn of the animal. This is the sign ordinarily used, but it was noticed that in conversing with one of the Dakotas the sign of the latter (*Dakota* VI) was used several times, to be more readily understood."

Place both hands, fingers fully extended and spread, close to the sides of the head. *Wied's* sign was readily understood as signifying the white flanks. (*Apache* I.)

In connection with the above signs Fig. 235 is presented, which was drawn by Running Antelope, an Uncpapa Dakota, as his personal totem, or proper name.

BAD, MEAN.

Make the sign for GOOD and then that of NOT. (*Long.*)

Close the hand, and open it whilst passing it downward. (*Wied.*) This is the same as my description; but differently worded, possibly notes a less forcible form. I say, however, that the arm is "extended." The precise direction in which the hand is moved is not, I think, essential. (*Matthews.*) This sign is invariably accompanied by a countenance expressive of contempt. (*F. Jacker.*)

Scatter the dexter fingers outward, as if spurting away water from them. (*Burton.*)

(1) Right hand partially elevated, fingers closed, thumb clasping the tips; (2) sudden motion downward and outward accompanied by equally sudden opening of fingers and snapping of the fingers from the thumb. (*Cheyenne* II.)

Right hand closed back to front is moved forcibly downward and forward, the fingers being violently opened at instant of stopping the motion of hand. (*Cheyenne* IV.)

Right hand closed (B) carried forward in front of the body toward the right and downward, during which the hand is opened, fingers downward, as if dropping out the contents. (*Dakota* I.) "Not worth keeping."

Half close the fingers of the right hand, hook the thumb over the fore and middle fingers; move the hand, back upward, a foot or so toward the object referred to, and suddenly let the fingers fly open. Scattered around, therefore bad. An Arapaho sign. (*Dakota* IV.)

Close the fingers of the right hand, resting the tips against the thumb, then throw the hand downward and outward toward the right to arm's length, and spring open the fingers. Fig. 236. (*Dakota* VI, VII, VIII; *Ponka* II; *Pani* I.)

FIG. 236,

The sign most commonly used for this idea is made by the hand being closed near the breast, with the back toward the breast, then as the arm is suddenly extended the hand is opened and the fingers separated from each other. (*Mandan and Hidatsa* I.)

Hands open, palms turned in; move one hand toward, and the other from, the body; then *vice versâ*. (*Omaha* I.)

Throw the clinched right hand forward, downward, and outward, and when near at arm's length, suddenly snap the fingers from the thumb as if sprinkling water. (*Wyandot* I.) "To throw away contemptuously; not worth keeping."

Raise hand in front of breast, fingers hooked, thumb resting against second finger, palm downward (G), then with a nervous movement throw the hand downward to the right and a little behind the body, with an expression of disgust on the face. During motion of hand the fingers are suddenly extended as though throwing something out of the hand, and in final position the fingers and thumb are straight and separated, palm backward (R 1). (*Sahaptin* I.) "Away with it!"

Another: Same motion of arm and hand as in *good*. But in the first position fingers are closed, and as the hand moves to the right they are thrown open, until in final position all are extended as in final for *good*. (*Sahaptin* I.)

Extend the right hand, palm downward, and move it in a horizontal line from the body, then suddenly turn the hand over as if throwing water from the back of it or the index. (*Comanche* I.) "Good, no."

Pass the flat right hand, interruptedly, downward and backward past the right side. (*Pima and Papago* I.) "Putting aside."

Deaf-mute natural signs:

Hold forward the closed hand with the little finger up, at the same time nodding the head. (*Ballard.*)

Draw the tongue out a little and then shake the head with a displeased look. (*Larson.*)

Use the sign for *handsome* (see first part of the sign for GOOD), at the same time shake the head as if to say "no." (*Ziegler.*)

Deaf-mute signs:

The hand closed (except the little finger which is extended and raised), and held forward with the fingers to the front is the sign for *bad* illustrated in the Report for 1879 of the Ohio Institution for the Deaf and Dumb. This sign is used among the deaf-mutes in England.

BEAR, animal.

Pass the hand before the face to mean ugliness, at the same time grinning and extending the fingers like claws. (*Burton.*)

Hands in front of and about eight inches above the elbows, fingers slightly bent and open, thumbs and palms to the front to represent claws,—or bear in standing position. Sometimes accompanied by clawing motion. (*Creel.*)

(1) Middle and third finger of right hand clasped down by the thumb, forefinger and little finger extended, crooked downward; (2) the motion of scratching made in the air. (*Cheyenne* II.) Fig. 237.

FIG. 237.

Fingers of both hands closed, except the thumb and little finger, which are extended, and point straight toward the front, hands horizontal, backs upward, are held in front of their respective sides near the body, and then moved directly forward with short, sharp jerking motions. (*Dakota* I.) "From the motion of the bear in running." This is also reported as an Arapaho sign. (*Dakota* IV.) The paws and claws are represented.

Seize a short piece of wood, say about two feet long, wave in the right hand, and strike a blow at an imaginary person. (*Omaha* I.)

Another: Seize a short thing about six inches long, hold it as dagger, pretend to thrust it downward under the breast-bone repeatedly, and each time farther, grunting or gasping in doing so; withdraw the stick, holding it up, and, showing the blood, point to the breast with the left forefinger, meaning to say *so do thou when you meet the bear.* (*Omaha* I.)

Another: Pretend to stab yourself with an arrow in various parts of the body, then point towards the body with the left-hand forefinger. (*Omaha* I.)

Arms are flexed and hands clasped about center of breast; then slowly fall with arms pendulous and both hands in type-position (Q). The sign is completed by slowly lifting the hands and arms several times in imitation of the animal's locomotion. Movement and appearance of animal's front feet. (*Oto* I.)

Hold the closed right hand at the height of the elbow before the right side, palm downward, extend and curve the thumb and little finger so that their tips are nearly directed toward one another before the knuckles of the closed fingers; then push the hand forward several times. (*Kaiowa* I; *Comanche* III; *Apache* II; *Wichita* II.) "Paw and long claws." Fig. 238.

FIG. 238.

FIG. 239.

Hold both closed hands before the body, palms down, and about eight inches apart; reach forward a short distance, relaxing the fingers as if grasping something with them, and draw them back again as the hands are withdrawn to their former position. Ordinarily but one hand is used, as in Fig. 239. (*Ute* I.) "Scratching, and grasping with the claws."

The right hand thrown in the position as for *horse,* as follows: Elevate the right-hand, extended, with fingers joined, outer edge toward the ground, in front of the body or right shoulder, and pointing forward, resting the curved thumb against the palmar side of the index, then extend both hands with fingers extended and curved, separated, palms down, and push them forward several times, making a short arch. (*Apache* I.) "The animal that scratches with long claws."

Fig. 240 is from a Moqui rock etching, contributed by Mr. G. FIG. 240. K. Gilbert, showing the pictorial mode of representing the animal.

Deaf-mute sign :

Claw both shoulders with the fingers.   (*Wing.*)

—— Grizzly.

Right hand flat and extended, held at height of shoulder, palm forward, then bring the palm to the mouth, lick it with the tongue, and return it to first position. (*Omaha* I.) "Showing blood on the paw."

Other remarks upon the signs for *bear* are made on pages 293 and 345.

BRAVE.

Close the fists, place the left near the breast, and move the right over

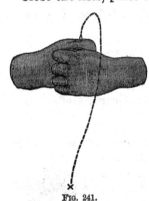

the left toward the left side. (*Wied.*) A motion something like this, which I do not now distinctly recall—a short of wrenching motion with the fists in front of the chest—I have seen used for *strong.* If *Wied's* sign-maker's hand first struck the region over the heart (as he may have done) he would then have indicated a "strong heart," which is the equivalent for *brave.* (*Matthews.*) This sign is used by the Sioux at the present day to denote *small.* (*McChesney.*) I have seen a similar sign repeatedly, the only variation being that the right fist is passed over and downward, in front of the left, instead of toward the left side. (*Hoffman.*) Fig. 241.

FIG. 241.

Clinch the right fist, and place it to the breast. (*Absaroka* I; *Shoshoni and Banak* I.)

Both hands fists, backs outward, obliquely upward, near together, right inside of left, are moved forward from in front of the chest, two or three times and back again to original position and then the right-hand fist is thrown with some force over the left on a curve. *Endurance* is expressed by this sign, and it is connected with the sun-dance trials of the young man in testing his bravery and powers of endurance before admission to the ranks of the warriors. (*Dakota* I.)

Push the two fists forward about a foot, at the height of the breast, the right about two inches behind the left, palms inward. (*Dakota* IV.) "The hands push all before them."

Hold the left arm in front as if supporting a shield, and the right drawn back as if grasping a weapon. Close the fists, lower the head, moving it a little forward (with a "lunge") as well as the arms and fists. (*Omaha* I.) "I am brave."

Another: Index and thumb extended parallel, palm to left, the other fingers bent. Shake the open fingers several times at the person referred to, the forearm being held at an angle of about 20°. (*Omaha* I.) "You are very brave; you do not fear death when you see the danger."

Strike the breast gently with the palmar side of the right fist. (*Wyandot* I.)

Place the left clinched hand horizontally before the breast, palm toward the body, and at the same time strike forcibly downward in front of it with the right fist, as in Fig. 242. Sometimes the right fist is placed back of the left, then thrown over the latter toward the front and downward, as in Fig. 241 above. The same gesture has also been made by throwing the palmar side of the right fist edgewise downward in front of the knuckles of the left, as in Fig. 243. In each instance the left fist is jerked upward very perceptibly as the right one is thrust downward. (*Kaiowa* I; *Comanche* III; *Apache* II; *Wichita* II.)

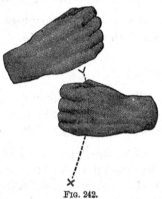

FIG. 242.

Strike the clinched fist forcibly toward the ground in front of and near the breast. (*Arikara* I.)

—————— He is the bravest of all.

Make the sign for BRAVE and then the left forefinger, upright, back inward about twelve inches in front of left breast, right index similarly held near the right breast, move them at the same time outward or forward, obliquely to the left. (*Dakota* I.)

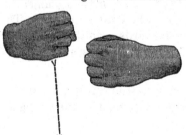

FIG. 243.

Raise right hand, fingers extended, palm downward (W 1), swing it around "over all," then point to the man, raise left fist (A 1, changed to left and palm inward) to a point in front of and near the body, close fingers of right hand and place the fist (A 2, palm inward) between left fist and body and then with violent movement throw it over left fist, as though breaking something, and stop at a point in front of and a little below left fist, and lastly point upward with right hand. (*Sahaptin* I.) "Of all here he is strongest."

The right fist, palm downward, is struck against the breast several times, and the index is then quickly elevated before the face, pointing upward. (*Apache* I.)

Move the fist, thumb to the head, across the forehead from right to left, and cast it toward the earth over the left shoulder. (*Apache* III.)

Deaf-mute natural signs:

Run forward with a bold expression of the countenance. (*Larson.*)

Not to run back but to run forward. (*Ziegler.*)

Deaf-mute sign:

Left hand held as if pressing a loaf against the chest. Make a motion with the right hand, palm upward as if cutting through the fingers of the left with a sawing motion. (*Wing.*)

Other remarks connected with the signs for *brave* appear on pages 352, 353, and 358, *supra.*

CHIEF.

The forefinger of the right hand extended, pass it perpendicularly downward, then turn it upward, and raise it in a right line as high as the head. (*Long.*) "Rising above others."

Raise the index finger of the right hand, holding it straight upward, then turn it in a circle and bring it straight down, a little toward the earth. (*Wied.*) The right hand is raised, and in position (J) describes a semicircle as in beginning the act of throwing. The arm is elevated perfectly erect aside of the head, the palm of the index and hand should be outward. There is an evident similarity in both execution and conception of this sign and *Wied's;* the little variation may be the result of different interpretation. The idea of superiority is most prominent in both. (*Boteler.*) "A prominent one before whom all succumb." The Arikaras understood this sign, and they afterwards used it in talking to me. (*Creel.*) *Wied's* air-picture reminds of the royal scepter with its sphere.

Raise the forefinger, pointed upwards, in a vertical direction, and then reverse both finger and motion; the greater the elevation the "bigger" the chief. (*Arapaho* I.)

Place the closed hand, with the index extended and pointing upward, near the right cheek, pass it upward as high as the head, then turn it forward and downward toward the ground, the movement terminating a little below the initial point. See Fig. 306 in TENDOY-HUERITO DIALOGUE, p. 487. (*Arapaho* II; *Cheyenne* V; *Ponka* II; *Shoshoni* I.)

(1) Sign for MAN, as follows: Right hand, palm inward, elevated to about the level of the breast, index carelessly pointing upward, suddenly pointed straight upward, and the whole hand moved a little forward, at the same time taking care to keep the back of the hand toward the person addressed; (2) middle, third, little finger, and thumb slightly closed

together, forefinger pointing forward and downward; (3) curved motion made forward, outward, and downward. (*Cheyenne* II.) "He who stands still and commands," as shown by similarity of signs to *sit here* or *stand here*.

Extend the index, remaining fingers closed, and raise it to the right side of the head and above it as far as the arm can reach. Have also seen the sign given by *Wyandot* I. (*Ojibwa* V.)

The extended forefinger of the right hand (J), of which the other fingers are closed, is raised to the right side of the head and above it as far as the arm can be extended, and then the hand is brought down in front of the body with the wrist bent, the back of hand in front and the extended forefinger pointing downward. (*Dakota* I.) "Raised above others."

Move the upright and extended right index, palm forward, from the shoulder upward as high as the top of the head, then forward six inches through a curve, and move it forward six inches, and then downward. its palm backward, to the height of the shoulder. An Arapaho sign, Above all others. He looks over or after us. (*Dakota* IV.)

Elevate the extended index before the shoulder, palm forward, pass it upward as high as the head, and forming a short curve to the front, then downward again slightly to the front to before the breast and about fifteen inches from it. (*Dakota* VI, VII, VIII; *Hidatsa* I; *Arikara* I.)

Right hand closed, forefinger pointing up, raise the hand from the waist in front of the body till it passes above the head. (*Omaha* I.)

Another: Bring the closed right hand, forefinger pointing up, on a level with the face; then bring the palm of the left hand with force against the right forefinger; next. send up the right hand above the head, leaving the left as it is. (*Omaha* I.)

The right arm is extended by side of head, with the hand in position (J). The arm and hand then descend, the finger describing a semicircle with the arm as a radius. The sign stops with arm hanging at full length. (*Oto* I.) "The arm of authority before whom all must fall."

Both hands elevated to a position in front of and as high as the shoulders, palms facing, fingers and thumbs spread and slightly curved; the hands are then drawn outward a short distance towards their respective sides and gently elevated as high as the top of the head. (*Wyandot* I.) "One who is elevated by others."

Elevate the closed hand—index only extended and pointing upward— to the front of the right side of the face or neck or shoulder; pass it quickly upward, and when as high as the top of the head, direct it forward and downward again toward the ground. (*Kaiowa* I; *Comanche* III; *Apache* II; *Wichita* II.)

27 A E

Close the right hand, index raised, extended, and placed before the breast, then move it forward from the mouth, pointing forward, until at arm's length. (*Ute* I.)

———, Head, of tribe.

Place the extended index, pointing upward, at some distance before the right shoulder, then place the left hand, with fingers and thumb extended and separated, just back of the index; then in passing the index upward as high as the head, draw the left hand downward a short distance, as in Fig. 244. Superior to others. (*Absaroka* I; *Arikara* I.)

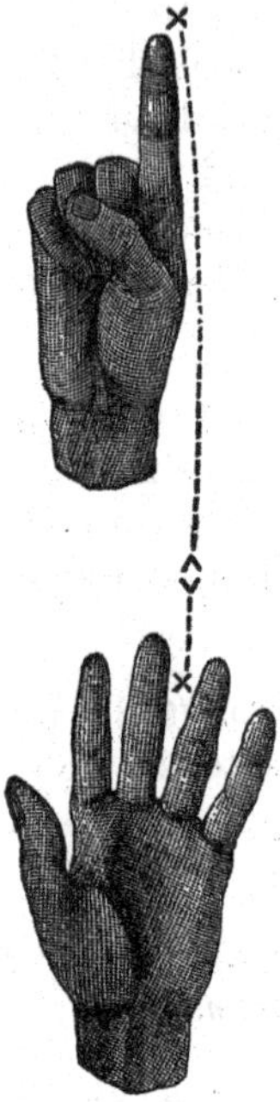

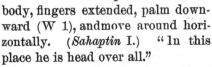

Place both flat hands before the body, palms down, and pass them horizontally outward toward their respective sides, then make the sign for CHIEF. (*Arikara* I.) "Chief of the wide region and those upon it."

After pointing out the man, point to the ground, all fingers closed except first (J 1, pointing downward in stead of upward), then point upward with same hand (J 2), then move hand to a point in front of body, fingers extended, palm downward (W 1), and move around horizontally. (*Sahaptin* I.) "In this place he is head over all."

FIG. 244.

Fig. 245.

Grasp the forelock with the right hand, palm backward, pass the hand upward about six inches and hold it in that position a moment. (*Pai-Ute* I.) Fig 245.

Elevate the extended index vertically above and in front of the head, holding the left hand, forefinger pointing upward, from one to two feet below and underneath the right, the position of the left, either elevated or depressed, also denoting the relative position of the second individual to that of the chief. (*Apache* I.)

———, War. Head of a war party; Partisan.

First make the sign of the *pipe*; then open the thumb and index finger of the right hand, back of the hand outward, moving it forward and upward in a curve. (*Wied.*) For remarks upon this sign see page 384.

Place the right hand, index only extended and pointing forward and upward, before the right side of the breast nearly at arm's length, then place the left hand, palm forward with fingers spread and extended, midway between the breast and the right hand. (*Arapaho* II; *Cheyenne* V; *Ponka* II; *Pani* I.)

First make the sign for BATTLE, viz: Both hands (A 1) brought to the median line of the body on a level with the breast and close together; describe with both hands at the same time a series of circular movements of small circumference; and then add the sign for CHIEF. (*Dakota* I.) "First in battle."

———— of a band.

Point toward the left and front with the extended forefinger of the left hand, palm down; then place the extended index about twelve inches behind the left hand, pointing in the same direction. (*Arapaho* II; *Cheyenne* V; *Ponka* II; *Pani* I.)

Place the extended index at some distance before the right shoulder, pointing forward and slightly upward, then place the left hand with fingers and thumb extended and separated over the

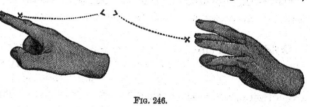

FIG. 246.

index, and while pushing the index to the front, draw the left hand backward toward body and to the left. Ahead of others. (*Absaroka* I; *Arikara* I.) Fig. 246.

FIG. 247.

Point the extended index forward and upward before the chest, then place the spread fingers of the left hand around the index, but at a short distance behind it, all pointing the same direction. Ahead of the remainder. (*Arikara* I.)

Grasp the forelock with the right hand, palm backward, and pretend to lay the hair down over the right side of the head by passing the hand in that direction. (*Pai-Ute* I.) Fig. 247.

The French deaf-mute sign for *order, command*, may be compared with several of the above signs. In it the index tip first touches the lower lip, then is raised above the head and brought down with violence. (*L'enseignment primaire des sourds-muets; par M. Pélissier. Paris*, 1856.)

Not only in Naples, but, according to De Jorio, in Italy generally the conception of *authority* in gesture is by pressing the right hand on the flank, accompanied by an erect and squared posture of the bust with the head slightly inclined to the right.   The idea of *substance* is conveyed.

————, Warrior lower than actual, but distinguished for bravery.

Place the left forefinger, pointing toward the left and front, before the left side of the chest, then place the extended index near (or against) the fore-

FIG. 248.

finger, and, while passing the latter outward toward the left, draw the index toward the right.   (*Absaroka* I; *Arikara* I; *Shoshoni* I.)   Fig. 248.

DEAD, DEATH.

Throw the forefinger from the perpendicular into a horizontal position toward the earth, with the back downward.   (*Long.*)

Hold the left hand flat over the face, back outward, and pass with the similarly held right hand below the former, gently striking or touching it.   (*Wied.*)   The sign given (*Oto and Missouri* I) has no similarity in execution or conception with *Wied's*.   (*Boteler.*)   This sign may convey the idea of *under* or *burial*, quite differently executed from most others reported.   Dr. McChesney conjectures this sign to be that of wonder or surprise at hearing of a death, but not a distinct sign for the latter.

The finger of the right hand passed to the left hand and then cast down.   (*Macgowan.*)

Hold the left hand slightly arched, palm down, fingers pointing toward the right about fifteen inches before the breast, then place the extended index nearer the breast, pointing toward the left, pass it quickly forward underneath the left hand and in an upward curve to termination.   (*Arapaho* II; *Cheyenne* V; *Ponka* II; *Pani* I.)

Place the palm of the hand at a short distance from the side of the head, then withdrawing it gently in an oblique downward direction and inclining the head and upper part of the body in the same direction. (*Ojibwa* II.)   See page 353 for remarks upon this sign.

Hold both hands open, with palms over ears, extend fingers back on brain, close eyes, and incline body a little forward and to right or left very low, and remain motionless a short time, pronouncing the word *Ke-nee-boo* slowly.   (*Ojibwa* IV.)

Left hand flattened and held back upward, thumb inward in front of and a few inches from the breast. Right hand slightly clasped, forefinger more extended than the others, and passed suddenly under the left hand, the latter being at the same time gently moved toward the breast. (*Cheyenne* II.) "Gone under."

Both hands horizontal in front of body, backs outward, index of each hand alone extended, the right index is passed under the left with a downward, outward and then upward and inward curved motion at the same time that the left is moved inward toward the body two or three inches, the movements being ended on the same level as begun. "Upset, keeled over." For *many deaths* repeat the sign many times. The sign of (*Cheyenne* II) expresses "gone under," but is not used in the sense of *death, dead,* but *going under a cover,* as entering a lodge, under a table, &c. (*Dakota* I.)

Make the sign for ALIVE, viz.: The right hand, back upward, is to be at the height of the elbow and forward, the index extended and pointing forward, the other fingers closed, thumb against middle finger; then, while rotating the hand outward, move it to a position about four inches in front of the face, the back looking forward and the index pointing upward; then the sign for No. (*Dakota* IV.)

Another: Hold the left hand pointing toward the right, palm obliquely downward and backward, about a foot in front of the lower part of the chest, and pass the right hand pointing toward the left, palm downward, from behind forward underneath it. Or from an upright position in front of the face, back forward, index extended and other fingers closed, carry the right hand downward and forward underneath the left and about four inches beyond it, gradually turning the right hand until its back is upward and its index points toward the left. An Arapaho sign. Gone under or buried. (*Dakota* IV.)

Hold the left hand slightly bent with the palm down, before the breast, then pass the extended right hand, pointing toward the left, forward under and beyond the left. (*Dakota* VI, VII.)

Hold the right hand, flat, palm downward, before the body; then throw it over on its back to the right, making a curve of about fifteen inches. (*Dakota* VI; *Hidatsa* I; *Arikara* I.) The gesture of reversal in this and other instances may be compared with picture-writings in which the reversed character for the name or totem of a person signifies his death. One of these is given in Fig. 249, taken from Schoolcraft's *Hist. Am. Tribes,* I, p. 356, showing the cedar burial post or *adjedatig* of Wabojeeg, an Ojibwa war chief, who died on Lake Superior about 1793. He belonged to the deer clan of his tribe and the animal is drawn reversed on the post.

Extend right hand, palm down, hand curved. Turn the palm up in moving the hand down towards the earth. (*Omaha* I.)

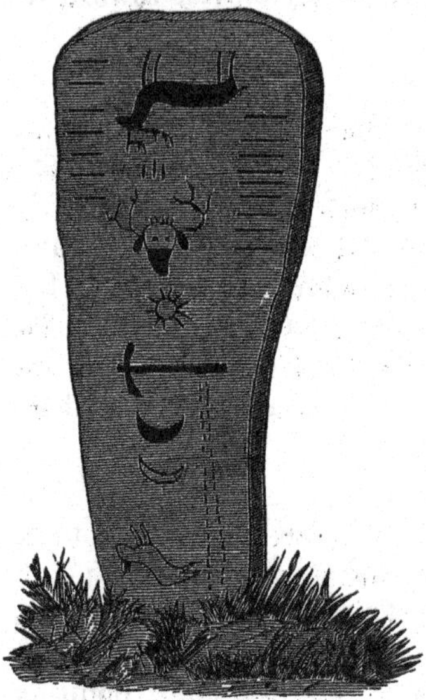

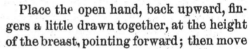

The countenance is brought to a sleeping composure with the eyes closed. This countenance being gradually assumed, the head next falls toward either shoulder. The arms having been closed and crossed upon the chest with the hands in type positions (B B) are relaxed and drop simultaneously towards the ground, with the fall of the head. This attitude is maintained some seconds. (*Oto and Missouri* I.) "The bodily appearance at death."

Place the open hand, back upward, fingers a little drawn together, at the height of the breast, pointing forward; then move it slowly forward and downward, turning it over at the same time. (*Iroquois* I.) "To express 'gone into the earth, face upward.'"

FIG. 249.

The flat right hand is waved outward and downward toward the same side, the head being inclined in the same direction at the time, with eyes closed. (*Wyandot* I.)

Hold the left hand loosely extended about fifteen inches in front of the breast, palm down, then pass the index, pointing to the left, in a short curve downward, forward, and upward beneath the left palm. (*Kaiowa* I; *Comanche* III; *Apache* II; *Wichita* II.)

Bring the left hand to the left breast, hand half clinched (H), then bring the right hand to the left with the thumb and forefinger in such a position as if you were going to take a bit of string from the fingers of the left hand, and pull the right hand off in a horizontal line as if you were stretching a string out, extend the hand to the full length of the arm from you and let the index finger point outward at the conclusion of the sign. (*Comanche* I.) "Soul going to happy hunting-grounds."

FIG. 250.

The left hand is held slightly arched, palm down, nearly at arm's length before the breast; the right extended, flat, palm down, and pointing forward, is pushed from the top of the breast, straightforward, underneath, and beyond the left. (*Shoshoni and Banak* I.) Fig. 250.

Close both eyes, and after a moment throw the palm of the right hand from the face downward and outward toward the right side, the head being dropped in the same direction. (*Ute* I.)

Touch the breast with the extended and joined fingers of the right hand, then throw the hand, palm to the left, outward toward the right, leaning the head in that direction at the same time. (*Apache* I.)

Close the eyes with the tips of the index and second finger, respectively, then both hands are placed side by side, horizontally, palms downward, fingers extended and united; hands separated by slow horizontal movement to right and left. (*Kutchin* I.)

Palm of hand upward, then a wave-like motion toward the ground. (*Zuñi* I.)

Deaf-mute natural signs :

Place the hand upon the cheek, and shut the eyes, and move the hand downward toward the ground. (*Ballard.*)

Let your head lie on the open hand with eyes shut. (*Cross.*)

Use the right shut hand as if to draw a screw down to fasten the lid to the coffin and keep the eyes upon the hand. (*Hasenstab.*)

Move the head toward the shoulder and then close the eyes. (*Larson.*)

Deaf mute signs :

The French deaf-mute conception is that of gently falling or sinking, the right index falling from the height of the right shoulder upon the left forefinger, toward which the head is inclined.

The deaf-mute sign commonly used in the United States is the same as *Dakota* VI; *Hidatsa* I; *Arikara* I; above. Italians with obvious conception, make the sign of the cross.

——— To Die.

Right hand, forefinger extended, side up, forming with the thumb a **U**; the other fingers slightly curved, touching each other, the little finger having its side toward the ground. Move the hand right and left then forward, several times; then turn it over suddenly, letting it fall toward the earth. (*Ojibwa* V; *Omaha* I.) "An animal wounded, but staggering a little before it falls and dies."

—— Dying.

Hold the left hand as in *dead*; pass the index in the same manner underneath the left, but in a slow, gentle, interrupted movement. (*Kai-*

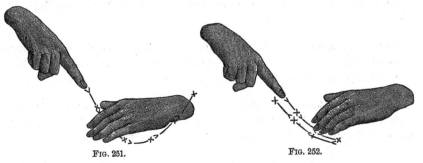

FIG. 251.   FIG. 252.

owa I; *Comanche* III; *Apache* II; *Wichita* II.) "Step by step; inch by inch." Fig. 251.

—— Nearly, but recovers.

Hold the left hand as in *dead*; pass the index with a slow, easy, interrupted movement downward, under the left palm, as in *dying*, but before passing from under the palm on the opposite side return the index in the same manner to point of starting; then elevate it. (*Kaiowa* I; *Comanche* III; *Apache* II; *Wichita* II.) Fig. 252.

Other remarks upon the signs for *dead* are given on page 353.

Good.

The hand held horizontally, back upward, describes with the arm a horizontal curve outward. (*Long.*) This is like the Eurasian motion of benediction, but may more suggestively be compared with several of the signs for *yes*, and in opposition to several of those for *bad* and *no*, showing the idea of acceptance or selection of objects presented, instead of their rejection.

Place the right hand horizontally in front of the breast and move it forward. (*Wied.*) This description is essentially the same as the one I furnished. (*Mandan and Hidatsa* I.) I stated, however, that the hand was moved outward (*i. e.*, to the right). I do not remember seeing it moved directly forward. In making the motion as I have described it the hand would have to go both outward and forward. (*Matthews.*) The left arm is elevated and the hand held in position (W). The arm and hand are thus extended from the body on a level with the chest; the elbow being slightly bent, the arm resembles a bent bow. The right arm is bent and the right hand, in position (W), sweeps smoothly over the left arm from the biceps muscle over the ends of the fingers. This sign and *Wied's* are noticeably similar. The difference is, the *Oto* sign uses the left arm in conjunction and both *more to the left.* The conception is of something that easily passes; smoothness, evenness, etc., in both. (*Boteler.*)

Wave the hand from the mouth, extending the thumb from the index and closing the other three fingers. This sign also means *I know.* (*Burton.*)

(1) Right-hand fingers pointing to the left placed on a level with mouth, thumb inward; (2) suddenly moved with curve outward so as to present palm to person addressed. (*Cheyenne* II.)

Pass the open right hand, palm downward, from the heart, twenty-four inches horizontally forward and to the right through an arc of about 90°. (*Dakota* IV.) "Heart easy or smooth."

Another: Gently strike the chest two or three times over the heart with the radial side of the right hand, the fingers partly flexed and pointing downward. An Arapaho sign. (*Dakota* IV.)

Place the flat right hand, palm down, thumb touching the breast, then move it forward and slightly upward and to the right. (*Arapaho* II; *Cheyenne* V; *Ojibwa* V; *Dakota* VI, VII, VIII; *Kaiowa* I; *Comanche* III; *Apache* II; *Wichita* II.)

Pass the flat hand, palm down, from the breast forward and in a slight curve to the right. (*Dakota* VI; *Hidatsa* I; *Arikara* I.)

The extended right hand, palm downward, thumb backward, fingers pointing to the left, is held nearly or quite in contact with the body about on a level with the stomach; it is then carried outward to the right a foot or two with a rapid sweep, in which the forearm is moved but not necessarily the humerus. (*Mandan and Hidatsa* I.)

Move right hand, palm down, over the blanket, right and left, several times. (*Omaha* I.)

Another: Hit the blanket, first on the right, then on the left, palm down, several times. (*Omaha* I.)

Another: Point at the object with the right forefinger, shaking it a little up and down, the other fingers being closed. (*Omaha* I.)

Another: Same as preceding, but with the hand open, the thumb crooked under and touching the forefinger; hand held at an angle of 45° while shaking a little back and forth. (*Omaha* I.)

Another: Hold the closed hands together, thumbs up; separate by turning the wrists down, and move the fists a little apart; then reverse movements till back to first position. (*Omaha* I.)

Another: Hold the left hand with back toward the ground, fingers and thumb apart, and curved; hold the right hand opposite it, palm down, hands about six inches apart; shake the hands held thus, up and down, keeping them the same distance apart. (*Omaha* I.)

Another: Hold the hands with the palms in, thumbs up, move hands right and left, keeping them about six inches apart. (*Omaha* I.)

Another: Look at the right hand, first on the back, then on the palm, then on the back again. (*Omaha* I.)

The flat right hand, palm down, is moved forward and upward, starting at a point about twelve inches before the breast. (*Wyandot* I.)

Hold the flat right hand forward and slightly outward from the shoulder, palm either upward or downward, and pass it edgewise horizontally to the right and left. This sign was made when no personality was involved. The same gesturer when claiming for himself the character of goodness made the following: Rapidly pat the breast with the flat right hand. (*Pima and Papago* I.)

Throw right hand from front to side, fingers extended and palm down, forearm horizontal. (*Sahaptin* I.)

Make an inclination of the body forward, moving at the same time both hands forward from the breast, open, with the palm upward, and gradually lowering them. This is also used for *glad, pleased*. (*Iroquois* I.)

Bring both hands to the front, arms extended, palms outward; elevate them upward and slightly forward; the face meanwhile expressive of wonder. (*Comanche* I.)

Bring the hand opposite the breast, a little below, hand extended, palm downward (W), and let it move off in a horizontal direction. If it be very good, this may be repeated. If comparatively good, repeat it more violently. (*Comanche* I.)

Hold the right hand palm down, pointing to the left, and placed horizontally before the breast, then raise it several times slightly. Good and glad. (*Kutchin* I.)

Deaf-mute natural signs:
Smack the lips. (*Ballard.*)

Close the hand while the thumb is up, and nod the head and smile as if to approve of something good. (*Hasenstab.*)

Point the forefinger to the mouth and move the lips with a pleased look as if tasting sweet fruit. (*Larson.*)

Use the sign for *handsome* by drawing the outstretched palm of the right hand down over the right cheek; at the same time nod the head as if to say "yes." (*Ziegler.*)

Deaf-mute signs:

Some of the Indian signs appear to be connected with a pleasant taste in the mouth, as is the sign of the French and American deaf-mutes, waving thence the hand, either with or without touching the lips, back upward, with fingers straight and joined, in a forward and downward curve. They make nearly the same gesture with hand sidewise for general assent: "Very well!"

The conventional sign for *good*, given in the illustration to the report of the Ohio Institution for the education of the deaf and dumb, is: The right hand raised forward and closed, except the thumb, which is extended upward, held vertically; its nail being toward the body; this is in opposition to the sign for *bad* in the same illustration, the one being merely the exhibition of the thumb toward and the other of the little finger away from the body. They are English signs, the traditional conception being acceptance and rejection respectively.

Italian signs :

The fingers gathered on the mouth, kissed and stretched out and spread, intimate a dainty morsel. The open hand stretched out horizontally, and gently shaken, intimates that a thing is so-so, not good and not bad. (*Butler.*) Compare also the Neapolitan sign given by De Jorio, see Fig. 62, p. 286, *supra.* Cardinal Wiseman gives as the Italian sign for *good* "the hand thrown upwards and the head back with a prolonged ah!" *Loc. cit.*, p. 543.

—— Heart is.

Strike with right hand on the heart and make the sign for GOOD from the heart outward. (*Cheyenne* II.)

Touch the left breast over the heart two or three times with the ends of the fingers of the right hand; then make the sign for GOOD. (*Dakota* IV.)

Place the fingers of the flat right hand over the breast, then make the sign for GOOD. (*Dakota* VII.)

Move hand to position in front of breast, fingers extended, palm downward (W), then with quick movement throw hand forward and to the side to a point 12 or 15 inches from body, hand same as in first position. (*Sahaptin* I.)

For further remarks on the signs for *good*, see page 286.

HABITATION, including HOUSE, LODGE, TIPI, WIGWAM.

—— HOUSE.

The hand half open and the forefinger extended and separated; then raise the hand upward and give it a half turn, as if screwing something. (*Dunbar.*)

Cross the ends of the extended fingers of the two hands, the hands to be nearly at right angle, radial side up, palms inward and backward, thumbs in palms. Represents the logs at the end of a log house. (*Oreel; Dakota* IV.)

Partly fold the hands, the fingers extended in imitation of the corner of an ordinary log house. (*Arapaho* I.)

Both hands outspread near each other, elevated to front of face; suddenly separated, turned at right angles, palms facing; brought down at right angles, suddenly stopped. Representing square form of a house. (*Cheyenne* II.)

The fingers of both hands extended and slightly separated, then those of the right are placed into the several spaces between those of the left, the tips extending to about the first joints. (*Absaroka* I.) "From the arrangement of the logs in a log building."

Both hands extended, fingers spread, place those of the right into the spaces between those of the left, then move the hands in this position a short distance upward. (*Wyandot* I.) "Arrangement of logs and elevation."

Both hands are held edgewise before the body, palms facing, spread the fingers, and place those of one hand into the spaces between those

FIG. 253.

of the other, so that the tips of each protrude about an inch beyond. (*Hidatsa* I; *Kaiowa* I; *Arikara* I; *Comanche* III; *Apache* II; *Wichita* II.) "The arrangement of logs in a frontier house." Fig. 253. In connection with this sign compare the pictograph, Fig. 204, page 379, *supra*. In ordinary conversation the sign for *white man's house* is often dropped, using instead the generic term employed for *lodge*, and this in turn is often abbreviated, as by the Kaiowas, Comanches, Wichitas, and others, by merely placing the tips of the extended forefingers together, leaving the other fingers and thumbs closed, with the wrists about three or four inches apart.

Both hands held pointing forward, edges down, fingers extended and slightly separated, then place the fingers of one hand into the spaces between the fingers of the other, allowing the tips of the fingers of either hand to protrude as far as the first joint, or near it. (*Shoshoni and Banak* I.) "From the appearance of a corner of a log house—protruding and alternate layers of logs."

Fingers of both hands interlaced at right angles several times; then the sign for LODGE. (*Kutchin* I.)

Deaf-mute natural signs:
Draw the outlines of a house in the air with hands tip to tip at a right angle. (*Ballard.*)

Put the open hands together toward the face, forming a right angle with the arms. (*Larson.*)

———, Stone; Fort.
Strike the back of the right fist against the palm of the left hand, the left palm backward, the fist upright ("idea of resistance or strength"); then with both hands opened, relaxed, horizontal, and palms backward, place the ends of the right fingers behind and against the ends of the left; then separate them, and moving them backward, each through a semicircle, bring their bases together. The latter sign is also that of the Arapahos for *house*. An inclosure. (*Dakota* IV.) The first part of this sign is that for *stone*.

——— LODGE, TIPI, WIGWAM.
The two hands are reared together in the form of the roof of a house, the ends of the fingers upward. (*Long.*)

Place the opened thumb and forefinger of each hand opposite each other, as if to make a circle, but leaving between them a small interval; afterward move them from above downward simultaneously (which is the sign for *village*); then elevate the finger to indicate the number—one. (*Wied.*) Probably he refers to an earthen lodge. I think that the sign I have given you is nearly the same with all the Upper Missouri Indians. (*Matthews.*)

Place the fingers of both hands ridge-fashion before the breast. (*Burton.*)

Indicate outlines (an inverted V, thus ʌ), with the forefingers touching or crossed at the tips, the other fingers closed. (*Creel; Arapaho* I.)

Both hands open, fingers upward, tips touching, brought downward, and at same time separated to describe outline of a cone, suddenly stopped. (*Cheyenne* II.)

Both hands approximated, held forward horizontally, fingers joined and slightly arched, backs upward, withdraw them in a sideward and downward direction, each hand moving to its corresponding side, thus combinedly describing a hemisphere. Carry up the right and, with its index pointing downward indicate a spiral line rising upward from the center of the previously formed arch. (*Ojibwa* V.) "From the dome-shaped form of the wigwam, and the smoke rising from the opening in the roof."

Both hands flat and extended, placing the tips of the fingers of one against those of the other, leaving the palms or wrists about four inches apart. (*Absaroka* I; *Wyandot* I; *Shoshoni and Banak* I.) "From its exterior outline."

Both hands carried to the front of the breast and placed V-shaped, inverted, thus Λ, with the palms looking toward each other, edge of fingers outward, thumbs inward. (*Dakota* I.) "From the outline of the tipi."

With the hands nearly upright, palms inward, cross the ends of the extended forefingers, the right one either in front or behind the left, or
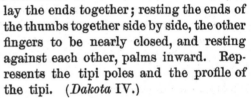
lay the ends together; resting the ends of the thumbs together side by side, the other fingers to be nearly closed, and resting against each other, palms inward. Represents the tipi poles and the profile of the tipi. (*Dakota* IV.)

FIG. 254.   Place the tips of the fingers of both hands together in front of the breast, with the wrists some distance apart. (*Dakota* V.) Fig. 254.

Fingers of both hands extended and separated; then interlace them so that the tips of the fingers of one hand protrude beyond the backs of those of the opposing one; hold the hands in front of the breast, pointing upward, leaving the wrists about six inches apart. (*Dakota* VII, VIII; *Hidatsa* I; *Ponka* II; *Arikara* I; *Pani* I.)

The extended hands, with finger tips upward and touching, the palms facing one another, and the wrists about two inches apart, are held before the chest. (*Mandan and Hidatsa* I)

Place the tip of the index against the tip of the forefinger of the left hand, the remaining fingers and thumbs closed, before the chest, leaving the wrists about six inches apart. (*Kaiowa* I; *Comanche* III; *Apache* II; *Wichita* II.) "Outline of lodge." This is an abbreviated sign, and care must be taken to distinguish it from *to meet*, in which the fingers are brought from their respective sides instead of upward to form the gesture.

Another: Place the tips of the fingers of the flat extended hands together before the breast, leaving the wrists about six inches apart. (*Kaiowa* I; *Comanche* III; *Apache* II; *Wichita* II.)

Another: Both hands flat and extended, fingers slightly separated; then place the fingers of the right hand between the fingers of the left as far as the second joints, so that the fingers of one hand protrude about an inch beyond those of the other; the wrists must be held about six inches apart. (*Kaiowa* I; *Comanche* III; *Apache* II; *Wichita* II.) "Outline of Indian lodge and crossing of tent poles above the covering." Fig. 255.

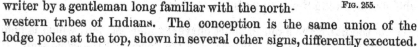

FIG. 255.

Fig. 256 represents a Sahaptin sign given to the writer by a gentleman long familiar with the northwestern tribes of Indians. The conception is the same union of the lodge poles at the top, shown in several other signs, differently executed.

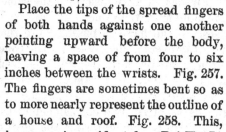

Place the tips of the spread fingers of both hands against one another pointing upward before the body, leaving a space of from four to six inches between the wrists. Fig. 257. The fingers are sometimes bent so as to more nearly represent the outline of a house and roof. Fig. 258. This, however, is accidental. (*Pai-Ute* I.)

FIG. 256.

FIG. 257.

"Represents the boughs and branches used in the construction of a Pai-Ute 'wik-i-up.'"

Place the tips of the two flat hands together before the body, leaving a space of about six inches between the wrists. (*Ute* I.) "Outline of the shape of the lodge."

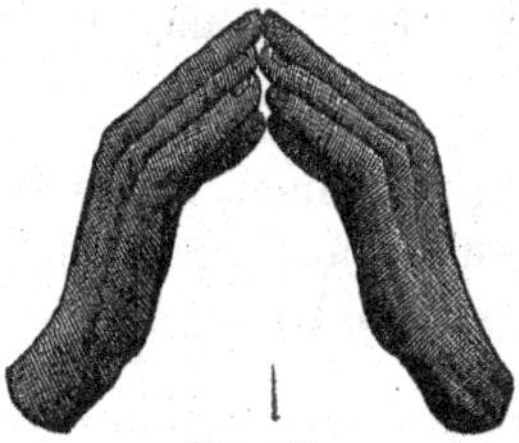

Left hand and right hand put together in shape of sloping shelter (*Kutchin* I.) Fig. 259.

FIG. 258.

FIG. 259.

—— Great Council House.
Place both flat and extended hands in front of the shoulders, pointing forward, palms facing; then pass them straight upward and slightly inward near the termination of the gesture. This appears to combine the gestures for *much, large,* and *lodge.* (*Arikara* I.)

——, Coming or going out of a.
Same as the sign for *entering a lodge,* only the fingers of the right hand point obliquely upward after passing under the left hand. (*Dakota* I.) "Coming out from under cover."

Hold the open left hand a foot or eighteen inches in front of the breast, palm downward or backward, fingers pointing toward the right and pass the right, back upward, with index extended, or all of the fingers extended, and pointing forward, about eighteen inches forward underneath the left through an arc from near the mouth. Some at the same time move the left hand toward the breast. (*Dakota* IV.)

————, Entering a.

The left hand is held with the back upward, and the right hand also with the back up is passed in a curvilinear direction down under the other, so as to rub against its palm, then up on the other side of it. The left hand here represents the low door of the skin lodge and the right the man stooping down to pass in. (*Long.*)

Pass the flat right hand in short curves under the left, which is held a short distance forward. (*Wied.*) I have described the same sign. It is not necessary to pass the hand more than once. By saying curves, he seems to imply many passes. If the hand is passed more than once it means repetition of the act. (*Mathews ; McChesney.*) The conception is of the stooping to pass through the low entrance, which is often covered by a flap of skin, sometimes stretched on a frame, and which must be shoved aside, and the subsequent rising when the entrance has been accomplished. A distinction is reported by a correspondent as follows: "If the intention is to speak of a person entering the gesturer's own lodge, the right hand is passed under the left and toward the body, near which the left hand is held; if of a person entering the lodge of another, the left hand is held further from the body and the right is passed under it and outward. In both cases both hands are slightly curved and compressed." As no such distinction is reported by others it may be an individual invention or peculiarity.

A gliding movement of the extended hand, fingers joined, backs up, downward, then ascending, indicative of the stooping and resumption of the upright position in entering the same. (*Arapaho* I.)

(1) Sign for LODGE, the left hand being still in position used in making sign for LODGE; (2) forefinger and thumb of right hand brought to a point and thrust through the outline of an imaginary lodge represented by the left hand. (*Cheyenne* II.)

First make the sign for LODGE, then place the left hand, horizontal and slightly arched, before the body, and pass the right hand with extended index underneath the left—forward and slightly upward beyond it. (*Absaroka* I; *Dakota* V; *Shoshoni and Banak* I; *Wyandot* I.)

Left hand (W), ends of fingers toward the right, stationary in front of the left breast; pass the right hand directly and quickly out from the breast under the stationary left hand, ending with the extended fingers of the right hand pointing outward and slightly downward, joined, palm downward flat, horizontal (W). (*Dakota* I.) "Gone under; covered."

Hold the open left hand a foot or eighteen inches in front of the breast, palm downward or backward, fingers pointing toward the right, and pass the right hand, palm upward, fingers bent sidewise and pointing backward, from before backward underneath it, through a curve until near the mouth. Some at the same time move the left hand a little forward. (*Dakota* IV.)

The left hand, palm downward, finger-tips forward, either quite extended or with the fingers slightly bent, is held before the body. Then the right hand nearly or quite extended, palm downward, finger-tips near the left thumb, and pointing toward it, is passed transversely under the left hand and one to four inches below it. The fingers of the right hand point slightly upward when the motion is completed. This sign usually, but not invariably, refers to entering a house. (*Mandan and Hidatsa* I.)

Place the slightly curved left hand, palm down, before the breast, pointing to the right, then pass the flat right hand, palm down, in a short curve forward, under and upward beyond the left. (*Ute* I.) "Evidently from the manner in which a person is obliged to stoop in entering an ordinary Indian lodge."

HORSE.
The right hand with the edge downward, the fingers joined, the thumb recumbent, extended forward. (*Dunbar.*)

Place the index and middle finger of the right hand astraddle the index finger of the left. [In the original the expression "third" finger is used, but it is ascertained in another connection that the author counts the thumb as the first finger and always means what is generally styled middle finger when he says third. The alteration is made to prevent confusion.] (*Wied.*) I have described this sign in words to the same effect. (*Matthews.*) The right arm is raised, and the hand, opened edgewise, with fingers parallel and approximated, is drawn from left to right before the body at the supposed height of the animal. There is no conceivable identity in the execution of this sign and *Wied's*, but his sign for *horse* is nearly identical with the sign for *ride a horse* among the Otos. (*Boteler.*) This sign is still used by the Cheyennes. (*Dodge.*)

A hand passed across the forehead. (*Macgowan.*)

Left-hand thumb and forefinger straightened out, held to the level of and in front of the breast; right-hand forefinger separated from the middle finger and thrown across the left hand to imitate the act of bestriding. They appear to have no other conception of a horse, and have thus indicated that they have known it only as an animal to be ridden. (*Creel; Cheyenne* II.)

28 A E

Draw the right hand from left to right across the body about the heart, the fingers all closed except the index. This is abbreviated by making a circular sweep of the right open hand from about the left elbow to the front of the body, probably indicating the mane. A Pani sign. (*Ohcyenne* IV.)

Place the first two fingers of the right hand, thumb extended (N 1), downward, astraddle the first two joined and straight fingers of the left hand (T 1), sidewise to the right. Many Sioux Indians use only the forefinger straightened. (*Dakota* I.) "Horse mounted."

The first and second fingers extended and separated, remaining fingers and thumb closed; left forefinger extended, horizontal, remaining fingers and thumb closed; place the right-hand fingers astride of the forefinger of the left, and both hands jerked together, up and down, to represent the motion of a horse. (*Dakota* III.)

The two hands being clinched and near together, palms downward, thumbs against the forefingers, throw them, each alternately, forward and backward about a foot, through an ellipsis two or three times, from about six inches in front of the chest, to imitate the galloping of a horse, or the hands may be held forward and not moved. (*Dakota* IV.)

Place the extended and separated index and second fingers of the

right hand astraddle of the extended forefinger of the left. Fig. 260. Sometimes all the fingers of the left hand are extended in making this sign, as in Fig. 261, though this may be the result of carelessness.

FIG. 260.   FIG. 261.

(*Dakota* VI, VII, VIII; *Hidatsa* I; *Ponka* II; *Arikara* I; *Pani* I.)

The left hand is placed before the chest, back upward in the position of an index-hand pointing forward; then the first and second fingers of the right hand only being extended, separated and pointing downward, are set one on each side of the left forefinger, the interdigital space resting on the forefinger. The palm faces downward and backward. This represents a rider astride of a horse. (*Mandan and Hidatsa* I.)

Close hands, except forefingers, which are curved downward; move them forward in rotation, imitating the fore feet of the horse, and make puffing sound of "Uh, uh"! (*Omaha* I.) "This sign represents the horse racing off to a safe distance, and puffing as he tosses his head."

The arm is flexed and with the hand extended is brought on a level with the mouth. The hand then assumes the position (W 1), modified by being held edges up and down, palm toward the chest, instead of flat. The arm and hand being held thus about the usual height of a horse are made to pass in an undulating manner across the face or body about one foot distant from contact. The latter movements are to resemble the animal's gait. (*Oto* I.) "Height of animal and movement of same."

The index and second fingers of the right hand are placed astraddle the extended forefinger of the left. (*Wyandot* I.)

Place the flat right hand, thumb down, edgewise before the right side of the shoulder, pointing toward the right. (*Kaiowa* I; *Comanche* III; *Apache* II; *Wichita* II.) Fig. 262.

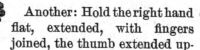

Another: Hold the right hand flat, extended, with fingers joined, the thumb extended up-

Fig. 263.

Fig. 262.

ward, then pass the hand at arm's length before the face from left to right. This is said by the authorities cited below to be also the Caddo sign, and that the other tribes mentioned originally obtained it from that tribe. (*Kaiowa* I; *Comanche* I, III; *Apache* II; *Wichita* II.) Fig. 263.

Another: Place the extended and separated index and second fingers astraddle the extended and horizontal forefinger of the left hand. This sign is only used when communicating with uninstructed white men, or with other Indians whose sign for *horse* is specifically distinct. (*Kaiowa* I; *Comanche* III; *Apache* II; *Wichita* II.)

Place the extended index and second fingers of the right hand across the extended first two fingers of the left. Fig. 264. Size of the animal is indicated by passing the right hand, palm down, with fingers loosely separated, forward from the right side, at any height as the case may necessitate, after which the sign for HORSE may be made. (*Pima and Papago* I.)

Fig. 264.

Fig. 265.

Place the right hand, palm down, before the right side of the chest; place the tips of the second and third fingers against the ball of the thumb, allowing the index and little fingers to project to represent the ears. Fig. 265. Frequently the middle fingers extend equally with and against the thumb, forming the head of the animal, the ears always being represented by the two outer fingers, viz, the index and little finger. Fig. 266. (*Ute* I.) A similar sign is reported by Colonel Dodge as used by the Utes.

Fig. 266.

Elevate the right hand, extended, with fingers joined, outer edge toward the ground, in front of the body or right shoulder, and pointing forward, resting the curved thumb against the palmar side of the index. This sign appears also to signify *animal* generically, being frequently employed as a preliminary sign when denoting other species. (*Apache* I.)

Deaf-mute natural signs :
Imitate the motion of the elbows of a man on horseback. (*Ballard.*)

Act in the manner of a driver, holding the lines in his hands and shouting to the horse. (*Cross.*)

Move the hands several times as if to hold the reins. (*Larson.*)

Deaf-mute signs :
The French deaf-mutes add to the straddling of the index the motion of a trot. American deaf-mutes indicate the ears by placing two fingers of each hand on each side of the head and moving them backward and forward. This is sometimes followed by straddling the left hand by the fore and middle fingers of the right.

————, A man on a.
Same sign as for HORSE, with the addition of erecting the thumb while making the gesture. (*Dodge.*)

————, Bay.
Make the sign for HORSE, and then rub the lower part of the cheek back and forth. (*Dakota* IV.)

————, Black.
Make the sign for HORSE, and then point to a black object or rub the back of the left hand with the palmar side of the fingers of the right. (*Dakota* IV.)

————, Bronco. An untamed horse.
Make the sign TO RIDE by placing the extended and separated index and second fingers of the right hand astraddle the extended forefinger of the left hand, then with both hands retained in their relative positions move them forward in high arches to show the bucking of the animal. (*Ute* I.)

————, Grazing of a.
Make the sign for HORSE, then lower the hand and pass it from side to side as if dipping it upon the surface. (*Ute* I.)

————, Packing a.
Hold the left hand, pointing forward, palm inward, a foot in front of the chest and lay the opened right hand, pointing forward, first obliquely along the right side of the upper edge of the left hand, then on top, and then obliquely along the left side. (*Dakota* IV.)

————, Racing, Fast horse.
The right arm is elevated and bent at right angle before the face; the hand, in position (S 1) modified by being horizontal, palm to the face,

is drawn across edgewise in front of the face. The hand is then closed
and in position (B) approaches the mouth from which it is opened and
closed successively forward several times, finally it is suddenly thrust
out in position (W 1) back concave. (*Oto and Missouri* I.) "Is expressed in the (*Oto* I) sign for HORSE, then the motion for quick running."

———— Racing.

Extend the two forefingers and after placing them parallel near
together in front of the chest, backs upward, push them rapidly forward about a foot. (*Dakota* IV.)

Place both hands, with the forefingers only extended and pointing
forward side by side with the palms down, before the body; then push
them alternately backward and forward, in imitation of the movement
of horses who are running "neck and neck." (*Ute* I; *Apache* I, II.)

————, Saddling a.

Hold the left hand as in the sign for HORSE, *Packing a*, and lay the
semiflexed right hand across its upper edge two or three times, the ends
of the right fingers toward the left. (*Dakota* IV.)

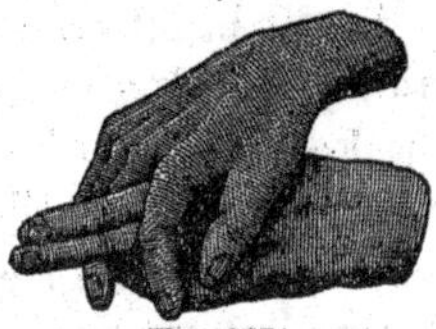

Place the extended and separated fingers rapidly
with a slapping sound astraddle the extended fore
and second fingers of the left hand. The sound is
produced by the palm of the right hand which comes
in contact with the upper surface of the left. (*Ute* I.)   Fig. 267.

FIG. 267.

————, Spotted; pied.

Make the sign for HORSE, then the sign for SPOTTED, see page 345.
(*Dakota* IV.)

KILL, KILLING.

The hands are held with the edge upward, and the right hand strikes
the other transversely, as in the act of chopping. This sign seems to be
more particularly applicable to convey the idea of death produced by
a blow of the tomahawk or war-club. (*Long.*)

Clinch the hand and strike from above downward. (*Wied.*) I do not
remember this. I have given you the sign for killing with a stroke.
(*Matthews.*) There is an evident similarity in conception and execution
between the (*Oto and Missouri* I) sign and *Wied's*. (*Boteler.*) I have
frequently seen this sign made by the Arikara, Gros Ventre, and Mandan Indians at Fort Berthold Agency. (*McChesney.*) This motion,
which may be more clearly expressed as the downward thrust of a knife
held in the clinched hand, is still used by many tribes for the general
idea of "kill," and illustrates the antiquity of the knife as a weapon.
Wied does not say whether the clinched hand is thrust downward with

the edge or the knuckles forward. The latter is now the almost universal usage among the same tribes from which he is supposed to have taken his list of signs, and indicates the thrust of a knife more decisively than if the fist were moved with the edge in advance. The actual employment of arrow, gun, or club in taking life, is, however, often specified by appropriate gesture.

Smite the sinister palm earthward with the dexter fist sharply, in sign of "going down"; or strike out with the dexter fist toward the ground, meaning to "shut down"; or pass the dexter under the left forefinger, meaning to "go under." (*Burton.*)

Right hand cast down. (*Macgowan.*)

Hold the right fist, palm down, knuckles forward, and make a thrust forward and downward. (*Arapaho* II; *Cheyenne* V; *Dakota* VI, VII, VIII; *Hidatsa* I; *Ponka* II; *Arikara* I; *Pani* I.) Fig. 268.

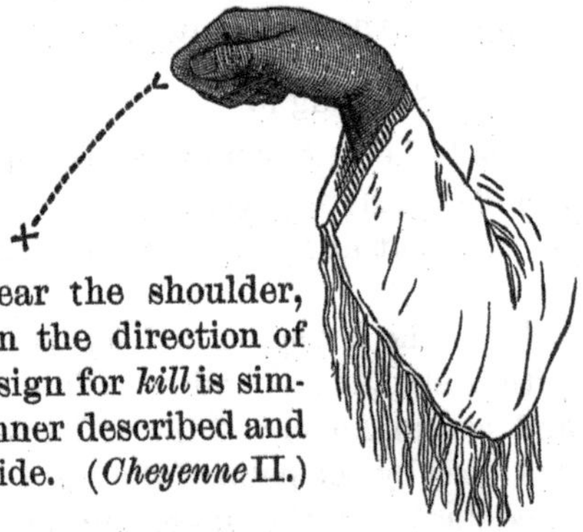

Right hand clinched, thumb lying along the finger tips, elevated to near the shoulder, strike downward and out vaguely in the direction of the object to be killed. The abstract sign for *kill* is simply to clinch the right hand in the manner described and strike it down and out from the right side. (*Cheyenne* II.)

FIG. 268.

Close the right hand, extending the forefinger alone; point toward the breast, then throw from you forward, bringing the hand toward the ground. (*Ojibwa* V; *Omaha* I.)

Both hands clinched, with the thumbs resting against the middle joints of the forefingers, hold the left transversely in front of and as high as the breast, then push the right, palm down, quickly over and down in front of the left. (*Absaroka* I; *Shoshoni and Banak* I.) "To force under—literally."

With the dexter fist carried to the front of the body at the right side, strike downward and outward several times, with back of hand upward, thumb toward the left, several times. (*Dakota* I.) "Strike down."

With the first and second joints of the fingers of the right hand bent, end of thumb against the middle of the index, palm downward, move the hand energetically forward and downward from a foot in front of the right breast. Striking with a stone—man's first weapon. (*Dakota* IV.)

The left hand, thumb up, back forward, not very rigidly extended, is held before the chest and struck in the palm with the outer edge of the right hand. (*Mandan and Hidatsa* I.) "To kill with a blow; to deal the death blow." Fig. 269.

Right hand, fingers open but slightly curved, palm to the left; move downward, describing a curve. (*Omaha* I.)

Another: Similar to the last, but the index finger is extended, pointing in front of
you, the other fingers but half open.
(*Omaha* I.)

Place the flat right hand, palm down, at
arm's length to the right, bring it quickly,
horizontally, to the side of the head, then
make the sign for DEAD. (*Ojibwa* V; *Wyandot* I.) "To strike with a club, dead."

FIG. 269.

Both hands, in positions (A A), with arms semiflexed toward the body, make the forward rotary sign with the clinched fists as in fighting; the right hand is then raised from the left outward, as clutching a knife with the blade pointing downward and inward toward the left fist; the left fist, being held *in situ*, is struck now by the right, edgewise as above described, and both suddenly fall together. (*Oto and Missouri* I.) "To strike down in battle with a knife. Indians seldom disagree or kill another in times of tribal peace."

Deaf-mute natural signs:
Strike a blow in the air with the clinched fist, and then incline the head to one side, and lower the open hand, palm upward. (*Ballard.*)

Strike the other hand with the fist, or point a gun, and, having shot, suddenly point to your breast with the finger, and hold your head side-wise on the hand. (*Cross.*)

Use the closed hand as if to strike, and then move back the head with the eyes shut and the mouth opened. (*Hasenstab.*)

Put the head down over the breast, and then move down the stretched hand along the neck. (*Larson.*)

Turkish sign:
Draw finger across the throat like cutting with a knife. (*Barnum.*)

—— In battle, To.
Make the sign for BATTLE by placing both hands at the height of the breast, palms facing, the left forward from the left shoulder, the right outward and forward from the right, fingers pointing up and spread, move them alternately toward and from one another; then strike the

back of the fingers of the right hand into the slightly curved palm of the left, immediately afterward throwing the right outward and downward toward the right. (*Ute* I.) "Killed and falling over."

—— You; I will kill you.
Direct the right hand toward the offender and spring the finger from the thumb, as in the act of sprinkling water. (*Long.*) The conception is perhaps "causing blood to flow," or, perhaps, "sputtering away the life," though there is a strong similarity to the motion used for the *discharge of a gun or arrow.*

Remarks and illustrations connected with the signs for *kill* appear on pages 377 and 378, *supra.*

——, to, with a knife.
Clinch the right hand and strike forcibly toward the ground before the breast from the height of the face. (*Ute* I.) "Appears to have originated when flint knives were still used."

No, NOT. (Compare NOTHING.)
The hand held up before the face, with the palm outward and vibrated to and fro. (*Dunbar.*)

The right hand waved outward to the right with the thumb upward. (*Long; Creel.*)

Wave the right hand quickly by and in front of the face toward the right. (*Wied.*) Refusing to accept the idea or statement presented.

Move the hand from right to left, as if motioning away. This sign also means "I'll have nothing to do with you." (*Burton.*)

A deprecatory wave of the right hand from front to right, fingers extended and joined. (*Arapaho* I; *Cheyenne* V.)

Right-hand fingers extended together, side of hand in front of and facing the face, in front of the mouth and waved suddenly to the right. (*Cheyenne* II.)

Place the right hand extended before the body, fingers pointing upward, palm to the front, then throw the hand outward to the right, and slightly downward. (*Absaroka* I; *Hidatsa* I; *Arikara* I.) See Fig. 65, page 290.

The right hand, horizontal, palm toward the left, is pushed sidewise outward and toward the right from in front of the left breast. *No, none, I have none,* etc., are all expressed by this sign. Often these Indians for *no* will simply shake the head to the right and left. This sign, although it may have originally been introduced from the white people's habit of shaking the head to express "no," has been in use among them for as long as the oldest people can remember, yet they do not use the variant to express "yes." (*Dakota* I.) "Dismissing the idea, etc."

Place the opened relaxed right hand, pointing toward the left, back forward, in front of the nose or as low as the breast, and throw it for-ward and outward about eighteen inches. Some at the same time turn the palm upward. Or make the sign at the height of the breast with both hands. Represents the shaking of the head. (*Dakota* IV.) The shaking of the head in negation is not so universal or "natural" as is popularly supposed, for the ancient Greeks, followed by the modern Turks and rustic Italians, threw the head back, instead of shaking it, for "no." Rabelais makes Pantagruel (Book 3) show by many quotations from the ancients how the shaking of the head was a frequent if not universal concomitant of oracular utterance—not connected with nega-tion.

Hold the flat hand edgewise, pointing upward before the right side of the chest, then throw it outward and downward to the right. (*Dakota* VI, VII.) Fig. 270.

The hand, extended or slightly curved, is held in front of the body a little to the right of the median line; it is then carried with a rapid sweep a foot or more farther to the right. (*Mandan and Hidatsa* I.)

Place the hand as in *yes*, as fol-lows: The hand open, palm down-ward, at the level of the breast, is moved forward with a quick down-ward motion from the wrist, imitat-

FIG. 270.

ing a bow of the head; then move it from side to side. (*Iroquois* I.) "A shake of the head."

Throw the flat right hand forward and outward to the right, palm to the front. (*Kaiowa* I; *Comanche* III; *Apache* II; *Wichita* II.)

Quick motion of open hand from the mouth forward, palm toward the mouth. (*Sahaptin* I.)

Place hand in front of body, fingers relaxed, palm toward body (Y 1), then with easy motion move to a point, say, a foot from the body, a little to right, fingers same, but palm upward. (*Sahaptin* I.) "We don't agree." To express *All gone*, use a similar motion with both hands. "Empty."

The hand waved outward with the thumb upward in a semi-curve. (*Comanche* I; *Wichita* I.)

Elevate the extended index and wave it quickly from side to side before the face. This is sometimes accompanied by shaking the head. (*Pai-Ute* I.) Fig. 271.

Extend the index, holding it vertically before the face, remaining fingers and thumb closed; pass the finger quickly from side to side a foot or so before the face. (*Apache* I.) This sign, as also that of (*Pai-Ute* I), is substantially the same as that with the same significance reported from Naples by De Jorio.

FIG. 271.   Another: The right hand, naturally relaxed, is thrown outward and forward toward the right. (*Apache* I.)

Wave extended index before the face from side to side. (*Apache* III.)

Another: Wave the index briskly before the right shoulder. This appears to be more common than the preceding. (*Apache* III.)

Right hand extended at the height of the eye, palm outward, then moved outward a little toward the right. (*Kutchin* I.)

Extend the palm of the right hand horizontally a foot from the waist, palm downward, then suddenly throw it half over from the body, as if tossing a chip from the back of the hand. (*Wichita* I.)

Deaf-mute natural signs :
Shake the head. (*Ballard.*)

Move both hands from each other, and, at the same time, shake the head. (*Hasenstab.*)

Deaf-mute signs :
French deaf-mutes wave the hand to the right and downward, with the first and second fingers joined and extended, the other fingers closed. This position of the fingers is that for the letter N in the finger alphabet, the initial for the word *non.* American deaf-mutes for emphatic negative wave the right hand before the face.

Turkish sign :
Throwing head back or elevating the chin and partly shutting the eyes. This also means, "Be silent." (*Barnum.*)

Japanese sign :
Move the right hand rapidly back and forth before the face. Communicated in a letter from Prof. E. S. MORSE, late of the University of Tokio, Japan. The same correspondent mentions that the Admiralty

Islanders pass the forefinger across the face, striking the nose in passing, for negation. If the *no* is a doubtful one they *rub* the nose in passing, a gesture common elsewhere.

For further illustrations and comparisons see pp. 290, 298, 299, 304, 355, and 356, *supra*.

NONE, NOTHING; I HAVE NONE.

Motion of rubbing out. (*Macgowan*.)

Little or *nothing* is signified by passing one hand over the other. (*Creel; Ojibwa* I.)

May be signified by smartly brushing the right hand across the left from the wrist toward the fingers, both hands extended, palms toward each other and fingers joined. (*Arapaho* I.)

Is included in *gone, destroyed*. (*Dakota* I.)

Place the open left hand about a foot in front of the navel, pointing obliquely forward toward the right, palm obliquely upward and backward, and sweep the palm of the open right hand over it and about a foot forward and to the right through a curve. All bare. (*Dakota* IV.)

Another: Pass the ulnar side of the right index along the left index several times from tip to base, while pronating and supinating the latter. Some roll the right index over on its back as they move it along the left. The hands are to be in front of the navel, backs forward and outward, the left index straight and pointing forward toward the right, the right index straight and pointing forward and toward the left; the other fingers loosely closed. Represents a bush bare of limbs. (*Dakota* IV.)

Another: With the right hand pointing obliquely forward to the left, the left forward to the right, palms upward, move them alternately several times up and down, each time striking the ends of the fingers. Or, the left hand being in the above position, rub the right palm in a circle on the left two or three times, and then move it forward and to the right. Rubbed out; that is all; it is all gone. (*Dakota* IV.)

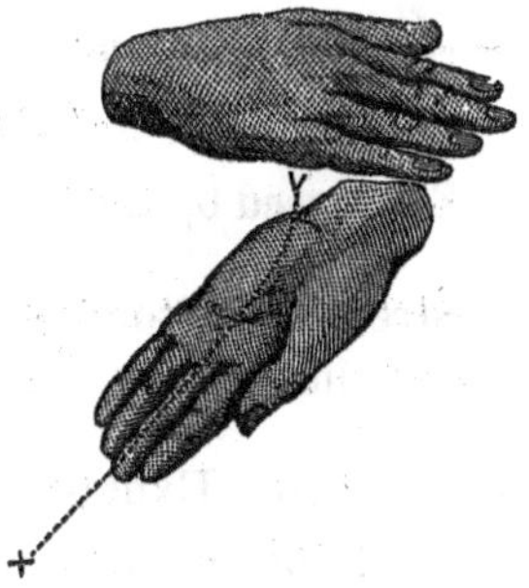

FIG. 272.

Pass the palm of the flat right hand over the left from the wrist toward and off of the tips of the fingers. (*Dakota* VI, VII, VIII; *Ponka* II; *Pani* I.) Fig. 272.

Brush the palm of the left hand from wrist to finger tips with the palm of the right. (*Wyandot* I.)

Another: Throw both hands outward toward their respective sides from the breast. (*Wyandot* I.)

Pass the flat right palm over the palm of the left hand from the wrist forward over the fingers. (*Kaiowa* I; *Comanche* III; *Apache* II; *Wichita* II.) "Wiped out."

Hold the left hand open, with the palm upward, at the height of the elbow and before the body; pass the right quickly over the left, palms touching, from the wrist toward the tips of the left, as if brushing off dust. (*Apache* I.)

Deaf-mute natural signs :
Place the hands near each other, palms downward, and move them over and apart, bringing the palms upward in opposite directions. (*Ballard.*)

Make a motion as in picking up something between the thumb and finger, carry it to the lips, blow it away, and show the open hand. (*Wing.*)

Australian sign :
Pannie (none or nothing). For instance, a native says *Bomako ingina* (give a tomahawk). I reply by shaking the hand, thumb, and all fingers, separated and loosely extended, palm down. (*Smyth, loc. cit.*) Fig. 273.

FIG. 273.

Turkish sign :
Blowing across open palm as though blowing off feathers; also means "Nothing, nothing left." (*Barnum.*)

————, I have none.

Deaf-mute natural signs :
Expressed by the signs for none, after pointing to one's self. (*Ballard.*)

Stretch the tongue and move it to and fro like a pendulum, then shake the head as if to say "no." (*Ziegler.*)

————Left. Exhausted for the present.
Hold both hands naturally relaxed nearly at arm's length before the body, palms toward the face, move them alternately to and fio a few inches, allowing the fingers to strike those of the opposite hand each time as far as the second joint. (*Kaiowa* I; *Comanche* III; *Apache* II; *Wichita* II.) Cleaned out.

QUANTITY, LARGE; MANY; MUCH.

The flat of the right hand patting the back of the left hand, which is repeated in proportion to the greater or lesser quantity. (*Dunbar.*) Simple repetition.

The hands and arms are passed in a curvilinear direction outward and downward, as if showing the form of a large globe; then the hands are closed and elevated, as if something was grasped in each hand and held up about as high as the face. (*Long; Creel.*)

Clutch at the air several times with both hands. The motion greatly resembles those of danseuses playing the castanets. (*Ojibwa* I.)

In the preceding signs the authorities have not distinguished between the ideas of "many" and "much." In the following there appears by the expressions of the authorities to be some distinction intended between a number of objects and a quantity in volume.

——— MANY.

A simultaneous movement of both hands, as if gathering or heaping up. (*Arapaho* I.) Literally "a heap."

Both hands, with spread and slightly curved fingers, are held pendent about two feet apart before the thighs; then draw them toward one another, horizontally, drawing them upward as they come together. (*Absaroka* I; *Shoshoni and Banak* I; *Kaiowa* I; *Comanche* III; *Apache* II; *Wichita* II.) "An accumulation of objects."

Hands about eighteen inches from the ground in front and about the same distance apart, held scoop-fashion, palms looking toward each other, fingers separated; then, with a diving motion, as if scooping up corn from the ground, bring the hands nearly together, with fingers nearly closed, as though holding the corn, and carry upward to the height of the breast, where the hands are turned over, fingers pointing downward, separated, as though the contents were allowed to drop to the ground. (*Dakota* I, II.)

Open the fingers of both hands, and hold the two hands before the breast, with the fingers upward and a little apart, and the palms turned toward each other, as if grasping a number of things. (*Iroquois* I.)

Place the hands on either side of and as high as the head, then open and close the fingers rapidly four or five times. (*Wyandot* I.) "Counting 'tens' an indefinite number of times."

Clasp the hands effusively before the breast. (*Apache* III.)

Deaf-mute natural signs:

Put the fingers of the two hands together, tip to tip, and rub them with a rapid motion. (*Ballard.*)

Make a rapid movement of the fingers and thumbs of both hands upward and downward, and at the same time cause both lips to touch each other in rapid succession, and both eyes to be half opened. (*Hasenstab.*)

Move the fingers of both hands forward and backward. (*Ziegler.*)

Add to *Ziegler's* sign: slightly opening and closing the hands. (*Wing.*)

—— Horses.
Raise the right arm above the head, palm forward, and thrust forward forcibly on a line with the shoulder. (*Omaha* I.)

—— Persons, etc.
Hands and fingers interlaced. (*Macgowan.*)

Take up a bunch of grass or a clod of earth; place it in the hand of the person addressed, who looks down upon it. (*Omaha* I.) "Represents as many or more than the particles contained in the mass."

—— MUCH.
Move both hands toward one another and slightly upward. (*Wied.*) I have seen this sign, but I think it is used only for articles that may be piled on the ground or formed into a heap. The sign most in use for the general idea of *much* or *many* I have given. (*Matthews.*)

Bring the hands up in front of the body with the fingers carefully kept distinct. (*Cheyenne* I.)

Both hands closed, brought up in a curved motion toward each other to the level of the neck or chin. (*Cheyenne* II.)

Both hands and arms are partly extended; each hand is then made to describe, simultaneously with the other, from the head downward, the arc of a circle curving outward. This is used for *large* in some senses. (*Ojibwa* V; *Mandan and Hidatsa* I.)

Both hands flat and extended, placed before the breast, finger tips touching, palms down; then separate them by passing outward and downward as if smoothing the outer surface of a globe. (*Absaroka* I; *Shoshoni and Banak* I; *Kaiowa* I; *Comanche* III; *Apache* II; *Wichita* II.) "A heap."

Much is included in *many* or *big*, as the case may require. (*Dakota* I.)

The hands, with fingers widely separated, slightly bent, pointing forward, and backs outward, are to be rapidly approximated through downward curves, from positions twelve to thirty-six inches apart, at the height of the navel, and quickly closed. Or the hands may be moved until the right is above the left. So much that it has to be gathered with both hands. (*Dakota* IV.)

Hands open, palms turned in, held about three feet apart and about two feet from the ground. Raise them about a foot, then bring in an upward curve toward each other. As they pass each other, palms down, the right hand is about three inches above the left. (*Omaha* I.)

Place both hands flat and extended, thumbs touching, palms downward, in front of and as high as the face; then move them outward and downward a short distance toward their respective sides, thus describing the upper half of a circle. (*Wyandot* I.) "A heap."

Both hands clinched, placed as high as and in front of the hips, palms facing opposite sides and about a foot apart, then bring them upward and inward, describing an arc, until the thumbs touch. (*Apache* I.) Fig. 274.

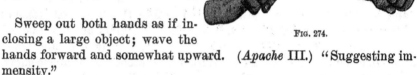

FIG. 274.

Sweep out both hands as if inclosing a large object; wave the hands forward and somewhat upward. (*Apache* III.) "Suggesting immensity."

Deaf-mute sign:

The French deaf-mutes place the two hands, with fingers united and extended in a slight curve, nearly together, left above right, in front of the body, and then raise the left in a direct line above the right, thus suggesting the idea of a large and slightly-rounded object being held between the two palms.

——— And heavy.

Hands open, palms turned in, held about three feet apart, and about two feet from the ground, raise them about a foot; close the fists, backs of hands down, as if lifting something heavy; then move a short distance up and down several times. (*Omaha* I.)

Remarks connected with the signs for *quantity* appear on pages 291, 359, and 382, *supra.*

QUESTION; INQUIRY; INTERROGATION.

The palm of the hand upward and carried circularly outward, and depressed. (*Dunbar.*)

The hand held up with the thumb near the face, and the palm directed toward the person of whom the inquiry is made; then rotated upon the wrist two or three times edgewise, to denote uncertainty. (*Long;* *Comanche* I; *Wichita* I.) The motion might be mistaken for the derisive, vulgar gesture called "taking a sight," "*donner un pied de nez,*" descending to our small boys from antiquity. The separate motion of the fingers in the vulgar gesture as used in our eastern cities is, however, more nearly correlated with some of the Indian signs for *fool*, one of which is the same as that for *Kaiowa*, see TRIBAL SIGNS. It may be noted that the Latin "*sagax*," from which is derived "sagacity," was chiefly used to denote the keen scent of dogs, so there is a relation established between the nasal organ and wisdom or its absence, and that "*suspendere naso*" was a classic phrase for hoaxing. The Italian expressions "*restare con un palmo di naso*," "*con tanto di naso*," etc., mentioned by the canon De Jorio, refer to the same vulgar gesture in which the face is supposed to be thrust forward sillily. Further remarks connected with this sign appear on pp. 304, 305, *supra*.

Extend the open hand perpendicularly with the palm outward, and move it from side to side several times. (*Wied.*) This sign is still used. For "outward," however, I would substitute "forward." The hand is usually, but not always, held before the face. (*Matthews.*) This is not the sign for *question*, but is used to attract attention before commencing a conversation or any other time during the talk, when found necessary. (*McChesney.*) With due deference to Dr. McChesney, this is the sign for *question*, as used by many tribes, and especially Dakotas. The Prince of Wied probably intended to convey the motion of *forward, to the front*, when he said *outward*. In making the sign for *attention* the hand is held more nearly horizontal, and is directed toward the individual whose attention is desired. (*Hoffman.*)

Right hand in front of right side of body, forearm horizontal, palm of hand to the left, fingers extended, joined and horizontal, thumb extending upward naturally, turn hand to the left about 60°, then resume first position. Continue this motion for about two to four seconds, depending on earnestness of inquiry. (*Creel.*)

Right hand, fingers pointing upward, palm outward, elevated to the level of the shoulder, extended toward the person addressed, and slightly shaken from side to side. (*Cheyenne* II.)

Hold the elbow of the right arm against the side, extending the right hand, palm inward, with all the fingers straight joined, as far as may be, while the elbow remains fixed against the side; then turn the extended hand to the right and left, repeating this movement several times, being performed by the muscles of the arm. (*Sac, Fox, and Kickapoo* I.)

Place the flat and extended right hand, palm forward, about twelve inches in front of and as high as the shoulder, then shake the hand from side to side as it is moved upward and forward. (*Apache* I.) See Fig. 304, in TENDOY-HUERITO DIALOGUE, p. 486. This may be compared with the ancient Greek sign, Fig. 67, and with the modern Neapolitan sign, Fig. 70, both of which are discussed on p. 291, *supra*.

Deaf-mute natural sign :

A quick motion of the lips with an inquiring look. (*Ballard.*)

Deaf-mute sign :

The French deaf-mutes for *inquiry*, "*qu'est-ce que c'est ?*" bring the hands to the lower part of the chest, with open palms about a foot separate and diverging outward.

Australian sign :

One is a sort of note of interrogation. For instance, if I were to meet a native and make the sign: Hand flat, fingers and thumb extended, the two middle fingers touching, the two outer slightly separated from the middle by turning the hand palm upward as I met him, it would mean: "Where are you going?" In other words I should say "*Minna?*" (what name?). (*Smyth.*) Fig. 275.

FIG. 275.

Some comparisons and illustrations connected with the signs for *question* appear on pages 291, 297, and 303, *supra*, and under PHRASES, *infra*. Quintilian remarks upon this subject as follows: "In questioning, we do not compose our gesture after any single manner; the position of the hand, for the most part is to be changed, however disposed before."

SOLDIER.

———, American.

The upright nearly closed hands, thumbs against the middle of the forefingers, being in front of the body, with their thumbs near together, palms forward, separate them about two feet horizontally on the same line. All in a line in front. (*Cheyenne* III; *Dakota* IV.)

Pass each hand down the outer seam of the pants. (*Sac, Fox, and Kickapoo* I.) "Stripes."

Sign for WHITE MAN as follows: The extended index (M turned inward) is drawn from the left side of the head around in front to the right side, about on a line with the brim of the hat, with the back of the hand outward; and then for FORT, viz, on level of the breasts in front of body, both hands with fingers turned inward, straight, backs joined, backs of hands outward, horizontal, turn outward the hands until the fingers are free, curve them, and bring the wrists together so as to describe a circle with a space left between the ends of the curved fingers. (*Dakota* I.) "From his fortified place of abode."

Another: Both hands in front of body, fists, backs outward, hands in contact, draw them apart on a straight line right to right, left to left about two feet, then draw the index, other fingers closed, across the

29 A E

forehead above the eyebrows. This is the sign preferred by the Sioux. (*Dakota* I.)

Extend the fingers of the right hand; place the thumb on the same plane close beside them, and then bring the thumb side of the hand horizontally against the middle of the forehead, palm downward and little finger to the front. (*Dakota* II; *Ute* I.) "Visor of forage cap."

First make the sign for SOLDIER substantially the same as (*Dakota* VI) below, then that for WHITE MAN, viz.: Draw the opened right hand horizontally from left to right across the forehead a little above the eyebrows, the back of the hand to be upward and the fingers pointing toward the left; or, close all the fingers except the index and draw it across the forehead in the same manner. (*Dakota* IV.) For illustrations of other signs for *white man* see Figs 315 and 329, *infra*.

Place the radial sides of the clinched hands together before the chest,

then draw them horizontally apart. (*Dakota* VI; *Arikara* I.) "All in a line." Fig. 276.

FIG. 276.

Put thumbs to temples, and forefingers forward, meeting in front, other fingers closed. (*Apache* III.) "Cap-visor."

———, Arikara.

Make the sign for ARIKARA (see TRIBAL SIGNS) and that for BRAVE. (*Arikara* I.)

———, Dakota.

Make the sign for DAKOTA-(see TRIBAL SIGNS) and that for SOLDIER. (*Dakota* VI.)

———, Indian.

Both fists before the body, palms down, thumbs touching, then draw them horizontally apart to the right and left. (*Arapaho* II; *Cheyenne* V; *Ponka* II; *Pani* I.) This is the same sign illustrated in Fig. 276, above, as given by tribes there cited for *white* or *American soldier*. The tribes now cited use it for *a soldier* of the same tribe as the gesturer, or perhaps for *soldier* generically, as they subjoin a tribal sign or the sign for *white man*, when desiring to refer to any other than their own tribe.

TRADE or BARTER; EXCHANGE.

——— TRADE.

First make the sign of EXCHANGE (see below), then pat the left arm with the right finger, with a rapid motion from the hand passing it toward the shoulder. (*Long*.)

Strike the extended index finger of the right hand several times upon that of the left. (*Wied.*) I have described the same sign in different terms and at greater length. It is only necessary, however, to place the fingers in contact once. The person whom the prince saw making this sign may have meant to indicate something more than the simple idea of trade, *i. e.*, trade often or habitually. The idea of frequency is often conveyed by the repetition of a sign (as in some Indian languages by repetition of the root). Or the sign-maker may have repeated the sign to demonstrate it more clearly. (*Matthews.*) Though some difference exists in the motions executed in *Wied's* sign and that of (*Oto and Missouri* I), there is sufficient similarity to justify a probable identity of conception and to make them easily understood. (*Boteler.*) In the author's mind *exchange* was probably intended for one transaction, in which each of two articles took the place before occupied by the other, and *trade* was intended for a more general and systematic barter, indicated by the repetition of strokes. Such distinction would not perhaps have occurred to most observers, but as the older authorities, such as Long and Wied, give distinct signs under the separate titles of *trade* and *exchange* they must be credited with having some reason for so doing. A pictograph connected with this sign is shown on page 381, *supra*.

Cross the forefingers of both hands before the breast. (*Burton.*) "Diamond cut diamond." This conception of one smart trader cutting into the profits of another is a mistake arising from the rough resemblance of the sign to that for *cutting*. Captain Burton is right, however, in reporting that this sign for *trade* is also used for *white man, American*, and that the same Indians using it orally call white men "shwop," from the English or American word "swap" or "swop." This is a legacy from the early traders, the first white men met by the Western tribes, and the expression extends even to the Sahaptins on the Yakama River, where it appears incorporated in their language as *swiapoin*. It must have penetrated to them through the Shoshoni.

Cross the index fingers. (*Macgowan.*)

Cross the forefingers at right angles. (*Arapaho* I.)

Both hands, palms facing each other, forefingers extended, crossed right above left before the breast. (*Cheyenne* II.)

The left hand, with forefinger extended, pointing toward the right (rest of fingers closed), horizontal, back outward, otherwise as (M), is held in front of left breast about a foot; and the right hand, with forefinger extended (J), in front of and near the right breast, is carried outward and struck over the top of the stationary left (+) crosswise, where it remains for a moment. (*Dakota* I.)

Hold the extended left index about a foot in front of the breast, pointing obliquely forward toward the right, and lay the extended right index at right angles across the left, first raising the right about a foot above the left, palms of both inward, other fingers half closed. This is also an Arapaho sign as well as Dakota. Yours is there and mine is there; take either. (*Dakota* IV.)

Place the first two fingers of the right hand across those of the left, both being slightly spread. The hands are sometimes used, but are placed edgewise. (*Dakota* V.) Fig. 277.

FIG. 277.

Another: The index of the right hand is laid across the forefinger of the left when the transaction includes but two persons trading single article for article. (*Dakota* V.)

Strike the back of the extended index at a right angle against the radial side of the extended forefinger of the left hand. (*Dakota* VI, VII.) Fig. 278.

FIG. 278.

The forefingers are extended, held obliquely upward, and crossed at right angles to one another, usually in front of the chest. (*Mandan and Hidatsa* I.)

Bring each hand as high as the breast, forefinger pointing up, the other fingers closed, then move quickly the right hand to the left, the left to the right, the forefingers making an acute angle as they cross. (*Omaha* I; *Ponka* I.)

The palm point of the right index extended touches the chest; it is then turned toward the second individual interested, then touches the object. The arms are now drawn toward the body, semiflexed, with the hands, in type-positions (W W), crossed, the right superposed to the left. The individual then casts an interrogating glance at the second person. (*Oto and Missouri* I.) "To cross something from one to another."

Close the hands, except the index fingers and the thumbs; with them open, move the hands several times past one another at the height of the breast, the index fingers pointing upward and the thumbs outward. (*Iroquois* I.) "The movement indicates 'exchanging.'"

Hold the left hand horizontally before the body, with the forefinger only extended and pointing to the right, palm downward; then, with the right hand closed, index only extended, palm to the right, place the index at right angles on the forefinger of the left, touching at the second joints. (*Kaiowa* I; *Comanche* III; *Apache* II; *Wichita* II.)

Pass the hands in front of the body, all the fingers closed except the forefingers. (*Sahaptin* I.)

Close the fingers of both hands (K); bring them opposite each shoulder; then bring the hands across each other's pathway, without permitting them to touch. At the close of the sign the left hand will be near and pointing at the right shoulder; right hand will be near and pointing at the left shoulder. (*Comanche* I.)

Close both hands, leaving the forefingers only extended; place the right before and several inches above the left, then pass the right hand toward the left elbow and the left hand toward the right elbow, each hand following the course made by a flourishing cut with a short sword. This sign, according to the informant, is also employed by the Banak and Umatilla Indians. (*Comanche* II; *Pai-Ute* I.)

The forefingers of both hands only extended, pass the left from left to right, and the right at the same time crossing its course from the tip toward the wrist of the left, stopping when the wrists cross. (*Ute* I.) "Exchange of articles."

Right hand carried across chest, hand extended, palm upward, fingers and thumb closed as if holding something; left hand, in same position, carried across the right, palm downward. (*Kutchin* I.)

Hands pronated and forefingers crossed. (*Zuñi* I.)

Deaf-mute natural sign :

Close the hand slightly, as if taking something, and move it forward and open the hand as if to drop or give away the thing, and again close and withdraw the hand as if to take something else. (*Ballard.*)

American instructed deaf-mutes use substantially the sign described by (*Mandan and Hidatsa* I).

—— To buy.

Hold the left hand about twelve inches before the breast, the thumb resting on the closed third and fourth fingers; the fore and second fingers separated and extended, palm toward the breast; then pass the extended index into the crotch formed by the separated fingers of the left hand. This

FIG. 279.

is an invented sign, and was given to illustrate the difference between buying and trading. (*Ute* I.) Fig. 279.

Deaf-mute natural sign :

Make a circle on the palm of the left hand with the forefinger of the right hand, to denote *coin,* and close the thumb and finger as if to take the money, and put the hand forward to signify giving it to some one, and move the hand a little apart from the place where it left the money, and then close and withdraw the hand, as if to take the thing purchased. (*Ballard.*)

Italian sign :

To indicate paying, in the language of the fingers, one makes as though he put something, piece after piece, from one hand into the other —a gesture, however, far less expressive than that when a man lacks money, and yet cannot make up a face to beg it; or simply to indicate want of money, which is to rub together the thumb and forefinger, at the same time stretching out the hand. (*Butler.*)   An illustration from De Jorio of the Neapolitan sign for *money* is given on page 297, *supra.*

—— EXCHANGE.

The two forefingers are extended perpendicularly, and the hands are then passed by each other transversely in front of the breast so as nearly to exchange positions. (*Long.*)

Pass both hands, with extended forefingers, across each other before the breast. (*Wied.*) See remarks on this author's sign for TRADE, *supra.*

Hands brought up to front of breast, forefingers extended and other fingers slightly closed; hands suddenly drawn toward and past each other until forearms are crossed in front of breast. (*Cheyenne* II.) "Exchange; right hand exchanging position with the left."

Left hand, with forefinger extended, others closed (M, except back of hand outward), is brought, arm extended, in front of the left breast, and the extended forefinger of the right hand, obliquely upward, others closed, is placed crosswise over the left and maintained in that position for a moment, when the fingers of the right hand are relaxed (as in Y), brought near the breast with hand horizontal, palm inward, and then carried out again in front of right breast twenty inches, with palm looking toward the left, fingers pointing forward, hand horizontal, and then the left hand performs the same movements on the left side of the body, (*Dakota* I.) "You give me, I give you."

The hands, backs forward, are held as index hands, pointing upward. the elbows being fully bent; each hand is then, simultaneously with the other, moved to the opposite shoulder, so that the forearms cross one another almost at right angles. (*Mandan and Hidatsa* I.)

YES; AFFIRMATION; IT IS SO. (Compare GOOD.)

The motion is somewhat like *truth,* viz: The forefinger in the attitude of pointing, from the mouth forward in a line curving a little upward, the other fingers being carefully closed; but the finger is held rather more upright, and is passed nearly straight forward from opposite the breast, and when at the end of its course it seems gently to strike something, though with rather a slow and not suddenly accelerated motion. (*Long.*)

Wave the hand straight forward from the face. (*Burton.*) This may be compared with the forward nod common over most of the world for assent, but that gesture is not universal, as the New Zealanders elevate the head and chin, and the Turks are reported by several travelers to shake the head somewhat like our negative. Rev. H. N. Barnum denies that report, giving below the gesture observed by him. He, however, describes the Turkish gesture sign for *truth* to be "gently bowing with head inclined to the right." This sidewise inclination may be what has been called the shake of the head in affirmation.

Another: Wave the hand from the mouth, extending the thumb from the index and closing the other three fingers. (*Burton.*)

Gesticulate vertically downward and in front of the body with the extended forefinger (right hand usually), the remaining fingers and thumb closed, their nails down. (*Creel*; *Arapaho* I.)

Right hand elevated to the level and in front of the shoulder, two first fingers somewhat extended, thumb resting against the middle finger; sudden motion in a curve forward and downward. (*Cheyenne* II.) It has been suggested that the correspondence between this gesture and the one given by the same gesturer for *sitting* (made by holding the right hand to one side, fingers and thumb drooping, and striking downward to the ground or object to be sat upon) seemingly indicates that the origin of the former is in connection with the idea of "resting," or "settling a question." It is however at least equally probable that the forward and downward curve is an abbreviation of the sign for *truth*, *true*, a typical description of which follows given by (*Dakota* I). The sign for *true* can often be interchanged with that for *yes*, in the same manner as the several words.

The index of the horizontal hand (M), other fingers closed, is carried straight outward from the mouth. This is also the sign for *truth*. (*Dakota* I.) "But one tongue."

Extend the right index, the thumb against it, nearly close the other fingers, and holding it about a foot in front of the right breast, bend the hand from the wrist downward until the end of the index has passed about six inches through an arc. Some at the same time move the hand forward a little. (*Dakota* IV.) "A nod; the hand representing the head and the index the nose."

Hold the naturally closed hand before the right side of the breast, or shoulder, leaving the index and thumb extended, then throw the hand downward, bring the index against the inner side of the thumb. (*Da-kota* VI, VII, VIII.) Fig. 280. Compare also Fig. 61, p. 286, *supra*, Quintilian's sign for approbation.

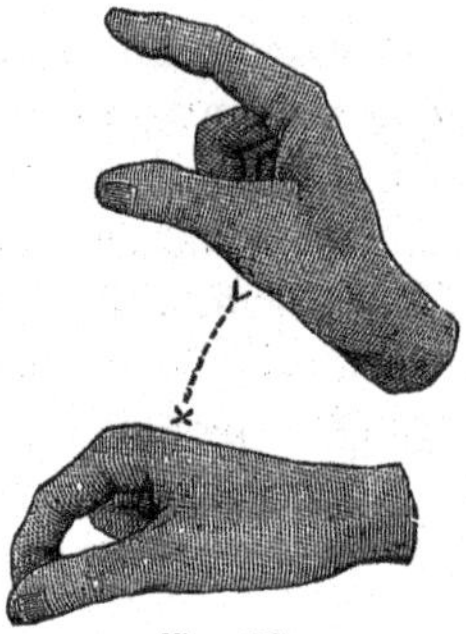

The right hand, with the forefinger only extended and pointing forward, is held before and near the chest. It is then moved forward one or two feet, usually with a slight curve downward. (*Mandan and Hidatsa* I.)

Bend the right arm, pointing toward the chest with the index finger; unbend, throwing the hand up and forward. (*Omaha* I.)

FIG. 280.

Another: Close the three fingers, close the thumb over them, extend forefinger, and then shake forward and down. This is more emphatic than the preceding, and signifies, *Yes, I know*. (*Omaha* I.)

The right arm is raised to head with the index finger in type-position (I 1), modified by being more opened. From aside the head the hands sweep in a curve to the right ear as of something entering or hearing something; the finger is then more open and carried direct to the ground as something emphatic or direct. (*Oto and Missouri* I.) "'I hear,' emphatically symbolized." It is doubted if this sign is more than an expression of understanding which may or may not imply positive assent. It would not probably be used as a direct affirmative, for instance, in response to a question.

The hand open, palm downward, at the level of the breast, is moved forward with a quick downward motion from the wrist, imitating a bow of the head. (*Iroquois* I.)

Throw the closed right hand, with the index extended and bent, as high as the face, and let it drop again naturally; but as the hand reaches its greatest elevation the index is fully extended and suddenly drawn into the palm, the gesture resembling a beckoning from above toward the ground. (*Kaiowa* I; *Comanche* III; *Apache* II; *Wichita* II.)

Quick motion of the right hand forward from the mouth; first position about six inches from the mouth and final as far again away. In first position the index finger is extended, the others closed; in final, the index loosely closed, thrown in that position as the hand is moved forward, as though hooking something with it; palm of hand out. (*Sahaptin* I.)

Another: Move right hand to a position in front of the body, letting arm hang loosely at the side, the thumb standing alone, all fingers hooked except forefinger, which is partially extended (E 1, palm upward). The sign consists in moving the forefinger from its partially extended position to one similar to the others, as though making a sly motion for some one to come to you. This is done once each time the assent is made. More emphatic than the preceding. (*Sahaptin* I.) "We are together, think alike."

Deaf-mute natural sign :

Indicate by nodding the head. (*Ballard.*)

Deaf-mute sign:

The French mutes unite the extremities of the index and thumb so as to form a circle and move the hand downward with back vertical and turned outward. It has been suggested in explanation that the circle formed and exhibited is merely the letter O, the initial of the word *oui*.

Fiji sign :

Assent is expressed, not by a downward nod as with ourselves, but by an upward nod; the head is jerked backward. Assent is also expressed by uplifting the eyebrows. (*Fison.*)

Turkish sign :

One or two nods of the head forward. (*Barnum.*)

Other remarks and illustrations upon the signs for *yes* are given on page 286, *supra*.

TRIBAL SIGNS.

ABSAROKA or CROW.

The hands held out each side, and striking the air in the manner of flying. (*Long.*)

Imitate the flapping of the bird's wings with the two hands, palms downward, brought close to the shoulder. (*Burton.*)

Imitate the flapping of a bird's wings with the two hands, palms to the front and brought close to the shoulder. (*Creel.*)

Place the flat hand as high as and in front or to the side of the right shoulder, move it up and down, the motion occurring at the wrist. For more thorough representation both hands are sometimes employed. (*Arapaho* II; *Cheyenne* V; *Dakota* V, VI, VIII; *Ponka* II; *Kaiowa* I; *Pani* I; *Comanche* III; *Apache* II; *Wichita* II.)   "Bird's wing."

Both hands extended, with fingers joined (W), held near the shoulders, and flapped to represent the wings of a crow. (*Dakota* II, III.)

At the height of the shoulders and a foot outward from them, move the upright hands forward and backward twice or three times from the wrist, palms forward, fingers and thumbs extended and separated a little; then place the back or the palm of the upright opened right hand against the upper part of the forehead; or half close the fingers, placing the end of the thumb against the ends of the fore and middle

FIG. 281.

fingers, and then place the back of the hand against the forehead. This sign is also made by the Arapahos. (*Dakota* IV.) "To imitate the flying of a bird, and also indicate the manner in which the Absaroka wear their hair."

Make with the arms the motion of flapping wings. (*Kutine* I.)

The flat right hand, palm outward to the front and right, is held in front of the right shoulder, and quickly waved back and forth a few times. When made for the information of one ignorant of the common sign, both hands are used, and the hands are moved outward from the body, though still near the shoulder. (*Shoshoni and Banak* I.) "Wings, *i. e.*, of a crow."   Fig. 281.

APACHE.

Make either of the signs for POOR, IN PROPERTY, by rubbing the index
back and forth over the extended
left forefinger; or, by passing
the extended index alternately
along the upper and lower sides
of the extended left forefinge
from tip to base. (*Kaiowa* I;
Comanche III; *Apache* II; *Wi-*

FIG. 282.

chita II.)   Fig. 282.   "It is said that when the first Apache came to
the region they now occupy he was asked who or what he was, and not
understanding the language he merely made the sign for *poor*, which
expressed his condition."

FIG. 283.

Rub the back of the extended left forefinger from end to end with the
extended index. (*Comanche* II; *Ute* I.)   "Poor, poverty-stricken."

———, Coyotero.

Place the back of the right hand near the end of the foot, the fingers
curved upward, to represent the turned-up toes of the moccasins. (*Pima
and Papago* I; *Apache* I.)   Fig. 283.

———, Mescalero.

Same sign as for LIPAN *q. v.* (*Kaiowa* I; *Comanche* III; *Apache* II;
Wichita II.)

———, Warm Spring.

Hand curved (Y, more flexed) and laid on its back on top of the foot (*moccasins much curved up at toe*); then draw hands up legs to near knee, and cut off with edges of hands (*boot tops*). (*Apache* III.) "Those who wear booted moccasins with turn-up toes."

ARAPAHO.

The fingers of one hand touch the breast in different parts, to indicate the tattooing of that part in points. (*Long.*)

Seize the nose with the thumb and forefinger. (Randolph B. Marcy, captain United States Army, in *The Prairie Traveler. New York*, 1859, p. 215.)

Rub the right side of the nose with the forefinger: some call this tribe the " Smellers," and make their sign consist of seizing the nose with the thumb and forefinger. (*Burton.*)

Finger to side of nose. (*Macgowan.*)

Touch the left breast, thus implying what they call themselves, viz: the "Good Hearts." (*Arapaho* I.)

Rub the side of the extended index against the right side of the nose. (*Arapaho* II; *Cheyenne* V; *Kaiowa* I; *Comanche* III; *Apache* II; *Wichita* II.)

Hold the left hand, palm down, and fingers extended; then with the right hand, fingers extended, palm inward and thumb up, make a sudden stroke from left to right across the back of the fingers of the left hand, as if cutting them off. (*Sac, Fox, and Kickapoo* I.) This is believed to be an error of the authority, and should apply to the CHEYENNE tribal sign.

Join the ends of the fingers (the thumb included) of the right hand, and, pointing toward the heart near the chest, throw the hand forward and to the right once, twice, or many times, through an arc of about six inches. (*Dakota* IV.) " Some say they use this sign because these Indians tattoo their breasts."

Collect the fingers and thumb of the right hand to a point, and tap the tips upon the left breast briskly. (*Comanche* II; *Ute* I.) " Goodhearted." It was stated by members of the various tribes at Washington, in 1880, that this sign is used to designate the Northern Arapahos, while that in which the index rubs against or passes upward alongside of the nose refers to the Southern Arapahos.

Another: Close the right hand, leaving the index only extended; then rub it up and down, held vertically, against the side of the nose where it joins the cheek. (*Comanche* II; *Ute* I.)

The fingers and thumb of the right hand are brought to a point, and tapped upon the right side of the breast. (*Shoshoni and Banak* I.)

ARIKARA. (Corruptly abbreviated REE.)

Imitate the manner of shelling corn, holding the left hand stationary, the shelling being done with the right. (*Creel.*) Fig. 284.

With the right hand closed, curve the thumb and index, join their tips so as to form a circle, and place to the lobe of the ear. (*Absaroka* I; *Hidatsa* I.) "Big ear-rings." Fig. 285.

Both hands, fists, (B, except thumbs) in front of body, backs looking toward the sides of the body, thumbs obliquely upward, left hand stationary, the backs of the fingers of the two hands touching, carry the right thumb forward and backward at the inner side of the left thumb and without moving the hand from the left, in imitation of the act of shelling corn. (*Dakota* I, VII, VIII.)

Collect the fingers and thumb of the right hand nearly to a point, and make a tattooing or dotting motion toward the up-

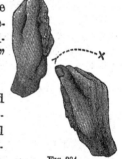

per portion of the cheek. This is the old sign, and was used by them previous to the adoption of the more modern one representing "corn-eaters." (*Arikara* I.)

Place the back of the closed right hand transversely before the mouth, and rotate it forward and backward several times. This gesture may be accompanied, as it sometimes is, by a motion

FIG. 285.

FIG. 284.

of the jaws as if eating, to illustrate more fully the meaning of the rotation of the fist. (*Kaiowa* I; *Comanche* III; *Wichita* II; *Apache* I.) "Corn-eater; eating corn from the ear."

Signified by the same motions with the thumbs and forefingers that are used in shelling corn. The dwarf Ree (Arikara) corn is their peculiar possession, which their tradition says was given to them by a superior being, who led them to the Missouri River and instructed them how to plant it. (Rev. C. L. Hall, in *The Missionary Herald, April*, 1880.) "They are the corn-shellers." Have seen this sign used by the Arikaras as a tribal designation. (*Dakota* II.)

ASSINABOIN.

Hands in front of abdomen, horizontal, backs outward, ends of fingers pointing toward one another, separated and arched (H), then moved up and down and from side to side as though covering a corpulent body. This sign is also used to indicate the Gros Ventres of the Prairie or At-sina. (*Dakota* I.)

Make the sign of *cutting the throat.* (*Kutine* I.) As the Assinaboins belong to the Dakotan stock, the sign generally given for the Sioux may be used for them also.

With the right hand flattened, form a curve by passing it from the top of the chest to the pubis, the fingers pointing to the left, and the back forward. (*Shoshoni and Banak* I.) "Big bellies."

ATSINA, LOWER GROS VENTRE.

Both hands closed, the tips of the fingers pointing toward the wrist and resting upon the base of the joint, the thumbs lying upon and extending over the middle joint of the forefingers; hold the left before the chest, pointing forward, palm up, placing the right, with palm down, just back of the left, and move as if picking small objects from the left with the tip of the right thumb. (*Absaroka* I; *Shoshoni and Banak* I.) "Corn-shellers."

Bring the extended and separated fingers and thumb loosely to a point, flexed at the metacarpal joints; point them toward the left clavicle, and imitate a dotting motion as if tattooing the skin. (*Kaiowa* I; *Comanche* III; *Apache* II; *Wichita* II.) "They used to tattoo themselves, and live in the country south of the Dakotas."

See also the sign of (*Dakota* I) under ASSINABOIN.

BANAK.

Make a whistling sound "phew" (beginning at a high note and ending about an octave lower); then draw the extended index across the throat from the left to the right and out to nearly at arm's length. They used to cut the throats of their prisoners. (*Pai-Ute* I.)

Major Haworth states that the *Banaks* make the following sign for themselves: Brush the flat right hand backward over the forehead as if forcing back the hair. This represents the manner of wearing the tuft of hair backward from the forehead. According to this informant, the Shoshoni use the same sign for BANAK as for themselves.

BLACKFEET. (This title refers to the Algonkian Blackfeet, properly called SATSIKA. For the Dakota Blackfeet, or Sihasapa, see under head of DAKOTA.)

The finger and thumb encircle the ankle. (*Long.*)

Pass the right hand, bent spoon-fashion, from the heel to the little toe of the right foot. (*Burton.*)

The palmar surfaces of the extended fore and second fingers of the right hand (others closed) are rubbed along the leg just above the ankle. This would not seem to be clear, but these Indians do not make any sign indicating *black* in connection with the above. The sign does not, however, interfere with any other sign as made by the Sioux. (*Creel; Dakota* I.) "Black feet."

Pass the flat hand over the outer edge of the right foot from the heel to beyond the toe, as if brushing off dust. (*Dakota* V, VII, VIII.) Fig. 2ᴈ6.

Fɪɢ. 286.

Touch the right foot with the right hand. (*Kutine* I.)

Close the right hand, thumb resting over the second joint of the fore-finger, palm toward the face, and rotate over the cheek, though an inch or two from it. (*Shoshoni and Banak* I.) "From manner of painting the cheeks." Fig. 287.

CADDO.

Pass the horizontally extended index from right to left under the nose. *Arapaho* II; *Cheyenne* V; *Kaiowa* I; *Comanche* I, II, III; *Apache* II; *Wichita* I, II.) "'Pierced noses,' from former custom of perforating the septum for the reception of rings." Fig. 288. This sign is also used for the Sahaptin. For some remarks see page 345.

FIG. 287.   FIG. 288.

CALISPEL.   See PEND D'OREILLE.

CHEYENNE.

Draw the hand across the arm, to imitate cutting it with a knife. (*Marcy* in *Prairie Traveller, loc. cit.*, p. 215.)

Draw the lower edge of the right hand across the left arm as if gashing it with a knife. (*Burton.*)

With the index-finger of the right hand proceed as if cutting the left arm in different places with a sawing motion from the wrist upward, to represent the cuts or burns on the arms of that nation. (*Long.*)

Bridge palm of left hand with index-finger of right. (*Macgowan.*)

Draw the extended right hand, fingers joined, across the left wrist as if cutting it. (*Arapaho* I.)

Pass the ulnar side of the extended index repeatedly across the extended finger and back of the left hand. Frequently, however, the index is drawn across the wrist or forearm. (*Arapaho* II; *Cheyenne* V; *Ponka* II; *Pani* I.) Fig. 289. See p. 345 for remarks.

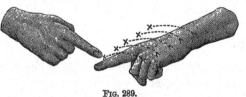

FIG. 289.

The extended index, palm upward, is drawn across the forefinger of the left hand (palm inward), several times, left hand stationary, right hand is drawn toward the body until the index is drawn clear off; then repeat. Some Cheyennes believe this to have reference to the former custom of cutting the arm as offerings to spirits, while others think it refers to a more ancient custom of cutting off the enemy's fingers for necklaces. (*Cheyenne* II.)

Place the extended index at the right side of the nose, where it joins the face, the tip reaching as high as the forehead, and close to the inner corner of the eye. This position makes the thumb of the right hand rest upon the chin, while the index is perpendicular. (*Sac, Fox, and Kickapoo* I.) It is considered that this sign, though given to the collaborator as expressed, was an error. It applies to the Southern Arapahos. Lieutenant Creel states the last remark to be correct, the gesture having reference to the Southern bands.

As though sawing through the left forearm at its middle with the edge of the right held back outward, thumb upward. Sign made at the left side of the body. (*Dakota* I.) "Same sign as for a *saw*. The Cheyenne Indians are known to the Sioux by the name of 'The Saws.'"

Right-hand fingers and thumb extended and joined (as in S), outer edge downward, and drawn sharply across the other fingers and forearm as if cutting with a knife. (*Dakota* III.)

Draw the extended right index or the ulnar (inner) edge of the open right hand several times across the base of the extended left index, or across the left forearm at different heights from left to right. This sign is also made by the Arapahos. (*Dakota* IV.) "Because their arms are marked with scars from cuts which they make as offerings to spirits."

Draw the extended index several times across the extended forefinger from the tip toward the palm, the latter pointing forward and slightly toward the right. From the custom of striping arms transversely with colors. (*Kaiowa* I; *Comanche* II, III; *Apache* II; *Ute* I; *Wichita* II.)

Another: Make the sign for Dog, viz: Close the right hand, leaving the index and second fingers only extended and joined, hold it forward from and lower than the hip and draw it backward, the course following the outline of a dog's form from head to tail; then add the sign To Eat, as follows: Collect the thumb, index, and second fingers to a point, hold them above and in front of the mouth and make a repeated dotting motion toward the mouth. This sign is generally used, but the other and more common one is also employed, especially so with individuals not fully conversant with the sign language as employed by the Comanches, &c. (*Kaiowa* I; *Comanche* III; *Apache* II; *Wichita* II.) "Dog-eaters."

Draw the extended index across the back of the left hand and arm as if cutting it. The index does not touch the arm as in signs given for the same tribe by other Indians, but is held at least four or five inches from it. (*Shoshoni and Banak* I.)

30 A E

CHIPEWAY. See OJIBWA.

COMANCHE.

Imitate, by the waving of the hand or forefinger, the forward crawling motion of a snake. (*Burton*, also *Blackmore* in introduction to Dodge's *Plains of the Great West. New York*, 1877, p. xxv.) The same sign is used for the Shoshoni, more commonly called "Snake", Indians, who as well as the Comanches belong to the Shoshonian linguistic family. "The silent stealth of the tribe." (*Dodge; Marcy* in *Thirty Years of Army Life on the Border. New York*, 1866, p. 33.) Rev. A. J. Holt remarks, however, that among the Comanches themselves the conception of this sign is the trailing of a rope, or lariat. This refers probably to their well-known horsemanship.

Motion of a snake. (*Macgowan*.)

Hold the elbow of the right arm near the right side, but not touching it; extend the forearm and hand, palm inward, fingers joined on a level with the elbow, then with a shoulder movement draw the forearm and hand back until the points of the fingers are behind the body; at the same time that the hand is thus being moved back, turn it right and left several times. (*Creel; Sac, Fox, and Kickapoo* I.) "Snake in the grass. A snake drawing itself back in the grass instead of crossing the road in front of you."

Another: The sign by and for the Comanches themselves is made by holding both hands and arms upward from the elbow, both palms inward, and passing both hands with their backs upward along the lower end of the hair to indicate *long hair*, as they never cut it. (*Sac, Fox, and Kickapoo* I.)

Right hand horizontal, flat, palm downward (W), advanced to the front by a motion to represent the crawling of a snake. (*Dakota* III.)

Extend the closed right hand to the front and left; extend the index, palm down, and rotate from side to side while drawing it back to the right hip. (*Arapaho* II; *Cheyenne* V; *Dakota* VI, VII, VIII; *Ponka* II; *Kaiowa* I; *Pani* I; *Comanche* III; *Apache* II; *Wichita* II.) This motion is just the reverse of the sign for *Shoshoni*, see Fig. 297 *infra*.

Make the reverse gesture for *Shoshoni*, i. e., begin away from the body, drawing the hand back to the side of the right hip while rotating it. (*Comanche* II.)

CREE, KNISTENO, KRISTENEAUX.

Sign for WAGON and then the sign for MAN. (*Dakota* I.) "This indicates the Red River half-breeds, with their carts, as these people are so known from their habit of traveling with carts."

Place the first and second fingers of the right hand in front of the mouth. (*Kutine* I.)

CROW. See ABSAROKA.

DAKOTA, or SIOUX.

The edge of the hand passed across the throat, as in the act of cutting that part. (*Long; Marcy* in *Army Life*, p. 33.)

Draw the lower edge of the hand across the throat. (*Burton.*)

Draw the extended right hand across the throat. (*Arapaho* I.) "The cut-throats."

Pass the flat right hand, with palm down, from left to right across the throat. (*Arapaho* II; *Cheyenne* V; *Dakota* VI, VIII; *Ponka* II; *Pani* I.)

Draw the forefinger of the left hand from right to left across the throat. (*Sac, Fox, and Kickapoo* I.) "A cut-throat."

Forefinger and thumb of right hand extended (others closed) is drawn from left to right across the throat as though cutting it. The Dakotas have been named the "cut-throats" by some of the surrounding tribes. (*Dakota* I.) "Cut-throats."

Right hand horizontal, flat, palm downward (as in W), and drawn across the throat as if cutting with a knife. (*Dakota* II, III.)

Draw the open right hand, or the right index, from left to right horizontally across the throat, back of hand upward, fingers pointing toward the left. This sign is also made by the Arapahos. (*Dakota* IV.) "It is said that after a battle the Utes took many Sioux prisoners and cut their throats; hence the sign "cut-throats."

Draw the extended right hand, palm downward, across the throat from left to right. (*Kaiowa* I; *Comanche* II, III; *Shoshoni and Banak* I; *Ute* I; *Apache* II; *Wichita* II.) "Cut-throats." Fig 290.

————, Blackfoot (Sihasapa).

Pass the flat right hand along the outer edge of the foot from the heel to beyond the toes. (*Dakota* VIII; *Hidatsa* I; *Ponka* II; *Arikara* I; *Pani* I.) Same as Fig. 286, above.

FIG. 290.

Pass the right hand quickly over the right foot from the great toe outward, turn the heel as if brushing something therefrom. (*Dakota* V.)

Pass the widely separated thumb and index of the right hand over the lower leg, from just below the knee nearly down to the heel. (*Kaiowa* I; *Comanche* III; *Apache* II; *Wichita* II.)

————, Brulé.

Rub the upper and outer part of the right thigh in a small circle with the open right hand, fingers pointing downward. This sign is also made by the Arapahos. (*Dakota* IV.) "These Indians were once caught in a prairie fire, many burned to death, and others badly burned about the thighs; hence the name Si-caⁿ-gu 'burnt thigh' and the sign. According to the Brulé chronology, this fire occurred in 1763, which they call 'The-People-were-burned-winter.'"

Pass the flat right hand quickly over the thigh from near the buttock forward, as if brushing dust from that part. (*Dakota* V, VI, VII, VIII.)

Brush the palm of the right hand over the right thigh, from near the buttock toward the front of the middle third of the thigh. (*Kaiowa* I; *Comanche* III; *Apache* II; *Wichita* II.)

————, Ogalala.

Fingers and thumb separated, straight (as in R), and dotted about over the face to represent the marks made by the small-pox. (*Arapaho* II; *Cheyenne* V; *Dakota* III, VI, VII, VIII.) "This band suffered from the disease many years ago."

With the thumb over the ends of the fingers, hold the right hand upright, its back forward, about six inches in front of the face, or on

one side of the nose near the face, and suddenly extend and spread all the fingers, thumb included. (*Dakota* IV.) "The word *Ogalala* means scattering or throwing at, and the name was given them, it is said, after a row in which they threw ashes into one another's faces."

FLATHEAD, or SELISH.

One hand placed on the top of the head, and the other on the back of the head. (*Long*.)

Place the right hand to the top of the head. (*Kutine* I.)

FIG. 291.

Pat the right side of the head above and back of the ear with the flat right hand. (*Shoshoni and Banak* I.) From the elongation of the occiput. Fig. 291.

FOX, or OUTAGAMI.

Same sign as for SAC. (*Sac, Fox, and Kickapoo* I.)

GROS VENTRE. See HIDATSA

HIDATSA, GROS VENTRE, or MINITARI.

Both hands flat and extended, palms toward the body, with the tips of the fingers pointing toward one another; pass from the top of the chest downward, outward, and inward toward the groin. (*Absaroka* I; *Dakota* V, VI, VII, VIII; *Shoshoni and Banak* I.) " Big belly."

Left and right hands in front of breast, left placed in position first, separated about four or five inches, left hand outside of the right, horizontal, backs outward, fingers extended and pointing left and right; strike the back of the right against the palm of the left several times, and then make the sign for GO, GOING, as follows: Both hands (A 1) brought to the median line of body on a level with the breast, some distance apart, then describe a series of half circles or forward arch-like movements with both hands. (*Dakota* I.) " The Gros Ventre Indians, Minitaris (the Hidatsa Indians of *Matthews*), are known to the Sioux as the Indians who went to the mountains to kill their enemies; hence the sign."

Express with the hand the sign of a big belly. (*Dakota* III.)

Pass the flat right hand, back forward, from the top of the breast, downward, outward, and inward to the pubis. (*Dakota* VI; *Hidatsa* I; *Arikara* I.) " Big belly."

INDIAN (generically).

Hand in type-position K, inverted, back forward, is raised above the head with forefinger directed perpendicularly to the crown. Describe with it a short gentle curve upward and backward in such a manner that the finger will point upward and backward, back outward, at the termination of the motion. (*Ojibwa* V.) "Indicates a feather planted upon the head—the characteristic adornment of the Indian."

Make the sign for WHITE MAN, viz: Draw the open right hand horizontally from left to right across the forehead a little above the eyebrows, the back of the hand to be upward and the fingers pointing toward the left, or close all the fingers except the index, and draw it across the forehead in the same manner; then make the sign for No; then move the upright index about a foot from side to side, in front of right shoulder, at the same time rotating the hand a little. (*Dakota* IV.)

Rub the back of the extended left hand with the palmar surfaces of the extended fingers of the right. (*Comanche* II.) "People of the same kind; dark-skinned."

Rub the back of the left hand with the index of the right. (*Pai-Ute* I; *Wichita* I.)

KAIOWA.

Make the signs of the PRAIRIE and of DRINKING WATER. (*Burton;
Blackmore* in Dodge's *Plains of the Great West. New York,* 1877, p. xxiv.)

Cheyennes make the same sign as (*Comanche* II), and think it was intended to convey the idea of cropping the hair. The men wear one side
of the hair of the head full length and done up as among the Cheyennes, the other side being kept cropped off about even with the neck
and hanging loose. (*Cheyenne* II.)

Right-hand fingers and thumb, extended and joined (as in W), placed
in front of right shoulder, and revolving loosely at the wrist. (*Dakota*
III.)

Place the flat hand with extended and separated fingers before the
face, pointing forward and upward, the wrist near the chin; pass it up-

ward and forward several times.
(*Kaiowa* I; *Comanche* III; *Apache* II;
Wichita II.)

Place the right hand a short distance above the right side of the head,
fingers and thumb separated and extended; shake it rapidly from side to
side, giving it a slight rotary motion
in doing so. (*Comanche* II.) "Rat-
tle-brained." Fig. 292. See p. 345 for
remarks upon this sign.

Same sign as (*Comanche* II), with
the exception that both hands are generally used instead of the right one
only. (*Ute* I.)

FIG. 292.

Make a rotary motion of the right hand, palm extended upward and
outward by the side of the head. (*Wichita* I.) "Crazy heads."

KICKAPOO.

With the thumb and finger go through the motion of clipping the
hair over the ear; then with the hand make a sign that the borders of
the leggings are wide. (*Sac, Fox, and Kickapoo* I.)

KNISTENO or KRISTENEAUX. See CREE.

KUTINE.

Place the index or second finger of the right hand on each side of the
left index finger to imitate riding a horse. (*Kutine* I.)

Hold the left fist, palm upward, at arm's length before the body, the right as if grasping the bowstring and drawn back. (*Shoshoni and Banak* I.) "From their pe-culiar manner of holding the long bow horizontally in shooting." Fig. 293.

FIG. 293.

LIPAN.

With the index and second fingers only extended and separated, hold the hand at arm's length to the front of the left side; draw it back in distinct jerks; each time the hand rests draw the fingers back against the inside of the thumb, and when the hand is again started on the next movement backward snap the fingers to full length. This is repeated five or six times during the one movement of the hand. The country which the Lipans at one time occupied contained large ponds or lakes, and along the shores of these the reptile was found which gave them this characteristic appellation. (*Kaiowa* I; *Comanche* III; *Apache* III; *Wichita* II.) "Frogs." Fig. 294.

FIG. 294.

MANDAN.

The first and second fingers of the right hand extended, separated, backs outward, other fingers and thumb closed, are drawn from the left shoulder obliquely downward in front of the body to the right hip. (*Dakota* I.) "The Mandan Indians are known to the Sioux as 'The people who wear a scarlet sash, with a train,' in the manner above described."

MINITARI. See HIDATSA.

NEZ PERCÉS. See SAHAPTIN.

OJIBWA, or CHIPPEWA.

Right hand horizontal, back outward, fingers separated, arched, tips pointing inward, is moved from right to left breast and generally over the front of the body with a trembling motion and at the same time a slight outward or forward movement of the hand as though drawing something out of the body, and then make the sign for MAN, viz: The right-hand is held in front of the right breast with the forefinger extended, straight upright (J), with the back of the hand outward; move the hand upward and downward with finger extended. (*Dakota* I.) "Perhaps the first Chippewa Indian seen by a Sioux had an eruption on his body, and from that his people were given the name of the 'People with a breaking out,' by which name the Chippewas have ever been known by the Sioux."

OSAGE, or WASAJI.

Pull at the eyebrows over the left eye with the thumb and forefinger of the left hand. This sign is also used by the Osages themselves. (*Sac, Fox, and Kickapoo* I.)

Hold the flat right hand, back forward, with the edge pointing backward, against the side of the head, then make repeated cuts, and the hand is moved backward toward the occiput. (*Kaiowa* I; *Comanche* III; *Apache* II; *Wichita* II.) "Former custom of shaving the hair from the sides of the head, leaving but an occipito-frontal ridge."

Pass the flat and extended right hand backward over the right side of the head, moving the index against the second finger in imitation of cutting with a pair of scissors. (*Comanche* II.) "Represents the manner of removing the hair from the sides of the head, leaving a ridge only from the forehead to the occiput."

OUTAGAMI.   See FOX.

PANI (Pawnee).

Imitate a wolf's ears with the two forefingers of the right hand extended together, upright, on the left side of the head. (*Burton.*)

Place a hand on each side of the forehead, with two fingers pointing to the front to represent the narrow, sharp ears of the wolf. (*Marcy* in *Prairie Traveler*, p. 215.)

Extend the index and second fingers of the right hand upward from the right side of the head. (*Arapaho* II; *Cheyenne* V; *Dakota* VII, VIII; *Ponka* II; *Pani* I; *Comanche* II.)

Right hand, as (N), is passed from the back part of the right side of the head, forward seven or eight inches. (*Dakota* I.) "The Pani Indians are known as the *Shaved-heads, i. e.,* leaving only the scalp locks on the head."

First and second fingers of right hand, straight upward and separated, remaining fingers and thumb closed (as in N), like the ears of a small wolf. (*Dakota* III.)

Place the closed right hand to the side of the temple, palm forward leaving the index and second fingers extended and slightly separated, pointing upward. This is ordinarily used, though, to be more explicit, both hands may be used. (*Kaiowa* I; *Comanche* III; *Ute* I; *Apache* II; *Wichita* II.) For illustration see Fig. 336, facing page 531.

PEND D'OREILLE, or CALISPEL.

Make the motion of paddling a canoe. (*Kutine* I.)

Both fists are held as if grasping a paddle vertically downward and working a canoe. Two strokes are made on each side of the body from the side backward. (*Shoshoni and Banak* I.) Fig. 295.

PUEBLO.

Place the clinched hand back of the occiput as if grasping the queue, then place both fists in front of the right shoulder, rotating them slightly to represent a loose mass of an imaginary substance. Represents the large mass of hair tied back of the head. (*Arapaho* II; *Cheyenne* V.)

REE. See ARIKARA.

FIG. 295.

SAC, or SAUKI.

Pass the extended palm of the right hand over the right side of the head from front to back, and the palm of the left hand in the same manner over the left side of the head. (*Sac, Fox, and Kickapoo* I.) "Shaved-headed Indians."

SAHAPTIN, or NEZ PERCÉS.

The right index, back outward, passed from right to left under the nose. Piercing the nose to receive the ring. (*Creel; Dakota* I.)

Place the thumb and forefinger to the nostrils. (*Kutine* I.)

Close the right hand, leaving the index straight but flexed at right

FIG. 296.

angles with the palm; pass it horizontally to the left by and under the nose. (*Comanche* II.) "Pierced nose." Fig. 296. This sign is made by the Nez Percés for themselves, according to Major Haworth. Information was received from Arapaho and Cheyenne Indians, who visited Washington in 1880, that this sign is also used to designate the *Caddos*, who practiced the same custom of perforating the nasal septum. The same informants also state that the *Shawnees* are sometimes indicated by the same sign.

Pass the extended index, pointing toward the left, remaining fingers and thumb closed, in front of and across the upper lip, just below the nose. The second finger is also sometimes extended. (*Shoshoni and Banak* I.) "From the custom of piercing the noses for the reception of ornaments."

See p. 345 for remarks upon the signs for *Sahaptin*.

SATSIKA. See BLACKFEET.

SELISH. See FLATHEAD.

SHEEPEATER. See under SHOSHONI.

SHAWNEE. See remarks under SAHAPTIN.

SHOSHONI, or SNAKE.

The forefinger is extended horizontally and passed along forward in a serpentine line. (*Long.*)

Right hand closed, palm down, placed in front of the right hip; extend the index and push it diagonally toward the left front, rotating it quickly from side to side in doing so. (*Absaroka* I; *Shoshoni and Banak* I.) "Snake." Fig. 297.

Right hand, horizontal, flat, palm downward (W), advanced to the front by a motion to represent the crawling of a snake. (*Dakota* III.)

With the right index pointing forward, the hand is to be moved forward about a foot in a sinuous manner, to imitate the crawling of a snake. Also made by the Arapahos. (*Dakota* IV.)

FIG. 297.

Place the closed right hand, palm down, in front of the right hip; extend the index, and move it forward and toward the left, rotating the hand and finger from side to side in doing so. (*Kaiowa* I; *Comanche* II, III; *Apache* II; *Wichita* II.)

Make the motion of a serpent with the right finger. (*Kutine* I.)

Close the right hand, leaving the index only extended and pointing forward, palm to the left, then move it forward and to the left. (*Pai-Ute* I.) The rotary motion of the hand does not occur in this description, which in this respect differs from the other authorities.

————, Sheepeater. Tukuarikai.

Both hands, half closed, pass from the top of the ears backward, downward, and forward, in a curve, to represent a ram's horns; then, with the index only extended and curved, place the hand above and in front of the mouth, back toward the face, and pass it downward and backward several times. (*Shoshoni and Banak* I.) " Sheep," and " to eat."

SIHASAPA. See under DAKOTA.

SIOUX. See DAKOTA.

TENNANAH.

Right hand hollowed, lifted to mouth, and describing waving line gradually descending from right to left; left hand describing mountainous outline, one peak rising above the other. (*Kutchin* I.) " Mountain-river-men."

UTE.

" They who live on mountains" have a complicated sign which denotes " living in mountains," and is composed of the signs SIT and MOUNTAIN. (*Burton.*)

Rub the back of the extended flat left hand with the extended fingers of the right, then touch some black object. Represents black skin. Although the same sign is generally used to signify *negro*, an addition is sometimes made as follows: place the index and second fingers to the hair on the right side of the head, and rub them against each other to signify *curly hair*. This addition is only made when the connection would cause a confusion between the " black skin" Indian (*Ute*) and negro. (*Arapaho* II; *Cheyenne* V.)

Left hand horizontal, flat, palm downward, and with the fingers of the right hand brush the other toward the wrist. (*Dakota* III.)

Place the flat and extended left hand at the height of the elbow before the body, pointing to the front and right, palm toward the ground; then pass the palmar surface of the flat and extended fingers of the right hand over the back of the left from near the wrist toward the tips of the fingers. (*Kaiowa* I; *Comanche* III; *Apache* II; *Wichita* II.) "Those who use sinew for sewing, and for strengthening the bow."

Indicate the color *black*, then separate the thumbs and forefingers of both hands as far as possible, leaving the remaining fingers closed, and pass upward over the lower part of the legs. (*Shoshoni and Banak* I.) " Black or dark leggings."

WASAJI. See OSAGE.

WICHITA.

Indicate a circle over the upper portion of the right cheek, with the index or several fingers of the right hand. The statement of the Indian authorities for the above is that years ago the Wichita women painted spiral lines on the breasts, starting at the nipple and extending several inches from it; but after an increase in modesty or a change in the upper garment, by which the breast ceased to be exposed, the cheek has been adopted as the locality for the sign. (*Creel; Kaiowa* I; *Comanche* III; *Apache* II; *Wichita* II.)

Extend the fingers and thumb of the right hand, semi-closed, and bring the hand toward the face nearly touching it, repeating this several times as if going through the motion of tattooing. The Comanches call the Wichitas "Painted Faces"; Caddos call them "Tattoed Faces," both tribes using the same sign. (*Comanche* I.)

WYANDOT.

Pass the flat right hand from the top of the forehead backward over the head and downward and backward as far as the length of the arm. (*Wyandot* I.) "From the manner of wearing the hair."

PROPER NAMES.

WASHINGTON, CITY OF.

The sign for *go* by closing the hand (as in type position B 1) and bending the arm; the hand is then brought horizontally to the epigastrium, after which both the hand and arm are suddenly extended; the sign for *house* or *lodge*; the sign for *cars*, consisting of the sign for *go* and *wagon, e. g.*, both arms are flexed at a right angle before the chest; the hands then assume type position (L) modified by the index being hooked and the middle finger partly opened and hooked similarly; the hands are held horizontally and rotated forward side by side to imitate two wheels, palms upward; and the sign for *council* as follows: The right arm is raised, flexed at elbow, and the hand brought to the mouth (in type position G 1, modified by being inverted), palm up, and the index being more open. The hand then passes from the mouth in jerks, opening and closing successively; then the right hand (in position S 1), horizontal, marks off divisions on the left arm extended. The sign for *father* is briefly executed by passing the open hand down and from the loins, then bringing it erect before the body; then the sign for *cars*, making with the mouth the noise of an engine. The hands then raised before the eyes and approximated at points, as in the sign for *lodge*; then diverge to indicate *extensive*; this being followed by the sign for *council*. (*Oto and Missouri* I.) "The home of our father, where we go on the puffing wagon to council."

MISSOURI RIVER.

Make the sign for *water* by placing the right hand upright six or eight inches in front of the mouth, back outward, index and thumb crooked, and their ends about an inch apart, the other fingers nearly closed; then move it toward the mouth, and then downward nearly to the top of the breast-bone, at the same time turning the hand over toward the mouth until the little finger is uppermost; and the sign for *large* as follows: The opened right hands, palms facing, fingers relaxed and slightly separated, being at the height of the breast and about two feet apart, separate them nearly to arm's length; and then rapidly rotate the right hand from right to left several times, its back upward, fingers spread and pointing forward to show that it is stirred up or muddy. (*Dakota* IV.)

EAGLE BULL, a Dakota chief.

Place the clinched fists to either side of the head with the forefingers extended and curved, as in Fig. 298; then extend the left hand, flat, palm down, before the left side, fingers pointing forward; the outer edge of the flat and extended right hand is then laid transversely across the back of the left hand, and slid forward over the fingers as in Fig. 299. (*Dakota* VI; *Arikara* I.) "Bull

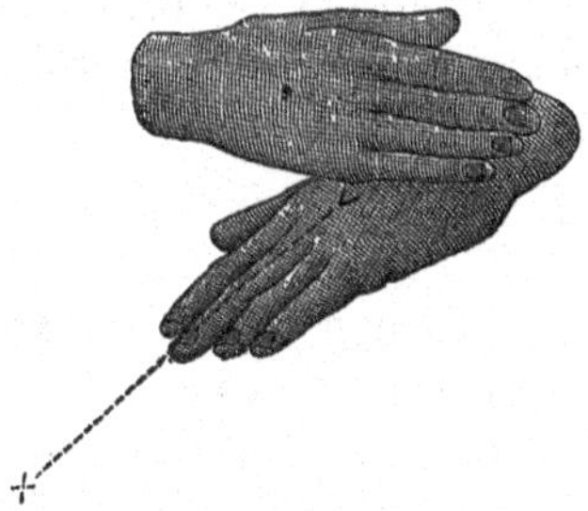

FIG. 299.　　　　　　　　　　FIG. 298.

and eagle—'*Haliaëtus leucocephalus*, (*Linn.*) *Sav.*'" In the picture-writing of the Moquis, Fig. 300 represents the eagle's tail as showing the difference of color which is indicated in the latter part of the above gesture.

FIG. 300.

RUSHING BEAR, an Arikara chief.

Place the right fist in front of the right side of the breast, palm down; extend and curve the thumb and little finger so that their tips point toward one another before the knuckles of the remaining closed fingers, then reach forward a short distance and pull toward the body several times rather quickly; suddenly push the fist, in this form, forward to arm's length twice. (*Dakota* VI; *Arikara* I.) "Bear, and rushing."

SPOTTED TAIL, a Dakota chief.

With the index only of the right hand extended, indicate a line or curve from the sacrum (or from the right buttock) downward, backward, and outward toward the right; then extend the left forefinger, pointing forward from the left side, and with the extended index draw imaginary lines transversely across the left forefinger. (*Absaroka* I; *Shoshoni* I; *Dakota* VI, VII; *Arikara* I.) "Tail, and spotted."

STUMBLING BEAR, a Kaiowa chief.

Place the right fist in front of the right side of the breast, palm down; extend and curve the thumb and little finger so that their tips point toward one another before the knuckles of the remaining closed fingers; then place the left flat hand edgewise before the breast, pointing to the right; hold the right hand flat pointing down nearer the body; move it forward toward the left, so that the right-hand fingers strike the left palm and fall downward beyond the left. (*Kaiowa* I.) "Bear, and stumble or stumbling."

SWIFT RUNNER, a Dakota warrior.

Place the right hand in front of the right side, palm down; close all the fingers excepting the index, which is slightly curved, pointing forward; then push the hand forward to arm's length twice, very quickly. (*Dakota* VI; *Arikara* I.) "Man running rapidly or swiftly."

WILD HORSE, a Comanche chief.

Place the extended and separated index and second fingers of the right hand astraddle the extended forefinger of the left hand. With the right hand loosely extended, held as high as and nearly at arm's length before the shoulder, make several cuts downward and toward the left. (*Comanche* III.) "Horse, and prairie or wild."

PHRASES.

PRESIDENT OF THE UNITED STATES; SECRETARY OF THE INTERIOR.

Close the right hand, leaving the thumb and index fully extended
and separated; place the index over the forehead so that the thumb
points to the right, palm toward the face; then draw the index across
the forehead toward the right; then elevate the extended index, pointing upward before the shoulder or neck; pass it upward as high as
the top of the head; make a short turn toward the front and pass it
pointing downward toward the ground, to a point farther to the front
and a little lower than at the beginning. (*Absaroka* I; *Dakota* VI, VII;
Shoshoni and Banak I; *Ute* I; *Apache* I.) "White man and chief."

Make the sign for *white man* (American), by passing the palmar surface of the extended index and thumb of the right hand across the forehead from left to right, then that for *chief*, and conclude by making that
for *parent* by collecting the fingers and thumb of the right hand nearly
to a point and drawing them forward from the left breast. (*Kaiowa* I;
Comanche III; *Apache* II; *Wichita* II.) "White man; chief; father."

SECRETARY OF THE INTERIOR.

Draw the palmar side of the index across the forehead from left to
right, resting the thumb upon the right temple, then make the sign for
chief—the white chief, "Secretary;" then make the sign for *great lodge,
council house*, by making the sign for *lodge*, then placing both hands
somewhat bent, palms facing, about ten inches apart, and passing them
upward from the waist as high as the face. (*Arikara* I.)

WHERE IS YOUR MOTHER?

After placing the index into the mouth—*mother*, point the index at
the individual addressed—*your*, then separate and extend the index and
second fingers of the right hand; hold them, pointing forward, about
twelve or fifteen inches before the face, and move them from side to
side, eyes following the same direction—*I see*, then throw the flat right
hand in a short curve outward to the right until the back points toward
the ground—*not*, and look inquiringly at the individual addressed.
(*Ute* I.) "Mother your I see not; where is she?"

ARE YOU BRAVE?

Point to the person and make sign for *brave*, at same time looking
with an inquiring expression. (*Absaroka* I; *Shoshoni and Banak* I.)

BISON, I HAVE SHOT A.

Move the open left hand, palm to the front, toward the left and away from the body slowly (motion of the buffalo when chased). Move right hand on wrist as axis, rapidly (man on pony chasing buffalo); then extend left hand to the left, draw right arm as if drawing a bow, snap the forefinger and middle finger of left hand, and thrust the right forefinger over the left hand. (*Omaha* I.)

GIVE ME SOMETHING TO EAT.

Bring the thumb, index and second fingers to a point as if grasping a small object, the remaining fingers naturally extended, then place the

FIG. 301.

hand just above the mouth and a few inches in front of it, and make repeated thrusts quickly toward the mouth several times; then place the naturally extended right hand nearly at arm's length before the body, palm up, fingers pointing toward the front and left, and make a short circular motion with the hand, as in Fig. 301, bringing the outer edge toward the body as far as the wrist will permit, throwing the hand forward again at a higher elevation. The motion being at the wrist only. (*Absaroka* I; *Dakota* VII, VIII; *Comanche* III.)

I WILL SEE YOU HERE AFTER NEXT YEAR.

Raise the right hand above the head (J 2), palm to the front, all the fingers closed except the index, hand slanting a little to backward, then move forward and downward toward the person addressed, describing a curve. (*Omaha* I.)

YOU GAVE US MANY CLOTHES, BUT WE DON'T WANT THEM.

Lean forward, and, holding the hands concavo-convex, draw them up over the limbs severally, then cross on the chest as wrapping a blanket. The arms are then extended before the body, with the hands in type-position (W), to a height indicating a large pile. The right hand then sweeps outward, showing a negative state of mind. The index of right hand finally touches the chest of the second party and approaches the body, in position (I), horizontal. (*Oto and Missouri* I.) "Something to put on that I don't want from you."

QUESTION. See also this title in EXTRACTS FROM DICTIONARY.

Hold the extended and flattened right hand, palm forward, at the height of the shoulder or face, and about fifteen inches from it, shaking the hand from side to side (at the wrist) as the arm is slightly raised, resembling the outline of an interrogation mark (?) made from below upward. (*Absaroka* I; *Dakota* V, VI, VII; *Hidatsa* I; *Kaiowa* I; *Arikara* I; *Comanche* II, III; *Pai-Ute* I; *Shoshoni and Banak* I; *Ute* I; *Apache* I, II; *Wichita* II.)

—— What? What is it?

First attract the person's notice by the sign for *attention*, viz: The right hand (T) carried directly out in front of the body, with arm fully extended and there moved sidewise with rapid motions; and then the right hand, fingers extended, pointing forward or outward, fingers joined, horizontal, is carried outward, obliquely in front of the right breast, and there turned partially over and under several times. (*Dakota* I.)

—— What are you doing? What do you want?

Throw the right hand about a foot from right to left several times, describing an arc with its convexity upward, palm inward, fingers slightly bent and separated, and pointing forward. (*Dakota* IV.)

—— When?

With its index extended and pointing forward, back upward, rotate the right hand several times to the right and left, describing an arc with the index. (*Dakota* IV.)

—— What are you? *i. e.*, What tribe do you belong to?

Shake the upright open right hand four to eight inches from side to side a few times, from twelve to eighteen inches in front of the chin, the palm forward, fingers relaxed and a little separated. (*Dakota* IV.)

It must be remarked that in the three preceding signs there is no essential difference, either between themselves or between them and the general sign for QUESTION above given, which can be applied to the several special questions above mentioned. A similar remark may be made regarding several signs given below, which are printed in deference to collaborators.

Pass the right hand from left to right across the face. (*Kutine* I.)

—— What do you want?

The arm is drawn to front of chest and the hand in position (N 1), modified by palms being downward and hand horizontal. From the chest center the hand is then passed spirally forward toward the one addressed; the hand's palm begins the spiral motion with a downward and ends in an upward aspect. (*Oto* I.) "To unwind or open."

—— Whence come you?

First the sign for *you*, viz: The hand open, held upward obliquely, and pointing forward; then the hand extended open and drawn to the breast, and lastly the sign for *bringing*, as follows: The hand half shut, with the thumb pressing against the forefinger, being first mod-

31 A E

erately extended either to the right or left, is brought with a moderate jerk to the opposite side, as if something was pulled along by the hand. (*Dunbar.*)

—— Who are you? or what is your name?

The right or left hand approximates close to center of the body; the arm is flexed and hand in position (D), or a little more closed. From inception of sign near center of body the hand slowly describes the arc of a quadrant, and fingers unfold as the hand recedes. We think the proper intention is for the inception of sign to be located at the heart, but it is seldom truly, anatomically thus located. (*Oto* I.) "To unfold one's self or make known."

—— Are you through?

With arms hanging at the side and forearms horizontal, place the fists near each other in front of body; then with a quick motion separate them as though breaking something asunder. (*Sahaptin* I.)

—— Do you know?

Shake the right hand in front of the face, a little to the right, the whole arm elevated so as to throw the hand even with the face, and the forearm standing almost perpendicular. Principal motion with hand, slight motion of forearm, palm out. (*Sahaptin* I.)

——— How far is it?

Sign for DO YOU KNOW? followed with a precise movement throwing right hand (palm toward face) to a position as far from body as convenient, signifying *far;* then with the same quick, precise motion, bring the hand to a position near the face—*near.* (*Sahaptin* I.)

——— How will you go—horseback or in wagon?

First make the sign for DO YOU KNOW? then throw right hand forward—"*go* or *going;* then throw fore and middle fingers of right astride the forefinger of the left hand, signifying, *will you ride?*; then swing the forefingers of each hand around each other, sign of *wheel running,* signifying, *or will you go in wagon?* (*Sahaptin* I.)

——— How many?

After making the sign for *question,* touch the tips of as many of the extended and separated fingers of the left hand held in front of the body upright, with back outward, with the right index as may be necessary. (*Dakota* I.) "Count them off to me—how many?"

FIG. 302.

Place the left hand carelessly before the breast, fingers extended and slightly separated, back to the front, then count off a few with the extended index, by laying down the fingers of the left, beginning at the little finger, as in Fig. 302. In asking the question, the sign for *question* must precede the sign for *many*, the latter being also accompanied by a look of interrogation. (*Shoshoni and Banak* I.)

—— Has he?

Deaf-mute natural sign:

Move to and fro the finger several times toward the person spoken of (*Larson.*)

—— Have you?

Deaf-mute natural sign:

Move the finger to and fro several times toward the person to whom the one is speaking. (*Larson.*)

—— Are you?

Deaf-mute natural signs:

Point to the person spoken to and slightly nod the head, with an inquiring look. (*Ballard.*)

Point with the forefinger, as if to point toward the second person, at the same time nod the head as if to say "yes." (*Ziegler.*)

The following was obtained at Washington during the winter of 1880–'81 from Ta-taⁿ-ka Wa-kaⁿ (Medicine Bull), a Brulé Dakota chief, by Dr. W. J. HOFFMAN.

I AM GOING HOME IN TWO DAYS.

(1) Place the flat hands in front of and as high as the elbows, palms down, pass each hand across to the opposite side of the body, the right above the left crossing near the wrist at the termination of the gesture (*night*), repeat in quick succession—*nights*, (2) elevate the extended index and second finger of the right hand, backs to the front—*two*, (3) place the tips of the extended and joined fingers of the right hand against the breast—*I*, (4) after touching the breast as in the preceding, pass the extended index from the breast, pointing downward, forward nearly to arm's length, and terminating by holding the hand but continuing the motion of the index until it points forward and upward—*am going to*, (5) throw the clinched right fist about six inches toward the earth at arm's length after the completion of the preceding gesture—*my home*.

ANALYSIS.

Haⁿ-he'-pi	noⁿ'-pa	mi'-ye	ti-ya'-ta	wa-gle'-kta.
(1)	(2)	(3)	(5)	(4)
nights	two	I	my home	am going to.

It will be noticed that the gesture No. 4, "am going to," was made before the gesture No. 5, "my home," although the Dakota words pronounced were in the reverse order, showing a difference in the syntax of the gestures and of the oral speech in this instance. The other gestures, 1, 2, and 3, had been made deliberately, the Dakota word translating each being in obvious connection with the several gestures, but the two final words were pronounced rapidly together as if they could not in the mind of the gesturer be applied separately to the reversed order of the signs for them.

The same authority obtained the above sentence in Ponka and Pani, together with the following signs for it, from individuals of those tribes. Those signs agreed between each other, but differed from the Dakota, as will be observed, in the signs *to my house*, as signifying *to my home*.

(1) Touch the breast with the tips of the extended fingers—*I*. This precedes the signs for Nos. 2, 3, 4, and 5, which correspond to Nos. 1, 2, 3, and 4 of the Dakota; then follows: (6) place the ·tips of the extended fingers of the flat hands together, leaving the wrists about six inches apart—*lodge*, (7) and conclude by placing the clinched fists nearly at arm's length before the body, the right several inches above the left, then throw them toward the ground—about six or eight inches—the fists retaining their relative positions—*my, mine*.

ANALYSIS.

The following is the Ponka sentence as given by the gesturer in connection with the several gestures as made:

....	Nan'-ba	jan ɥi	a-g¢e'	ta miñ'-ke	ɥi	wi'-wi-a tĕ'-ɫa.
(1)	(3)	(2)	(4)	(5)	(6)	(7)

The following is the full sentence as spoken by Ponkas without regard to gesture, and its literal translation:

Nan'-ba	jan	ɥi	a-g¢e'	ta'	miñ'-ke	ɥi	wi'-wi-ɫa	tĕ'-ɫa	..
Two	night, sleep	if, when	I go homeward	will	I who	lodge	my own	the, one, standing object,	to.

The Pani gestures were given with the accompanying words, viz:

	Pit' ku-rĕt'	ka'-ha	wi	ta-tukh'-ta	a-ka'-ru	ru-rĕt'-i-ru.
(1)	(3)	(2)	(4)	(5)	(6)	(7)
I	(In) two	nights	I	am going	house	to my.

The orthography in the above sentences, as in others where the original text is given (excepting the Dakota and Ojibwa), is that adopted by Maj. J. W. POWELL in the second edition of the *Introduction to the Study of Indian Languages. Washington,* 1880. The characters more particularly requiring explanation are the following, viz:

¢, as *th* in *then, though.*

ñ, as *ng* in *sing, singer ;* Sp. *luengo.*

ɥ, an intermediate sound between *k* and *g* in *gig.*

kh, as the German *ch,* in *nacht.*

ɫ, an intermediate sound betwen *t* and *d.*

Nasalized vowels are written with a superior *n*, thus: a^n, e^n.

The following phrases were obtained by the same authority from Antonito, son of Antonio Azul, chief of the Pimas in Arizona.

I AM HUNGRY, GIVE ME SOMETHING TO EAT.

(1) Touch the breast with the tips of the extended fingers of the right hand—*I*, (2) place the outer edge of the flat and extended right hand against the pit of the stomach, palm upward, then make a sawing motion from side to side with the hand—*hunger*, (3) place the right hand before the face, back upward, and fingers pointing toward the mouth, then thrust the fingers rapidly to and from the mouth several times—*eat*.

ANALYSIS.

Aⁿ-anʹ-t	piʹ-hu-kiʹum	......
(1)	(2)	(3)
I (have)	hunger	eat.

The last sign is so intimately connected with that for hunger, that no translation can be made.

GIVE ME A DRINK OF WATER.

(1) Place the tips of the index and thumb together, the remaining fingers curved, forming a cup, then pass it from a point about six inches before the chin, in a curve upward, backward and downward past the mouth—*water*, (2) then place the flat right hand at the height of the elbow in front of or slightly to the right of the body, palm up, and in passing it slowly from left to right, give the hand a lateral motion at the wrist—*give me*.

ANALYSIS.

Shuʹ-wu-to	doʹ-iʹ.
(1)	(2)
water	give me.

The following was also obtained by Dr. W. J. HOFFMAN from Ta-taⁿ-ka Wa-kaⁿ, before referred to, at the time of his visit to Washington.

I AM GOING HOME.

(1) Touch the breast with the extended index—*I*, (2) then pass it in a downward curve, outward and upward toward the right nearly to arm's length, as high as the shoulder—*am going (to)*, (3) and when at that point suddenly clinch the hand and throw it edgewise a short distance toward the ground—*my country, my home.* Fig 303.

FIG. 303.

ANALYSIS.

Ma-koʹ-ce		mi-taʹ-wa		kin		e-ktaʹ		wa-gleʹ		kta.
	(3)					(2)			(1)	
Country	‖	my own	‖	the	‖	to	‖	I go home	‖	will.

DIALOGUES.

TENDOY-HUERITO DIALOGUE.

The following conversation took place at Washington in April, 1880, between TENDOY, chief of the Shoshoni and Banak Indians of Idaho, and HUERITO, one of the Apache chiefs from New Mexico, in the presence of Dr. W. J. HOFFMAN. Neither of these Indians spoke any language known to the other, or had ever met or heard of one another before that occasion:

Huerito.—WHO ARE YOU?

Place the flat and extended right hand, palm forward, about twelve inches in front of and as high as the shoulder, then shake the hand from side to side as it is moved forward and upward—
question, who are you?   Fig. 304.

FIG. 304.

FIG. 305.

Tendoy.—SHOSHONI CHIEF.

Place the closed right hand near the right hip, leaving the index only extended, palm down; then pass the hand toward the front and left, rotating it from side to side—*Shoshoni,* Fig. 305; then place the closed hand, with the index extended and pointing upward, near the right cheek, pass it upward as high as the head, then turn it forward and downward toward the ground, terminating with the movement a little below the initial point—*chief.*   Fig. 306.

Huerito.—HOW OLD ARE YOU?

Clinch both hands and cross the forearms before the breast with a trembling motion—*cold—winter, year,* Fig. 307; then elevate the left hand as high as the neck and about twelve or fifteen inches before it, palm toward the face, with fingers extended and pointing upward ; then, with the index, turn down one finger after another slowly, beginning at the little finger, until three or four are folded against the palm, and look inquiringly at the person addressed—*how many ?* See Fig. 302.

Fig. 306.

Fig. 307.

Tendoy.—FIFTY-SIX.

Close and extend the fingers and thumbs of both hands, with the palms forward, five times—*fifty*; then extend the fingers and thumb of the left

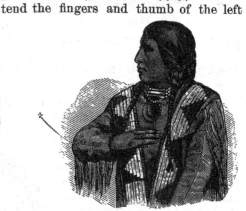

Fig. 308.

Fig. 309.

hand, close the right, and place the extended thumb alongside of and near the left thumb—*six*. Fig. 308.

Huerito.—VERY WELL. ARE THERE ANY BUFFALO IN YOUR COUNTRY ?

Place the flat right hand, pointing to the left, with the palm down, against the breast-bone; then move it forward and slightly to the right and in an upward curve; make the gesture rather slow and nearly to arm's length (otherwise, *i. e.*, if made hastily and but a short distance, it would only mean *good*)—*very good*, Fig. 309; place both closed hands to their respective sides of the head, palms toward the hair, leaving the forefingers curved—*buffalo*, see Fig. 298, p. 477; then reach out the fist to arm's length toward the west, and throw it forcibly toward the ground for a distance of about six inches, edge downward—*country, away to the west;* then point the curved index rather quickly and carelessly toward the person addressed—*your.*

Tendoy.—YES; MANY BLACK BUFFALO.

Pass the closed right hand, with the index partly flexed, to a position about eight inches before the right collar-bone, and, as the hand reaches that elevation, quickly close the index—*yes;* then make the same sign as in the preceding question for *buffalo;* touch the hair on the right side of the head with the palms of the extended fingers of the right hand—*black;* spread the curved fingers and thumbs of both hands, place them before either thigh, pointing downward; then draw them toward one another and upward as high as the stomach, so that the fingers will point toward one another, or may be interlaced—*many.* Fig. 310.

FIG. 310.

Tendoy.—DID YOU HEAR ANYTHING FROM THE SECRETARY? IF SO, TELL ME.

Close the right hand, leaving the index and thumb widely separated, pass it by the ear from the back of the ear downward and toward the chin, palm toward the head—*hear,* see Fig. 316, p. 492; point to the individual addressed—*you;* close the hand again, leaving the index and thumb separated as in the sign for *hear* and placing the palmar surface of the finger horizontally across the forehead, pointing to the left, allow the thumb to rest against the right temple; then draw the index across the forehead from left to right, leaving the thumb touching the head—*white man;* then place the closed hand, with elevated in

FIG. 311.

dex, before the right side of the neck or in front of the top of the shoulder; pass the index, pointing upward, as high as the top of the head; turn it forward and downward as far as the breast—*chief;* pass the extended index, pointing upward and forward, forward from the mouth twice—*talk;* then open and flatten the hand, palm up, outer edge toward the face, place it about fifteen inches in front of the chin, and draw it horizontally inward until the hand nearly touches the neck—*tell me.*

Huerito.—HE TOLD ME THAT IN FOUR DAYS I WOULD GO TO MY COUNTRY.

Close the right hand, leaving the index curved; place it about six inches from the ear and move it in toward the external meatus—*told me, hear, I heard,* Fig. 311; with the right hand still closed, form a circle with the index and thumb by allowing their tips to touch; pass the hand from east to west at arm's length—*day;* place the left hand before the breast, the fingers extended, and the thumb resting against the palm, back forward, and, with the index, turn down one finger after another, beginning at the little finger—*four;* touch the breast with the tips of the finger and thumb of the left hand collected to a point—*I;* drop the hand a short distance and move it forward to arm's length and slightly upward until it points above the horizon—*go to*;* then as the arm is extended, throw the fist edgewise toward the ground—*my country.*

Tendoy.—IN TWO DAYS I GO TO MY COUNTRY JUST AS YOU GO TO YOURS. I GO TO MINE WHERE THERE IS A GREAT DEAL OF SNOW, AND WE SHALL SEE EACH OTHER NO MORE.

Place the flat hands horizontally, about two feet apart, move them quickly in an upward curve toward one another until the right lies

FIG. 312.　　　　　　　FIG. 313.

across the left—*night,* Fig. 312, repeat this sign—*two nights* (literally *two sleeps hence*); point toward the individual addressed with the right hand—*you;* and in a continuous movement pass the hand to the right, *i. e.,* toward the south, nearly to arm's length—*go;* then throw the fist edgewise toward the ground at that distance—*your country;* then touch the breast with the tips of the fingers of the left hand—*I;* move the hand off slowly toward the left, *i. e.,* toward the north to arm's length—*go to* ;* and throw the clinched hand toward the ground—*my country;* then hold both hands toward the left as high as the head, palms down, with fingers and thumbs pendent and separated; move them toward the ground two or three times—*rain,* Fig. 313; then place the flat hands

FIG. 314.

horizontally to the left of the body about two feet from the ground—*deep;* (literally, *deep rain*) *snow*—and raise them until about three feet from the ground—*very deep*—*much;* place the hands before the body about twelve inches apart, palms down, with forefingers only extended and pointing toward one another; push them toward and from one another several times—*see each other,* Fig. 314; then hold the flat right hand in front of the breast, pointing forward, palm to the left, and throw it over on its back toward the right—*not, no more.*

EXPLANATORY NOTE.—Where the asterisks appear in the above dialogue the preposition *to* is included in the gesture. After touching the breast for *I,* the slow movement forward signifies *going to,* and *country* is signified by locating it at arm's length toward the west, to the left of the gesturer, as the stopping-place, also *possession* by the clinched fist being directed toward the ground. It is the same as for *my* or *mine,* though made before the body in the latter signs. The direction of Tendoy's hands, first to the south and afterwards to the north, was understood not as pointing to the exact locality of the two parts of the country, but to the difference in their respective climates.

OMAHA COLLOQUY.

The following is contributed by Rev. J. OWEN DORSEY:

Question. FROM WHAT QUARTER IS THE WIND?

Raise the curved right hand, palm in, in front of the left shoulder. Draw in toward the body a little, then from the body several times in different directions.

Answer. FROM THAT QUARTER.

Hand as above; draw in towards the body *once,* and *farther* with *emphasis,* according to the direction of the wind.

BRULÉ DAKOTA COLLOQUY.

The following signs, forming a question and answer, were obtained by Dr. W. J. HOFFMAN, from Ta-tan-ka Wa-kan (Medicine Bull), a Brulé Dakota chief who visited Washington during the winter of 1880–'81:

Question. WE WENT TO THE DEPARTMENT [OF THE INTERIOR], SHOOK HANDS WITH THE SECRETARY AND HAD A CONVERSATION WITH HIM, DID YOU HEAR OF IT?

(1) Extend and separate the thumb and index, leaving the remaining fingers closed, place the ball of the thumb against the temple above the outer corner of the eye, and the index across the forehead, the tip resting on the left temple, then draw the index across to the right until its tip touches the thumb—*white man*, Fig. 315; (2) Elevate the extended index before the shoulder, palm forward, pass it upward, as high as the head, and forming a short curve to the front, then downward again slightly to the front to before the breast and about fifteen inches from it—*chief*; (3) Fingers of both hands extended and separated; then interlace them so that the tips of the fingers of one hand protrude beyond the backs of those of the opposing one; hold the hands in front of the breast, pointing upward, leaving the wrists about six inches apart—

FIG. 315.

lodge; (4) Place the left hand a short distance before the breast, palm down and slightly arched, fingers directed toward the right and front, then pass the flat and extended right hand forward, under and beyond the left, forming a downward curve, the right hand being as high as the left at the commencement and termination of the gesture—*enter, entered*; (5) Clasp the hands before the body, left uppermost—*shook hands, friendly*; (6) Place the flat right hand before the chin, palm up with fingers directed to the left, then pass the hand forward several times—*talk, talked to him*; (7) Reverse this motion, beginning away from the body, drawing the hand edgewise toward the chin several times—*talked to me*; (8) Separate the extended thumb and index as far as possible, leaving the remaining fingers closed, place the hand about six inches opposite the right ear, palm toward the head, then pass it in a curve forward and downward, terminating at the height of the elbow—*hear, heard*; (9) then in a continuous movement direct the extended index at the individual addressed, the face expressing a look of inquiry—*you.*

ANALYSIS.

Wa-śi'-ćuⁿ		i-taⁿ-caⁿ		ti-el'	ti'-ma-hel		unk-i'-pi	na
(1)	‖	(2)	‖		(3)	‖	(4)	
White man		chief		lodge in	lodge within		we were at that place	and ‖

na'-pe-uⁿ-za-pi		na		ki-ci		wo-un-gla-ka-pi		kiⁿ
(5)						(6, 7)		
hand we hold it, take hold of		and		to each other		we talk		the thing

na-ya-ḣoⁿ-hu-o
(8, 9)
you hear it ?

It will be observed that the interrogation point is placed under the last syllable, hu-o, the latter implying a question, though the gesture was not made to accompany it, the gestures for *hear* and *you*, with a look of inquiry, being deemed sufficient to express the desire on the part of the speaker.

FIG. 316.

Answer. YES, I HEARD OF IT, BUT DID NOT SEE IT.

(1) Hold the naturally closed hand before the right side of the breast or shoulder, leaving the index and thumb loosely extended, then, as the hand is thrown downward and forward, bring the index against the inner side of the thumb—*yes.* (2) Repeat gesture No. 8—*heard*, Fig. 316; (3) pass the extended index forward from the right eye—*saw;* (4) then in a continuous motion extend all the fingers so as to place the flat hand edgewise, and pointing forward about twelve inches before the right side of the breast, and throw it outward and slightly downward—*no, not.*

ANALYSIS.

Ha-ṇ,	na-wa'-ḣoⁿ	tka	waⁿ-mla'-ke	śni
(1)	(2)		(3)	(4)
Yes,	I heard	(but)	I saw it.	not.

DIALOGUE BETWEEN ALASKAN INDIANS.

The following introductory notes are furnished by Mr. IVAN PETROFF, who contributes the Dialogue :

It has been repeatedly stated that among the natives of Alaska no trace of gesture or sign language can be found. The universal spread of the Russian language in former times as a medium of trade and general intercourse has certainly prevented observations of this primitive linguistic feature in all the vast regions visited by the Russians. On the other hand, the homogeneous elements of the Innuit tongue, spoken along the whole seacoast from the Arctic to the Alaskan Peninsula, and the Island of Kadiak, has, to a great extent, abolished all causes for the employment of sign language between tribes in their mutual intercourse. Basing their opinions upon what they saw while touching upon the coast here and there, even the acknowledged authorities on Alaskan matters have declared that sign language did not and could not exist in all that country. Without entering into any lengthened dispute upon this question, I venture to present in the subjoined pages a succinct account of at least one instance where I saw natives of different tribes converse with each other only by means of signs and gestures within the boundaries of Alaska.

In the month of September, 1866, there arrived on the Lower Kinnik River, a stream emptying its waters into Cook's Inlet, two Indians from a distant region, who did not speak the Kenaitze language. The people of the settlement at which the strangers made their first appearance were equally at a loss to understand the visitors. At last a chief of great age, bearing the name of Chatidoolts (mentioned by Vancouver as a youth), was found to be able to interpret some of the signs made by the strangers, and after a little practice he entered into a continued conversation with them in rather a roundabout way, being himself blind. He informed me that it was the second or third time within his recollection that strangers like those then present had come to Kinnik from the northeast, but that in his youth he had frequently "talked with his hands" to their visitors from the west and east. He also told me that he had acquired this art from his father, who, as the old man expressed himself, had "seen every country, and spoken to all the tribes of the earth." The conversation was carried on with the help of the old man's sons, who described to their blind parent the gestures of the strangers, and were instructed in turn by him with what gestures to reply.

This being an entirely new experience to me I at once proceeded to carefully make notes of the desultory talk, extending over several days. My object, primarily, was to make use of the signs for purposes of trade in the future.

The notes thus obtained contain a narrative of the two strangers, interpreted to me at the time by Chatidoolts. I shall present each sign or sentence as I noted it at the time, with only casual reference to that incomplete and frequently erroneous interpretation.

The two Indians wore the pointed hunting shirt of tanned moose-skin, ornamented with beads and fringes which is still common to the Kutchin tribes. They were not tattooed, but ears and noses were encumbered with pendants of dentalium and a small red glass bead. Their feet were clothed in moccasins. One of them had a rifle of English manufacture, and his companion carried two huge knives, one of them of copper evidently of native manufacture.

(1) *Kenaitze.*—Left hand raised to height of eye, palm outward, moved several times from right to left rapidly; fingers extended and closed; pointing to strangers with left hand. Right hand describes a curve from north to east—*Which of the northeastern tribes is yours?*

(2) *Tennanah.*—Right hand, hollowed, lifted to mouth, then extended and describing waving line gradually descending from right to left. Left hand describing mountainous outline, apparently one peak rising above the other, said by Chatidoolts to mean—*Tenan-tnu-kohtana, Mountain-river-men.*

(3) *K.*—Left hand raised to height of eye, palm outward, moved from right to left, fingers extended. Left index describes curve from east to west. Outline of mountain and river as in preceding sign—*How many days from Mountain-river?*

(4) *T.*—Right hand raised toward sky, index and thumb forming first crescent and then ring. This repeated three times—*moon, new and full three times.*

(5) Right hand raised, palm to front, index raised and lowered at regular intervals—*walked.* Both hands imitating paddling of canoe, alternately right and left—*traveled three months on foot and by canoe.*

(6) Both arms crossed over breast, simulating shivering—*cold, winter.*

(7) Right index pointing toward speaker—*I.* Left hand pointing to the west—*traveled westward.*

(8) Right hand lifted cup-shaped to mouth—*water.* Right hand describing waving line from right to left gradually descending, pointing to the west—*river running westward.*

(9) Right hand gradually pushed forward, palm upward, from height of breast. Left hand shading eyes; looking at great distance—*very wide.*

(10) Left and right hands put together in shape of sloping shelter—*lodge, camp.* See Fig. 259, on p. 431.

(11) Both hands lifted, height of eye, palm inward, fingers spread—*many times.*

(12) Both hands closed, palm outward, height of hips—*surprised.*

(13) Index pointing from eye forward—*see.*

(14) Right hand held up, height of shoulder, three fingers extended, left hand pointing to me—*three white men.*

(15) *K.*—Right hand pointing to me, left hand held up, three fingers extended—*three white men.*

(16) Making Russian sign of cross—*Russians.* *Were the three white men Russians?*

(17) *T.*—Left hand raised, palm inward, two fingers extended, sign of cross with right—*two Russians.*

(18) Right hand extended, height of eye, palm outward, moved outward a little to right—*no.*

(19) One finger of left hand raised—*one.*

(20) Sign of cross with right—*Russian.*

(21) Right hand height of eye, fingers closed and extended, palm outward a little to right—*no.*

(22) Right hand carried across chest, hand extended, palm upward, fingers and thumb closed as if holding something. Left hand in same position carried across the right, palm downward—*trade.*

(23) Left hand upholding one finger, right pointing to me—*one white man.*

(24) Right hand held horizontally, palm downward, about four feet from ground—*small.*

(25) Forming rings before eyes with index and thumb—*eye-glasses.*

(26) Right hand clinched, palm upward, in front of chest, thumb pointing inward—*gave one.*

(27) Forming cup with right hand, similating drinking—*drink.*

(28) Right hand grasping chest repeatedly, fingers curved and spread—*strong.*

(29) Both hands pressed to temple and head moved from side to side—*drunk, headache.*

(30) Both index fingers placed together, extended, pointing forward—*together.*

(31) Fingers interlaced repeatedly—*build.*

(32) Left hand extended, fingers closed, pointing outward (vertically), right hand extended, fingers closed, placed slopingly against left—*camp.*

(33) Both wrists placed against temples, hands curved upward and outward, fingers spread—*horns.*

(34) Both hands horizontally lifted to height of shoulder, right arm extended gradually full length to the right, hand drooping a little at the end—*long back, moose.*

(35) Both hands upright, palm outward, fingers extended and spread, placing one before the other alternately—*trees, forest, dense forest.*

(36) Sign of cross—*Russian.*

(37) Motions of shooting a gun—*shot.*

(38) Sign for *moose* (Nos. 33, 34), showing two fingers of left hand—*two.*

(39) Sign for *camp* as before (No. 10) *camp.*

(40) Right hand describing curve from east to west, twice—*two days.*

(41) Left hand lifted height of mouth, back outward, fingers closed as if holding something; right hand simulating motion of tearing off and placing in mouth—*eating moose meat.*

(42) Right hand placed horizontally against heart, fingers closed, moved forward a little and raised a little several times—*glad at heart.*

(43) Fingers of left hand and index of right hand extended and placed together horizontally, pointing forward, height of chest. Hands separated, right pointing eastward and left westward—*three men and speaker parted, going west and east.*

(44) Pressing both arms against chest and shivering—*very cold.*

(45) Drawing index of each hand around corresponding legs below the knee—*deep snow.*

(46) Drawing imaginary line with index of right hand across each foot, just behind the toes—*snow shoes.*

(47) Head lowered to right side into palm of hand three times—*slept three times.*

(48) Sign for *camp,* as before (No. 10)—*camp.*

(49) Pointing to speaker—*I.*

(50) Fingers of right hand extended and joined and pointed forward from mouth, left hand lowered horizontally to a foot from the ground —*fox.*

(51) Left hand raised height of eye, back to the left, fingers closed, with exception of middle finger held upright; then middle finger suddenly closed—*trap.*

(52) Both hands lifted height of eye, palm inward, fingers spread—*many.*

(53) Right hand pointing to speaker—*I.*

(54) Sign for *trap* (No. 51), as above—*trap.*

(55) Right hand lowered to within a few inches of the ground and moved from left to right about two feet. Motions of both hands descriptive of playful jumping of marten around a tree or stump—*marten.*

(56) Holding up the fingers of both hands three times until aggregating thirty—*thirty.*

(57) Left forearm held up vertically, palm to front, fingers spread—*tree.*

(58) Motion of chopping with hatchet—*cut.*

(59) Driving invisible wedge around small circle—*peeling birch bark.*

(60) Right hand, fingers extended and joined, moved slowly from left to right horizontally while blowing upon it with mouth—*pitching seams of canoe.*

(61) Motions of using paddle very vigorously—*paddle up stream.*

(62) Lifting both arms above head on respective sides, hands closed as if grasping something and lifting the body—*poling canoe.*

(63) Sign for *moon* (No. 4), (crescent and ring) once—*one month.*

(64) Right hand vertically, height of chest, palm to left, fingers extended, closed. Left hand horizontally, palm downward, pushed against right—*stopped.*

(65) Right hand, index extended, drawing outline of mountains, one above other—*high mountains.*

(66) Left hand lifted to left shoulder, back to front, fingers bent and closed. Right hand, fingers bent and closed, placed over left and then slowly drawn across chest to right shoulder. Motion with both hands as if adjusting pack—*pack, knapsack.*

(67) Sign for *water* as before (No. 8). Both hands brought forward, palms down, arms passed outward horizontally to respective sides, palms down—*lake.* Both hands describing circular line backward until touching collar bone—*big and deep.*

(68) Left hand raised slightly about height of nipple, three fingers closed; index and thumb holding tip of index of right hand. Both hands moved across chest from left to right—*beaver*.*

(69) Previous sign for *many* (No. 52) repeated several times—*very plentiful*.

(70) Both hands held up with fingers spread, palm forward, twice and left hand once—height of eye—*twenty-five*.

(71) Pointing to himself—*I*.

(72) Sign for *trap* as before (No. 51)—*trapped*.

(73) Sign for temporary *shelter* (No. 10)—*camped*.

(74) Sign for new and full moon (No. 4), once—*one month*.

(75) Right hand passed slowly over the hair and chin. Left hand touching a pendant of white beads—*old man*.

(76) Index of right hand held up—*one*.

(77) Both hands partially closed and placed against breast, back of hands to front, a few inches apart—*women*.

(78) Index and middle finger of right hand held up, palm forward; eyes directed as if counting—*two*.

(79) Sign for *trap* as before (No. 51)—*trapping*.

(80) Left forearm vertically in front of chest, palm of hand to front, fingers spread, elbow resting upon the back of the right hand—*tree*.

(81) Arms and hands spanning imaginary tree of some size—*big*.

(82) Sign for *tree* as before (No. 57), left forearm suddenly brought down across extended right hand—*fell*.

(83) Right hand laid on top of head, then passed over the hair and chin, left hand touching white beads—*on the head of the old man*.

(84) Sign for *old man* as before (No. 75)—*old man*.

(85) Closing both eyes with fore and middle finger of right hand; both hands placed side by side, horizontally, palms downward, fingers extended and united, hands separated by slow horizontal movement to right and left—*dead*.

(86) Sign for *women* as before (No. 77)—*women*.

(87) Fingers of both hands interlaced at right angles several times—*built*.

(88) Sign for *lodge* as before (No. 10)—*lodge*.†

(89) Right index describing circle around the head, height of eye (cutting hair). Right hand passed over forehead and face. Left index pointing to black scabbard (blacking faces)—*mourning*.

(90) Index and middle finger of right hand passed from eyes downward across cheeks—*weeping*.

(91) Pointing to himself—*I*.

(92) Make the signs for *shoot* (Nos. 33, 34), and *moose* (No. 37)—*shot a moose*.

(93) Left hand extended horizontally, palm upward, right hand placed across left vertically, about the middle—*divided in two*.

(94) Right hand closed, palm downward, moved forward from right breast the length of the arm and then opened—*I gave*.

32 A E

(95) Sign for *women* (No. 77)—*to women.*

(96) Right hand, palm down, pointing to left, placed horizontally before heart and slightly raised several times—*good and glad.*

(97) Pointing to his companion—*he.*

(98) Motion of *paddling—in canoe.*

(99) Right arm and hand extended in N. E. direction, gradually curved back until index touches speaker—*came to me from the northeast.*

(100) Sign for *together* as above (No. 30)—*together.*

(101) Motion of *paddling—paddled.*

(102) Pointing to ground—*to this place.*

(103) *K.* Motion of drinking water out of hand—*water.*

(104) Describing circle with right index on palm of left hand extended horizontally—*lake.*

(105) Left hand raised to height of eye, palm to front, fingers leaning slightly backward. Fingers of left hand closed alternately—*how many ?*

(106) *T.* Holding up right hand back to front, showing four fingers, eyes looking at them as if counting—*four.*

(107) Sign for packing with wooden breast-brace as above; three fingers of right hand shown as above—*three portages.*

(108) *K.* Right hand pointing to gun of stranger—*gun.* Left hand raised height of eye, palm to front, and moved rapidly several times to right and left—*interrogation.*

(109) Sign for *trade* as before (No. 22)—*trade; i. e., where did you buy the gun?*

(110) *T.* Sign for *Mountain-river* as above (No. 2). Pointing eastward—*from the eastward.*

(111) Pointing to sun and then raising both hands, backs to front, fingers spread—*ten days.*

(112) Pointing to me—*white man.*

(113) Left hand held up vertically, palm outward, fingers joined. Right index placed horizontally across fingers of left hand in front, about the middle joint—*pallisaded.*

(114) Describing square with right index on flat palm of left hand—*building.*

(115) Pointing to his gun, powder-horn, blanket, and beads—*trading goods.*

(116) Both hands horizontal, brought forward and upward from chest and then downward—*plenty.*

* Chatidoolts explained this to his sons as well as to me, saying that the mountain men had a peculiar mode of catching beavers with long sticks.

†They never occupy a house in which one of the other Indians died.

In giving this narrative I have observed the original sequence, but there were frequent interruptions, caused by consultation between Chatidoolts and his sons, and before the strangers departed again they had obtained a knowledge of some words of the Kenaitze language.

OJIBWA DIALOGUE.

[Communicated by the Very Rev. EDWARD JACKER.]

The following short dialogue forms part of the scanty tradition the civilized Ojibwas possess regarding their ancestors' sign language:

Two Indians of different tongue meet on a journey. First Indian points to second Indian with the outstretched forefinger of the right hand, bringing it within a few inches of his breast; next he extends both forearms horizontally, clinches all but the forefingers, and bends the hands inward; then he brings them slowly and in a straight line together, until the tips of the outstretched forefingers meet. This gesture is accompanied with a look of inquiry—*You met somebody?*

Second Indian, facing the south, points to the east, and with the outstretched hand forms a half-circle from east to west (corresponding to the the daily course of the sun); then he raises the arm and points to a certain height above the southern horizon. Then the sign for *meeting* (as above) may be made, or omitted. After this he bends the right hand downward, and repeatedly moves the outstretched forefinger and middle finger in opposite directions (in imitation of the motion of the legs in the act of walking). Finally he raises the right hand and stretches up the forefinger (or several fingers). *To-day, when the sun stood at such a height, I met one (or several) persons traveling on foot.* If the travelers met were on horseback he makes the sign for *horse* as described by (*Dakota* III), see EXTRACTS FROM DICTIONARY, or the identical one for *going* given by (*Ojibwa* I), which is as follows: To describe a journey on horseback the first two fingers of the right hand are placed astride of the forefinger of the left hand, and both represent the galloping movement of a horse. If it is a foot journey, wave the two fingers several times through the air.

NARRATIVES.

The following, which is presented as a good descriptive model, was obtained by Dr. W. J. HOFFMAN, of the Bureau of Ethnology, from Natci, a Pai-Ute chief connected with the delegation of that tribe to Washington in January, 1880, and refers to an expedition made by him by direction of his father, Winnimukka, Head Chief of the Pai-Utes, to the northern camp of his tribe, partly for the purpose of preventing the hostile outbreak of the Banaks which occurred in 1878, and more particularly to prevent those Pai-Utes from being drawn into any difficulty with the United States by being leagued with the Banaks.

NATCI'S NARRATIVE.

(1) Close the right hand, leaving the index extended, pointed westward at arm's length a little above the horizon, head thrown back with the eyes partly closed and following the direction—*Away to the west,* (2) indicate a large circle on the ground with the forefinger of the right hand pointing downward—*place* (locative), (3) the tips of the spread fingers of both hands placed against one another, pointing upward before the body, leaving a space of four or five inches between the wrists —*house* (brush tent or wik'-i-up), see Fig. 257, p. 431, (4) with the right hand closed, index extended or slightly bent, tap the breast several times—*mine.* (5) Draw an imaginary line, with the right index toward the ground, from some distance in front of the body to a position nearer to it—*from there I came,* (6) indicate a spot on the ground by quickly raising and depressing the right hand with the index pointing downward—*to a stopping place,* (7) grasp the forelock with the right hand, palm to the forehead, and raise it about six inches, still holding the hair upward—*the chief of the tribe* (Winnimukka), see Fig. 245, p. 418, (8) touch the breast with the index—*me,* (9) the right hand held forward from the hip at the level of the elbow, closed, palm downward, with the middle finger extended and quickly moved up and down a short distance—*telegraphed,* (10) head inclined toward the right, at the same time making movement toward and from the ear with the extended index pointing toward it—*I heard,* i. e., understood.

(11) An imaginary line indicated with the extended and inverted index from a short distance before the body to a place on the right—*I went,* (12) repeat gesture No. 6—*a stopping place,* (13) inclining the head, with eyes closed, toward the right, bring the extended right hand, palm up, to within six inches of the right ear—*where I slept.* (14) Place the spread and extended index and thumb of the right hand, palm downward, across the right side of the forehead—*white man* (American), (15)

elevating both hands before the breast, palms forward, thumbs touching, the little finger of the right hand closed—*nine*, (16) touch the breast with the right forefinger suddenly—*and myself*, (17) lowering the hand, and pointing downward and forward with the index still extended (the remaining fingers and thumb being loosely closed) indicate an imaginary line along the ground toward the extreme right—*went*, (18) extend the forefinger of the closed left hand, and place the separated fore and second fingers of the right astraddle the forefinger of the left, and make a series of arched or curved movements toward the right—*rode horseback*, (19) keeping the hands in their relative position, place them a short distance below the right ear, the head being inclined toward that side—*sleep*, (20) repeat the signs for *riding* (No. 18) and *sleeping* (No. 19) three times—*four days and nights*, (21) make sign No. 18, and stopping suddenly point toward the east with the extended index-finger of the right (others being closed) and follow the course of the sun until it reaches the zenith—*arrived at noon of the fifth day*.

(22) Indicate a circle as in No. 2—*a camp*, (23) the hands then placed together as in No. 3, and in this position, both moved in short irregular upward and downward jerks from side to side—*many wik'-i-ups*, (24) then indicate the chief of the tribe as in No. 7—meaning that *it was one of the camps of the chief of the tribe*. (25) Make a peculiar whistling sound of "phew" and draw the extended index of the right hand across the throat from left to right—*Banak*, (26) draw an imaginary line with the same extended index, pointing toward the ground, from the right to the body—*came from the north*, (27) again make gesture No. 2—*camp*, (28) and follow it twice by sign given as No. 18 (forward from the body, but a short distance)—*two rode*. (29) Rub the back of the right hand with the extended index of the left—*Indian*, i. e., the narrator's own tribe, Pai-Ute, (30) elevate both hands side by side before the breast, palms forward, thumbs touching, then, after a short pause, close all the fingers and thumbs except the two outer fingers of the right hand—*twelve*, (31) again place the hands side by side with fingers all spread or separated, and move them in a horizontal curve toward the right—*went out of camp*, (32) and make the sign given as No. 25—*Banak*, (33) that of No. 2—*camp*, (34) then join the hands as in No. 31, from the right toward the front—*Pai-Utes returned*, (35) close the right hand, leaving the index only extended, move it forward and downward from the mouth three or four times, pointing forward, each time ending the movement at a different point—*I talked to them*, (36) both hands pointing upward, fingers and thumbs separated, palms facing and about four inches apart, held in front of the body as far as possible in that position—*the men in council*, (37) point toward the east with the index apparently curving downward over the horizon, then gradually elevate it to an altitude of 45°—*talked all night and until nine o'clock next morning*, (38) bring the closed hands, with forefingers extended, upward and forward from their respective sides, and place them side by side, palms forward, in front—

my brother, Fig. 317, (39) (see also pp. 385, 386) followed by the gesture, No. 18, directed toward the left and front—*rode*, (40) by No. 7—*the head chief*, (41) and No. 2—*camp*.

(42) Continue by placing the hands, slightly curved, palm to palm, holding them about six inches below the right ear, the head being inclined considerably in that direction—*one sleep (night)*, (43) make sign No. 14—*white man*, (44) raise the left hand to the level of the elbow forward from the left hip, fingers pointing upward, thumb and forefinger closed—*three*, (45) and in this position draw them toward the body and slightly to the right—*came*, (46) then make gesture No. 42—*sleep;* (47) point with the right index to the eastern horizon—*in the morning*, (48) make sign No. 14—*white man*, (49) hold the left hand nearly at arm's length before the body, back up, thumb and forefinger closed, the remaining fingers pointing downward—*three*, (50) with the right index finger make gesture No. 35, the movement being directed towards the left hand—*talked to them*, (51) motion along the ground with the left hand, from the body toward the left and front, retaining the position of the fingers just stated (in No. 49)—*they went*, (52) tap toward the ground, as in gesture No. 6, with the left hand nearly at arm's length—*to their camp*.

FIG. 317.

(53) Make gesture No. 18 toward the front—*I rode*, (54) extend the right hand to the left and front, and tap towards the earth several times as in sign No. 6, having the fingers and thumb collected to a point—*camp of the white men*. (55) Close both hands, with the forefingers of each partly extended and crooked, and place one on either side of the forehead, palms forward—*cattle (a steer)*, (56) hold the left hand loosely extended, back forward, about twenty inches before the breast, and strike the back of the partly extended right hand into the left—*shot*, (57) make a short upward curved movement with both hands, their position unchanged, over and downward toward the right—*fell over, killed*, (58) then hold the left hand a short distance before the body at the height of the elbow, palm downward, fingers closed, with the thumb lying over the second joint of the forefinger, extend the flattened right hand, edge down, before the body, just by the knuckles of the left, and draw the hand towards the body, repeating the movement—*skinned*, (59) make the sign given in No. 25—*Banak*, (60) place both hands with spread fingers upward and palms forward, thumb to thumb, before the right shoulder, moving them with a tremulous motion toward the left and front—*came in*, (61) make three short movements toward the ground in front, with the left hand, fingers loosely curved, and pointing downward—*camp of the three white men*, (62) then with the right hand open and flattened, edge down, cut towards the body as well as to the right and left—*cut up the meat*, (63) and make the pantomimic gesture of *handing it around to the visitors*.

(64) Make sign No. 35, the movement being directed to the left hand,

as held in No. 49—*told the white men*, (65) grasping the hair on the right side of the head with the left hand, and drawing the extended right hand with the edge towards and across the side of the head from behind forward—*to scalp ;* (66) close the right hand, leaving the index partly extended, and wave it several times quickly from side to side a short distance before the face, slightly shaking the head at the same time— *no*, Fig. 318, (67) make gesture No. 4—*me*, (68) repeat No. 65—*scalp*, (69) and raising the forelock high with the left hand, straighten the whole frame with a triumphant air—*make me a great chief*. (70) Close the right hand with the index fully extended, place the tip to the mouth and direct it firmly forward and downward toward the ground—*stop*, (71) then placing the hands, pointing upward, side by side, thumbs touching, and all the fingers separated, move them from near the breast outward toward the right, palms facing that direction at termination of movement—*the Banaks went to one side*, (72) with the right hand closed, index curved, palm downward, point toward the western hori-

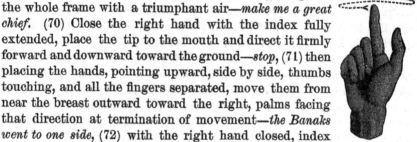

FIG. 318.

zon, and at arm's length dip the finger downward—*after sunset*, (73) make the gesture given as No. 14—*white men*, (74) pointing to the heart as in No. 4—*and I*, (75) conclude by making gesture No. 18 from near body toward the left, four times, at the end of each movement the hands remaining in the same position, thrown slightly upward—*we four escaped on horseback*.

The above was paraphrased orally by the narrator as follows: "Hearing of the trouble in the north, I started eastward from my camp in Western Nevada, when, upon arriving at Winnemucca Station, I received telegraphic orders from the head chief to go north to induce our bands in that region to escape the approaching difficulties with the Banaks. I started for Camp McDermit, where I remained one night. Leaving next morning in company with nine others, we rode on for four days and a half. Soon after our arrival at the Pai-Ute camp, two Banaks came in, when I sent twelve Pai-Utes to their camp to ask them all to come in to hold council. These messengers soon returned, when I collected all the Pai-Utes and talked to them all night regarding the dangers of an alliance with the Banaks and of their continuance in that locality. Next morning I sent my brother to the chief, Winnimukka, with a report of proceedings.

"On the following day three white men rode into camp, who had come up to aid in persuading the Pai-Utes to move away from the border. Next morning I consulted with them respecting future operations, after which they went away a short distance to their camp. I then followed them, where I shot and killed a steer, and while skinning it the Banaks came in, when the meat was distributed. The Banaks being disposed to become violent at any moment, the white men became alarmed, when

I told them that rather than allow them to be scalped I would be scalped myself in defending them, for which action I would be considered as great a chief as Winnemukka by my people.   When I told the Banaks to cease threatening the white men they all moved to one side a short distance to hold a war council, and after the sun went down the white men and I mounted our horses and fled toward the south, whence we came."

Some of the above signs seem to require explanation. Natci was facing the west during the whole of this narration, and by the right he signified the north; this will explain the significance of his gesture to the right in Nos. 11 and 17, and to the left in No. 75.

No. 2 (repeated in Nos. 22, 27, 33, and 41) designates an Indian brush lodge, and although Natci has not occupied one for some years, the gesture illustrates the original conception in the round form of the foundation of poles, branches, and brush, the interlacing of which in the construction of the *wik'-i-up* has survived in gestures Nos. 3 and 23 (the latter referring to more than one, *i. e.*, an encampment).

The sign for Banak, No. 25 (also 32 and 59), has its origin from the tradition among the Pai-Utes that the Banaks were in the habit of cutting the throats of their victims. This sign is made with the index instead of the similar gesture with the flat hand, which among several tribes denotes the Sioux, but the Pai-Utes examined had no specific sign for that body of Indians, not having been in sufficient contact with them.

"A stopping place," referred to in Nos. 6, 12, 52, and 54, represents the temporary station, or camp of white men, and is contradistinguished from a village, or perhaps from any permanent encampment of a number of persons, by merely dotting toward the ground instead of indicating a circle.

It will also be seen that in several instances, after indicating the nationality, the fingers previously used in representing the number were repeated without its previously accompanying specific gesture, as in No. 61, where the three fingers of the left hand represented the men (white), and the three movements toward the ground signified the camp or tents of the three (white) men.

This also occurs in the gesture (Nos. 59, 60, and 71) employed for the Banaks, which, having been once specified, is used subsequently without its specific preceding sign for the tribe represented.

The rapid connection of the signs Nos. 57 and 58 and of Nos. 74 and 75 indicates the conjunction, so that they are severally readily understood as "shot *and* killed," and "the white men *and* I." The same remark applies to Nos. 15 and 16, "the nine *and* I."

PATRICIO'S NARRATIVE.

This narrative was obtained in July, 1880, by Dr. FRANCIS H. ATKINS, acting assistant surgeon, United States Army, at South Fork, New Mexico, from TI-PE-BES-TLEL (Sheepskin-leggings), habitually called Patricio, an intelligent young Mescalero Apache. It gives an account of what is locally termed the "April Round-up," which was the disarming and imprisoning by a cavalry command of the United States Army, of the small Apache subtribe to which the narrator belonged.

(1) Left hand on edge, curved, palm forward, extended backward length of arm toward the West (*far westward*).

(2) Arm same, turned hand, tips down, and moved it from north to south (*river*).

(3) Dipped same hand several times above and beyond last line (*beyond*).

(4) Hand curved (Y, more flexed) and laid on its back on top of his foot (*moccasins much curved up at toe*); then drew hands up legs to near knee, and cut off with edges of hands (*boot tops*), (*Warm Spring Apaches*, who wear booted moccasins with turn-up toes.)

(5) Hands held before him, tips near together, fingers gathered (U); then alternately opened and gathered fingers of both hands (P to U, U to P), and thrusting them toward each other a few times (*shot or killed many*).

(6) Held hands six inches from side of head, thumbs and forefingers widely separated (*Mexican, i. e.*, wears a broad hat).

(7) Held right hand on edge, palm toward him, threw it on its back forward and downward sharply toward earth (T on edge to X), (*dead, so many dead*).

(8) Put thumbs to temples and indexes forward, meeting in front, other fingers closed (*soldiers, i. e.*, cap-visor).

(9) Repeated No. 5 and No. 7 (*were also shot dead*).

(10) Placed first and second fingers of right hand, others closed, astride of left index, held horizontally (*horses*).

(11) Held hands on edge and forward (T on edge forward), pushed them forward, waving vertically (*marching, i. e.*, ran off with soldiers' horses or others). N. B.—Using both hands indicates double ranks of troops marching also.

(12) Struck right fist across in front of chin from right to left sharply (*bad*).

(13) Repeated No. 4 (*Warm Spring Apache*).

(14) Moved fist, thumb to head, from center of forehead to right temple and a little backward (*fool*).

(15) Repeated No. 8 and No. 11 (*soldiers riding in double column*).

(16) Thrust right hand down over and beyond left, both palms down (W) (*came here*).

(17) Repeated No. 8 (*soldier*).

(18) Touched hair (*hair*).

(19) Touched tent (*quite white*).

(20) Touched top of shoulder (*commissioned officer*, i. e., shoulder-straps).

(21) Thrust both hands up high (*high rank*).

(22) Right forefinger to forehead; waved it about in front of face and rolled head about (primarily *fool*, but qualified in this case by the interpreter as *no sabe much*).

(23) Drew hands up his thighs and body and pointed to himself (*Mescalero Indian*).

(24) Approximated hands before him, palms down, with thumbs and indexes widely separated, as if inclosing a circle (*captured*, i. e., *corralled, surrounded*).

(25) Placed tips of hands together, wrists apart, held them erect (T, both hands inclined), (*house;* in this case *the agency*).

(26) Threw both hands, palms back, forward and downward, moving from knuckles (metacarpo-phalangeal joint) only, several times (*issuing rations*).

(27) Thrust two fingers (N) toward mouth and downward (*food*).

(28) Repeated No. 25 (*house*); outlined a hemispherical object (*wik-i-up*); repeated these several times, bringing the hands with emphasis several times down toward the earth (*village permanently here*).

(29) Repeated No. 25 several times and pointed to a neighboring hillside (*village over there*).

(30) Repeated Nos. 17 to 21, inclusive (*General X*).

(31) Thrust two fingers forward from his eyes (primarily *I see;* also *I saw*, or *there were*).

(32) Repeated No. 11 (*toward said hillside*), (*troops went over there with General X*).

(33) Repeated No. 4, adding, swept indexes around head and touched red paper on a tobacco wrapper (*San Carlos Apaches*, scouts especially distinguished by wearing a red fillet about the head); also added, drew indexes across each cheek from nose outward (*were much painted*).

(34) Repeated No. 24 and No. 23 (*to capture the Mescalero Indians*).

(35) Repeated No. 31 (*there were*).

(36) Repeated No. 33 (*San Carlos scouts*).

(37) Repeated No. 8 (*and soldiers*).

(38) Clasped his hands effusively before his breast (*so many!* i. e., *a great many*).

(39) Repeated No. 31 (*I saw*).

(40) Repeated No. 23 (*my people*).

(41) Brought fists together under chin, and hugged his arms close to his breast, with a shrinking motion of body (*afraid*).

(42) Struck off half of left index with right index (*half*, or *a portion*).

(43) Waved off laterally and upward with both hands briskly (*fled*).

(44) Projected circled right thumb and index to eastern horizon, thence to zenith (*next morning, i. e.*, sunrise to noon).

(45) Repeated No. 23 (*the Mescaleros*).

(46) Held hands in position of aiming a gun—left oblique—(*shoot*).

(47) Waved right index briskly before right shoulder (*no, did not; negation*).

(48) Swept his hand from behind forward, palm up (Y) (*the others came*).

(49) Repeated No. 5 (*and shot*).

(50) Repeated No. 23 (*the Mescaleros*).

(51) Repeated No. 7 (*many dead*).

(52) Repeated No. 8 (*soldiers*).

(53) Repeated No. 10 (*horse, mounted*).

(54) Hand forward, palm down (W) moved forward and up and down (*walking, i. e., infantry*).

(55) Beckoned with right hand, two fingers curved (N horizontal and curved) (*came*).

(56) Repeated No. 11 (*marching*).

(57) Repeated No. 28 (*to this camp*, or *village*).

(58) Repeated No. 23 (*with Mescaleros*).

(59) Repeated No. 24 (*as prisoners, surrounded*).

(60) Repeated No. 33 (*San Carlos scouts*).

(61) Placed hands, spread out (R inverted), tips down, about waist (*many cartridges*).

(62) Repeated No. 46 (*and guns*).

(63) Repeated No. 5 (*shot many*).

(64) Repeated No. 4 (*Warm Spring Apaches*).

(65) Repeated No. 23 (*and Mescaleros*).

(66) Moved fist—thumb to head—across his forehead from right to left, and cast it toward earth over left shoulder (*brave, i. e., the San Carlos scouts are brave*).

CONTINUOUS TRANSLATION OF THE ABOVE.

Far westward beyond the Rio Grande are the Warm Spring Apaches, who killed many Mexicans and soldiers and stole their horses. They (the Warm Spring Apaches) are bad and fools.

Some cavalry came here under an aged officer of high rank, but of inferior intelligence, to capture the Mescalero Indians.

The Mescaleros wished to have their village permanently here by the agency, and to receive their rations, *i. e.*, were peacefully inclined.

Our village was over there. I saw the general come with troops and San Carlos scouts to surround (or capture) the Mescalero Indians. There were a great many San Carlos scouts and soldiers.

I saw that my people were afraid, and half of them fled.

Next morning the Mescaleros did not shoot (were not hostile). The others came and killed many Mescaleros. The cavalry and infantry brought us (the Mescaleros) to this camp as prisoners.

The San Carlos scouts were well supplied with ammunition and guns, and shot many Warm Spring Indians and Mescaleros.

The San Carlos scouts are brave men.

NA-WA-GI-JIG'S STORY.

The following is contributed by Mr. FRANCIS JACKER:

This narrative was related to me by *John Na-wa-gi-jig* (literally "noon-day sky"), an aged Ojibwa, with whom I have been intimately connected for a long period of years. He delivered his story, referring to one of the many incidents in his perilous life, orally, but with pantomimes so graphic and vivid that it may be presented truly as a specimen of gesture language. Indeed, to any one familiar with Indian mimicry, the story might have been intelligible without the expedient of verbal language, while the oral exposition, incoherent as it was, could hardly be styled anything better than the subordinate part of the delivery. I have endeavored to reproduce these gestures in their original connections from memory, omitting the verbal accompaniment as far as practicable. In order to facilitate a clear understanding it is stated that the gesturer was in a sitting posture before a camp fire by the lake shore, and facing the locality where the event referred to had actually occurred, viz, a portion of Keweenaw Bay, Lake Superior, in the neighborhood of Portage Entry, as seen by the annexed diagram, Fig. 319. The time of the relation (latter part of April) also coincided with the *actual* time. In speaking of "arm," "hand," "finger," &c., the "right" is understood if not otherwise specified. "Finger" stands for "forefinger."

(1) With the exclamation "*me-wi-ja*" (a long time ago), uttered in a slow and peculiarly emphatic manner, he elevated the arm above and toward the right at the head, accompanying the motion with an upward wave of the hand and held it thus suspended a moment—*a long time ago*. (This gesture resembles sign for *time, a long*, of which it seems to be an abbreviation and it is not sufficiently clear without the accompanying exclamation.) Withdrawing it slowly, he placed the hand back upon his knee.

(2) He then brought up the left hand toward the temple and tapped his hair, which was gray, with the finger—*hair gray*.

(3) From thence he carried it down upon the thigh, placing the extended finger perpendicularly upon a fold of his trousers, which the thumb and finger of the right held grasped in such a manner as to advantageously present the smooth black surface of the cloth—*of that color, i. e., black.*

(4) Next, with a powerful strain of the muscles, he slowly stretched

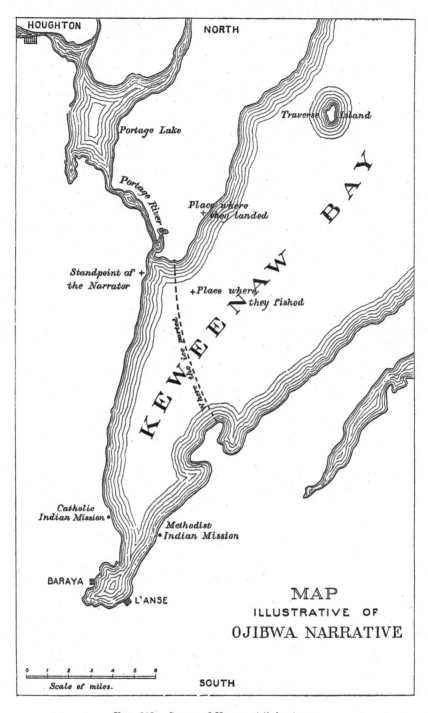

HOUGHTON   NORTH

Portage Lake

Traverse Island

Portage River

KEWEENAW BAY

Place where
+ they landed

Standpoint of +
the Narrator

+Place where
they fished

Where the ice parted

Catholic
Indian Mission •

Methodist
• Indian Mission

BARAYA

L'ANSE

MAP
ILLUSTRATIVE OF
OJIBWA NARRATIVE

0 1 2 3 4 5 6
Scale of miles.   SOUTH

Fig. 319.—Scene of Na-wa-gi-jig's story.

out the right arm and fist and grasping the arm about the elbow with the left, he raised the forearm perpendicularly upward, then brought it down with force, tightening the grasp in doing so (fingers pressing upon knuckle, thumb against pit of elbow)—*strength.*

(5) Pointing first at me—*you.*

(6) He next held out the hand horizontally and flat, palm downward, about four feet above the ground, correcting the measure a moment afterward by elevating hand a few inches higher, and estimated the height thus indicated with a telling look, leaning the head toward the side—*about that height, i. e., a youth of about that size.*

(7) He then rapidly extended the arm about two-thirds of its length forward and toward the right, terminating the motion with a jerk of the hand upward, palm turned outward, and accompanied the motion with a nod of the head, the hand in its downfall closing and dropping upon knee—*very well.*

(8) Musing a few moments, he next slowly extended the arm and pointed with the fingers toward and along the surface of the frozen bay—*out there.*

(9) In an easterly direction—*eastward.*

(10) Thence turning the arm to the right he nodded the finger toward a projection of land southward at a distance of about two miles—following in each case the direction of the finger with the eyes—and immediately after placed the hand again eastward, indicating the spot with the same emphatic nod of the finger as though carrying the visible distance to a spot upon the expanse of the bay, which, bearing no object, could not be marked otherwise—*two miles out there.*

(11) Carrying the finger toward the body, he touched his breast—*I myself.*

(12) Thence erected the hand, turning its palm forward, forefinger perpendicularly extended, others slightly closed, and nodded it downward in an explanatory manner, all in an uninterrupted movement—*one,* meaning in connection with the preceding gesture—*I for one.*

(13) Again, with an emphatic movement, he turned the hand upward, slightly erecting the index, thumb pointing forward, remaining fingers partially and naturally opened and more or less separated—*furthermore.*

(14) Then quickly and after a moment's stop brought down the hand to a horizontal position, first and second fingers joining and fully extending during the movement, and pointing forward—*another, i. e., joined by another.* Repeating this motion, he at the same time called out the name *Ga-bi-wa-bi-ko-ke.*

(15) Following the exclamation with a repetition of No. 2—*gray hair*—repeatedly touching the hair, meaning in this case—*an old man.*

(16) Pointed with the finger toward the right, directing it obliquely toward the ground—*at a short distance toward my right.*

(17) Repeated No. 13—*furthermore.*

(18) Repeated No. 14, adding the third finger to joined fore and middle

fingers, thumb resting upon tip of fourth—*another, i. e., joined by a third,* and pronounced the words "*o-gwis-san Sa-ba-dis* (this is a corruption of the French "Jean Baptiste," a favorite name among Christianized Indians)—*John Baptist, his son,* while repeating the movement.

(19) Held up the three separated fingers perpendicularly in front of the face, pushing the hand forward a little—*three in all.*

(20) Presently lowered the hand, fingers relaxing, and carried it a short distance toward the left, thence back to the right, fingers pointing obliquely toward the ground in each case—*placed to the right and left of me at a short distance.*

(21) He then brought the hand—back toward the right, index horizontally extended, remaining fingers closed, thumb placed against second finger—in front of abdomen, and moved it slowly up and down two or three times, giving it a slight jerk at the upward motion, and raising the arm partially in doing so. At the same time he inclined the body forward a little, eyes looking down—*fishing.* This refers to fishing on the ice, and, as may be inferred from it, to the use of hook and line. A short stick to which the line is attached serves as a rod and is moved up and down in the manner described.

(22) After a short pause he elevated the hand, directing the index toward that point of the meridian which the sun passes at about the tenth hour of the day, and following the direction with the eye—*about ten o'clock.*

(23) Turning his face toward the southwest and holding up the flat and extended hand some distance in front of it, back outward, he waved it briskly and several times toward the face—*fresh breeze from the southwest.*

(24) Repeated No. 21 (*fishing*), playing the imaginary fish-line up and down regularly for a while, till all at once he changed the movement by raising the hand in an oblique course, which movement he repeated several times, each time increasing the divergence and the length of the motion—*the fish-hook don't sink perpendicularly any longer, i. e., it is moving.*

(25) Quickly erecting his body he looked around him with surprise—*looking with surprise.*

(26) Shading his eyes with the hand, gazed intensively toward the south—*fixedly gazing toward the south.*

(27) Threw up his arm almost perpendicularly the next moment—*greatly astonished.*

(28) Extended and slowly moved the arm from southeast to northwest as far as he could reach, at the same time exclaiming "*mig-wam*" "ice"— *the ice from shore to shore.*

(29) Approximated the flat and horizontally extended hands, backs upward, with their inner edges touching, whereupon, suddenly turning the edges downward, he withdrew them laterally, backs nearly opposed to each other—*parting.*

(30) Pushed the left hand, palm outward, fingers joined, edges up and down, forward and toward its side with a full sweep of the arm, head following the movement—*pushed in that direction, i. e., northeastward.*

(31) Repeated No. 23, but waved the hand only once and with a quick and more powerful movement toward the face—*by the force of the wind.*

(32) Rotated hands in front of body, rolling them tips over tips very rapidly, fingers with thumbs nearly collected to a point—*winding up the hook-line in a hurry.*

(33) Quickly passed the hand toward the left breast of his coat—*putting it in pocket.*

(34) And bending the body forward made motion as if picking up something—*picking up.*

(35) Raised the hand closed to fist, arm elevated so as to form a right angle with elbow, and made a short stroke downward and toward the left—*hatchet.*

(36) Thence moved the hand to side of breast and pushed it down the waist—*putting it into belt.*

(37) Placed the closed hands to each side of the waist (thumbs upward with tips facing each other) and approximated them rapidly and with a jerk in front of navel—*tightening the belt.*

(38) With both hands lowered to the ground, he described an elongated oval around his foot by placing tips of forefingers together in front of the toes and passing them around each side, meeting the fingers behind the heel and running them jointly backward a few inches to indicate a tail—*snow-shoe.*

(39) Raised up the heel, resting the foot on the toes and turning it a little toward the right, brought it back in a downward movement with a jerk—*putting it on.*

(40) Waved the left hand emphatically forward, palm backward, fingers joined and pointing downward, extending them forward at termination of motion, at the same time pushing forward the head—*starting.*

(41) Directed the finger of the same hand toward the light-house—*toward that point.*

(42) Pointed with extended first two fingers of the same hand, thumb with remaining fingers partially extended to right and to left—*companions.*

(43) Repeated No. 40 (*starting*) less emphatically.

(44) Made several very quick jumping movements forward with the extended left fingers, joined, back upward—*going very fast.*

(45) Repeated No. 23 (*wind*), increasing the force of the movement and terminating the sign with the second repetition (wave)—*wind increasing.*

(46) Raised up the hand in front of head and then arrested it a moment, palm outward, fingers extended, upward and forward—*halt.*

(47) Partially turning the body toward the north he lowered the extended hand, back forward, fingers joined and pointing downward toward the left of his feet and moved it closely in front of them, and with

a cutting motion toward the right, following the movement with the eye—*cut off right before feet, i. e., standing on the very edge.*

(48) Still facing the north, he carried the hand, back upward, fingers joined and extended, from left side of body outward and toward the right horizontally, indicating the rippled surface of turbulent water by an appropriate motion, and extending the arm to full length, fingers pointing northeastward (toward the right) at termination of motion, and accompanied the movement with a corresponding turn of the head, eyes gazing far into distance—*water all along the shore.*

(49) Pushed the extended finger, back upward, forward (*i. e.*, northward) in a slightly arched movement—*across.*

(50) Directing it toward an object (tree) at a distance of about one hundred yards the next moment—*a distance of about one hundred yards.*

(51) Repeated No. 49 (*across*) without interrupting the motion—*that distance placed across.*

(52) Motions as follows: Hands naturally relaxed, edges up and down, backs outward, are with a quick movement and simultaneously carried from the epigastrium forward and toward their sides, arms being extended from elbows only. The hands change their position during the movement and are ultimately placed palms upward, thumbs and fingers extended and widely separated, pointing forward. This is the general sign for *doubt.* He also turned the face from one side to the other as though interrogating his companions—*what are we to do?*

(53) Repeated No. 35 (*hatchet*).

(54) Raised up the finger perpendicularly, other fingers closed, thumb resting against second, and emphatically inclined it forward—*only one.*

(55) Elevated the arm from the elbow toward the head, hand naturally relaxed, back obliquely upward, inclining the face sideward with a look of consternation, simultaneously, and again mechanically lowered it, dropping palm of hand heavily upon the knee—*"bad fix."*

(56) Placed the hand to his hip and raised it up, closed to fist, by a rapid and very energetic movement, ejaculating *haw!*—*quick to the work* (referring to the ax or hatchet).

(57) Turning the body downward, he passed the hand, with forefinger directed toward the ground, forward, sideward, and backward, in three movements, each time turning at a right angle—*measuring off a square piece on the ground, i. e., on the ice.*

(58) Looked and pointed toward an object some twenty feet off, then opposed palms of hands horizontally, and at a short distance from each other, connecting both movements in such a manner as to clearly illustrate their meaning—*about twenty feet wide.*

(59) Moved the hand—fist, thumb upward—several times quickly up and down a few inches, the arm progressing forward at every stroke—*cutting it off.*

(60) Repeated No. 55 (*bad fix*), meaning in this case—*bad job.*

(61) Opposed the palms of both hands, vertically, at a distance of

eight inches, holding them thus steady a moment and estimating the thus indicated measure with the eyes—*eight inches thick.*

(62) Then struck the palm of left with the back of arched right forcibly—*solid ice.*

(63) Laid the joined and extended first two fingers, palm up, across side of leg, a foot above heel, accompanying the movement with the eye—*one foot deep.*

(64) Pushed downward perpendicularly and from same point the flat, extended hand—*sinking,* or *giving in*—and turning the hand upward at wrist, back downward, he flirted up the fingers several times quickly—*water—slush and water.*

(65) Passed one hand over the other as in the act of pulling off mittens—*mittens.*

(66) Made the motion of wringing out a wet piece of cloth—*wringing wet.*

(67) Grasped a fold of his trowsers (below the knee) and wrung it—*trowsers also wet.*

(68) Placed palms of both hands upon legs, near to the ankles, and dragged them up to the knees—*up to the knees.*

(69) Shivered—*feeling cold.*

(70) Pointed with thumb backward and toward the right (designating his companion) and repeated No. 2 (*hair gray*)—*my old companion, i. e., Ga-bi-wa-bi-ko-ke.*

(71) Repeated No. 69 (*feeling cold*) more emphatically—*more so, i. e., suffering worse from the cold.*

(72) Repeated No. 59 (*cutting the ice*).

(73) Made sign for *tired*—*getting tired,* as follows: The left arm is partly extended forward, and is gently struck near the bend of the elbow, usually above it, with the palm of the right hand, at the same time the head is usually inclined to the left side, then in similar manner the right arm is extended and struck by the left hand, and the head in turn inclined to the right.

(74) Repeated No. 35—(*hatchet*).

(75) Turned the slightly closed left (thumb obliquely upward) over to its side, partially opening it in so doing, fingers pointing to left—*passing it over to his companion at the left, i. e., Sabadis.*

(76) Flung forefingers of both hands, backs forward, thumbs upward, remaining fingers partially closed, toward their respective sides alternately—*by turns.*

(77) Repeated No. 59 (*cutting the ice*).

(78) Elevated the hand above head, thumb and first two fingers extended and directed toward the western meridian, and shook it emphatically and with a tremulous motion up and down while thus suspended—*at a late hour.*

(79) Followed with the sign for *done, finished,* as follows: Left hand, with forearm horizontally extended toward the right, is held naturally

33 A E

relaxed, back outward, a few inches in front of body and at a right angle with opposite hand, which is placed on a higher level, slightly arched, edge downward, fingers joined and extended forward. Pass the right quickly and with a cutting motion downward and toward its side, at the same time withdraw the left a few inches toward the opposite direction—*finished our work.*

(80) Quickly threw up his arm, ejaculating "haw!"—*let us start.*

(81) Passed both hands approximated in front of body, naturally relaxed, backs outward, forward and toward their respective sides, extending and widely separating the fingers during the movement, and again approximating them with quickly accelerated speed and arresting them, closed to fists, in front of body and with a jerk upward—*with united efforts.*

(82) Placing the fists, thumbs upward, pointing forward and placed upon side of forefingers, with their wrists against the breast, he pushed them forward and downward a few inches, head slightly participating in the movement—*pushing off.*

(83) Repeated No. 38 (*snow-shoe*)—*with snow-shoes.*

(84) Immediately reassumed the position of "pushing off" as in No. 82, slowly passing forward the fists further and further—*pushing and gradually moving off.*

(85) Quickly passed and turned the closed left forward, upward, and backward, opening and again closing the fingers in so doing, and executing at almost the same instant a similar, but smaller, revolution with the right—*turning over the snow-shoe, tail up.*

(86) With both hands closed to fists, left obliquely over the right and on the right side of the body, made motion as if paddling—*paddling.*

(87) Moved and pointed finger of left towards its side, *i. e.,* northward —*toward the shore.*

(88) Moved both hands, flat and extended, backs upward, toward the left side, by an even and very slow movement—*moving along very slowly toward that direction.*

(89) Repeated No. 23—*southwest wind.*

(90) Repeated No. 30—*pushing northeastward.*

(91) Turned the thumb of left over to the left—*Sabadis.*

(92) Repeated No. 32 (*winding up*), reversing the motion—*winding off the hook-line.*

(93) Approximated both hands with their tips horizontally in front of body, first two fingers with thumb collected to a point, and moving the fingers as in the act of twisting a cord, gradually receded the hands— *twisting.*

(94) Thrust forward three fingers of the right—*three, i. e., hook-lines.*

(95) Repeated No. 93, then rubbed palm of flat and extended right forward over the thigh repeatedly and with a slight pressure—*twisting them tightly.*

(96) Approximated both hands closed to fists, thumbs upward, in

front of body and pulled them asunder repeatedly by short, quick, and sudden jerks—*proving strength of line*.

(97) Hooked the forefinger, hand turned downward at wrist, remaining fingers closed, thumb resting upon first—*fish-hook*.

(98) Raised and curved three fingers and thrust them forward a little separated, back to the front—*three, i. e., hooks*.

(99) Collecting fore and middle fingers of each hand to a point with thumb, he opposed tips of both hands, vertically describing with the upper hand several short circular movements around the tip of the lower—*tying together*.

(100) Hooked the separated fore and middle fingers of the right, pointing upward, back forward, and placed the hooked finger of the left, palm forward, in front and partially between the fork of the first—*in the shape of an anchor*.

(101) Thrust both hands, backs upward, fingers extended and separated, forward (*i. e.,* northward), vigorously, left being foremost—*throwing toward the shore*.

(102) Thence elevating the right toward the head, he thrust it downward in an oblique direction, fore and middle fingers extended and joined with the thumb—*sinking*.

(103) Placing hands in the position attained last in No. 100 (*throwing out toward shore*), he closed the fingers, drawing the hands back toward the body and leaning backward simultaneously—*hauling in*.

(104) Elevated the naturally closed hand to side of head, fingers opening and separating during the movement—at the same time and with a slight jerk of the shoulders inclining the head sideward—and again closed and slowly dropped it upon knee—*in vain*.

(105) Dropped the finger perpendicularly downward, following the movement with the eye—*bottom*.

(106) Passed the flat hand, palm down, from side to side in a smooth and horizontal movement—*smooth*.

(107) Made the sign for *stone, rock*, as follows: With the back of the arched right hand (H) strike repeatedly in the palm of the left, held horizontal, back outward, at the height of the breast and about a foot in front, the ends of the fingers pointing in opposite directions.

(108) Repeated No. 100—*anchor*.

(109) Dragged the curved fore and middle fingers over the back of the extended left—*dragging*.

(110) Waved the left—bent at the wrist, back outward—forward and upward from body, extending the arm to full length, at the same time inclining and pushing forward the head, and repeated the gesture more emphatically—*trying again and again*.

(111) Waved both hands—backs outward, fingers slightly joined, tips facing each other and closely approximated in front of breast—forward and toward their respective sides a short distance, turning the palms upward during the movement, thumb and fingers being extended and

widely separated toward the last. At the same time he inclined the head to one side, face expressing disappointment—*all in vain.*

(112) Repeated No. 80—*Let us start anew!*

(113) Repeated No. 86—*paddling.*

(114) Repeated the preceding gesture, executing the movement only once very emphatically—*vigorously.*

(115) Waved the finger toward the place of the setting sun, following the direction with the eye—*day is near its close.*

(116) Repeated No. 69, more emphatically—*feeling very cold.*

(117) Repeated No. 70—*Ga-bi-wa bi-ko-ke.*

(118) Made sign for *without*, dropping the hands powerless at the sides, with a corresponding movement of head—*exhausted.*

(119) Pointed with finger toward the light-house and drawing back the finger a little, pushed it forward in the same direction, fully extending the arm—*that distance, i. e., one mile beyond light-house.*

(120) Elevated both hands to height of shoulder, fingers extended toward the right, backs upward, moving them horizontally forward—left foremost—with an impetuous motion toward the last—*drifted out.*

(121) Repeated No. 86, executing the movement a series of times without interruption and very energetically—*paddling steadily and vigorously.*

(122) Pointed with the left forefinger to his breast—*I myself.*

(123) Waved the thumb of the same hand over to left side without interrupting motion of hand—*and Sabadis.*

(124) Moved the extended left—back upward, fingers slightly joined—toward left side, and downward a few inches—*shore.*

(125) Elevated it to level of eyes, fingers joined and extended, palm toward the right, approaching it toward the face by a slow interrupted movement—*drawing nearer and nearer.*

(126) Drawing a deep breath—*relieved.*

(127) Repeated No. 86 very emphatically—*paddling with increased courage and vigor.*

(128) Gazed and pointed northeastward, shading the eyes with the hand, at the same time pushing the left—bent downward at wrist, palm backward—forward in that direction, arm fully extended, fingers separated and pointing ahead at termination of motion—*out there at a great distance.*

(129) Made a lateral movement with the hand flat and extended over the field of ice in front of him—*the ice-field.*

(130) Described a series of waves with the flat and extended left, back upward, horizontally outward—*sea getting turbulent.*

(131) Joyously flourished the hand above head, while pronouncing the word *ke-ya-bi*—*only yet.*

(132) Pointed the finger toward the upturned root of a tree a few yards off, thence carrying it forward directed it toward the shore in front—*a few yards from shore.*

(133) Pointing toward the sun first, he placed palms of both hands in opposition vertically, a space of only an inch or two intervening, with a glance sideways at the height thus indicated—*the sun just setting*.

(134) Made three vigorous strokes with the imaginary paddle—*three more paddle-strokes*.

(135) Moved both hands (flat and extended, backs upward) evenly and horizontally toward the left, terminating the movement by turning hands almost perpendicularly upward at wrist, thus arresting them suddenly—*the ice-raft runs up against the shore*.

(136) Lastly threw up the hand perpendicularly above head, and bringing it down, placed the palm gently over the heart with an air of solemnity—*we are saved*.

Free translation of the story.

Many years ago—my hair, then black and smooth, has since turned gray; I was then in the prime of life; you, I suppose, were a young lad at that time—the following incident occurred to me:

Yonder on the ice, two miles eastward, I was one day fishing in company with two others, the old Gabiwabikoke and his son John Baptist. It was about ten o'clock in the morning—a fresh breeze from the southwest had previously been getting up—when the hook-line which I was playing up and down began to take an oblique course as though it were moved by a current. Surprised, I looked up and around me. When glancing toward the south I saw a dark streak stretching from shore to shore across the bay; the ice had parted and the wind was carrying it out toward the open lake. In an instant I had wound up my hook-line, picked up my hatchet and snow-shoes, which I put on my feet, and hurried—the others following my example—toward the nearest point of land, yonder where the light-house stands. The wind was increasing and we traveled as fast as we could. There we arrived at the very edge of the ice, a streak of water about one hundred yards in width extending northward along the shore as far as we could see. What to begin with, nothing but a single hatchet? We were in a bad situation. Well, something had to be done. I measured off a square piece on the ice and began cutting it off with the hatchet, a hard and tedious labor. The ice was only eight inches thick, but slush and water covered it to the depth of a foot. I soon had my mittens and trowsers wringing wet and began to feel cold and tired. The old Gabiwabikoke was in a worse state than I. His son next took the hatchet and we all worked by turns. It was about two o'clock in the afternoon when we finished our work. With the help of our snow-shoes (stemming their tail-ends against the edge of the solid ice), we succeeded in pushing off our raft. Turning our snow-shoes the other way (using their tails as handles), we commenced paddling with them toward the shore. It was a very slow progress, as the wind drifted us outward continually. John Baptist managed to twist our three hook-lines into a strong cord, and tying the hooks together in the shape of an anchor, he threw it out toward the shore. Hauling in the line the hooks dragged over the smooth rock bottom and would not catch. Repeated trials were of no avail. We all resumed our former attempt and paddled away with increased energy. The day was drawing near its close, and we began to feel the cold more bitterly. Gabi-wabikoke was suffering badly from its effects and was entirely played out. We had already drifted more than a mile beyond the light-house point. John Baptist and I continued paddling steadily and vigorously, and felt relieved and encouraged when we saw the shore draw near and nearer. The ice-field, by this time, was miles away to the northeast, and a sea was getting up. At last, just when the sun was setting, only a few yards separated us from the shore; three more paddle-strokes and our raft ran up against the beach. We were safe.

The oral part of the story in the language of the narrator, with a literal translation into English.

(1) *Me^n'wija*
  a long time ago

(2) *aw ninisis'san*
  this my hair

(3) *me'gwa giijina'gwak tibi'shko aw*
  while it looked like that

(4) *me'gwa gimashkaw'isian*
  while I possessed strength

(5) *kin dash*
  you and (*i. e.*, and you)

(6) *ga'nabatch kikwiwi'se^nsiwina'ban*
  perhaps (probably) were a boy

(7) *mi'iw*
  very well

(8)–(10) *iwe'di*
  there

(11) (12) *nin be'jig*
    I one

(13) *mi'nawa*
  again (furthermore)

(14) *Gabiwa'bikoke*
  "The Miner"

(15) *akiwe^n'si*
  old man

(16) Expressed by gesture only.

(17) The same as No. 13.

(18) *ogwis'san ga'ie, Sabadis*
  his son too, John Baptist.

(19) *mi minik'*
  so many

(20) (21) Gestures only.

(22) *mi wa'pi*
  thus far, *i. e.*, at that time.

(23) *we'ai gion'din*
  then the wind blew from

(24) *me'gwa nin wewe'banabina'ban*
  while I was (in the act of)
    fishing with the hook
  nin'goting gonin'gotchi
  at one time somewhere (out of
    its course)
  oda'bigamo nimigis'skane'ab
  was drawn my hook line

(25) *a'nin ejiwe'bak ?*
  how it happens ?

(26) Gesture only.

(27) *taai'!*
  ho!

(28) *mi'gwam*
  the ice

(29) *ma'dja*
  goes

(30) (31) Gestures only.

(32) *we'wib*
  quickly

(33) (34) Gestures only.

(35) *wagak'wadŏⁿs*
hatchet

(36) (37) Gestures only.

(38) (39) *nin bita'gime*
I put on snowshoes

(40) *nin madja'min*
we go (start)

(41) Gestures only.

(42) (43) *mamaw'e*
together

(44) Gesture only.

(45) *esh'kam ki'tchi no'din*
more   big   wind

(46) Gesture only.

(47) *mi ja'igwa gima'djishkad (i. e.,*
mi'gwam)
already has moved off (i. e.,
the ice)

(48) (49) Gestures only.

(50) *mi'wapi*
thus far, *i. e.*, at such a distance

(51) Gesture only.

(52) *a'nin dash gediji'tchigeiang?*
how (*i. e.*, what) shall we do ?

(53) (54) *mi e'ta be'jigwang wagak'-*
wadŏⁿs
only   one   hatchet

(55) *ge'get gisan'agissimin*
indeed we are badly off.

(56) *haw !   bak'wewada mi'-*
gwam!
well! (hallo!) let us cut the ice!

(57) (58) (59) Gestures only.

(60) *sa'nagad*
it is bad (hard)

(61) *mi epi'tading*
so it is thick (so thick is it)

(62) Gesture only.

(63) *mi dash mi'nawa minik'*
that   again   much   (that
much again)

(64) *nibi' gon ga'ie*
water snow too (water and
snow)

(65) *nimidjik a'wanag*
my   mittens

(66) *a'pitchi*
very much

(67) *nindas'san   gaie*
my trowsers two

(68) Gestures only.

(69) *nin gi'katch ja'igwa*
I   feel cold already

(70) *aw sa kiweⁿsi*
the   old man

(71) *nawatch' win'*
more yet he

(72) Gesture only.

(73) *nind aie'kos   ja'igwa*
I   am tired already

(74) Gesture only.

(75) *Sa'badis*
John Baptist

(76) *memesh'kwat kaki'na*
by turns   all

(77) Gesture only.

(78) *wi'ka ga'ishkwanawo'kweg*
late   in the afternoon

(79) *mi   gibakwewangid*
now it is cut loose

(80) *haw!*
well! (ho!)

(81) *mama'we*
together

(82) Gesture only.

(83) *a'gimag*
snowshoes

(84) *ma'djishka*
it is moving

(85)–(87) Gestures only.

(88) *aga'wa ma'djishka*
scarcely it moves
(very little)

(89) *no'din*
wind

(90) Gesture only.

(91) *Sa'badis*
John Baptist

(92) *migiss'kaneyab*
  hook-line

(93) (94) *oginisswa'biginan*
  he twisted three cords together

(95)–(98) Gestures only.

(99) *oginisso'bidonan* (*i. e.*, *migas-kanan*)
  he tied together three (*i. e.*, hooks)

(100) Gesture only.

(101) *ogiaba'gidonan dash*
  he threw it out

(102) Gesture only.

(103) *owikobi'donan*
  he wants to draw it in

(104) *kawes'sa*
  in vain ("no go")

(105)–(108) Gestures only.

(109) *ka'win sagakwidis'sinon*
  (not) it don't catch on the rock-bottom

(110) *mi'nawa—mo'jag*
  again—often (repeatedly)

(111) The same as No. 104.

(112) The same as No. 80.

(113) Gesture only.

(114) *e'nigok*
  vigorously

(115) *ja'igwa ona'kwishi*
  already evening

(116) *esh'kam kis'sina*
  more   cold (getting colder)

(117) The same as No. 70.

(118) *mi ja'igwa gianiji'tang*
  already he has given up

(119) *was'sa ja'igwa*
  far   already

(120) *niwebas'himin*
  we have drifted out

(121) Gesture only.

(122) (123) *mi'sa e'ta mij'iang*
  (now) only we are two

(124) Gesture only.

(125) *ja'igwa tchi'gibig*
  already near to shore

(126) *mi ja'igwa anibonen'damang*
  now we catch new spirits

(127) *esh'kam nigijijaw'isimin*
  more   we are strong (*i. e.*, our strength and courage increases)

(128) (129) *e-eh! was'sa ja'igwa'*
  oh!   far   already
  mi'gwam!
  the ice!

(130) *ja'igwa*
  already

(131) *ke'abi*
  yet

(132) *go'mapi*
  so far perhaps

(133) *ge'ga bangi'shimo*
  nearly sundown

(134) Gesture only.

(135) *mi gibima'jagang*
  we have landed

(136) *mi gibima'disiang*
  we have saved our lives.

DISCOURSES.

ADDRESS OF KIN CHĒ-ĔSS.

The following is the farewell address of KIN CHĒ-ĔSS (Spectacles), medicine-man of the Wichitas, to Rev. A. J. HOLT, missionary, on his departure from the Wichita Agency, in the words of the latter:

He placed one hand on my breast, the other on his own, then clasped his two hands together after the manner of our congratulations—*We are friends*, Fig. 320. He placed one hand on me, the other on himself, then placed the first two fingers of his right hand between his lips—*We are brothers.* He placed his right hand over my heart, his left hand over his own heart, then linked the first fingers of his right and left hands—*Our hearts are linked together.* See Fig. 232, p. 386. He laid his right hand on

FIG. 320.

me lightly, then put it to his mouth, with the knuckles lightly against his lips, and made the motion of flipping water from the right-hand forefinger, each flip casting the hand and arm from the mouth a foot or so, then bringing it back in the same position. (This repeated three or more times, signifying *talk* or *talking*.) Fig. 321. He then made a motion with his right hand as if he were fanning his right ear; this repeated. He then extended his right hand with his index finger pointing upward, his eyes also being turned upward—*You told me of the Great Father.* Pointing to himself, he hugged both hands to his bosom,

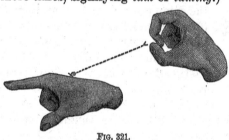

FIG. 321.

as if he were affectionately clasping something he loved, and then pointed upward in the way before described—*I love him* (the Great Father). Laying his right hand on me, he clasped his hands to his bosom as before—*I love you.* Placing his right hand on my shoulder, he threw it over his own right shoulder as if he were casting behind him a little chip, only when his hand was over his shoulder his index finger was pointing behind him—*You go away.* Pointing to his breast, he clinched the same hand as if it held a stick, and made a motion as if he were trying to strike something on the ground with the bottom of the stick held in an upright position—*I stay*, or *I stay right here*, Fig. 322.

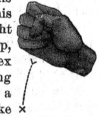

FIG. 322.

Placing his right hand on me, he placed both his hands on his breast and breathed deeply two or three times, then using the index finger and thumb of each hand as if he were holding a small pin, he placed the two hands in this position as if he were holding a thread in each hand and between the thumb and forefinger of each hand close together, and then let his hands recede from each other, still holding his fingers in the same position, as if he were letting a thread slip between them until his hands were two feet apart—*You live long time*, Fig. 323. Laying

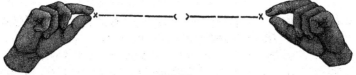

FIG. 323.

his right hand on his breast, then extending his forefinger of the same hand, holding it from him at half-arm's length, the finger pointing nearly upward, then moving his hand, with the finger thus extended, from side to side about as rapidly as a man steps in walking, each time letting his hand get farther from him for three or four times, then suddenly placing his left hand in a horizontal position with the fingers extended and together so that the palm was sidewise, he used the right-hand palm extended, fingers together, as a hatchet, and brought it down smartly, just missing the ends of the fingers of the left hand, Fig. 324. Then

FIG. 324.

placing his left hand, with the thumb and forefinger closed, to his heart, he brought his right hand, fingers in the same position, to his left, then, as if he were holding something between his thumb and forefinger, he moved his right hand away as if he were slowly casting a hair from him, his left hand remaining at his breast, and his eyes following his right—*I go about a little while longer, but will be cut off shortly and my spirit will go away* (or will die). Placing the thumbs and forefingers again in such a position as if he held a small thread between the thumb and forefinger of each hand, and the hands touching each other, he drew his hands slowly from each other, as if he were stretching a piece of gum-elastic; then laying his right hand on me, he extended the left hand in a horizontal position, fingers extended and closed, and brought down his right hand with fingers extended and together, so as to just miss the tips of the fingers of his left hand; then placing his left forefinger and thumb against his heart, he acted as if he took a hair from the forefinger and thumb of his left hand with the forefinger and thumb of the right, and slowly cast it from him, only letting his left hand remain at his breast, and let the index finger of the right hand point outward toward the distant horizon—*After a long time you die.* When placing his left hand upon himself and his right hand upon me, he extended them upward over his head and clasped them there—*We then meet in heaven.* Pointing upward, then to himself, then to me, he closed the third and little finger of his right hand, laying his thumb over them, then extending his first and second fingers about as far apart as the eyes, he brought his hand to his eyes, fingers pointing outward, and shot his hand outward—*I see you up there.* Pointing to me, then giving the last above-described sign of *look*, then pointing to himself, he made the sign as if stretching out a piece of gum-elastic between the fingers of his left and right hands, and then made the sign of *cut-off* before described, and then extended the palm of the right hand horizontally a foot from his waist, inside downward, then suddenly threw it half over and from him, as if you were to toss a chip from the back of the hand (this is the negative sign everywhere used among these Indians)—*I would see him a long time, which should never be cut off, i. e., always.*

Pointing upward, then rubbing the back of his left hand lightly with the forefinger of his right, he again gave the negative sign.—*No Indian there* (in heaven). Pointing upward, then rubbing his forefinger over the back of my hand, he again made the negative sign—*No white man there.* He made the same sign again, only he felt his hair with the forefinger and thumb of his right hand, rolling the hair several times between the fingers—*No black man in heaven.* Then rubbing the back of his hand and making the negative sign, rubbing the back of my hand and making the negative sign, feeling of one of his hairs with the thumb and forefinger of his right hand, and making the negative sign, then using both hands as if he were reaching around a hogshead, he brought the forefinger of his right hand to the front in an upright position after their manner of counting, and said thereby—*No Indian, no white man, no black man, all one.* Making the "hogshead" sign, and that for *look*, he placed the forefinger of each hand side by side pointing upward—*All look the same*, or alike. Running his hands over his wild Indian costume and over my clothes, he made the "hogshead" sign, and that for *same*, and said thereby—*All dress alike there.* Then making the "hogshead" sign, and that for *love*, (hugging his hands), he extended both hands outward, palms turned downward, and made a sign exactly similar to the way ladies smooth a bed in making it; this is the sign for *happy—All will be happy alike there.* He then made the sign for *talk* and for *Father*, pointing to himself and to me—*You pray for me.* He then made the sign for *go away*, pointing to me, he threw right hand over his right shoulder so his index finger pointed behind him—*You go away.* Calling his name he made the sign for *look* and the sign of *negation* after pointing to me—*Kin Chē-ĕss see you no more.*

Fig. 322, an illustration in the preceding address, also represents a common gesture for *sit down*, if made to the right of the hip, toward the locality to be occupied by the individual invited. The latter closely corresponds to an Australian gesture described by Smyth (*The Aborigines of Victoria*, London, 1878, Vol. II, p. 308, Fig. 260), as follows: "*Minnie-minnie* (wait a little). It is shaken downwards rapidly two or three times. Done more slowly towards the ground, it means 'Sit down.'" This is reproduced in Fig. 325.

FIG. 325.

TSO-DI-A'-KO'S REPORT.

The following statement was made to Dr. W. J. HOFFMAN by TSO-DI-A'-KO (Shaved-head Boy), chief of the Wichitas in Indian Territory, while on a visit to Washington, D. C., in June 1880.

The Indian being asked whether there was any timber in his part of the Territory, replied in signs as follows:

(1) Move the right hand, fingers loosely extended, separated and pointing upward, back to the front, upward from the height of the waist to the front of the face—*tree* (for illustration see Fig. 112, p. 343); repeat this two or three times—*trees*; (2) then hold the hand, fingers extended and joined, pointing upward, with the back to the front, and push it forward toward different points on a level with the face—*standing at various places*; (3) both hands, with spread and slightly curved fingers, are held about two feet apart, before the thighs, palms facing, then draw them toward one another horizontally and gradually upward until the wrists cross, as if grasping a bunch of grass and pulling it up—*many*; (4) point to the southwest with the index, elevating it a little above the horizon—*country*; (5) then throw the fist edgewise toward the surface, in that direction—*my, mine*; (6) place both hands, extended, flat, edgewise before the body, the left below the right, and both edges pointing toward the ground a short distance to the left of the body, then make repeated cuts toward that direction from different points, the termination of each cut ending at nearly the same point—*cut down*, Fig. 326; (7) hold the left hand

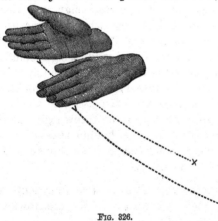

with the fingers and thumb collected to a point, directed horizontally forward, and make several cutting motions with the edge of the flat right hand transversely by the tips of the left, and upon the wrist—*cut off the ends*; (8) then cut upon the left hand, still held in the same position, with the right, the cuts being parallel to the longitudinal axis of the palm—*split*; (9) both hands closed in front of the body, about four inches apart,

FIG. 326.

with forefingers and thumbs approximating half circles, palms toward the ground, move them forward so that the back of the hand comes forward and the half circles imitate the movement of wheels—*wagon*, Fig. 327; (10) hold the left flat hand before the body, pointing horizontally forward, with the palm down, then bring the right flat hand from the right side and slap the palm upon the back of the left several

times—*load upon*, Fig. 328; (11) partly close the right hand as if grasping a thick rod, palm toward the ground, and push it straight forward
nearly to arm's length—*take;* (12) hold both hands with fingers naturally extended and slightly separated nearly at arm's length before the
body, palms down, the right lying upon the left, then pass the upper

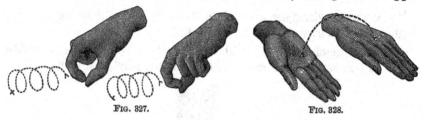

FIG. 327.   FIG. 328.

forward and downward from the left quickly, so that the wrist of the
right is raised and the fingers point earthward—*throw off;* (13) cut the
left palm repeatedly with the outer edge of the extended right hand—
build; (14) hold both hands edgewise before the body, palms facing,
spread the fingers and place those of one hand into the spaces between
those of the left, so that the tips of one protrude beyond the backs of
the fingers of the other—*log house*, see Fig. 253, p. 428; (15) then place
the flat right hand, palm down and fingers pointing to the left, against
the breast and move it forward, and slightly upward and to the right—
good.

ANALYSIS OF THE FOREGOING.

[There is] much | timber | [in] my | country | [of which I] cut down
       (3)   (1, 2)   (5)   (4)   (6)
[some], | trimmed, | split, | loaded it upon | a wagon [and] | took it
   (7)   (8)   (10)   (9)   (11)
away, | [where I] threw [it] off | [and] built | [a] good | house | .
     (12)   (13)   (15)   (14)

NOTES.—As will be seen, the word *timber* is composed of signs No. 1
and 2, signifying *trees standing.* Sign No. 3, for *many*, in this instance,
as in similar other examples, becomes *much.* The word " in," in connection with *country* and *my*, is expressed by the gesture of pointing (passing the hand less quickly than in ordinary sign language) before making
sign No. 5. That sign commonly given for *possession*, would, without
the prefix of indication, imply *my country*, and with that prefix signifies
in my country. Sign No. 7, *trimmed*, is indicated by chopping off the ends,
and facial expression denoting *satisfaction.* In sign Nos. 11 and 12 the
gestures were continuous, but at the termination of the latter the narrator straightened himself somewhat, denoting that he had overcome the
greater part of the labor. Sign No. 14 denotes *log-house*, from the manner of interlacing the finger-ends, thus representing the corner of a log-
house, and the arrangement of the ends of the same. *Indian lodge*
would be indicated by another sign, although the latter is often used as
an abbreviation for the former, when the subject of conversation is
known to all present.

LEAN WOLF'S COMPLAINT.

The following remarks were obtained by Dr. W. J. HOFFMAN from TCE-CAQ-A-DAQ-A-QIC (Lean Wolf), chief of the Hidatsa Indians of Dakota Territory, who visited Washington in 1880:

FOUR YEARS AGO THE AMERICAN PEOPLE AGREED TO BE FRIENDS WITH US, BUT THEY LIED. THAT IS ALL.

(1) Place the closed hand, with the thumb resting over the middle of the index, on the left side of the forehead, palmar side down, then

FIG. 329.

draw the thumb across the forehead to the right, a short distance beyond the head—*white man*, American, Fig. 329.

FIG. 330.

(2) Place the naturally extended hand, fingers and thumb slightly separated and pointing to the left, about fifteen inches before the right

side of the body, bringing it to within a short distance—*with us*, Fig. 330.

(3) Extend the flat right hand to the front and right as if about to grasp the hand of another individual—*friend, friends*, Fig. 331. For remarks connected with this sign see pp. 384–386.

FIG. 331.

(4) Place the flat right hand, with fingers only extended, back to the front, about eighteen inches before the right shoulder—*four* [years], Fig. 332.

FIG. 332.

(5) Close the right hand, leaving the index and second fingers extended and slightly separated, place it, back forward, about eight inches before

the right side of the body, and pass it quickly to the left in a slightly downward curve—*lie*, Fig. 333.

FIG. 333.

(6) Place the clinched fists together before the breast, palms down, then separate them in a curve outward and downward to their respective sides—*done, finished, "that is all"*, Fig. 334.

FIG. 334.

SIGNALS.

The collaborators in the work above explained have not generally responded to the request to communicate material under this head. It is, however, hoped that by now printing some extracts from published works and the few contributions recently procured, the attention of observers will be directed to the prosecution of research in this direction.

The term "signal" is here used in distinction from the signs noted in the DICTIONARY, extracts from which are given above, as being some action or manifestation intended to be seen at a distance, and not allowing of the minuteness or detail possible in close converse. Signals may be executed, first, exclusively by bodily action; second, by action of the person in connection with objects, such as a blanket, or a lance, or the direction imparted to a horse; third, by various devices, such as smoke, fire or dust, when the person of the signalist is not visible. When not simply intended to attract attention they are generally conventional, and while their study has not the same kind of importance as that of gesture signs, it possesses some peculiar interest.

SIGNALS EXECUTED BY BODILY ACTION.

Some of these are identical, or nearly so, with the gesture signs used by the same people.

ALARM. See NOTES ON CHEYENNE AND ARAPAHO SIGNALS, *infra*.

ANGER.

Close the hand, place it against the forehead, and turn it back and forth while in that position. (Col. R. B. Marcy, U. S. A., *Thirty Years of Army Life on the Border, New York*, 1866, p. 34.)

COME HERE.

The right hand is to be advanced about eighteen inches at the height of the navel, horizontal, relaxed, palm downward, thumb in the palm; then draw it near the side and at the same time drop the hand to bring the palm backward. The farther away the person called is, the higher the hand is raised. If very far off, the hand is raised high up over the head and then swung forward, downward, and backward to the side. (*Dakota* I, IV.)

DANGER.

There is something dangerous in that place.—Right-hand index-finger and thumb forming a curve, the other fingers closed; move the right

34 A E

hand forward, pointing in the direction of the dangerous place or animal. (*Omaha* I.)

DEFIANCE.

Right-hand index and middle fingers open; motion toward the enemy signifies "I do not fear you." Reverse the motion, bringing the hand toward the subject, means " Do your worst to me." (*Omaha* I.)

DIRECTION.

Pass around that object or place near you—she-í-he ti-dhá-ga.—When a man is at a distance, I say to him " Go around that way." Describe a curve by raising the hand above the head, forefinger open, move to right or left according to direction intended and hand that is used, *i. e.*, move to the left, use right hand; move to the right, use left hand. (*Omaha* I; *Ponka* I.)

HALT!

——— To inquire disposition.

Raise the right hand with the palm in front and gradually push it forward and back several times; if they are not hostile it will at once be obeyed. (Randolph B. Marcy, *The Prairie Traveler*. *New York*, 1859, p. 214.)

——— Stand there! He is coming to you.

Right hand extended, flat, edgewise, moved downward several times. (*Omaha* I.)

——— Stand there! He is going toward you.

Hold the open right hand, palm to the left, with the tips of the fingers toward the person signaled to; thrust the hand forward in either an upward or downward curve. (*Omaha* I; *Ponka* I.)

——— Lie down flat where you are—she-dhu bis-pé zha$^{n\prime}$-ga.

Extend the right arm in the direction of the person signaled to, having the palm down; move downward by degrees to about the knees. (*Omaha* I; *Ponka* I.)

PEACE; FRIENDSHIP.

Hold up palm of hand.—Observed as made by an Indian of the Kansas tribe in 1833. (John T. Irving, *Indian Sketches*. *Philadelphia*, 1835, vol. ii, p. 253.)

Elevate the extended hands at arm's length above and on either side of the head. Observed by Dr. W. J. Hoffman, as made in Northern Arizona in 1871 by the Apaches, Mojaves, Hualpais, and Seviches. "No arms"—corresponding with "hands up" of road-agents. Fig. 335.

FIG. 335.—A signal of peace.

FIG. 336.—Signal, "Who are you?" Answer, "Pani."

The right hand held aloft, empty. (General G. A. Custer, *My Life on the Plains*, *New York*, 1874, p. 238.) This may be collated with the lines in Walt Whitman's *Salut au Monde*—

> Toward all
> I raise high the perpendicular hand,—I make the signal.

The Natchez in 1682 made signals of friendship to La Salle's party by the joining of the two hands of the signalist, much embarrassing Tonty, La Salle's lieutenant, in command of the advance in the descent of the Mississippi, who could not return the signal, having but one hand. His men responded in his stead. (Margry, *Decouvertes et Établissments des Français dans l'ouest et dans le sud de l'Amérique Septentrionale*, &c.)

QUESTION.

—— I do not know you. Who are you?

After halting a party coming: Right hand raised, palm in front and slowly moved to the right and left. [Answered by tribal sign.] (Marcy's *Prairie Traveler*, loc. cit., 214.) Fig. 336. In this illustration the answer is made by giving the tribal sign for Pani.

—— To inquire if coming party is peaceful.

Raise both hands, grasped in the manner of shaking hands, or by locking the two forefingers firmly while the hands are held up. If friendly they will respond with the same signal. (Marcy's *Prairie Traveler*, loc. cit., 214.)

SUBMISSION.

The United States steamer Saranac in 1874, cruising in Alaskan waters, dropped anchor in July, 1874, in Freshwater Harbor, back of Sitka, in latitude 59° north. An armed party landed at a T'linkit village, deserted by all the inhabitants except one old man and two women, the latter seated at the feet of the former. The man was in great fear, turned his back and held up his hands as a sign of utter helplessness. (Extract from notes kindly furnished by Lieutenant-Commander WM. BAINBRIDGE HOFF, U. S. N., who was senior aid to Rear-Admiral Pennock, on the cruise mentioned.)

SURRENDER.

The palm of the hand is held toward the person [to whom the surrender is made]. (*Long.*)

Hold the palm of the hand toward the person as high above the head as the arm can be raised. (*Dakota* I.)

SIGNALS IN WHICH OBJECTS ARE USED IN CONNECTION WITH PERSONAL ACTION.

BUFFALO DISCOVERED. See also NOTES ON CHEYENNE AND ARAPAHO SIGNALS.

When the Ponkas or Omahas discover buffalo the watcher stands erect on the hill, with his face toward the camp, holding his blanket with an end in each hand, his arms being stretched out (right and left) on a line with shoulders. (*Dakota* VIII; *Omaha* I; *Ponka* I.) See Fig. 337.

Same as (*Omaha* I), and (*Ponka* I); with the addition that after the blanket is held out at arm's length the arms are crossed in front of the body. (*Dakota* I.)

CAMP!

When it is intended to encamp, a blanket is elevated upon a pole so as to be visible to all the individuals of a moving party. (*Dakota* VIII.)

COME! TO BECKON TO A PERSON.

Hold out the lower edge of the robe or blanket, then wave it in to the legs. This is made when there is a desire to avoid general observation. (*Matthews.*)

COME BACK!

Gather or grasp the left side of the unbuttoned coat (or blanket) with the right hand, and, either standing or sitting in position so that the signal can be seen, wave it to the left and right as often as may be necessary for the sign to be recognized. When made standing the person should not move his body. (*Dakota* I.)

DANGER. See also NOTES ON CHEYENNE AND ARAPAHO SIGNALS.

—— Horseman at a distance, galloping, passing and repassing, and crossing each other—*enemy comes*. But for notice of herd of buffalo, they gallop back and forward abreast—do not cross each other. (H. M. Brackenridge's *Views of Louisiana. Pittsburgh*, 1814, p. 250.)

—— Riding rapidly round in a circle, "Danger! Get together as quickly as possible." (Richard Irving Dodge, lieutenant-colonel United States Army, *The Plains of the Great West. New York*, 1877, p. 368.)

—— Point the right index in the direction of the danger, and then throw the arm over the front of the body diagonally, so that the hand rests near the left shoulder, back outward. If the person to be notified of the danger should be in the rear precede the above signal with that

FIG. 337.—Signal for " buffalo discovered."

FIG. 338.—Signal of discovery or alarm.

for "*Attention.*" This signal can also be made with a blanket, properly grasped so as to form a long narrow roll. Perhaps this signal would more properly belong under "*Caution,*" as it would be used to denote the presence of a dangerous beast or snake, and not that of a human enemy. (*Dakota* I.)

―――― Passing and repassing one another, either on foot or mounted, is used as a war-signal; which is expressed in the Hidatsa—mạkimakǎ'da-halidié. (*Mandan and Hidatsa* I.)

DIRECTION.

―――― Pass around that place.

Point the folded blanket in the direction of the object or place to be avoided, then draw it near the body, and wave it rapidly several times in front of the body only, and then throwing it out toward the side on which you wish the person to approach you, and repeat a sufficient number of times for the signal to be understood. (*Dakota* I.)

DISCOVERY.

The discovery of enemies, game, or anything else, is announced by riding rapidly to and fro, or in a circle. The idea that there is a difference in the signification of these two directions of riding appears, according to many of the Dakota Indians of the Missouri Valley, to be erroneous. Parties away from their regular encampment are generally in search of some special object, such as game, or of another party, either friendly or hostile, which is generally understood, and when that object is found, the announcement is made to their companions in either of the above ways. The reason that a horseman may ride from side to side is, that the party to whom he desires to communicate may be at a particular locality, and his movement—at right angles to the direction to the party—would be perfectly clear. Should the party be separated into smaller bands, or have flankers or scouts at various points, the only way in which the rider's signal could be recognized as a motion from side to side, by all the persons to whom the signal was directed, would be for him to ride in a circle, which he naturally does. (*Dakota* VI, VII, VIII.) Fig. 338.

The latter was noticed by Dr. Hoffman in 1873, on the Yellowstone River, while attached to the Stanley Expedition. The Indians had again concentrated after their first repulse by General Custer, and taken possession of the woods and bluffs on the opposite side of the river. As the column came up, one Indian was seen upon a high bluff to ride rapidly round in a circle, occasionally firing off his revolver. The signal announced the discovery of the advancing force, which had been expected, and he could be distinctly seen from the surrounding region. As many of the enemy were still scattered over the neighborhood, some of them would not have been able to recognize this signal had he ridden to and from an observer, but the circle produced a lateral movement visible from any point.

——— Of enemies, or other game than Buffalo. See also NOTES ON CHEYENNE AND ARAPAHO SIGNALS.

The discovery of enemies is indicated by riding rapidly around in a circle, so that the signal could be seen by their friends, but out of sight of the discovered enemy. (*Dakota* I.)

When enemies are discovered, or other game than buffalo, the sentinel waves his blanket over his head up and down, holding an end in each hand. (*Omaha* I; *Ponka* I.)

——— Of game, wood, water, &c.

This is communicated by riding rapidly forward and backward on the top of the highest hill. The same would be communicated with a blanket by waving it right and left, and then directly toward the game or whatever the party might be searching for, indicating that it is not to the right or to the left, but directly in front. (*Dakota* I.)

DRILL, MILITARY.

"It is done by signals, devised after a system of the Indian's own invention, and communicated in various ways.

"Wonderful as the statement may appear, the signaling on a bright day, when the sun is in the proper direction, is done with a piece of looking-glass held in the hollow of the hand. The reflection of the sun's rays thrown on the ranks communicates in some mysterious way the wishes of the chief. Once standing on a little knoll overlooking the valley of the South Platte, I witnessed almost at my feet a drill of about one hundred warriors by a Sioux chief, who sat on his horse on a knoll opposite me, and about two hundred yards from his command in the plain below. For more than half an hour he commanded a drill, which for variety and promptness of action could not be equaled by any civilized cavalry of the world. All I could see was an occasional movement of the right arm. He himself afterwards told me that he used a looking-glass." (Dodge's *Plains of the Great West, loc. cit.,* pp. 307, 308.)

FRIENDSHIP.

If two Indians [of the plains] are approaching one another on horseback, and they may, for instance, be one mile apart, or as far as they can see each other. At that safe distance one wants to indicate to the other that he wishes to be friendly. He does this by turning his horse around and traveling about fifty paces back and forth, repeating this two or three times; this shows to the other Indian that he is not for hostility, but for friendly relations. If the second Indian accepts this proffered overture of friendship, he indicates the same by locking the fingers of both hands as far as to the first joints, and in that position raises his hands and lets them rest on his forehead with the palms either in or out, indifferently, as if he were trying to shield his eyes from the excessive light of the sun. This implies, "I, too, am for peace," or "I accept your overture." (*Sac, Fox, and Kickapoo* I.) It is interesting in this connection to note the reception of Father Marquette by an Illinois chief who is reported to have raised his hands to his eyes as if to shield them from overpowering splendor. That action was supposed to be made in a combination of humility and admiration, and a pretended inability to gaze on the face of the illustrious guest has been taken to be the conception of the gesture, which in fact was probably only the holding the interlocked hands in the most demonstrative posture. An oriental gesture in which the flat hand is actually interposed as a shield to the eyes before a superior is probably made with the poetical conception erroneously attributed to the Indian.

The display of green branches to signalize friendly or pacific intentions does not appear to have been noticed among the North American Indians by trustworthy observers. Captain Cook makes frequent mention of it as the ceremonial greeting among islands he visited. See his *Voyage toward the South Pole. London*, 1784, Vol. II, pp. 30 and 35. Green branches were also waved in signal of *friendship* by the natives of the island of New Britain to the members of the expedition in charge of Mr. Wilfred Powell in 1878. *Proceedings of the Royal Geological Society*, February, 1881, p. 89.

HALT!

—— Stand there! he is coming this way.

Grasp the end of the blanket or robe; wave it downward several times. (*Omaha* I.)

—— To inquire disposition.

Wave the folded blanket to the right and left in front of the body, then point toward the person.or persons approaching, and carry it from a horizontal position in front of the body rapidly downward and upward several times. (*Dakota* I.)

MANY.

Wave the blanket directly in front of the body upward and downward several times. Many of *anything*. (*Dakota* I.)

PEACE, COUPLED WITH INVITATION.

Motion of spreading a real or imaginary robe or skin on the ground. Noticed by Lewis and Clark on their first meeting with the Shoshoni in 1805. (*Lewis and Clark's Travels*, &c., London, 1817, vol. ii, p. 74.) This signal is more particularly described as follows : Grasp the blanket by the two corners with the hands, throw it above the head, allowing it to unfold as it falls to the ground as if in the act of spreading it.

QUESTION.

The ordinary manner of opening communication with parties known or supposed to be hostile is to ride toward them in zigzag manner, or to ride in a circle. (Custer's *My Life on the Plains, loc. cit.,* p. 58.)

This author mentions (p. 202) a systematic manner of waving a blanket, by which the son of Satana, the Kaiowa chief, conveyed information to him, and a similar performance by Yellow Bear, a chief of the Arapahos (p. 219), neither of which he explains in detail.

———— I do not know you. Who are you?

Point the folded blanket at arm's length toward the person, and then wave it toward the right and left in front of the face. You—I don't know. Take an end of the blanket in each hand, and extend the arms to full capacity at the sides of the body, letting the other ends hang down in front of the body to the ground, means, Where do you come from? or who are you? (*Dakota* I.)

SAFETY. ALL QUIET. See NOTES ON CHEYENNE AND ARAPAHO SIGNALS.

SURRENDER.

Hold the folded blanket or a piece of cloth high above the head. "This really means 'I want to die right now.'" (*Dakota* I.)

SURROUNDED, We are.

Take an end of the blanket in each hand, extend the arms at the sides of the body, allowing the blanket to hang down in front of the body, and then wave it in a circular manner. (*Dakota* I.)

SIGNALS MADE WHEN THE PERSON OF THE SIGNALIST IS NOT VISIBLE.

Those noted consist of SMOKE, FIRE, or DUST signals.

SMOKE SIGNALS GENERALLY.

They [the Indians] had abandoned the coast, along which bale-fires were left burning and sending up their columns of smoke to advise the distant bands of the arrival of their old enemy. (Schoolcraft's *History,* &c., vol. iii, p. 35, giving a condensed account of De Soto's expedition.)

"Their systems of telegraphs are very peculiar, and though they might seem impracticable at first, yet so thoroughly are they understood by the savages that it is availed of frequently to immense advantage. The most remarkable is by raising smokes, by which many important facts are communicated to a considerable distance and made intelligible by the manner, size, number, or repetition of the smokes, which are commonly raised by firing spots of dry grass." (Josiah Gregg's *Commerce of the Prairies. New York*, 1844, vol. ii, p. 286.)

The highest elevations of land are selected as stations from which signals with smoke are made. These can be seen at a distance of from twenty to fifty miles. By varying the number of columns of smoke different meanings are conveyed. The most simple as well as the most varied mode, and resembling the telegraphic alphabet, is arranged by building a small fire, which is not allowed to blaze; then by placing an armful of partially green grass or weeds over the fire, as if to smother it, a dense white smoke is created, which ordinarily will ascend in a continuous vertical column for hundreds of feet. Having established a current of smoke, the Indian simply takes his blanket and by spreading it over the small pile of weeds or grass from which the smoke takes its source, and properly controlling the edges and corners of the blanket, he confines the smoke, and is in this way able to retain it for several moments. By rapidly displacing the blanket, the operator is enabled to cause a dense volume of smoke to rise, the length or shortness of which, as well as the number and frequency of the columns, he can regulate perfectly, simply by a proper use of the blanket. (Custer's *My Life on the Plains*, loc. cit., p. 187.)

They gathered an armful of dried grass and weeds, which were placed and carried upon the highest point of the peak, where, everything being in readiness, the match was applied close to the ground; but the blaze was no sooner well lighted and about to envelop the entire amount of grass collected than it was smothered with the unlighted portion. A slender column of gray smoke then began to ascend in a perpendicular column. This was not enough, as it might be taken for the smoke rising from a simple camp-fire. The smoldering grass was then covered with a blanket, the corners of which were held so closely to the ground as to almost completely confine and cut off the column of smoke. Waiting a few moments, until the smoke was beginning to escape from beneath, the blanket was suddenly thrown aside, when a beautiful balloon-shaped column puffed upward like the white cloud of smoke which attends the discharge of a field-piece. Again casting the blanket on the pile of grass, the column was interrupted as before, and again in due time released, so that a succession of elongated, egg-shaped puffs of smoke kept ascending toward the sky in the most regular manner. This bead-like column of smoke, considering the height from which it began to ascend, was visible from points on the level plain fifty miles distant. (*Ib.*, p. 217.)

The following extracts are made from Fremont's *First and Second Expeditions*, 1842–3–4, Ex. Doc., 28th Cong. 2d Session, Senate, Washington, 1845:

"Columns of smoke rose over the country at scattered intervals—signals by which the Indians here, as elsewhere, communicate to each other that enemies are in the country," p. 220. This was January 18, 1844, in the vicinity of Pyramid Lake, and perhaps the signalists were Pai-Utes.

"While we were speaking, a smoke rose suddenly from the cotton-wood grove below, which plainly told us what had befallen him [Tableau]; it was raised to inform the surrounding Indians that a blow had been struck, and to tell them to be on their guard," p. 268, 269. This was on May 5, 1844, near the Rio Virgen, Utah, and was narrated of "Diggers," probably Chemehuevas.

ARRIVAL OF A PARTY AT AN APPOINTED PLACE, WHEN ALL IS SAFE.

This is made by sending upward one column of smoke from a fire partially smothered by green grass. This is only used by previous agreement, and if seen by friends of the party, the signal is answered in the same manner. But should either party discover the presence of enemies, no signal would be made, but the fact would be communicated by a runner. (*Dakota* I.)

SUCCESS OF A WAR PARTY.

Whenever a war party, consisting of either Pima, Papago, or Maricopa Indians, returned from an expedition into the Apache country, their success was announced from the first and most distant elevation visible from their settlements. The number of scalps secured was shown by a corresponding number of columns of smoke, arranged in a horizontal line, side by side, so as to be distinguishable by the observers. When the returning party was unsuccessful, no such signals were made. (*Pima and Papago* I.) Fig. 339. A similar custom appears to have existed among the Ponkas, although the custom has apparently been discontinued by them, as shown in the following proper name: Oú-de gá-xe, Smoke maker; He who made a smoke by burning grass returning from war.

SMOKE SIGNALS OF THE APACHES.

The following information was obtained by Dr. W. J. HOFFMAN, from the Apache chiefs named on page 407, under the title of TINNEAN, (*Apache* I):

The materials used in making smoke of sufficient density and color consist of pine or cedar boughs, leaves and grass, which can nearly always be obtained in the regions occupied by the Apaches of Northern New Mexico. These Indians state that they employ but three kinds of signals, each of which consists of columns of smoke, numbering from one to three or more.

ALARM.

This signal is made by causing three or more columns of smoke to ascend, and signifies danger or the approach of an enemy, and also requires the concentration of those who see them. These signals are communicated from one camp to another, and the most distant bands are guided by their location. The greater the haste desired the greater

FIG. 339.—Signal of successful war-party.

the number of columns of smoke. These are often so hastily made that they may resemble puffs of smoke, and are caused by throwing heaps of grass and leaves upon the embers again and again.

ATTENTION.

This signal is generally made by producing one continuous column, and signifies attention for several purposes, viz, when a band had become tired of one locality, or the grass may have been consumed by the ponies, or some other cause necessitated removal, or should an enemy be reported, which would require further watching before a decision as to future action would be made. The intention or knowledge of anything unusual would be communicated to neighboring bands by causing one column of smoke to ascend.

ESTABLISHMENT OF A CAMP; QUIET; SAFETY.

When a removal of camp has been made, after the signal for ATTENTION has been given, and the party have selected a place where they propose to remain until there may be a necessity or desire for their removal, two columns of smoke are made, to inform their friends that they propose to remain at that place. Two columns are also made at other times during a long continued residence, to inform the neighboring bands that a camp still exists, and that all is favorable and quiet.

FOREIGN SMOKE SIGNALS.

The following examples of smoke signals in foreign lands are added for comparison.

Miss Haigh, speaking of the Guanches of the Canary Islands at the time of the Spanish conquest, says: "When an enemy approached, they alarmed the country by raising a thick smoke or by whistling, which was repeated from one to another. This latter method is still in use among the people of Teneriffe, and may be heard at an almost incredible distance." (*Trans. Eth. Soc. Lond.* vii, 1869, sec. ser., pp. 109, 110.)

"The natives have an easy method of telegraphing news to their distant friends. When Sir Thomas Mitchell was traveling through Eastern Australia he often saw columns of smoke ascending through the trees in the forests, and he soon learned that the natives used the smoke of fires for the purpose of making known his movements to their friends. Near Mount Frazer he observed a dense column of smoke, and subsequently other smokes arose, extending in a telegraphic line far to the south, along the base of the mountains, and thus communicating to the natives who might be upon his route homeward the tidings of his return.

"When Sir Thomas reached Portland Bay he noticed that when a whale appeared in the bay the natives were accustomed to send up a column of smoke, thus giving timely intimation to all the whalers. If the whale should be pursued by one boat's crew only it might be taken; but if pursued by several, it would probably be run ashore and become food for the blacks." (Smyth, *loc. cit.*, vol. 1, pp. 152, 153, quoting Maj. T. L. Mitchell's *Eastern Australia*, vol. ii, p. 241.)

Jardine, writing of the natives of Cape York, says that a "communica. tion between the islanders and the natives of the mainland is frequent; and the rapid manner in which news is carried from tribe to tribe, to great distances, is astonishing. I was informed of the approach of Her Majesty's Steamer Salamander, on her last visit, two days before her arrival here. Intelligence is conveyed by means of fires made to throw up smoke in different forms, and by messengers who perform long and rapid journeys." (Smyth, *loc. cit.*, vol. 1, p. 153, quoting from *Overland Expedition*, p. 85.)

Messengers in all parts of Australia appear to have used this mode of signaling. In Victoria, when traveling through the forests, they were accustomed to raise smoke by filling the hollow of a tree with green boughs and setting fire to the trunk at its base; and in this way, as they always selected an elevated position for the fire when they could, their movements were made known.

When engaged in hunting, when traveling on secret expeditions, when approaching an encampment, when threatened with danger, or when foes menaced their friends, the natives made signals by raising a smoke. And their fires were lighted in such a way as to give forth signals that would be understood by people of their own tribe and by friendly tribes. They exhibited great ability in managing their system of telegraphy; and in former times it was not seldom used to the injury of the white settlers, who at first had no idea that the thin column of smoke rising through the foliage of the adjacent bush, and raised perhaps by some feeble old woman, was an intimation to the warriors to advance and attack the Europeans. (R. Brough Smyth, F. L. S., F. G. S., *The Aborigines of Victoria. Melbourne*, 1878, vol. i, pp. 152, 153.)

FIRE ARROWS.

"Travelers on the prairie have often seen the Indians throwing up signal lights at night, and have wondered how it was done. * * * They take off the head of the arrow and dip the shaft in gunpowder, mixed with glue. * * * The gunpowder adheres to the wood, and coats it three or four inches from its end to the depth of one-fourth of an inch. Chewed bark mixed with dry gunpowder is then fastened to the stick, and the arrow is ready for use. When it is to be fired, a warrior places it on his bowstring and draws his bow ready to let it fly; the point of the arrow is then lowered, another warrior lights the dry bark, and it is shot high in the air. When it has gone up a little distance, it bursts out into a flame, and burns brightly until it falls to the ground. Various meanings are attached to these fire-arrow signals. Thus, one arrow meant, among the Santees, 'The enemy are about'; two arrows from the same point, 'Danger'; three, 'Great danger'; many, 'They are too strong, or we are falling back'; two arrows sent up at the same moment, 'We will attack'; three, 'Soon'; four, 'Now'; if shot diagonally, 'In that direction.' These signals are constantly changed, and are always agreed upon when the party goes out or before it separates. The Indians send their signals very intelligently, and seldom make mistakes in telegraphing each other by these silent monitors. The amount of information they can communicate by fires and burning arrows is perfectly wonderful. Every war party carries with it bundles of signal arrows." (*Belden, The White Chief; or Twelve Years among the Wild Indians of the Plains. Cincinnati and New York*, 1871, pp. 106, 107.)

With regard to the above, it is possible that white influence has been felt in the mode of signaling as well as in the use of gunpowder, but it would be interesting to learn if any Indians adopted a similar expedient before gunpowder was known to them. They frequently used arrows, to which flaming material was attached, to set fire to the wooden houses of the early colonists. The Caribs were acquainted with this same mode of destruction as appears by the following quotation:

"Their arrows were commonly poisoned, except when they made their military excursions hy night; on these occasions they converted them into instruments of still greater mischief; for, by arming the points with pledgets of cotton dipped in oil, and set on fire, they fired whole villages of their enemies at a distance." (*Alcedo. The Geograph. and Hist. Dict. of America and the West Indies.* Thompson's trans. *London*, 1812, Vol. I, p. 314.)

DUST SIGNALS.

When an enemy, game, or anything else which was the special object of search is discovered, handfulls of dust are thrown into the air to announce that discovery. This signal has the same general signification as when riding to and fro, or, round in a circle on an elevated portion of ground, or a bluff. (*Dakota* VII, VIII.)

When any game or any enemy is discovered, and should the sentinel be without a blanket, he throws a handful of dust up into the air. When the Brulés attacked the Ponkas, in 1872, they stood on the bluff and threw up dust. (*Omaha* I; *Ponka* I.)

There appears to be among the Bushmen a custom of throwing up sand or earth into the air when at a distance from home and in need of help of some kind from those who were there. (*Miss L. C. Lloyd,, MS. Letter*, dated July 10, 1880, from Charlton House, Mowbray, near Cape Town, Africa.)

NOTES ON CHEYENNE AND ARAPAHO SIGNALS.

The following information was obtained from WA-Uⁿ' (*Bobtail*), Mo-HI'-NUK-MA-HA'-IT (*Big Horse*), Cheyennes, and O-QO-HIS'-SA (*The Mare,* better known as "Little Raven"), and NA'-WATO (*Left Hand*), Arapahos, chiefs and members of a delegation who visited Washington, D. C., in September, 1880, in the interest of their tribes dwelling in Indian Territory:

A party of Indians going on the war-path leave camp, announcing their project to the remaining individuals and informing neighboring friends by sending runners. A party is not systematically organized until several days away from its headquarters, unless circumstances should require immediate action. The pipe-bearers are appointed, who precede the party while on the march, carrying the pipes, and no one is allowed to cross ahead of these individuals, or to join the party by riding up before the head of the column, as it would endanger the success of the expedition. All new arrivals fall in from either side or the rear. Upon coming in sight of any elevations of land likely to afford a good view of the surrounding country the warriors come to a halt and secrete themselves as much as possible. The scouts who have already been selected, advance just before daybreak to within a moderate distance of the elevation to ascertain if any of the enemy has preceded them. This is only discovered by carefully watching the summit to see if any objects are in motion; if not, the flight of birds is observed, and if any should alight upon the hill or butte it would indicate the absence of anything that might ordinarily scare them away. Should a large bird, as a raven, crow, or eagle, fly toward the hill-top and make a sudden swerve to either side and disappear, it would indicate the presence of something sufficient to require further examination. When it is learned that there is reason to suspect an enemy the scout, who has all the time been closely watched by the party in the rear, makes a signal for them to lie still, signifying *danger* or *caution*. It is made by grasping the blanket with the right hand and waving it earthward from a position in front of and as high as the shoulder. This is nearly the same as civilized Americans use the hand for a similar purpose in battle or hunting to direct "lie quiet"!

Should the hill, however, be clear of any one, the Indian will ascend slowly, and under cover as much as possible, and gain a view of the country. If there is no one to be seen, the blanket is grasped and waved horizontally from right to left and back again repeatedly, showing a clear surface. If the enemy is discovered, the scout will give the *alarm* by running down the hill, upon a side visible to the watchers, in a zigzag manner, which communicates the state of affairs.

Should any expedition or advance be attempted at night, the same signals as are made with the blanket are made with a firebrand, which is constructed of a bunch of grass tied to a short pole.

When a war party encamps for a night or a day or more, a piece of wood is stuck into the ground, pointing in the direction pursued, with a number of cuts, notches, or marks corresponding to the number of days which the party spent after leaving the last camp until leaving the present camp, serving to show to the recruits to the main party the course to be followed, and the distance.

A hunting party in advancing takes the same precautions as a war party, so as not to be surprised by an enemy. If a scout ascends a prominent elevation and discovers no game, the blanket is grasped and waved horizontally from side to side at the height of the shoulders or head; and if game is discovered the Indian rides back and forth (from left to right) a short distance so that the distant observers can view the maneuver. If a large herd of buffalo is found, the extent traveled over in going to and fro increases in proportion to the size of the herd. A quicker gait is traveled when the herd is very large or haste on the part of the hunters is desired.

It is stated that these Indians also use mirrors to signal from one elevation to another, but the system could not be learned, as they say they have no longer use for it, having ceased warfare (?).

SCHEME OF ILLUSTRATION.

In the following pages the scheme of graphic illustration, intended both to save labor and secure accuracy, which was presented in the *Introduction to the Study of Sign Language*, is reproduced with some improvements. It is given for the use of observers who may not see that publication, the material parts of which being included in the present paper it is not necessary that the former should now be furnished. The TYPES OF HAND POSITIONS were prepared for reference by the corresponding letters of the alphabet to avoid tedious description, should any of them exactly correspond, or by alteration, as suggested in the note following them. These, as well as the OUTLINES OF ARM POSITIONS, giving front and side outlines with arms pendant, were distributed in separate sheets to observers for their convenience in recording, and this will still be cheerfully done when request is made to the present writer. When the sheets are not accessible the TYPES can be used for graphic changes by tracing the one selected, or by a few words indicating the change, as shown in the EXAMPLES. The OUTLINES OF ARM POSITIONS can also be readily traced for the same use as if the sheets had been provided. It is hoped that this scheme, promoting uniformity in description and illustration, will be adopted by all observers who cannot be specially addressed.

Collaborators in the gestures of foreign uncivilized peoples will confer a favor by sending at least one photograph or sketch in native costume of a typical individual of the tribe, the gestures of which are reported upon, in order that it may be reproduced in the complete work. Such photograph or sketch need not be made in the execution of any particular gesture, which can be done by artists engaged on the work, but would be still more acceptable if it could be so made.

OUTLINES FOR ARM POSITIONS IN SIGN LANGUAGE.

The gestures, to be indicated by corrected positions of arms and by dotted lines showing the motion from the initial to the final positions (which are severally marked by an arrow-head and a cross—see EXAMPLES), will always be shown as they appear to an observer facing the gesturer, the front outline, Fig. 340, or side, Fig. 341, or both, being used as most convenient. The special positions of hands and fingers will be designated by reference to the TYPES OF HAND POSITIONS. For brevity in the written description, "hand" may be used for "right hand," when that one alone is employed in any particular gesture. When more convenient to use the profile figure in which the right arm is exhibited for a gesture actually made by the left hand and arm it can be done, the fact, however, being noted.

FIG. 340.　　　　　FIG. 341.

In cases where the conception or origin of any sign is ascertained or suggested it should be annexed to the description, and when obtained from the gesturer will be so stated affirmatively, otherwise it will be considered to be presented by the observer. The graphic illustration of associated facial expression or bodily posture which may accentuate or qualify a gesture is necessarily left to the ingenuity of the contributor.

35 A E

ORDER OF ARRANGEMENT.

The following order of arrangement for written descriptions is suggested. The use of a separate sheet or part sheet of paper for each sign described and illustrated would be convenient in the collation. It should always be affimatively stated whether the "conception or orgin" of the sign was procured from the sign-maker, or is suggested or inferred by the observer.

Word or idea expressed by Sign: ....

DESCRIPTION:

....

....

....

CONCEPTION OR ORIGIN:

....

Tribe: ....

Locality: ....

Date: .... 188 .

....

Observer.

TYPES OF HAND POSITIONS IN SIGN LANGUAGE.

A—Fist, palm outward, horizontal.

B—Fist, back outward, oblique
upward.

C—Clinched, with thumb extended against forefinger,
upright, edge outward.

D—Clinched, ball of thumb
against middle of fore-
finger, oblique, upward,
palm down.

E—Hooked, thumb against
end of forefinger, upright,
edge outward.

F—Hooked, thumb against
side of forefinger, oblique,
palm outward.

G—Fingers resting against
ball of thumb, back up-
ward.

H—Arched, thumb horizontal
against end of forefinger,
back upward.

I—Closed, except forefinger
crooked against end of
thumb, upright, palm out-
ward.

J—Forefinger straight, upright, others closed, edge
outward.

K—Forefinger obliquely extended upward, others
closed, edge outward.

L—Thumb vertical, forefinger
horizontal, others closed,
edge outward.

FIG. 342a.

M—Forefinger horizontal, fingers and thumb closed, palm outward.

N—First and second fingers straight upward aud separated, remaining fingers and thumb closed, palm outward.

O—Thumb, first and second fingers separated, straight upward, remaining fingers curved edge outward.

P—Fingers and thumb partially curved upward and separated, knuckles outward.

Q—Fingers and thumb, separated, slightly curved, downward.

R—Fingers and thumb extended straight, separated, upward.

S—Hand and fingers upright, joined, back outward,

T—Hand and fingers upright, joined, palm outward.

U—Fingers collected to a point, thumb resting in middle.

V—Arched, joined, thumb resting near end of forefinger, downward.

W—Hand horizontal, flat, palm downward.

X—Hand horizontal, flat, palm upward.

Y—Naturally relaxed, normal; used when hand simply follows arm with no intentional disposition.

FIG. 342b.

NOTE CONCERNING THE FOREGOING TYPES.

The positions are given as they appear to an observer facing the gesturer, and are designed to show the relations of the fingers to the hand rather than the positions of the hand relative to the body, which must be shown by the outlines (see OUTLINES OF ARM POSITIONS) or description. The right and left hands are figured above without discrimination, but in description or reference the right hand will be understood when the left is not specified. The hands as figured can also with proper intimation be applied with changes either upward, downward, or inclined to either side, so long as the relative positions of the fingers are retained, and when in that respect no one of the types exactly corresponds with a sign observed, modifications may be made by pen or pencil on that one of the types, or a tracing of it, found most convenient, as indicated in the EXAMPLES, and referred to by the letter of the alphabet under the type changed, with the addition of a numeral —e g., A 1, and if that type, i. e., A, were changed a second time by the observer (which change would necessarily be drawn on another sheet of types or another tracing of a type selected when there are no sheets provided), it should be referred to as A 2.

EXAMPLES.

Word or idea expressed by sign : To cut, with an ax.

DESCRIPTION.

With the right hand flattened (X changed to right instead of left), palm upward, move it downward to the left side repeatedly from different elevations, ending each stroke at the same point. Fig. 343.

CONCEPTION OR ORIGIN.

From the act of felling a tree.

FIG. 343.

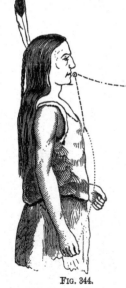

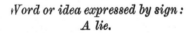

Word or idea expressed by sign : A lie.

DESCRIPTION.

Touch the left breast over the heart, and pass the hand forward from the mouth, the two first fingers only being extended and slightly separated (L, 1—with thumb resting on third finger, Fig. 344 *a*). Fig. 344.

L 1, FIG. 344*a*.

CONCEPTION OR ORIGIN.

Double-tongued.

FIG. 344.

Word or idea expressed by sign: To ride.

DESCRIPTION.

Place the first two fingers of the right hand, thumb extended (N 1, Fig. 345a) downward, astraddle the first two joined and straight fingers of the left (T 1, Fig. 345b), sidewise, to the right, then make several short, arched movements forward with hands so joined. Fig. 345.

N 1, FIG. 345a.

CONCEPTION OR ORIGIN.

The horse mounted and in motion.

T 1, FIG. 345b.

FIG. 345.

Word or idea expressed by signs: I am going home.

DESCRIPTION.

(1) Touch the middle of the breast with the extended index (K), then (2) pass it slowly downward and outward to the right, and when the hand is at arm's length, at the height of the shoulder, (3) clinch it (A) suddenly and throw it edgewise toward the ground. Fig. 346.

CONCEPTION OR ORIGIN.

(1) I, personality; (2) motion and direction; (3) locality of my possessions—home.

FIG. 346.

EXPLANATION OF MARKS.

The following indicative marks are used in the above examples:

----------------- Dotted lines indicate movements to place the hand and arm in position to commence the sign and not forming part of it.

------------------ Short dashes indicate the course of hand employed in the sign, when made rapidly.

------------- Longer dashes indicate a less rapid movement.

___ ___ ___ ___ Broken lines represent slow movement.

> Indicates commencement of movement in representing sign, or part of sign.

× Represents the termination of movements.

⊙ Indicates the point in the gesture line at which the hand position is changed.

A CATALOG OF SELECTED
DOVER BOOKS
IN ALL FIELDS OF INTEREST

A CATALOG OF SELECTED DOVER BOOKS IN ALL FIELDS OF INTEREST

100 BEST-LOVED POEMS, Edited by Philip Smith. "The Passionate Shepherd to His Love," "Shall I compare thee to a summer's day?" "Death, be not proud," "The Raven," "The Road Not Taken," plus works by Blake, Wordsworth, Byron, Shelley, Keats, many others. 96pp. $5\frac{3}{16}$ x $8\frac{1}{4}$. 0-486-28553-7

100 SMALL HOUSES OF THE THIRTIES, Brown-Blodgett Company. Exterior photographs and floor plans for 100 charming structures. Illustrations of models accompanied by descriptions of interiors, color schemes, closet space, and other amenities. 200 illustrations. 112pp. $8\frac{3}{8}$ x 11. 0-486-44131-8

1000 TURN-OF-THE-CENTURY HOUSES: With Illustrations and Floor Plans, Herbert C. Chivers. Reproduced from a rare edition, this showcase of homes ranges from cottages and bungalows to sprawling mansions. Each house is meticulously illustrated and accompanied by complete floor plans. 256pp. $9\frac{3}{8}$ x $12\frac{1}{4}$. 0-486-45596-3

101 GREAT AMERICAN POEMS, Edited by The American Poetry & Literacy Project. Rich treasury of verse from the 19th and 20th centuries includes works by Edgar Allan Poe, Robert Frost, Walt Whitman, Langston Hughes, Emily Dickinson, T. S. Eliot, other notables. 96pp. $5\frac{3}{16}$ x $8\frac{1}{4}$. 0-486-40158-8

101 GREAT SAMURAI PRINTS, Utagawa Kuniyoshi. Kuniyoshi was a master of the warrior woodblock print — and these 18th-century illustrations represent the pinnacle of his craft. Full-color portraits of renowned Japanese samurais pulse with movement, passion, and remarkably fine detail. 112pp. $8\frac{3}{8}$ x 11. 0-486-46523-3

ABC OF BALLET, Janet Grosser. Clearly worded, abundantly illustrated little guide defines basic ballet-related terms: arabesque, battement, pas de chat, relevé, sissonne, many others. Pronunciation guide included. Excellent primer. 48pp. $4\frac{3}{16}$ x $5\frac{3}{4}$. 0-486-40871-X

ACCESSORIES OF DRESS: An Illustrated Encyclopedia, Katherine Lester and Bess Viola Oerke. Illustrations of hats, veils, wigs, cravats, shawls, shoes, gloves, and other accessories enhance an engaging commentary that reveals the humor and charm of the many-sided story of accessorized apparel. 644 figures and 59 plates. 608pp. $6\frac{1}{8}$ x $9\frac{1}{4}$. 0-486-43378-1

ADVENTURES OF HUCKLEBERRY FINN, Mark Twain. Join Huck and Jim as their boyhood adventures along the Mississippi River lead them into a world of excitement, danger, and self-discovery. Humorous narrative, lyrical descriptions of the Mississippi valley, and memorable characters. 224pp. $5\frac{3}{16}$ x $8\frac{1}{4}$. 0-486-28061-6

ALICE STARMORE'S BOOK OF FAIR ISLE KNITTING, Alice Starmore. A noted designer from the region of Scotland's Fair Isle explores the history and techniques of this distinctive, stranded-color knitting style and provides copious illustrated instructions for 14 original knitwear designs. 208pp. $8\frac{3}{8}$ x $10\frac{7}{8}$. 0-486-47218-3

Browse over 9,000 books at www.doverpublications.com

CATALOG OF DOVER BOOKS

ALICE'S ADVENTURES IN WONDERLAND, Lewis Carroll. Beloved classic about a little girl lost in a topsy-turvy land and her encounters with the White Rabbit, March Hare, Mad Hatter, Cheshire Cat, and other delightfully improbable characters. 42 illustrations by Sir John Tenniel. 96pp. 5³⁄₁₆ x 8¼. 0-486-27543-4

AMERICA'S LIGHTHOUSES: An Illustrated History, Francis Ross Holland. Profusely illustrated fact-filled survey of American lighthouses since 1716. Over 200 stations — East, Gulf, and West coasts, Great Lakes, Hawaii, Alaska, Puerto Rico, the Virgin Islands, and the Mississippi and St. Lawrence Rivers. 240pp. 8 x 10¾. 0-486-25576-X

AN ENCYCLOPEDIA OF THE VIOLIN, Alberto Bachmann. Translated by Frederick H. Martens. Introduction by Eugene Ysaye. First published in 1925, this renowned reference remains unsurpassed as a source of essential information, from construction and evolution to repertoire and technique. Includes a glossary and 73 illustrations. 496pp. 6⅛ x 9¼. 0-486-46618-3

ANIMALS: 1,419 Copyright-Free Illustrations of Mammals, Birds, Fish, Insects, etc., Selected by Jim Harter. Selected for its visual impact and ease of use, this outstanding collection of wood engravings presents over 1,000 species of animals in extremely lifelike poses. Includes mammals, birds, reptiles, amphibians, fish, insects, and other invertebrates. 284pp. 9 x 12. 0-486-23766-4

THE ANNALS, Tacitus. Translated by Alfred John Church and William Jackson Brodribb. This vital chronicle of Imperial Rome, written by the era's great historian, spans A.D. 14-68 and paints incisive psychological portraits of major figures, from Tiberius to Nero. 416pp. 5³⁄₁₆ x 8¼. 0-486-45236-0

ANTIGONE, Sophocles. Filled with passionate speeches and sensitive probing of moral and philosophical issues, this powerful and often-performed Greek drama reveals the grim fate that befalls the children of Oedipus. Footnotes. 64pp. 5³⁄₁₆ x 8 ¼. 0-486-27804-2

ART DECO DECORATIVE PATTERNS IN FULL COLOR, Christian Stoll. Reprinted from a rare 1910 portfolio, 160 sensuous and exotic images depict a breathtaking array of florals, geometrics, and abstracts — all elegant in their stark simplicity. 64pp. 8⅜ x 11. 0-486-44862-2

THE ARTHUR RACKHAM TREASURY: 86 Full-Color Illustrations, Arthur Rackham. Selected and Edited by Jeff A. Menges. A stunning treasury of 86 full-page plates span the famed English artist's career, from *Rip Van Winkle* (1905) to masterworks such as *Undine, A Midsummer Night's Dream,* and *Wind in the Willows* (1939). 96pp. 8⅜ x 11. 0-486-44685-9

THE AUTHENTIC GILBERT & SULLIVAN SONGBOOK, W. S. Gilbert and A. S. Sullivan. The most comprehensive collection available, this songbook includes selections from every one of Gilbert and Sullivan's light operas. Ninety-two numbers are presented uncut and unedited, and in their original keys. 410pp. 9 x 12. 0-486-23482-7

THE AWAKENING, Kate Chopin. First published in 1899, this controversial novel of a New Orleans wife's search for love outside a stifling marriage shocked readers. Today, it remains a first-rate narrative with superb characterization. New introductory Note. 128pp. 5³⁄₁₆ x 8¼. 0-486-27786-0

BASIC DRAWING, Louis Priscilla. Beginning with perspective, this commonsense manual progresses to the figure in movement, light and shade, anatomy, drapery, composition, trees and landscape, and outdoor sketching. Black-and-white illustrations throughout. 128pp. 8⅜ x 11. 0-486-45815-6

Browse over 9,000 books at www.doverpublications.com